ATLANTIC 2/07

W9-BOM-969

A TO Z
OF
MATHEMATICIANS

NOTABLE SCIENTISTS

A TO Z
OF
MATHEMATICIANS

TUCKER MCELROY, Ph.D.

Facts On File, Inc.

A TO Z OF MATHEMATICIANS

Notable Scientists

Facts On File, Inc.
132 West 31st Street
New York NY 10001

Library of Congress Cataloging-in-Publication Data

McElroy, Tucker.
    A to Z of mathematicians / Tucker McElroy.
      p. cm.—(Notable scientists)
    Includes bibliographical references and index.
    ISBN 0-8160-5338-3 (acid-free paper)
    1. Mathematicians—Biography.   I. Title.   II. Series.
QA28.M395 2005
510'.92'2—dc22
                                 2004005460

Text design by Joan M. Toro
Cover design by Cathy Rincon
Chronology by Sholto Ainslie

Printed in the United States of America

VB TECHBOOKS 10 9 8 7 6 5 4 3 2 1

This book is printed on acid-free paper.

CONTENTS

LIST OF ENTRIES

ACKNOWLEDGMENTS

I thank God, who gives me strength and hope each day. I am grateful to my wife, Autumn, who encouraged me to complete this book. Thanks also go to Jim Dennison for title translations, as well as Diane Kit Moser and Lisa Yount for advice on photographs. Finally, my thanks go to Frank K. Darmstadt, Executive Editor, for his great patience and helpfulness, as well as the rest of the Facts On File staff for their work in making this book possible.

INTRODUCTION

A to Z of Mathematicians contains the fascinating biographies of 150 mathematicians: men and women from a variety of cultures, time periods, and socioeconomic backgrounds, all of whom have substantially influenced the history of mathematics. Some made numerous discoveries during a lifetime of creative work; others made a single contribution. The great Carl Gauss (1777–1855) developed the statistical method of least squares and discovered countless theorems in algebra, geometry, and analysis. Sir Isaac Newton (1643–1727), renowned as the primary inventor of calculus, was a profound researcher and one of the greatest scientists of all time. From the classical era there is Archimedes (287 B.C.E.–212 B.C.E.), who paved the way for calculus and made amazing investigations into mechanics and hydrodynamics. These three are considered by many mathematicians to be the princes of the field; most of the persons in this volume do not attain to the princes' glory, but nevertheless have had their share in the unfolding of history.

THE MATHEMATICIANS

A to Z of Mathematicians focuses on individuals whose historical importance is firmly established, including classical figures from the ancient Greek, Indian, and Chinese cultures as well as the plethora of 17th-, 18th-, and 19th-century mathematicians. I have chosen to exclude those born in the 20th century (with the exception of Kurt Gödel), so that the likes of Dame Mary Cartwright, Andrey Kolmogorov, and John Von Neumann are omitted; this choice reflects the opinion that true greatness is made lucid only through the passage of time. The earlier mathematicians were often scientists as well, also contributing to astronomy, philosophy, and physics, among other disciplines; however, the latter persons, especially those of the 19th century, were increasingly specialized in one particular aspect of pure or applied mathematics. Modern figures who were principally known for fields other than mathematics—such as Albert Einstein and Richard Feynman—have been omitted, despite their mathematical accomplishments. Being of the opinion that statistics is one of the mathematical sciences, I have included a smattering of great statisticians. Several sources were consulted in order to compile a diverse list of persons—a list that nevertheless delivers the main thrust of mathematical history.

I have attempted to make this material accessible to a general audience, and as a result the mathematical ideas are presented in simple terms that cut to the core of the matter. In some cases precision was sacrificed for accessibility. However, due to the abstruse nature of 19th- and 20th-century mathematics, many readers may still have difficulty. I suggest that they refer to Facts On File's handbooks in algebra, calculus, and geometry for unfamiliar terminology. It is helpful for readers to have knowledge of high school geometry and algebra, as well as calculus.

After each entry, a short list of additional references for further reading is provided. The majority of the individuals can be found in the *Dictionary of Scientific Biography* (New York, 1970–90), the *Encyclopaedia Britannica* (http://www.eb.com), and the online MacTutor History of Mathematics archive (http://www-gap.dcs. st-and.ac.uk/~history); so these references have not been repeated each time. In compiling references I tried to restrict sources to those articles written in English that were easily accessible to college undergraduates.

A

Abel, Niels Henrik
(1802–1829)
Norwegian
Algebra

The modest Norwegian mathematician Niels Abel made outstanding contributions to the theory of elliptic functions, one of the most popular mathematical subjects of the 19th century. Struggle, hardship, and uncertainty characterized his life; but under difficult conditions he still managed to produce a prolific and brilliant body of mathematical research. Sadly, he died young, without being able to attain the glory and recognition for which he had labored.

Niels Henrik Abel was born the son of Sören Abel, a Lutheran pastor, and Ane Marie Simonson, the daughter of a wealthy merchant. Pastor Abel's first parish was in the island of Finnöy, where Niels Abel was born in 1802. Shortly afterward, Abel's father became involved in politics.

Up to this time Abel and his brothers had received instruction from their father, but in 1815 they were sent to school in Oslo. Abel's performance at the school was marginal, but in 1817 the arrival of a new mathematics teacher, Bernt Holmboe, greatly changed Abel's fate. Holmboe recognized Abel's gift for mathematics, and they commenced studying LEONHARD EULER and the French mathematicians. Soon Abel had surpassed his teacher. At this time he was greatly interested in the theory of algebraic equations. Holmboe was delighted with his discovery of the young mathematician, and he enthusiastically acquainted the other faculty with the genius of Abel.

During his last year at school Abel attempted to solve the quintic equation, an outstanding problem from antiquity; but he failed (the equation has no rational solutions). Nevertheless, his efforts introduced him to the theory of elliptic functions. Meanwhile, Abel's father fell into public disgrace due to alcoholism, and after his death in 1820 the family was left in difficult financial circumstances.

Abel entered the University of Sweden in 1821, and was granted a free room due to his extreme poverty. The faculty even supported him out of its own resources; he was a frequent guest of the household of Christoffer Hansteen, the leading scientist at the university. Within the first year, Abel had completed his preliminary degree, allowing him the time to pursue his own advanced studies. He voraciously read everything he could find concerning mathematics, and published his first few papers in Hansteen's journal after 1823.

In summer 1823 Abel received assistance from the faculty to travel to Copenhagen, in

1

Niels Abel, one of the founders of the theory of elliptic functions, a generalization of trigonometric functions *(Courtesy of the Library of Congress)*

order to meet the Danish mathematicians. The trip was inspirational; he also met his future fiancée, Christine Kemp. When he returned to Oslo, Abel began work on the quintic equation once again, but this time, he attempted to prove that there was no radical expression for the solution. He was successful, and had his result published in French at his own expense. Sadly, there was no reaction from his intended audience— even CARL FRIEDRICH GAUSS was indifferent.

Abel's financial problems were complicated by his engagement to Kemp, but he managed to secure a small stipend to study languages in preparation for travel abroad. After this, he would receive a modest grant for two years of foreign study. In 1825 he departed with some friends for Berlin, and on his way through

Copenhagen made the acquaintance of August Crelle, an influential engineer with a keen interest for mathematics. The two became lifelong friends, and Crelle agreed to start a German journal for the publication of pure mathematics. Many of Abel's papers were published in the first volumes, including an expanded version of his work on the quintic.

One of Abel's notable papers in *Crelle's Journal* generalized the binomial formula, which gives an expansion for the nth power of a binomial expression. Abel turned his thought toward infinite series, and was concerned that the sums had never been stringently determined. The result of his research was a classic paper on power series, with the determination of the sum of the binomial series for arbitrary exponents. Meanwhile, Abel failed to obtain a vacant position at the University of Sweden; his former teacher Holmboe was instead selected. It is noteworthy that Abel maintained his nobility of character throughout his frustrating life.

In spring 1826 Abel journeyed to Paris and presented a paper to the French Academy of Sciences that he considered his masterpiece: It treated the sum of integrals of a given algebraic function, and thereby generalized Euler's relation for elliptic integrals. This paper, over which Abel labored for many months but never published, was presented in October 1826, and AUGUSTIN-LOUIS CAUCHY and ADRIEN-MARIE LEGENDRE were appointed as referees. A report was not forthcoming, and was not issued until after Abel's death. It seems that Cauchy was to blame for the tardiness, and apparently lost the manuscript. Abel later rewrote the paper (neither was this work published), and the theorem described above came to be known as Abel's theorem.

After this disappointing stint in France, Abel returned to Berlin and there fell ill with his first attack of tuberculosis. Crelle assisted him with his illness, and tried to procure a position for him in Berlin, but Abel longed to return to Norway. Abel's new research transformed the theory of elliptic integrals to the theory of elliptic functions by using their inverses. Through this duality, elliptic functions became an important generalization of trigonometric functions. As a student in Oslo, Abel had already developed much of the theory, and this paper presented his thought in great detail.

Upon his return to Oslo in 1827, Abel had no prospects of a position, and managed to survive by tutoring schoolboys. In a few months Hansteen went on leave to Siberia and Abel became his substitute at the university. Meanwhile, Abel's work had started to stimulate interest among European mathematicians. In early 1828 Abel discovered that he had a young German competitor, CARL JACOBI, in the field of elliptic functions. Aware of the race at hand, Abel wrote a rapid succession of papers on elliptic functions and prepared a book-length memoir that would be published posthumously.

It seems that Abel had the priority of discovery over Jacobi in the area of elliptic functions; however, it is also known that Gauss was aware of the principles of elliptic functions long before either Abel or Jacobi, and had decided not to publish. At this time Abel started a correspondence with Legendre, who was also interested in elliptic functions. The mathematicians in France, along with Crelle, attempted to secure employment for Abel, and even petitioned the monarch of Sweden.

Abel's health was deteriorating, but he continued to write papers frantically. He spent summer 1828 with his fiancée, and when visiting her at Christmastime he became feverish due to exposure to the cold. As he prepared for his return to Oslo, Abel suffered a violent hemorrhage, and was confined to bed. At the age of 26 he died of tuberculosis on April 26, 1829; two days later, Crelle wrote him jubilantly that he had secured Abel an appointment in Berlin. In 1830 the French Academy of Sciences awarded its Grand Prix to Abel and Jacobi for their brilliant mathematical discoveries.

Abel became recognized as one of the greatest mathematicians after his death, and he truly accomplished much despite his short lifespan. The theory of elliptic functions would expand greatly during the later 19th century, and Abel's work contributed significantly to this development.

Further Reading

Bell, E. *Men of Mathematics*. New York: Simon and Schuster, 1965.

Ore, O. *Niels Henrik Abel, Mathematician Extraordinary*. Minneapolis: University of Minnesota Press, 1974.

Rosen, M. I. "Niels Henrik Abel and the Equation of the Fifth Degree," *American Mathematical Monthly* 102 (1995): 495–505.

Stander, D. "Makers of Modern Mathematics: Niels Henrik Abel," *Bulletin of the Institute of Mathematics and Its Applications* 23, nos. 6–7 (1987): 107–109.

⊠ **Adelard of Bath**
(unknown–ca. 1146)
British
Arithmetic

Little is known of the personal life of Adelard of Bath, but his work has been of great importance to the early revival of mathematics and natural philosophy during the medieval period. His translation of Greek and Arabic classics into Latin enabled the knowledge of earlier societies to be preserved and disseminated in Europe.

Adelard was a native of Bath, England, but his exact birth date is not known. He traveled widely in his life, first spending time in France, where he studied at Tours. For the next seven years he journeyed afar, visiting Salerno, Sicily, Cilicia, Syria, and perhaps even Palestine; it is thought that he also dwelt in Spain. His latter travels gave him an acquaintance with Arabic language and culture, though he may have learned Arabic while still in Sicily. By 1130 he had returned to Bath, and his writings from that time have some association with the royal court. One of his works, called *Astrolabe,* was apparently composed between 1142 and 1146; this is the latest recorded date of his activity.

Adelard made two contributions—*De eodem et diverso* (On sameness and diversity) and the *Questiones naturales* (Natural questions)—to medieval philosophy, written around 1116 and 1137, respectively. In *De eodem et diverso,* there is no evidence of Arabic influence, and he expresses the views of a quasi-Platonist. The *Questiones naturales* treats various topics in natural philosophy and shows the impact of his Arabic studies. Adelard's contribution to medieval science seems to lie chiefly in his translation of various works from Arabic.

His early endeavors in arithmetic, published in *Regule abaci* (By rule of the abacus), were quite traditional—his work reflected current arithmetical knowledge in Europe. These writings were doubtlessly composed prior to his familiarity with Arabic mathematics. Adelard also wrote on the topics of arithmetic, geometry, music, and astronomy. Here, the subject of Indian numerals and their basic operations is introduced as of fundamental importance.

Many scholars believe that Adelard was the first translator to present a full Latin version of EUCLID OF ALEXANDRIA's *Elements.* This began the process whereby the *Elements* would come to dominate late medieval mathematics; prior to Adelard's translation from the Arabic, there were only incomplete versions taken from the Greek. The first version was a verbatim transcription from the Arabic, whereas Adelard's second version replaces some of the proofs with instructions or summaries. This latter edition became the most popular, and was most commonly studied in schools. A third version appears to be a commentary and is attributed to Adelard; it enjoyed some popularity as well.

All the later mathematicians of Europe would read Euclid, either in Latin or Greek; indeed, this compendium of geometric knowledge would become a staple of mathematical education up to the present time. The Renaissance, and the consequent revival of mathematical discovery, was only made possible through the rediscovery of ancient classics and their translations. For his work as a translator and commentator, Adelard is remembered as an influential figure in the history of mathematics.

Further Reading

Burnett, C. *Adelard of Bath: An English Scientist and Arabist of the Early Twelfth Century.* London: Warburg Institute, University of London, 1987.

⊠ Agnesi, Maria Gaetana
(1718–1799)
Italian
Algebra, Analysis

Maria Gaetana Agnesi is known as a talented mathematician of the 18th century, and indeed was one of the first female mathematicians in the Western world. A mathematical prodigy with great linguistic talents, Agnesi made her greatest contribution through her clear exposition of algebra, geometry, and calculus; her colleagues acknowledged the value of her work within her own lifetime.

Born the eldest child of Pietro Agnesi and Anna Fortunato Brivio, Agnesi showed early interest in science. Her father, a wealthy professor of mathematics at the University of Bologna, encouraged and developed these interests. He established a cultural salon in his home, where his daughter would present and defend theses on a variety of scientific and philosophical topics. Some of the guests were foreigners, and Maria demonstrated her talent for languages by conversing with them in their own tongue; by age 11 she was familiar with Greek, German, Spanish, and Hebrew, having already mastered French by age five. At age nine she prepared a lengthy speech in Latin that promulgated higher education for women.

The topics of these theses, which were usually defended in Latin, included logic, ontology, mechanics, hydromechanics, elasticity, celestial mechanics and universal gravitation, chemistry, botany, zoology, and mineralogy. Her second published work, the *Propositiones philosophicae* (Propositions of philosophy, 1738), included almost 200 of these disputations. Agnesi's mathematical interests were developing at this time; at age 14 she was solving difficult problems in ballistics and analytic geometry. But after the publication of the *Propositiones philosophicae*, she decided to withdraw from her father's salon, since the social atmosphere was unappealing to her—in fact, she was eager to join a convent, but her father dissuaded her.

Nevertheless, Agnesi withdrew from the extroverted social life of her childhood, and devoted

Maria Agnesi studied the bell-shaped cubic curve called the *versiera,* which is more commonly known as the "witch of Agnesi." *(Courtesy of the Library of Congress)*

the next 10 years of her life to mathematics. After a decade of intense effort, she produced her *Instituzioni analitiche ad uso della gioventù italiana* (Analytical methods for the use of young Italians) in 1748. The two-volume work won immediate praise among mathematicians and brought Agnesi public acclaim. The objective of the thousand-page book was to present a complete and comprehensive treatment of algebra and analysis, including and emphasizing the new concepts of the 18th century. Of course, the development of differential and integral calculus was still in progress at this time; Agnesi would incorporate this contemporary mathematics into her treatment of analysis.

The material spanned elementary algebra and the classical theory of equations, coordinate geometry, the differential and integral calculus, infinite series, and the solution of elementary differential equations. Many of the methods and results were due solely to Agnesi, although her humble nature made her overly thorough in giving credit to her predecessors. Her name is often associated with a certain cubic curve called the *versiera* and known more commonly as the "witch of Agnesi." She was unaware that PIERRE DE FERMAT had studied the equation previously in 1665. This bell-shaped curve has many interesting properties and some applications in physics, and has been an ongoing source of fascination for many mathematicians.

Agnesi's treatise received wide acclaim for its excellent treatment and clear exposition. Translations into French and English from the original Italian were considered to be of great importance to the serious student of mathematics. Pope Benedict XIV sent her a congratulatory note in 1749, and in 1750 she was appointed to the chair of mathematics and natural philosophy at the University of Bologna.

However, Agnesi's reclusive and humble personality led her to accept the position only in honor, and she never actually taught at the university. After her father's death in 1752, she began to withdraw from all scientific activity—she became more interested in religious studies and social work. She was particularly concerned with the poor, and looked after the education of her numerous younger brothers. By 1762 she was quite removed from mathematics, so that she declined the University of Turin's request that she act as referee for JOSEPH-LOUIS LAGRANGE's work on the calculus of variations. In 1771 Agnesi became the director of a Milanese home for the sick, a position she held until her death in 1799.

It is interesting to note that the sustained activity of her intellect over 10 years was able to produce the *Instituzioni*, a work of great excellence and quality. However, she lost all interest in mathematics soon afterward and made no further contributions to that discipline. Agnesi's primary contribution to mathematics is the *Instituzioni*, which helped to disseminate mathematical knowledge and train future generations of mathematicians.

Further Reading

Grinstein, L., and P. Campbell. *Women of Mathematics.* New York: Greenwood Press, 1987.

Truesdell, C. "Correction and Additions for Maria Gaetana Agnesi," *Archive for History of Exact Science* 43 (1991): 385–386.

⊠ Alembert, Jean d' (Jean Le Rond d'Alembert)
(1717–1783)
French
Mechanics, Calculus

In the wave of effort following SIR ISAAC NEWTON's pioneering work in mechanics, many mathematicians attempted to flesh out the mathematical aspects of the new science. Jean d'Alembert was noteworthy as one of these intellectuals, who contributed to astronomy, fluid mechanics, and calculus; he was one of the first

Jean d'Alembert formulated several laws of motion, including d'Alembert's principle for decomposing constrained motions. *(Courtesy of the National Library of Medicine)*

persons to realize the importance of the limit in calculus.

Jean Le Rond d'Alembert was born in Paris on November 17, 1717. He was the illegitimate son of a famous salon hostess and a cavalry officer named Destouches-Canon. An artisan named Rousseau raised the young d'Alembert, but his father oversaw his education; he attended a Jansenist school, where he learned the classics, rhetoric, and mathematics.

D'Alembert decided on a career as a mathematician, and began communicating with the Académie des Sciences in 1739. During the next few years he wrote several papers treating the integration of differential equations. Although he had no formal training in higher mathematics, d'Alembert was familiar with the works of Newton, as well as the works of JAKOB BERNOULLI and JOHANN BERNOULLI.

In 1741 he was made a member of the Académie, and he concentrated his efforts on some problems in rational mechanics. The *Traité de dynamique* (Treatise on dynamics) was the fruit of his labor, a significant scientific work that formalized the new science of mechanics. The lengthy preface disclosed d'Alembert's philosophy of sensationalism (this idea states that sense perception, not reason, is the starting point for the acquisition of knowledge). He developed mechanics from the simple concepts of space and time, and avoided the notion of force. D'Alembert also presented his three laws of motion, which treated inertia, the parallelogram law of motion, and equilibrium. It is noteworthy that d'Alembert produced mathematical proofs for these laws.

The well-known d'Alembert's principle was also introduced in this work, which states that any constrained motion can be decomposed in terms of its inertial motion and a resisting (or constraining) force. He was careful not to overvalue the impact of mathematics on physics—he said that geometry's rigor was tied to its simplicity. Since reality was always more complicated than a mathematical abstraction, it is more difficult to establish truth.

In 1744 he produced a new volume called the *Traité de l'équilibre et du mouvement des fluides* (Treatise on the equilibrium and movement of fluids). In the 18th century a large amount of interest focused on fluid mechanics, since fluids were used to model heat, magnetism, and electricity. His treatment was different from that of DANIEL BERNOULLI, though the conclusions were similar. D'Alembert also examined the wave equation, considering string oscillation problems in 1747. Then in 1749 he turned toward celestial mechanics, publishing the *Recherches sur la précession des équinoxes et sur la nutation de l'axe de la terre* (*Research on the precession of the equinoxes and on the nodding of the earth's axis*), which treated the topic of the gradual change in the position of the earth's orbit.

Next, d'Alembert competed for a prize at the Prussian Academy, but blamed LEONHARD EULER for his failure to win. D'Alembert published his *Essai d'une nouvelle théorie de la résistance des fluides* (Essay on a new theory of the resistance of fluids) in 1752, in which the differential hydrodynamic equations were first expressed in terms of a field. The so-called hydrodynamic paradox was herein formulated—namely, that the flow before and behind an obstruction should be the same, resulting in the absence of any resistance. D'Alembert did not solve this problem, and was to some extent inhibited by his bias toward continuity; when discontinuities arose in the solutions of differential equations, he simply threw the solution away.

In the 1750s, interested in several nonscientific topics, d'Alembert became the science editor of the *Encyclopédie* (Encyclopedia). Later he wrote on the topics of music, law, and religion, presenting himself as an avid proponent of Enlightenment ideals, including a disdain for medieval thought.

Among his original contributions to mathematics, the ratio test for the convergence of an infinite series is noteworthy; d'Alembert viewed divergent series as nonsensical and disregarded them (this differs markedly from Euler's viewpoint). D'Alembert was virtually alone in his view of the derivative as the limit of a function, and his stress on the importance of continuity probably led him to this perspective. In the theory of probability d'Alembert was quite handicapped, being unable to accept standard solutions of gambling problems.

D'Alembert was known to be a charming, witty man. He never married, although he lived with his lover Julie de Lespinasse until her death in 1776. In 1772 he became the secretary of the Académie Française (the French Academy), and he increasingly turned toward humanitarian concerns. His later years were marked by bitterness and despair; he died in Paris on October 29, 1783.

Although he was well known as a preeminent scientist and philosopher, d'Alembert's mathematical achievements deserve special recognition. He greatly advanced the theory of mechanics in several of its branches, by contributing to its mathematical formulation and by consideration of several concrete problems.

Further Reading

Grimsley, R. *Jean d'Alembert, 1717–83*. Oxford: Clarendon Press, 1963.

Hankins, T. *Jean d'Alembert: Science and the Enlightenment*. Oxford: Clarendon Press, 1970.

Pappas, J. *Voltaire and d'Alembert*. Bloomington: Indiana University Press, 1962.

Wilson, C. "D'Alembert versus Euler on the Precession of the Equinoxes and the Mechanics of Rigid Bodies," *Archive for History of Exact Sciences* 37, no. 3 (1987): 233–273.

⊠ Apollonius of Perga
(ca. 262 B.C.E.–190 B.C.E.)
Greek
Geometry

Greek mathematics continued its development from the time of EUCLID OF ALEXANDRIA, and after ARCHIMEDES OF SYRACUSE one of the greatest mathematicians was Apollonius of Perga. He is mainly known for his contributions to the theory of conic sections (those plane figures obtained by slicing a cone at various angles). The fascination in this subject, revived in the 16th and 17th centuries, has continued into modern times with the onset of projective geometry.

Little information on his life has been preserved from the ravages of time, but it seems that Apollonius flourished sometime between the second half of the third century and the early second century B.C.E. Perga, a small Greek city in the southern portion of what is now Turkey, was his town of birth. Apollonius dwelt for some time in Alexandria, where he may have studied with the pupils of Euclid, and he later visited both Pergamum and Ephesus.

His most famous work, the *Conics*, was composed in the early second century B.C.E., and it soon became recognized as a classic text. Archimedes, who died around 212 B.C.E., appears to be the immediate mathematical predecessor of Apollonius, who developed many of the Syracusan's ideas. The *Conics* was originally divided into eight books, and had been intended as a treatise on conic sections. Before Apollonius's time, the basics of the theory of conic sections were known: Parabolas, hyperbolas, and ellipses could be obtained by appropriately slicing a cone with right, obtuse, or acute vertex angles, respectively. Apollonius employed an alternative method of construction that involved slicing a double cone at various angles, keeping the vertex angle fixed (this is the approach taken in modern times). This method had the advantage of making these curves accessible to the "application of areas," a geometrical formulation of quadratic equations that in modern time would be expressed algebraically. It is apparent that Apollonius's approach was refreshingly original, although the actual content of the *Conics* may have been well known. Much terminology, such as *parabola, hyperbola*, and *ellipse*, is due to Apollonius, and he generalizes the methods for generating sections.

The *Conics* contains much material that was already known, though the organization was according to Apollonius's method, which smoothly joined together numerous fragments of geometrical knowledge. Certain elementary results were omitted, and some few novel facts were included. Besides the material on the generation of sections, Apollonius described theorems on the rectangles contained by the segments of intersecting chords of a conic, the harmonic properties of pole and polar, properties of the focus, and the locus of three and four lines. He discusses the formation of a normal line to a conic, as well as certain inequalities of conjugate diameters. This work, compared with other Greek literature, is quite difficult to read, since the lack of modern notation makes the text burdensome, and the content itself is quite convoluted. Nevertheless, persistent study has rewarded many gifted mathematicians, including SIR ISAAC NEWTON, PIERRE DE FERMAT, and BLAISE PASCAL, who drew enormous inspiration from Apollonius's classic text.

In the work of PAPPUS OF ALEXANDRIA is contained a summary of Apollonius's other mathematical works: *Cutting off of a Ratio*, *Cutting off of an Area*, *Determinate Section*, *Tangencies*, *Inclinations*, and *Plane Loci*. These deal with various geometrical problems, and some of them involve the "application of an area." He uses the Greek method of analysis and synthesis: The problem in question is first presumed solved, and a more easily constructed condition is deduced from the solution ("analysis"); then from the latter construction, the original is developed ("synthesis"). It seems that Apollonius wrote still other documents, but no vestige of their content has survived to the present day. Apparently, he devised a number system for the representation of enormous quantities, similar to the notational system of Archimedes, though Apollonius generalized the idea. There are also references to the inscribing of the dodecahedron in the sphere, the study of the cylindrical helix, and a general treatise on the foundations of geometry.

So Apollonius was familiar with all aspects of Greek geometry, but he also contributed to the Euclidean theory of irrational numbers and derived approximations for pi more accurate than Archimedes'. His thought also penetrated the science of optics, where his deep knowledge of conics assisted the determination of various reflections caused by parabolic and spherical mirrors. Apollonius was renowned in his own time as a foremost astronomer, and he even earned the epithet of Epsilon, since the Greek letter of that name bears a resemblance in shape to the Moon. He calculates the distance of Earth to Moon as roughly 600,000 miles, and made various computations of the orbits of the planets. In fact, Apollonius is an important player in the development of geometrical models to explain planetary motion; HIPPARCHUS OF RHODES and CLAUDIUS PTOLEMY, improving upon his theories, arrived at the Ptolemaic system, a feat of the ancient world's scientific investigation possessed of sweeping grandeur and considerable longevity.

There was no immediate successor to Apollonius, though his *Conics* was recognized as a superb accomplishment. Various simple commentaries were produced, but interest declined after the fall of Rome, and only the first four books continued to be translated in Byzantium. Another three books of the *Conics* were translated into Arabic, and Islamic mathematicians remained intrigued by his work, though they made few advancements; the final (eighth) book has been lost. In the late 16th and early 17th centuries, several translations of Apollonius's *Conics* appeared in Europe and were voraciously studied by French mathematicians such as RENÉ DESCARTES, Pierre de Fermat, GIRARD DESARGUES, and Blaise Pascal. When Descartes propounded his analytic geometry, which took an algebraic, rather than constructive or geometrical, approach to curves and sections, interest in Apollonius's classic treatise began to wane. However, later in the 19th century, the *Conics* experienced a resurrection of curiosity with the introduction of projective geometry.

Further Reading

Heath, T. *Treatise on Conic Section*. New York: Barnes & Noble, 1961.

———. *A History of Greek Mathematics*. Oxford: Clarendon Press, 1921.

Hogendijk, J. "Arabic Traces of Lost Works of Apollonius," *Archive for History of Exact Sciences* 35, no. 3 (1986): 187–253.

⊠ Archimedes of Syracuse
(ca. 287 B.C.E.–212 B.C.E.)
Greek
Geometry, Mechanics

Of the mathematicians of Greek antiquity, Archimedes should be considered the greatest. His contributions to geometry and mechanics, as well as hydrostatics, place him on a higher pedestal than his contemporaries. And as his works were gradually translated and introduced into the West, he exerted as great an influence there as his thought already had in Byzantium and Arabia. In his method of exhaustion can be seen a classical predecessor of the integral calculus, which would be formally developed by BLAISE PASCAL, GOTTFRIED WILHELM VON LEIBNIZ, SIR ISAAC NEWTON, and others in the 17th cen-

Archimedes is the great Greek mathematician who formulated the principles of hydromechanics and invented early techniques of integral calculus. *(Courtesy of the National Library of Medicine)*

tury. His life story alone has inspired many mathematicians.

As with many ancient persons, the exact details of Archimedes' life are difficult to ascertain, since there are several accounts of variable quality. His father was the astronomer Phidias, and it is possible that Archimedes was a kinsman of the tyrant of Syracuse, King Hieron II. Certainly he was intimate with the king, as his work *The Sandreckoner* was dedicated to Hieron's son Gelon. Born in Syracuse, Archimedes departed to Alexandria in order to pursue an education in mathematics; there he studied EUCLID OF ALEXANDRIA and assisted the development of Euclidean mathematics. But it was in Syracuse, where he soon returned, that he made most of his discoveries.

Although renowned for his contributions to mathematics, Archimedes also designed numerous mechanical inventions. The water snail, invented in Egypt to aid irrigation, was a screwlike contraption used to raise water. More impressive are the stories relating his construction and application of the compound pulley: Hieron had requested Archimedes to demonstrate how a small force could move a large weight. The mathematician attached a rope to a large merchant ship that was loaded with freight and passengers, and ran the line through a system of pulleys. In this manner, seated at a distance from the vessel, Archimedes was able to effortlessly draw the boat smoothly off the shore into the harbor.

Similar to the pulley, Archimedes discovered the usefulness of the lever, noting that the longer the distance from the fulcrum, the more weight the lever could move. Logically extending this principle, he asserted that it was feasible to move the world, given a sufficiently long lever. Another popular story relates that Hieron gave Archimedes the task of ascertaining whether a certain crown was made of pure gold, or whether it had been fraudulently alloyed with silver. As Archimedes pondered this puzzle, he came upon the bath, and noticed that the amount of water displaced was equal to the amount of his body that was immersed. This immediately put him in mind of a method to solve Hieron's problems, and he leapt out of the tub in joy, running naked toward his home, shrieking "Eureka!"

His skill in mechanical objects was unequaled, and Hieron often put him to use in improving the defenses of the city, insisting that Archimedes' intellect should be put to some practical application. When Marcellus and the Romans later came to attack Syracuse, they found the city impregnable due to the multiplicity of catapults, mechanical arms, burning mirrors, and various ballistic devices that Archimedes had built. Archimedes wrote a book entitled *On Spheremaking*, in which he describes how to construct a model planetarium designed to simulate the movement of Sun, Moon, and planets. It seems that Archimedes was familiar with Archytas's heliocentrism, and made use of this in his planetarium.

According to Plutarch, Archimedes was dedicated to pure theory and disdained the practical applications of mathematics to engineering; only those subjects free of any utility to society were considered worthy of wholehearted pursuit. Archimedes' mathematical works consist mainly of studies of area and volume, and the geometrical analysis of statics and hydrostatics. In computing the area or volume of various plane and solid figures, he makes use of the so-called Lemma of Archimedes and the "method of exhaustion." This lemma states that the difference of two unequal magnitudes can be formed into a ratio with any similar magnitude; thus, the difference of two lines will always be a line and not a point. The method of exhaustion involves subtracting a quantity larger than half of a given magnitude indefinitely, and points to the idea of the eternal divisibility of the continuum (that one can always take away half of a number and still have something left). These ideas border on notions of the infinitesimal—the infinitely small—and the idea of a limit, which are key ingredients of integral calculus; however, the Greeks were averse to the notion of infinity and infinitesimals, and Archimedes shied away from doing anything that he felt would be regarded as absurd.

The method of exhaustion, which was used rarely in Euclid's *Elements*, will be illustrated through the following example: In *On the Measurement of the Circle*, Archimedes assumes, for the sake of contradiction, that the area of a right triangle with base equal to the circumference and height equal to the radius of the circle is actually greater than the area of the circle. Then he is able, using the Lemma of Archimedes, to inscribe a polygon in the circle, with the same area as the triangle; this contradiction shows that the area of the triangle cannot be greater than the circle, and he makes a similar argument that it cannot be less.

The basic concept of the method of approximation, which is similar to the method of exhaustion, is to inscribe regular figures within a given plane figure and solid such that the remaining area or volume is steadily reduced; the area or volume of the regular figures can be easily calculated, and this will be an increasingly accurate approximation. The remaining area or volume is "exhausted." Of course, the modern way to obtain an exact determination of measure is via the limit; Archimedes avoided this issue by demonstrating that the remaining area or volume could be made as small as desired by inscribing more regular figures. Of course, one could perform the same procedure with circumscribing regular figures.

He also applied these methods to solids, computing the surface area and volume of the sphere, and the volume of cones and pyramids. Archimedes' methods were sometimes purely geometrical, but at times used principles from statics, such as a "balancing method." His knowledge of the law of the lever and the center of gravity for the triangle, together with his approximation and exhaustion methods, enabled him to improve the proofs of known theorems as well as establish completely new results.

Archimedes also made some contributions in the realm of numerical calculations, producing some highly accurate approximations for pi and the square root of three. In *The Sandreckoner* he devises a notation for enormous numbers and estimates the number of grains of sand to fill the universe. In *On the Equilibrium of Planes* he proves the law of the lever from geometrical principles, and in *On Floating Bodies* he explains the concept of hydrostatic pressure. The so-called Principle of Archimedes states that solids placed in a fluid will be lighter in the fluid by an amount equal to the weight of the fluid displaced.

His influence on later mathematics was extensive, although Archimedes may not have enjoyed much fame in his own lifetime. Later Greeks, including PAPPUS OF ALEXANDRIA and Theon of Alexandria, wrote commentaries on his writings, and later still, Byzantine authors studied his work. From Byzantium his texts came into the West before the start of the Renaissance; meanwhile, Arabic mathematicians were familiar with Archimedes, and they exploited his methods in their own researches into conic sections. In the 12th century translations from Arabic into Latin appeared, which LEONARDO FIBONACCI made use of in the 13th century. By the 1400s knowledge of Archimedes had expanded throughout parts of Europe, and his mathematics later influenced SIMON STEVIN, Johannes Kepler, GALILEO GALILEI, and BONAVENTURA CAVALIERI.

Perhaps the best-known story concerning Archimedes relates his death, which occurred in 212 B.C.E. during the siege of Syracuse by the Romans. Apparently, he was not concerned with the civic situation, and was busily making sand diagrams in his home (at this time he was at least 75 years old). Although the Roman general Marcellus had given strict orders that the famous Sicilian mathematician was not to be harmed, a Roman soldier broke into Archimedes' house and spoiled his diagram. When the aged math-ematician vocally expressed his displeasure, the soldier promptly slew him.

Archimedes was an outstanding mathematician and scientist. Indeed, he is considered by many to be one of the greatest three mathematicians of all time, along with CARL FRIEDRICH GAUSS and Newton. Once discovered by medieval Europeans, his works propelled the discovery of calculus. It is interesting that this profound intellect was remote in time and space from the great classical Greek mathematicians; Archimedes worked on the island of Syracuse, far from Athens, the source of much Greek thought, and he worked centuries after the decline of the Greek culture.

Further Reading

Aaboe, A. *Episodes from the Early History of Mathematics.* Washington, D.C.: Mathematical Association of America, 1964.

Brumbaugh, R. *The Philosophers of Greece.* New York: Crowell, 1964.

Dijksterhuis, E. *Archimedes.* Copenhagen: E. Munksgaard, 1956.

Heath, T. A *History of Greek Mathematics.* Oxford: Clarendon Press, 1921.

Hollingdale, S. "Archimedes of Syracuse: A Tribute on the 22nd Century of His Death," *Bulletin of the Institute of Mathematics and Its Applications* 25, no. 9 (1989): 217–225.

Laird, W. "Archimedes among the Humanists," *Isis* 82, no. 314 (1991): 629–638.

Neugebauer, O. "Archimedes and Aristarchus," *Isis* 34 (1942): 4–6.

Osborne, C. "Archimedes on the Dimension of the Cosmos," *Isis* 74, no. 272 (1983): 234–242.

⊠   Aristarchus of Samos
(ca. 310 B.C.E.–230 B.C.E.)
Greek
Trigonometry

Renowned as the first person to propose a he-liocentric theory (that the planets revolve around the Sun) of the solar system, Aristarchus was both an important astronomer and a first-rate mathematician. Little is known of his life, but his works have survived, in which he calculates various astronomical distances millennia before the invention of modern telescopes.

Apparently, Aristarchus was born on the island of Samos, which lies in the Aegean Sea close to the city of Miletus, a center for science and learning in the Ionian civilization. He studied under Strato of Lampsacos, director of the Lyceum founded by Aristotle. It is thought that Aristarchus was taught by Strato in Alexandria rather than Athens. His approximate dates are determined by the records of CLAUDIUS PTOLEMY and ARCHIMEDES OF SYRACUSE. Aristarchus's only work still in existence is his treatise *On the Sizes and Distances of the Sun and Moon*.

Among his peers, Aristarchus was known as "the mathematician," which may have been merely descriptive. At that time, the discipline of astronomy was considered part of mathematics, and Aristarchus's *On Sizes and Distances* primarily treats astronomical calculations. According to Vitruvius, a Roman architect, Aristarchus was an expert in all branches of mathematics, and was the inventor of a popular sundial consisting of a hemispherical bowl with a vertical needle poised in the center. It seems that his discoveries in *On Sizes and Distances* of the vast scale of the universe fostered an interest in the physical orientation of the solar system, eventually leading to his heliocentric conception of the Sun in the center.

Heliocentrism has its roots in the early Pythagoreans, a religious/philosophical cult that thrived in the fifth century B.C.E. in southern Italy. Philolaus (ca. 440 B.C.E.) is attributed with the idea that the Earth, Moon, Sun, and planets orbited around a central "hearth of the universe." Hicetas, a contemporary of Philolaus, believed in the axial rotation of the Earth. The ancient historians credit Heraclides of Pontus (ca. 340 B.C.E.) with the Earth's rotation about the Sun,

but Aristarchus is said to be the first to develop a complete heliocentric theory: The Earth orbits the Sun while at the same time spinning about its axis.

It is interesting that the heliocentric theory did not catch on. The idea did not attract much attention, and the philosophical speculations of the Ionian era were already waning, to be replaced by the increasingly mathematical feats of APOLLONIUS OF PERGA, HIPPARCHUS OF RHODES, and Ptolemy. Due to trends in intellectual and religious circles, geocentrism became increasingly popular. Not until Nicolaus Copernicus, who lived 18 centuries later, resurrected Aristarchus's hypothesis did opinion turn away from considering the Earth as the center of the universe.

Living after EUCLID OF ALEXANDRIA and before Archimedes, Aristarchus was able to produce rigorous arguments and geometrical constructions, a distinguishing characteristic of the better mathematicians. The attempt to make various measurements of the solar system without a telescope seems incredible, but it involved the simple geometry of triangles. With the Sun (S), Earth (E), and Moon (M) as the three vertices of a triangle, the angle EMS will be a right angle when the Moon is exactly half in shadow. Through careful observation, it is possible to measure the angle MES, and thus the third angle ESM can be deduced. Once these angles are known, the ratio of the length of the legs, that is, the distance to the Moon and the distance to the Sun, can be determined. Of course, this procedure is fraught with difficulties, and any slight error in estimating the angles will throw off the whole calculation. Aristarchus estimated angle MES to be approximately 87 degrees, when it is actually 89 degrees and 50 minutes. From this, he deduces that the distance to the Sun is about 20 times greater than the distance to the Moon, when in actuality it is 400 times greater. His theory was sound, but Aristarchus was inhibited by his crude equipment.

This is discussed in *On Sizes and Distances*, where he states several assumptions and from these proves the above estimate on the distance to the Sun and also states that the diameter of Sun and Moon are related in the same manner (the Sun is about 20 times as wide across as the Moon). He also computes that the ratio of the diameter of the Sun to the diameter of the Earth is between 19:3 and 43:6, an underestimate.

It is noteworthy that trigonometry had not yet been developed, and yet Aristarchus developed methods that essentially estimated the sines of small angles. Without precise means of calculation, Aristarchus was unable to attain accurate results, although his method was brilliant. Because heliocentrism was not accepted at the time, Aristarchus failed to achieve much fame in his own lifetime. Nevertheless, he was one of the first mathematicians to obtain highly accurate astronomical measurements.

Further Reading

Heath, T. *Aristarchus of Samos, the Ancient Copernicus*. Oxford: Clarendon Press, 1966.

———. *A History of Greek Mathematics*. Oxford: Clarendon Press, 1921.

Neugebauer, O. *A History of Ancient Mathematical Astronomy*. New York: Springer-Verlag, 1975.

———. "Archimedes and Aristarchus," *Isis* 34 (1942): 4–6.

⊠   **Aryabhata I**
(476–550)
Indian
Algebra, Geometry

Little is known of the life of Aryabhata, who is called Aryabhata I in order to distinguish him from another mathematician of the same name who lived four centuries later. Aryabhata played a role in the development of the modern current number system and made contributions to number theory at a time when much of Europe was enveloped in ignorance.

He was born in India and had a connection with the city Kusumapura, the capital of the Guptas during the fourth and fifth centuries; this place is thought to be the city of his birth. Certainly, his *Aryabhatiya* was written in Kusumapura, which later became a center of mathematical learning.

Aryabhata wrote two works: the *Aryabhatiya* in 499, when he was 23 years old, and another treatise, which has been lost. The former work is a short summary of Hindu mathematics, consisting of three sections on mathematics, time and planetary models, and the sphere. The sections on mathematics contain 66 mathematical rules without proof, dealing with arithmetic, algebra, plane trigonometry, and spherical trigonometry. However, it also contains more advanced knowledge, such as continued fractions, quadratic equations, infinite series, and a table of sines. In 800 this work was translated into Arabic, and had numerous Indian commentators.

Aryabhata's number system, the one he used in his book, gives a number for each of the 33 letters of the Indian alphabet, representing the first 25 numbers as well as 30, 40, 50, 60, 70, 80, 90, and 100. It is noteworthy that he was familiar with a place-value system, so that very large numbers could easily be described and manipulated using this alphabetical notation. Indeed, it seems likely that Aryabhata was familiar with zero as a placeholder. The Indian place-value number system, which would later greatly influence the construction of the modern system, facilitated calculations that would be infeasible under more primitive models, such as Roman numerals. Aryabhata appears to be the originator of this place-value system.

In his examination of algebra, Aryabhata first investigates linear equations with integer coefficients—apparently, the *Aryabhatiya* is the first written work to do so. The question arose from certain problems of astronomy, such as the computation of the period of the planets. The technique is called *kuttaka*, which means "to pulverize," and consists of breaking the equation into related problems with smaller coefficients; the method is similar to the Euclidean algorithm for finding the greatest common divisor, but is also related to the theory of continued fractions.

In addition, Aryabhata gave a value for pi that was accurate to eight decimal places, improving on ARCHIMEDES OF SYRACUSE's and APOLLONIUS OF PERGA's approximations. Scholars have argued that he obtained this independently of the Greeks, having some particular method for approximating pi, but it is not known exactly how he did it; Aryabhata also realized that pi was an irrational number. His table of sines gives approximate values at intervals of less than four degrees, and uses a trigonometric formula to accomplish this.

Aryabhata also discusses rules for summing the first *n* integers, the first *n* squares, and the first *n* cubes; he gives formulas for the area of triangles and of circles. His results for the volumes of a sphere and of a pyramid are incorrect, but this may have been due to a translation error. Of course, these latter results were well known to the Greeks and might have come to Aryabhata through the Arabs.

As far as the astronomy present in the text, which the mathematics is designed to elucidate, there are several interesting results. Aryabhata gives an excellent approximation to the circumference of the Earth (62,832 miles), and explains the rotation of the heavens through a theory of the axial rotation of the Earth. Ironically, this (correct) theory was thought ludicrous by later commentators, who altered the text in order to remedy Aryabhata's mistakes. Equally remarkable is his description of the planetary orbits as ellipses—only highly accurate astronomical data provided by superior telescopes allowed European astronomers to differentiate between circular and elliptical orbits. Aryahbhata gives a correct explanation of the solar and lunar eclipses, and attributes the light of the Moon to reflected sunlight.

Aryabhata was of great influence to later Indian mathematicians and astronomers. Perhaps most relevant for the later development of mathematics was his place-number system. His theories were exceedingly advanced considering the time in which he lived, and the accurate computations of astronomical measurements illustrated the power of his number system.

Further Reading

Gupta, R. C. "Aryabhata, Ancient India's Great Astronomer and Mathematician," *Mathematical Education* 10, no. 4 (1976): B69–B73.

———. "A Preliminary Bibliography on Aryabhata I," *Mathematical Education* 10, no. 2 (1976): B21–B26.

Ifrah, G. *A Universal History of Numbers: From Prehistory to the Invention of the Computer.* New York: John Wiley, 2000.

van der Waerden, B. "The 'Day of Brahman' in the Work of Aryabhata," *Archive for History of Exact Sciences* 38, no. 1 (1988): 13–22.

B

⊠ **Babbage, Charles**
(1792–1871)
British
Analysis

The name of Charles Babbage is associated with the early computer. Living during the industrial age, in a time when there was unbridled optimism in the potential of machinery to improve civilization, Babbage was an advocate of mechanistic progress, and spent much of his lifetime pursuing the invention of an "analytic engine." Although his ambitious project eventually ended in failure, his ideas were important to the subsequent develop of computer logic and technology.

Born on December 26, 1792, in Teignmouth, England, to affluent parents, Babbage exhibited great curiosity for how things worked. He was educated privately by his parents, and by the time he registered at Cambridge in 1810, he was far ahead of his peers. In fact, it seems that he knew more than even his teachers, as mathematics in England had lagged far behind the rest of Europe. Along with George Peacock and John Herschel, he campaigned vigorously for the resuscitation of English mathematics. Together with Peacock and Herschel, he translated Lacroix's *Differential and Integral Calculus*, and became an ardent proponent of GOTTFRIED WILHELM VON LEIBNIZ's notation over SIR ISAAC NEWTON's.

Upon graduating, Babbage became involved in many diverse activities: He wrote several papers on the theory of functions and applied mathematics and helped to found several progressive learned societies, such as the Astronomical Society in 1820, the British Association in 1831, and the Statistical Society of London in 1834. He was recognized for his excellent contributions to mathematics, being made a fellow of the Royal Society in 1816 and Lucasian professor of mathematics at Cambridge in 1827; he held this latter position for 12 years without teaching, because he was becoming increasingly absorbed by the topic of mechanizing computation.

Babbage viewed science as an essential part of civilization and culture, and even thought that it was the government's responsibility to encourage and advance science by offering grants and prizes. Although this viewpoint is fairly common today, Babbage was one of its first advocates; before his time, much of science and mathematics was conducted in private research by men of leisure. He also advocated pedagogical reform, realizing that great teaching was crucial for the future development of mathematics; however, he did little with his chair at Cambridge toward realizing this goal.

His interests were remarkably diverse, including probability, cryptanalysis, geophysics, astronomy, altimetry, ophthalmoscopy, statistical

Charles Babbage, inventor of an early mechanical computer and founder of computer science *(Courtesy of the Library of Congress)*

linguistics, meteorology, actuarial science, lighthouse technology, and climatology. Babbage devised a convenient notation that simplified the drawing and reading of engineering charts. His literature on operational research, concerned with mass production in the context of pin manufacture, the post office, and the printing trade, has been especially influential.

Babbage was, as a young man, lively and sociable, but his growing obsession with constructing computational aids made him bitter and grumpy. Once he realized the extent of errors in existing mathematical tables, his mind turned to the task of using machinery to accomplish faultless calculations. Initially, he imagined a steam-powered calculator for the computation of trigonometric quantities; he began to envision a machine that would calculate functions and also print out the results.

The theory behind his machine was the method of finite differences—a discrete analog of the continuous differential calculus. Any polynomial of nth degree can be reduced, through successive differences, to a constant; the inverse of this procedure, taking successive sums, would be capable of computing the values of a polynomial, given some initial conditions. In addition, this concept could be extended to most nonrational functions, including logarithms; this would allow the mechanistic computation of the value of an arbitrary function.

Unfortunately, Babbage did not succeed. He continually thought up improvements for the system, becoming more ambitious for the final "Difference Engine Number One." This machine would handle sixth-order differences and 20 decimal numbers—a goal more grandiose than feasible. He never completed the project, though a Swedish engineer, in Babbage's own lifetime, built a modest working version based on a magazine account of the Englishman's dream. It seems that the principal reason for Babbage's failure was the prohibitive cost, though another cause is found in his new design to build an "analytical engine."

The analytical engine, in its design and planning, was a forerunner of the modern computer. Based on Joseph-Marie Jacquard's punch cards used in weaving machinery, Babbage's machine would be run by inserting cards with small holes; springy wires would move through the holes to operate certain levers. This concept described a machine of great versatility and power. The mill, the center of the machine, was to possess 1,000 columns with 50 geared wheels apiece: up to 1,000 50-digit numbers could be operated on with one of the four main arithmetic operations. Data, operation, and function cards could be inserted to provide information on variables, programs, and constants to the mill. The output would be printed, and another part of the machine would check for errors, store information, and make decisions. This corresponds to the memory and logic flow components of a modern computer. However, in one important aspect Babbage's analytical engine differs from the digital computer: His was based on a decimal system, whereas computers operate on a binary system.

Although the plans for this machine impressed all who viewed them, Babbage did not receive any financial support for its construction. He died on October 18, 1871, in London, without seeing the completion of his mechanistic projects. However, his son later built a small mill and printer, which is kept in the Science Museum of London.

Babbage was a highly creative mathematician whose ideas foreshadowed the major thrust of computer science in the second half of the 20th century. His work in pure mathematics has had little impact on successive generations of mathematicians, but his ideas on the analytical engine would be revisited over the next century, culminating in the design of early computers in the mid-1900s.

Further Reading

Babbage, H. *Babbage's Calculating Engines*. Los Angeles: Tomash, 1982.

Buxton, H. *Memoir of the Life and Labors of the Late Charles Babbage Esq., F.R.S.* Los Angeles: Tomash, 1988.

Dubbey, J. *The Mathematical Work of Charles Babbage*. Cambridge: Cambridge University Press, 1978.

Hyman, A. *Charles Babbage: Pioneer of the Computer*. Princeton, N.J.: Princeton University Press, 1982.

Morrison, P., and E. Morrison. *Charles Babbage and His Calculating Engines*. New York: Dover Publications, 1961.

Wilkes, M. "Babbage as a Computer Pioneer," *Historia Mathematica* 4, no. 4 (1977): 415–440.

⊠   Bacon, Roger
(ca. 1214–ca. 1292)
British
Arithmetic

In 13th-century Europe, there was no pursuit of science as there is today: the medieval church,

Roger Bacon proposed that mathematical knowledge should be arrived at through reason rather than authority. *(Courtesy of the National Library of Medicine)*

having gone so far as to make reason irrelevant in matters of faith and knowledge, substituting the unmitigated authority of papal decree and canon law, reigned over a stifling intellectual climate. However, the use of reason and empiricism, when coupled with the knowledge of a rational God's creation of a rational world, would prove to be the epistemology of science for the next several centuries, which resulted in numerous discoveries. Roger Bacon was an early figure in this paradigm shift, vigorously acting as a key proponent of the utility of mathematics and logic within the spheres of human knowledge. Natural philosophy, which in his view was subservient to theology, could serve toward the advancement of the human task generally speaking (the dominion and ordering of the Earth and, more specifically, the development of the church). Later scientific endeavor, starting in the 18th and 19th centuries, would abandon these theistic roots in favor of reason as the sole authority in man's pedagogical quest; but Bacon's promotion of the use of mathematics in partnership with faith in God was to remain the guiding epistemology for several centuries.

Bacon's birth has been calculated to be approximately 1214, though scholars differ on this detail since there is no exact record. This Englishman came of a family that had suffered persecution from the baronial party, due to their failed support of Henry III. His early instruction in the Latin classics, including Seneca and Cicero, led to his lifelong fascination with natural philosophy and mathematics, further inculcated at Oxford. After receiving his M.A. degree in about 1240, he apparently lectured in the Faculty of the Arts at Paris from 1241 to 1246. He discussed various topics from Aristotle's works, and he was a vehement advocate of complete instruction in foreign languages. Bacon underwent a drastic change in his conception of knowledge after reading the works of Robert Grosseteste (a leading philosopher and mathematician of the region) when he returned to Oxford in 1247; he invested considerable sums of money for experimental equipment, instruments, and books, and sought out acquaintance with various learned persons. Under Grosseteste's influence, Bacon developed the belief that languages, optics, and mathematics were the most important scientific subjects, a view he maintained his whole life.

By 1251 he had returned to Paris, and he entered the Franciscan order in 1257. The chapter of Narbonne was presided over by Bonaventure, who was opposed to inquiries not directly related to theology; he disagreed sharply with Bacon on the topics of alchemy and astrology, which he viewed as a complete waste of time. Bacon, on the other hand, while agreeing that they had no

discernible or predictable impact on the fates of individuals, thought it possible for the stars to exert a generic influence over the affairs of the world; he also experimented in alchemy, the quest to transmute lead into gold. Due to these political difficulties, Bacon made various proposals on education and science to Cardinal Guy de Folques, who was soon elected Pope Clement IV in 1265. As pope he formally requested Bacon to submit his philosophical writings, and the Englishman soon produced three famous works: *Opus maius* (Great work), *Opus minus* (Smaller work), and *Opus tertium* (Third work) within the next few years.

The *Opus maius* treated his opinions on natural philosophy and educational reform. Authority and custom were identified as impediments to learning; although Bacon submitted to the authority of the Holy Scriptures, he believed the wisdom contained therein needed to be developed by reason, rightly informed by faith. In this one sees some early seeds of Protestant thought about the proper balance of authority and reason. However, Bacon was not a believer in pure deduction detached from the observed world, like the Greek philosophers and mathematicians of antiquity; rather, he argued for requisition of experience. Information obtained through the exterior senses could be measured and quantified through instruments and experimental devices and analyzed through the implementation of mathematics. By studying the natural world, it was possible, Bacon argued, to arrive at some understanding of the Creator of that natural world. Thus, all of human knowledge was conceived in a harmonious unity, guided and led by theology as the regent of science. Hence it was necessary to deepen the understanding of languages, mathematics, optics, experimental science, alchemy, metaphysics, and moral philosophy.

Bacon's view on authority was somewhat progressive: without moderation, authority would prevent the plowing of intellectual furrows given provenience by rational disputation.

However, it must not be thought that a predecessor of nihilism, moral relativism, or other antiauthoritative systems can be found in Bacon—he believed in one truth (Christianity), but sought to use reason as a fit tool for advancing the interests of the kingdom of God and the civilization of man. The heathen should be converted by argument and persuasion, never by force.

Mathematics was to play an important role in Bacon's entire system. Of course, he understood the term in a broad sense, as inclusive of astronomy and astrology, optics, physical causation, and calendar reform, with even applications to purely religious matters. His work in optics relied heavily on geometry, and stood on the shoulders of EUCLID OF ALEXANDRIA, CLAUDIUS PTOLEMY, and ABU ALI AL-HAYTHAM, as well as Grosseteste. Along with Grosseteste, he advocated the use of lenses for incendiary and visual purposes. Bacon's ideas on refraction and reflection constituted a wholly new law of nature. His work on experimental science laid down three main goals: to certify deductive reasoning from other subjects, such as mathematics, by experimental observation; to add new knowledge not attainable by deduction; and to probe the secrets of nature through new sciences. The last prerogative can be seen as an effort toward attaining practical magic—the requisitioning of nature toward spectacular and utilitarian ends.

Bacon lists four realms of mathematical activity: human business, divine affairs (such as chronology, arithmetic, music), ecclesiastical tasks (such as the certification of faith and repair of the calendar), and state works (including astrology and geography). Mathematics, the "alphabet of philosophy," had no limits to its range of applicability, although experience was still necessary in Bacon's epistemology. Despite his glowing praise of "the door and key of the sciences," it appears that Bacon's facility in mathematics was not great. Although he has some original results in engineering, optics, and astronomy, he does not furnish any proofs or theorems of his own devising.

He also made some contributions in the areas of geography and calendar reform. He stated the possibility of journeying from Spain to India, which may have influenced Columbus centuries later. Bacon's figures on the radius of the Earth and ratio of land and sea were fairly accurate, but based on a careful selection of ancient authorities. His map of the known world, now lost, seems to have included lines of latitude and longitude, with the positions of famous towns and cities. Bacon discussed the errors of the Julian calendar with great perspicuity, and recommended the removal of one day in 125 years, similar to the Gregorian system.

Certainly, after his death, Bacon had many admirers and followers in the subsequent centuries. He continued writing various communications on his scientific theories, but sometime after 1277 he was condemned and imprisoned in Paris by his own Franciscan order, possibly for violating a censure. His last known writing was published in 1292, and he died sometime afterward.

Bacon contributed generally to the advance of reason and a rational approach to knowledge in Europe; his efforts influenced not only the course of mathematics but also the history of science more generally. The writings of Bacon would be familiar to later generations of mathematicians working in the early 17th century.

Further Reading

Bridges, J. *The Life and Work of Roger Bacon: An Introduction to the Opus Majus.* Merrick, N.Y.: Richwood Publishing Company, 1976.

Easton, S. *Roger Bacon and His Search for a Universal Science; a Reconsideration of the Life and Work of Roger Bacon in the Light of His Own Stated Purposes.* Westport, Conn.: Greenwood Press, 1970.

Lindberg, D. *Roger Bacon's Philosophy of Nature: A Critical Edition.* Oxford: Clarendon Press, 1983.

———. "Science As Handmaiden: Roger Bacon and the Patristic Tradition," *Isis* 78, no. 294 (1987): 518–536.

⊠ Baire, René-Louis
(1874–1932)
French
Analysis

In the late 19th century some of the ideas on the limits of sequences of functions were still vague and ill formulated. René Baire greatly advanced the theory of functions by considering issues of continuity and limit; his efforts helped to solidify the intuitive notions then in circulation.

René-Louis Baire was born in Paris on January 21, 1874, one of three children in a middle-class family. His parents endured hardship in order to send Baire to school, but he won a scholarship in 1886 that allowed him to enter the Lycée Lakanal. He completed his studies with high marks and entered the École Normale Supérieure in 1892.

During his next three years, Baire became one of the leading students in mathematics, earning first place in his written examination. He was a quiet, introspective young man of delicate health, which would plague him throughout his life. In the course of his oral presentation of exponential functions, Baire realized that the demonstration of continuity that he had learned was insufficient; this realization led him to study the continuity of functions more intensely and to investigate the general nature of functions.

In 1899 Baire defended his doctoral thesis, which was concerned with the properties of limits of sequences of continuous functions. He embarked on a teaching career at local lycées, but found the schedule too demanding; eventually he obtained an appointment as professor of analysis at the Faculty of Science in Dijon in 1905. Meanwhile, Baire had already written some papers on discontinuities of functions, and had also suffered a serious illness involving the constriction of his esophagus. In 1908 he completed a major treatise on mathematical

analysis that breathed new life into that subject. From 1909 to 1914 his health was in continual decline, and Baire struggled to fulfill his teaching duties; in 1914 he obtained a leave of absence and departed for Lausanne. Unfortunately, the eruption of war prevented his return, and he was forced to remain there in difficult financial circumstances for the next four years.

His mathematical contributions were mainly focused around the analysis of functions. Baire developed the concept of semicontinuity, and perceived that limits and continuity of functions had to be treated more carefully than they had been. His use of the transfinite number exercised great influence on the French school of mathematics over the next several decades. Baire's most lasting contributions are concerned with the limits of continuous functions, which he divided into various categories. He provided the proper framework for studying the theory of functions of a real variable; previously, interest was peripheral, as mathematicians were only interested in real functions that came up in the course of some other investigation. Thus, Baire effected a reorientation of thought.

Baire's illness made him incapable of resuming his grand project, and after the war he focused instead on calendar reform. He later received the ribbon of the Legion of Honor and was elected to the Academy of Sciences; sadly, his last years were characterized by pain and financial struggles. As a result, he was able to devote only limited amounts of time to mathematical research. He died in Chambéry, France, on July 5, 1932.

Baire's work played an important role in the history of modern mathematics, as it represents a significant step in the maturation of thought. His ideas were highly regarded by ÉMILE BOREL and HENRI LEBESGUE, and exerted much influence on subsequent French and foreign mathematicians.

⊠   **Banach, Stefan**
(1892–1945)
Polish
Analysis

Stefan Banach is known as the principal founder of functional analysis, the study of certain spaces of functions. He influenced many students during his intense career as a research mathematician, and many of the most important results of functional analysis bear his name.

Little is known of Banach's personality, other than that he was hardworking and dedicated to mathematics. Born in Krakow on March 30, 1892, to a railway official, Banach was turned over to a laundress by his parents; this woman, who became his foster mother, reared him and gave him his surname, Banach. At the age of 15 he supported himself by giving private lessons. He graduated from secondary school in 1910. After this he matriculated at the Institute of Technology at Lvov, in the Ukraine, but did not graduate. Four years later he returned to his hometown. There he met the Polish mathematician Hugo Steinhaus in 1916. From this time he became devoted to mathematics; it seems that he already possessed a wide knowledge of the discipline, and together with Steinhaus he wrote his first paper on the convergence of Fourier series.

In 1919 Banach was appointed to a lectureship at the Institute of Technology in Lvov, where he taught mathematics and mechanics. In this same year he received his doctorate in mathematics, even though his university education was incomplete. His thesis, said to have signaled the birth of functional analysis, dealt with integral equations; this is discussed in greater length below. In 1922 Banach was promoted in consideration of an excellent paper on measure theory (measures are special functions that compute the lengths, areas, and volumes of sets). After this he was made associate professor, and then full professor in 1927 at the University of Lvov.

Also, in 1924 he was elected to the Polish Academy of Sciences and Arts.

Banach made contributions to orthogonal series and topology, investigating the properties of locally meager sets. He researched a more general version of differentiation in measure spaces, and discovered classic results on absolute continuity. The Radon-Nikodym theorem was stimulated by his contributions in the area of measure and integration. He also established connections between the existence of measures and axiomatic set theory.

However, functional analysis was Banach's most important contribution. Little had been done in a unified way in functional analysis: VITO VOLTERRA had a few papers from the 1890s on integral equations, and IVAR FREDHOLM and DAVID HILBERT had looked at linear spaces. From 1922 onward, Banach researched normed linear spaces with the property of completeness—now called Banach spaces. Although some other contemporary mathematicians, such as Hans Hahn, RENÉ-MAURICE FRÉCHET, Eduard Helly, and NORBERT WIENER, were simultaneously developing concepts in functional analysis, none performed the task as thoroughly and systematically as Banach and his students. His three fundamental results were the theorem on the extension of continuous linear functionals (now called the Hahn-Banach theorem, as both Banach and Hahn proved it independently); the theorem on bounded families of mappings (called the Banach-Steinhaus theorem); and the theorem on continuous linear mappings of Banach spaces. He introduced the notions of weak convergence and weak closure, which deal with the topology of normed linear spaces.

Banach and Steinhaus founded the journal *Studia mathematica* (Mathematical studies) but Banach was often distracted from his scientific work due to his writing of college and secondary school texts. From 1939 to 1941 he served as dean of the faculty at Lvov, and during this time was elected as a member of the Ukrainian

Academy of Sciences. However, World War II interrupted his brilliant career; in 1941 the Germans occupied Lvov. For three years Banach was forced to research infectious diseases in a German institute, where he fed lice. When the Soviets recaptured Lvov in 1944, Banach returned to his post in the university; unfortunately, his health was shattered by the poor conditions under the German army, and he died on August 31, 1945.

Banach's work later became more widely known to mathematicians laboring in the field of functional analysis. His name is attached to several mathematical objects and theorems, giving evidence to his importance as one of the principal founders of functional analysis.

Further Reading

Hoare, G., and N. Lord. "Stefan Banach (1892–1945): A Commemoration of His Life and Work," *The Mathematical Gazette* 79 (1995): 456–470.

Kauza, R. *Through a Reporter's Eyes: The Life of Stefan Banach.* Boston: Birkhäuser, 1996.

Ulam, S. *Adventures of a Mathematician.* Berkeley: University of California Press, 1991.

Isaac Barrow, early discoverer of certain rules and results of calculus *(Courtesy of the Library of Congress)*

⊠   **Barrow, Isaac**
(1630–1677)
British
Calculus

Isaac Barrow was the first to discover certain aspects of differential calculus. There is some controversy about this, and also about the extent of his influence on SIR ISAAC NEWTON, who was his successor at Cambridge. However, Barrow's lectures on geometry contain some of the first theorems of calculus, and for this he is renowned.

Barrow was born in October 1630 (the exact date is unknown) to Thomas Barrow, a prosperous linen draper and staunch royalist. His mother, Anne, died in childbirth. A rebel in his younger days, Barrow later became disciplined and learned Greek, Latin, logic, and rhetoric. In 1643 he entered Trinity College, where he would remain for 12 years. Barrow, like his father, was a supporter of the king, but at Trinity the atmosphere became increasingly antiroyalist. He earned his B.A. degree in 1648, was elected college fellow in 1649, and received his M.A. degree in mathematics in 1652. With these credentials, he entered his final position as college lecturer and university examiner.

It is likely that his next appointment would have been a professorship of Greek, but Barrow was ejected from his position by Cromwell's government in 1655. Barrow sold his books and embarked on a tour of Europe, which lasted for four years. When he returned from his travels, Charles II had just been restored to power; Barrow took holy orders and thereby obtained the Regius professorship. In 1662 he also accepted the

Gresham professorship of geometry in London, and the next year was appointed as first Lucasian professor of mathematics at Cambridge. During the next six years Barrow concentrated his efforts on writing the three series of *Lectiones*, a collection of lectures that are discussed below.

Barrow's education had been quite traditional, centered on Aristotle and Renaissance thinkers, and on some topics he remained very conservative. But he was greatly intrigued by the revival of atomism and RENÉ DESCARTES's natural philosophy—his master's thesis studied Descartes in particular. By 1652 he had read many commentaries of EUCLID OF ALEXANDRIA, as well as more advanced Greek authors such as ARCHIMEDES OF SYRACUSE. His *Euclidis elementorum libri XV* (Euclid's first principles in 15 books), written in 1654, was designed as an undergraduate text, stressing deductive structure over content. He later produced commentaries on Euclid, Archimedes, and APOLLONIUS OF PERGA.

Apparently, Barrow's scientific fame was due to the *Lectiones* (Lectures), though they have not survived. The first Lucasian series, the *Lectiones mathematicae* (Mathematical lectures)—given from 1664 to 1666—is concerned with the foundations of mathematics from a Greek viewpoint. Barrow considers the ontological status of mathematical objects, the nature of deduction, spatial magnitude and numerical quantity, infinity and the infinitesimal, proportionality and incommensurability, as well as continuous and discrete entities. His *Lectiones geometricae* (Geometrical lectures) were a technical study of higher geometry.

In 1664 he found a method for determining the tangent line of a curve, a problem that was to be solved completely by the differential calculus; his technique involves the rotation and translation of lines. Barrow's later lectures are a generalization of tangent, quadrature, and rectification procedures compiled from his reading of Evangelista Torricelli, Descartes, Frans van Schooten, Johann Hudde, JOHN WALLIS, Christopher Wren, PIERRE DE FERMAT, CHRISTIAAN

HUYGENS, BLAISE PASCAL, and JAMES GREGORY. The material of these lectures was not totally original, being heavily based on the above authors, especially Gregory, and Barrow's *Lectiones geometricae* were not widely read.

Barrow also contributed to the field of optics, though his *Lectiones opticae* (Lectures on optics) was soon eclipsed by Newton's work. The introduction describes a lucid body, consisting of "collections of particles minute almost beyond conceivability," as the source of light rays; color is a dilution of thickness. The work is developed from six axioms, including the Euclidean law of reflection and sine law of refraction. Much of the material is taken from ABU ALI AL-HAYTHAM, Johannes Kepler, and Descartes, but Barrow's method for finding the point of refraction at a plane interface is original.

Much has been hypothesized of the relationship between Barrow and Newton; some say that Newton derived many of his ideas about calculus from Barrow, but there is little evidence of this. By late 1669 the two collaborated briefly, but it is not clear if they had any interaction before that time. In that year Barrow had resigned his chair, being replaced by Newton, in order to become the Royal Chaplain of London, and in 1675 became university vice-chancellor.

Barrow never married, being content with the life of a bachelor. His personality was blunt, and his theological sermons were extremely lucid and insightful, although he was not a popular preacher. Barrow was also one of the first members of the Royal Society, incorporated in 1662. He was small and wiry, and enjoyed good health; his early death on May 4, 1677, was due to an overdose of drugs.

Barrow's mathematical contribution seems somewhat marginal compared with the prodigious output of his contemporary Newton. However, he was an important mathematician of his time, earning fame through his popular *Lectiones*, and was the first to derive certain propositions of differential calculus.

Further Reading

Feingold, M. *Before Newton: The Life and Times of Isaac Barrow*. New York: Cambridge University Press, 1990.

———. "Newton, Leibniz, and Barrow Too: An Attempt at a Reinterpretation," *Isis* 84, no. 2 (1993): 310–338.

Hollingdale, S. "Isaac Barrow (1630–1677)," *Bulletin of the Institute of Mathematics and Its Applications* 13, nos. 11–12 (1977): 258–262.

Malet, A. "Barrow, Wallis, and the Remaking of Seventeenth Century Indivisibles," *Centaurus* 39, no. 1 (1997): 67–92.

⊠ **Bayes, Thomas**
(1702 1761)
British
Probability, Statistics

The field of statistics is split between two factions: Bayesians and Frequentists. The latter group, sometimes known as the Orthodox, maintains a classical perspective on probability, whereas the former group owes its genesis to Thomas Bayes, a nonconformist preacher and amateur statistician. Though his writings were not copious, in distinction to many of the famous mathematicians of history, the extensive influence of one remarkable essay has earned Bayes no small quantity of fame.

Born in 1702 to a dissenting theologian and preacher (he opposed certain doctrines and traditions of the established Anglican Church), Bayes was raised in his father's nontraditional views. With a decent private education, Bayes assisted his father in his pastoral duties in Holborn, London, and later became the minister at Tunbridge Wells. He never married, but possessed a wide circle of friends.

Apparently, Bayes was familiar with the current mathematics of the age, including the differential and integral calculus of SIR ISAAC NEWTON and the well-laid ideas of classical probability. Bayes's mathematical work, *Introduction to the Doctrine of Fluxions*, was published in 1736. Newton's work on calculus, which included the concept of infinitesimals, sometimes called fluxions, was controversial, as many scientists abhorred the concept of infinitely small quantities as intellectually repugnant. In fact, Bishop Berkeley—a contemporaneous philosopher—had written the *Analyst*, a thorough critique of Newton's work; Bayes's *Doctrine of Fluxions* was a mathematical rebuttal of Berkeley, and was appreciated as one of the soundest apologies for Newton's calculus.

But Bayes acquired some fame for his paper "Essay Towards Solving a Problem in the Doctrine of Chances," published posthumously in 1763. Although probability theory was already well founded with recent texts by JAKOB BERNOULLI and ABRAHAM DE MOIVRE, theoretical bastions of a similar ilk were lacking for the branch of statistics. The task that Bayes set for himself was to determine the probability, or chance, of statistical hypotheses' truth in light of the observed data. The framework of hypothesis testing, whereby scientific claims could be rejected or accepted (technically, "not rejected") on the basis of data, was vaguely understood in some special cases—SIR RONALD AYLMER FISHER would later formulate hypothesis testing with mathematical rigor, providing precision and generality. Of course, to either reject or not reject a claim gives a black or white decision to a concept more amenable to shades of gray (perhaps to a given statistical hypothesis a probability could be attached, which would indicate the practitioner's degree of confidence, given the data, of the truth of the proposition). This is the question that Bayes endeavored to answer.

The basic idea is that prior notions of the probability of an event are often brought to a situation—if biasing presuppositions exist, they color the assessment of the likelihood of certain unforeseen outcomes, and affect the interpretation of observations. In the absence of prior knowledge, one could assume a so-called noninformative prior distribution for the hypothesis, which would logically be the uniform probability distribution. Bayes demonstrated how to compute the probability of a hypothesis after observations have been made, which was designated by the term posterior distribution of the hypothesis. His method of calculation involved a formula that expressed the posterior probability in terms of the prior probability and the assumed distribution of the data; this was subsequently called Bayes's theorem.

Whereas the mathematics involved is fairly elementary (many students learn Bayes's theorem in the first two weeks of a course on probability and statistics), the revolutionary concept was that scientific hypotheses should be assigned probabilities of two species—the prior and the posterior. It seems that Bayes was not satisfied with his argument for this formulation, and declined to publish the essay, even though this theoretical work gave a firm foundation for statistical inference. A friend sent the paper to the Royal Society after Bayes's death, and the work was popularized by the influential PIERRE-SIMON LAPLACE. Bayes was a wealthy bachelor, and spent most of his life performing religious duties in the provinces. He was honored by inclusion to the Royal Society of London in 1742, perhaps for his *Doctrine of Fluxions*. He died on April 17, 1761, in Tunbridge Wells, England.

Much controversy has arisen over Bayes's methodology. The Bayesians show the logical foundation of the theory, which agrees with the general practice of science. The Frequentist opposition decries the variation in statistical results, which will be contingent upon the subjective choice of prior. It is appropriate to point out that, not only the analyses of classical statistics (especially nonparametric statistics) and mathematics, but the results of scientific endeavor more generally, are always contingent upon presuppositional assumptions that cannot

be completely justified. Some Bayesians conceive of probabilities as objective degrees of confidence, whereas others conceive of purely subjective beliefs—the Bayesian framework corresponds to the updating of belief structures through the accumulation of empirical information. It seems that Bayes himself was indifferent or at a median between these two philosophical extremes.

Further Reading

Barnard, G. "Thomas Bayes—a Biographical Note," *Biometrika* 45 (1958): 293–315.

Dale, A. "Thomas Bayes: A Memorial," *The Mathematical Intelligencer* 11, no. 3 (1989): 18–19.

Gillies, D. "Was Bayes a Bayesian?" *Historia Mathematica* 14, no. 4 (1987): 325–346.

Savage, L. *The Foundations of Statistics*. New York: Dover Publications, 1972.

Smith, G. "Thomas Bayes and Fluxions," *Historia Mathematica* 7, no. 4 (1980): 379–388.

Stigler, S. *The History of Statistics: The Measurement of Uncertainty before 1900*. Cambridge, Mass.: Belknap Press of Harvard University Press, 1986.

———. "Thomas Bayes's Bayesian Inference," *Journal of the Royal Statistical Society. Series A. Statistics in Society* 145, no. 2 (1982): 250–258.

Bernoulli, Daniel
(1700–1782)
Swiss
Mechanics, Probability

The 18th century was relatively bereft of mathematical talent in comparison with the intellectual wealth of the 1600s; however, Daniel Bernoulli was among the few rare geniuses of that time, making significant contributions to medicine, mathematics, and the natural sciences. In particular, his labors in the mechanical aspects of physiology, infinite series, rational mechanics, hydrodynamics, oscillatory systems, and probability have earned him great renown as an outstanding scientist.

Daniel Bernoulli, known for his outstanding contributions to hydrodynamics and the theory of oscillations *(Courtesy of the National Library of Medicine)*

Daniel Bernoulli was born on February 8, 1700, in Groningen, the Netherlands, into the well-known Bernoulli family: his father was the famous mathematician JOHANN BERNOULLI, who was then a professor at Groningen, and his mother was Dorothea Falkner, member of an affluent Swiss family. Daniel Bernoulli was close to his older brother Nikolaus, but later fell victim to his father's jealous competitiveness. In 1705 Johann Bernoulli relocated the family in Basel, occupying the chair of mathematics recently held by his deceased brother Jakob. Daniel Bernoulli commenced the study of logic and philosophy in 1713 and passed his baccalaureate in 1716. Meanwhile he studied mathematics under the supervision of his father and Nikolaus. Daniel Bernoulli was not destined for business, as a failed apprenticeship in commerce

testified; instead, he continued his Basel studies in medicine, later journeying to Heidelberg (1718) and Strasbourg (1719) to pursue knowledge. The next year he returned to Basel, and he earned his doctorate in 1721 with the dissertation *De respiratione* (Of respiration).

His application for the professorship of anatomy and botany was denied, and neither was he able to obtain the chair of logic. In 1723 he traveled to Venice to continue his medical studies under Michelotti. His 1724 publication of *Exercitationes mathematicae* (Mathematical exercises) earned him enough fame that he received an offer from the St. Petersburg Academy, and he stayed in Russia from 1725 to 1732, making the acquaintance of LEONHARD EULER. His dear brother Nikolaus suddenly died, and the severe climate was not to Bernoulli's liking; these factors encouraged Bernoulli to return home. After three failed applications to Basel, he obtained the chair of anatomy and botany in 1732.

The Russian period was quite fruitful for Bernoulli. During this time he accomplished important work in hydrodynamics, the theory of oscillations, and probability. His return to Basel evolved into a tour of Europe, where he was cordially received by numerous scholars. At this time his father competed with Bernoulli over the priority of the work on hydrodynamics called *Hydrodynamica* (Hydrodynamics); completed in 1734 and published in 1738, his father's own *Hydraulica* (Hydraulics) was predated to 1732.

In the field of medicine, in which he was forced to work for some periods of his life, Bernoulli turned his intellect toward mechanical aspects of physiology. His 1721 dissertation was a review of the mechanics of breathing, and a 1728 paper addressed the mechanics of muscle contraction, dispensing with the notion of fermentation in the blood corpuscles. Bernoulli also determined the shape and location of the entrance of the optic nerve into the bulbus, and lectured on the calculation of work done by the heart; he later established the maximum amount of work (activity over a sustained period) that a human could perform in a day.

However, Bernoulli's interests were absorbed by mathematical problems motivated by scientific questions. His four-volume *Exercitationes mathematicae* treats a variety of topics: the game of faro, the outflow of water, differential equations, and the lunulae (figures bounded by two circular arcs). He later investigated divergent series, such as the infinitely continued alternating sum and subtraction of the number one, which Euler and GOTTFRIED WILHELM VON LEIBNIZ thought summed to one-half. Bernoulli obtained sums for trigonometric series and investigated the theory of infinite continued fractions.

His contribution to mechanics lay in the areas of oscillations of rigid bodies and the mechanics of flexible and elastic bodies; these new areas were thoroughly addressed by the collaborative efforts of Bernoulli and Euler. Bernoulli explains the principle of gravity and magnetism, dispensing with the vortex theory of RENÉ DESCARTES and CHRISTIAAN HUYGENS. The theory of rotating bodies, the center of instantaneous rotation, and the conservation of live force are some of his other contributions, as well as the friction of solid bodies. He obtained wide fame from *Hydrodynamica*, which gives a history of hydraulics, formulas for the outflow of a fluid, oscillations of water in a tube, theory for hydraulic machinery (such as pumps, including the screw of ARCHIMEDES OF SYRACUSE), motions of "elastic fluids" (gases), and the derivation of the Bernoulli equation for stationary currents. This book also contains the determination of pressure on a container caused by a fluid, and the pressure of a water jet on an inclined plane—put into practice to propel boats many years later.

Together with Euler, Bernoulli dominated the mechanics of elastic bodies, deriving equilibrium curves for such bodies in 1728. He determined the curvature of a horizontal elastic band fixed at one end, and defined the "simple modes" and

frequencies of oscillation of a system with more than one body. After leaving St. Petersburg, Bernoulli's ongoing correspondence with Euler resulted in more literature: the small vibrations of both a plate immersed in water and a rod suspended from a flexible thread. Here he stressed the difference between simple and composite vibrations. In papers written between 1741 and 1743, Bernoulli treats the transversal vibrations of elastic strings, considering a horizontal rod affixed to a vertical wall. To derive the equation for vibration, he implemented the relation between curvature and moment. His 1753 treatise on oscillations resulted in a description of the general motion as the superposition of numerous single vibrations, given by an infinite trigonometric series. Later Bernoulli considered the oscillations of organ pipes and the vibrations of strings of uneven thickness.

Bernoulli also advanced the theory of probability and statistics; his most novel work in this area was *De mensura sortis* (Concerning the measure of chance), which addresses a problem in capital gains, and introduces the concept of a utility function—described by Bernoulli as the moral value of a quantity of capital. In 1760 he examined a problem of mortality in medical statistics, giving a differential equation relating the relevant variables. He later used an urn model in applications to population statistics, attempting to determine the average duration of marriage for each age group. It is interesting that Bernoulli uses the infinitesimal calculus in probability, taking an early step toward the notion of a continuous random variable and the statistical theory of errors. The latter subject he viewed as part of probability, using a semicircle as an approximation to the distribution of errors; this is similar to the modern theory, which uses Carl Friedrich Gauss's probability curve.

In 1743 Bernoulli switched to lecturing in physiology, and in 1750 he finally obtained the chair of physics; he continued lecturing until 1776, displaying fascinating physics experiments that attracted a large audience at Basel. For example, he was able to conjecture Coulomb's law of electrostatics as a result of experimental evidence from his lectures. He died on March 17, 1782, having received numerous prizes and honors in his lifetime, for example winning the Grand Prize of the Paris Academy in 1734 and 1737. In fact, Bernoulli won 10 prizes for essays entered in the competitions of the Paris Academy, which were usually given on topics of public interest, such as the best form of an anchor and the relationship between tides and lunar attraction. He won two prizes on the topic of magnetism and improved the construction of the compass.

Bernoulli was an outstanding scientist and mathematician. His principal mathematical contributions lay in differential equations, mechanics, and probability. Bernoulli's efforts, along with the work of Euler, would influence subsequent mathematicians of the 19th century.

Further Reading

Cannon, J., and S. Dostrovsky. *The Evolution of Dynamics: Vibration Theory from 1687 to 1742.* New York: Springer-Verlag, 1981.

Gower, B. "Planets and Probability: Daniel Bernoulli on the Inclinations of the Planetary Orbits," *Studies in History and Philosophy of Science* 18, no. 4 (1987): 441–454.

⊠   **Bernoulli, Jakob (Jacques Bernoulli)**
(1654–1705)
Swiss
Differential Equations, Probability

The Bernoulli family produced many mathematicians who contributed to diverse branches of mathematics such as probability, calculus, and number theory, and Jakob Bernoulli was the first member of that impressive congregation. His genius lay in the clever solution of certain highly specific problems, many of which possessed a relevancy to the external world.

Originally from Amsterdam, the Bernoullis were a thriving family of drug merchants who had immigrated to Basel. Jakob Bernoulli was born on December 27, 1654, in Basel, to Nikolaus Bernoulli, a city magistrate, and Margaretha Schönauer, a banker's daughter. Jakob Bernoulli was intended for a mercantile career as well, but his proclivities for scientific investigation would mark his destiny for another path. After attaining the master of arts degree in philosophy in 1671, he went on to receive a licentiate in theology five years later. However, it seems that Bernoulli had little interest or predilection toward evangelical ministry; he has been described as self-willed, stubborn, and aggressive, with an inferiority complex. During this time he studied mathematics and astronomy, although his father attempted to dissuade him from it. In 1676 he came to Geneva as a tutor, and there started his scientific diary called *Meditationes*; next he journeyed to France, where he spent two years learning the methodologies of Cartesian scientific philosophy. A second educational journey to the Netherlands and England in 1681 put him in contact with contemporary mathematicians. As a result, Bernoulli soon formulated a theory of comets (1682) and gravity (1683). Returning to Basel, Jakob began to lecture on the mechanics of solid and liquid bodies; he sent reports of his investigations to scientific journals, and meanwhile worked through RENÉ DESCARTES's *Géométrie* (Geometry). His contributions in geometry and algebra (he showed how a triangle could be divided into four equal parts by two straight perpendicular lines) were placed in an appendix to the fourth edition of the *Géométrie*.

Bernoulli next presented four studies in formal logic, published in the media of a disputation, from 1684 to 1686, and his first work in probability appeared in 1685. He was also familiar with the writings of JOHN WALLIS and ISAAC BARROW on infinitesimals in optical and mechanical problems, and in this way was introduced to calculus.

In 1684 Bernoulli married Judith Stupanus, the daughter of a wealthy pharmacist. One of his younger brothers, JOHANN BERNOULLI, started to attend the University of Basel; as a respondent to Jakob Bernoulli's logical debates, Johann Bernoulli earned his master of arts degree in 1685. Formally he studied medicine, but in secret pursued mathematics under the tutelage of Jakob Bernoulli. The relationship between the two brothers would prove fraught, as their similar personalities led to implacable friction and rivalry.

In 1687 Bernoulli was appointed professor of mathematics at the University of Basel, and at this time he studied and mastered the differential calculus of GOTTFRIED WILHELM VON LEIBNIZ; as a result, in 1689 Bernoulli produced a theory of infinite series, established the law of large numbers from probability theory, and brought attention to the importance of complete induction. The analysis of CHRISTIAAN HUYGENS's solution of the problem of the curve of constant descent in a gravitational field furnishes an excellent example of Bernoulli's mastery of Leibnizian calculus—it was in this context that the term *integral* first appeared. He later investigated elasticity through a simple differential equation (1694), and also researched the parabolic and logarithmic spirals (1691). His procedure of evolutes for determining the focal line of incident parallel rays of light on a semicircular mirror consists of generating an algebraic curve through the envelope of its circles of curvature. This later led to a differential equation that described the form of a sail that was inflated by the wind (1692, 1695). Bernoulli worked carefully on a wide range of ancient as well as modern problems, including the so-called Bernoulli differential equation, using the tools of differential calculus with expert facility.

Jakob Bernoulli and Johann Bernoulli's affections became increasingly sundered, mainly due to their mutual conflict of personality. Though inferior to his younger brother in terms of intuition and speed of thought, Jakob Bernoulli's mind could more deeply penetrate a subject. A famous 1696 problem proposed by Johann Bernoulli, called the brachistochrone, was concerned with the determination of a curve of quickest descent between two points. Jakob Bernoulli solved this in 1697, and also corrected Johann Bernoulli's solution of the isoperimetric problem in 1701, which the latter refused to recognize until long after Jakob Bernoulli's death. Their mutual antipathy soon led to criticism of each other's work, and they continued the debate in print from 1699 to 1700.

Bernoulli's main achievements lie in his clever analysis of particular problems of mathematical, classical, and mechanical interest. He developed a theory of natural phenomena based on the collision of ether particles, discussed the center point of oscillation, and discovered properties of the resistance of elastic bodies. The center of gravity of two bodies in uniform motion, the shape of a stretched cord, centrally accelerated motion, and the collective impulse of many shocks are some of the mechanical problems that he considered. In engineering, he treated the drawbridge problem in 1695, which was to determine the curve of a sliding weight hanging on a cable that holds the drawbridge in balance.

In the *Theory of Series* (published in five dissertations from 1682 to 1704), he develops series for pi and the logarithm of 2, investigates compound interest, exponential series, and the harmonic series. The *Ars conjectandi* (Art of conjecturing), published posthumously in 1713, is Bernoulli's most original work: the theory of combinations, exponential series, Bernoullian numbers, expected profit from various games of chance, probability as measure of confidence, a priori and a posteriori probability, and the law of large numbers are among the outstanding elements of this work. He died in Basel, on December 27, 1705, from tuberculosis.

Perhaps his contribution to probability is his most significant legacy, as this field has been extensively developed from his early efforts. Certainly, he advanced algebra, infinitesimal calculus, the calculus of variations, mechanics, and infinite series as well. Bernoulli was widely read by later generations of mathematicians, and is recognized today for his contributions to calculus and probability.

Further Reading

Boswell, T. "The Brothers James and John Bernoulli on the Parallelism between Logic and Algebra," *History and Philosophy of Logic* 11, no. 2 (1990): 173–184.

Hacking, I. "Jacques Bernoulli's 'Art of Conjecturing,'" *British Journal for the Philosophy of Science* 22 (1971): 209–229.

Stigler, S. *The History of Statistics: The Measurement of Uncertainty before 1900.* Cambridge, Mass.: Belknap Press of Harvard University Press, 1986.

Johann Bernoulli contributed to the development of calculus and used the method of integration as an inverse operation of differentiation to solve differential equations. *(Courtesy of the National Library of Medicine)*

⊠ **Bernoulli, Johann** (Jean Bernoulli)
(1667–1748)
Swiss
Differential Equations

The second of the famous Bernoulli brothers, Johann Bernoulli was part of a remarkable family of mathematicians. It was his fate to spend his early career under the shadow of his accomplished brother JAKOB BERNOULLI, but he eventually became renowned for his own genius. A leading proponent of Leibnizian differential calculus in later life, Bernoulli was at one point the most eminent mathematician of Europe.

Johann Bernoulli was born on August 6, 1667, in Basel, the 10th child of a wealthy mercantile family. The Bernoullis were originally from Holland, but Johann Bernoulli's father, Nikolaus Bernoulli, had settled in Switzerland as a druggist and married the affluent Margaretha

Schönauer. Originally, Johann Bernoulli was intended for a career in business, but after a failed apprenticeship as a salesman, he was permitted in 1683 to enroll at the university. His older brother Jakob Bernoulli was lecturing there on experimental physics, and Johann Bernoulli benefited from his elder's tutelage in mathematics. Responding to one of Jakob Bernoulli's 1685 logical disputations, Johann Bernoulli was elevated to *magister artium* and commenced the study of medicine. His first publication of fermentation processes appeared in 1690, and he earned his doctorate in 1694 with a mathematical dissertation in the field of medicine.

Meanwhile, Johann Bernoulli was avidly pursuing the study of mathematics (without his father's approval), and together with Jakob Bernoulli mastered GOTTFRIED WILHELM VON LEIBNIZ's differential calculus. Johann Bernoulli's solution of the *catenaria* problem, posed by Jakob Bernoulli in 1691, demonstrated his talent and marked him as a leading mathematician of Europe. At that time he was in Geneva, but soon he moved to Paris, where he won recognition thanks to his "golden theorem": the determination of a formula for the radius of curvature of an arbitrary curve. Bernoulli met Guillaume de L'Hôpital, and was employed by the latter to tutor him in infinitesimal calculus, for which Bernoulli was handsomely rewarded. When Bernoulli later returned to Basel, their correspondence continued, and became the source for a first calculus textbook titled *Analyse des infiniment petits* (Analysis of the infinitely small). Bernoulli was a faithful and eager communicator, writing 2,500 letters with 110 scholars over the course of his life; among these persons was Leibniz, with whom Bernoulli exchanged his scientific views starting in 1693.

During this period, a hiatus from his medical studies, Bernoulli obtained several mathematical results, which were published as short papers. Of principal significance is his work on exponential functions and the series development of such by integration. Integration was viewed as the inverse operation to differentiation, and thus could be used to solve differential equations. This idea was borne out by his solution of several outstanding problems, including Jakob Bernoulli's "Bernoulli equation"—Johann Bernoulli's piercing intuition allowed an elegance of solution that Jakob Bernoulli's more brutal techniques could not attain, which illustrated the contrast between the two brothers' intellects. Johann Bernoulli's formulation of exponential calculus, which is simply the application of Leibniz's differential calculus to exponential functions, further extended the applicability of infinitesimal methods. In 1695 he summed the infinite harmonic series, developed addition theorems for trigonometric and hyperbolic functions, and described the geometric generation of pairs of curves. The summation of reciprocal squares remained impervious to both Bernoullis' efforts, and was later to be computed by LEONHARD EULER, Johann Bernoulli's ablest student.

Having completed his degree in medicine, Bernoulli accepted the chair of mathematics at the University of Groningen. He had already married Dorothea Falkner when he departed for Holland, and was brimming with resentment toward Jakob Bernoulli. The relationship with his brother had already begun to disintegrate: both men had quarrelsome, pugnacious personalities, and Johann Bernoulli was an avid debater and polemicist. However, Johann Bernoulli's feistiness extended beyond his brother; in 1702 he was involved in theological quarrels with Groningen professors, and was labeled a follower of Spinoza.

In June 1696 Bernoulli posed the following problem, known as the brachistochrone: to determine the path of quickest descent between two fixed locations. Dedicating the problem "to the shrewdest mathematicians of all the world," Bernoulli gave a half-year time limit to find the solution; Leibniz, who solved the problem immediately, accurately predicted that only five persons in the world were capable of success— SIR ISAAC NEWTON, Leibniz himself, the Bernoulli brothers, and L'Hôpital. The brachistochrone provides another contrast of the brothers' abilities: Jakob Bernoulli's cumbersome analysis laid the foundations for the calculus of variations, whereas Johann Bernoulli's approach ingeniously reduced the problem to a question in optics, and he deduced the correct differential equation from the law of refraction. Jakob Bernoulli subsequently posed the isoperimetric problem, whose solution required the new calculus of variations, which had been characteristically underestimated by Johann Bernoulli. His published solution was therefore inadequate, resulting in Jakob Bernoulli's unbridled disparagement in published critique. It was not until many years after Jakob Bernoulli's death that Johann Bernoulli would admit the supremacy of the calculus of variations—so deep ran the enmity aroused by wounded ego and controversy. In 1718 Johann Bernoulli produced an elegant solution of the isoperimetric problem utilizing Jakob Bernoulli's methodology, and this work contained the early notions for the modern calculus of variations.

Johann Bernoulli's work on the cycloid, in his description the "fateful curve of the 17th century," promulgated his development of integration of rational functions via the method of partial fractions. A formal algebraic approach to such calculations was typical of Johann Bernoulli, and his influence in the common techniques of calculus has been felt through modern times.

After Jakob Bernoulli's death in 1705, Johann Bernoulli succeeded him at the chair of mathematics in Basel, apparently a decision motivated by his family. He soon became involved in the politically fraught priority dispute between Newton and Leibniz, and he openly criticized Taylor's support of the method of fluxions (the Newtonian calculus). In later debates and competitions, Bernoulli was able to successfully analyze certain problems, such as the trajectory of the ballistic curve in the general case, to which the Newtonian calculus was insufficient. After Newton's death in 1727, Bernoulli would be recognized as the leading mathematician of Europe. At Basel he researched theoretical and applied mechanics, and in 1714 he published his only book, *Théorie de la manoeuvre des vaisseaux* (Theory of the maneuver of vessels). In this work he criticizes French navigational theories and developed the principle of virtual velocities, with applications to conservative mechanical systems. In other papers he investigated the transmission of momentum, the motion of planets, and the phenomenon of the luminous barometer.

Bernoulli was greatly honored during his lifetime, being granted membership of the academies of Paris, Berlin, London, St. Petersburg, and Bologna. He benefited from a high social status in Basel, due to his marital connections and family wealth, and held various civic offices there. He died on January 1, 1748, in Basel. His genius in solving particular mathematical problems made him one of the top mathematicians of his time. In terms of legacy, he was not as successful as his brother Jakob Bernoulli, but nevertheless left influential work on mechanics and differential equations behind.

Further Reading

Boswell, T. "The Brothers James and John Bernoulli on the Parallelism between Logic and Algebra," *History and Philosophy of Logic* 11, no. 2 (1990): 173–184.

⊠ **Bessel, Friedrich Wilhelm**
(1784–1846)
German
Analysis

The field of astronomy had developed quickly by the 19th century, and mathematics retained its vital importance to this sister science. Friedrich Bessel not only became one of the greatest astronomers, accurately calculating various astronomical distances and labeled as the founder of the German school of practical astronomy, but also developed outstanding mathematical theories to explain the perturbations of planetary orbits.

On July 22, 1784, Friedrich Bessel was born in Minden, Germany. His father was a civil servant of that town, and his mother was a minister's daughter. Bessel had a large family, consisting of six sisters and two brothers. Bessel attended the Gymnasium (German high school) in Minden, but after four years he departed to become a merchant's apprentice. While in school, he had an inclination toward mathematics and physics, but did not exhibit any noteworthy degree of ability until he was 15 years of age. In 1799 he commenced his apprenticeship

Friedrich Bessel, a great astronomer, invented Bessel functions to study the perturbations of planetary orbits. *(Courtesy of the Library of Congress)*

with Kulenkamp, a famous mercantilist firm; he quickly demonstrated his facility with calculations and accounting, and as a result was provided a meager salary, emancipating him from dependence on his parents.

Meanwhile, Bessel spent evenings studying various subjects in preparation for his future career as a cargo officer. He soon mastered geography, Spanish, and English, as well as the art of navigation—this discipline first aroused his fascination for astronomy. Not content simply to know the technology of his trade, Bessel set about researching the deeper aspects of astronomy and mathematics, considering this foundational knowledge to be essential. Among his first achievements in the field of astronomy was the determination of the longitude of Bremen, using a sextant that he had built. He also began to peruse the astronomical literature, and in this

manner discovered the astronomer Thomas Harriot's 1607 observations of Halley's comet. After completing the reduction of Harriot's observations (a process that involves compensating for the refraction of light caused by the Earth's atmosphere and generally freeing the observations of errors), he presented the astronomer Heinrich Olbers with his own calculation of the orbit in 1804. The result was in close agreement with Halley's work, and Olbers encouraged Bessel to supplement these reductions with some additional observations; the fruit of this labor was an article printed in the *Monatliche Correspondenz* (Monthly correspondence). In depth of material worthy of a doctoral dissertation, this paper attracted the notice of many readers and marked a transition in Bessel's life.

In early 1806, before the termination of his apprenticeship, Bessel became an assistant at a private observatory near Bremen, which was owned by a wealthy civil servant with an interest in astronomy who had contacts with many scientists. At the observatory Bessel acquired a thorough schooling in the observation of planets and comets, and meanwhile made further contributions toward the calculation of cometary orbits. In 1807 he commenced the reduction of James Bradley's observations on 3,222 stars, which marked one of Bessel's greatest achievements. Friedrich Wilhelm III of Prussia constructed a new observatory in Königsberg, and Bessel was appointed as its director and as professor of astronomy in 1809. Since he did not have a doctorate, the University of Göttingen gave him one at the suggestion of CARL FRIEDRICH GAUSS, who had earlier met Bessel in 1807.

During construction of the observatory, Bessel continued his work in the reduction of Bradley's data; for his resulting tables of refraction, he was awarded the Lalande Prize in 1811 by the Institut de France. In 1813 he began his observations in the completed observatory, and remained in Königsberg as a teacher and researcher for the rest of his life. In 1812 he married Johanna Hagen, by whom he had two sons and three daughters. This felicitous marriage was shadowed by illness and his sons' early deaths, and Bessel found distraction in walking and hunting.

Bessel accomplished much in the field of astronomy. The reduction of Bradley's data allowed a proper determination of the stars' positions and motions, but Bessel's own program of observation and immediate reduction resulted in highly accurate data. He also gave the first accurate estimate of the distance of a fixed star, using triangulation techniques and a heliometer. He was also involved in geodesy, the measurement of the Earth, completing an 1830 triangulation of East Prussia with a new measuring apparatus and Gauss's method of least squares. Bessel's resulting estimate of the parameters of the Earth's dimensions earned him international fame.

Bessel was interested in mathematics through its close connection to astronomy. The problem of perturbation in astronomy was amenable to analysis using certain special confluent hypergeometric functions, later called Bessel functions. There were two effects of an intruding planet on the elliptical orbit of a given planet: the direct effect of the gravitational perturbation and the indirect effect arising from the motion of the sun caused by the perturbing planet. Bessel separated the two influences, and Bessel functions appear as coefficients in the series expansion of the indirect effect. In his study of the problem, Bessel made an intensive study of these special functions, which are described in his Berlin treatise of 1824. Special cases of these functions had been known for more than a century, having been discovered by JOHANN BERNOULLI and GOTTFRIED WILHELM VON LEIBNIZ; DANIEL BERNOULLI (1732) and LEONHARD EULER (1744) had also investigated Bessel coefficients. But Bessel's motivation arose from their application to astronomy, not as a detached study in pure mathematics.

His health was in decline from 1840, and his last major journey to England was in 1842; as a result of his participation in the Congress of the British Association in Manchester, Bessel was encouraged to complete and publish some remaining research. After two agonizing years battling cancer, he died on March 17, 1846, in Königsberg.

Although Bessel is principally known as an astronomer, like Gauss he made outstanding contributions to pure mathematics that could be applied to astronomy. His name is attached to the special functions mentioned above, as well as to an inequality that is today used in Fourier analysis and the theory of Hilbert spaces. Both the Bessel functions and the Bessel inequality have enduring relevance for modern mathematicians.

Further Reading

Clerke, A. *A Popular History of Astronomy during the Nineteenth Century*. Decorah, Iowa: Sattre Press, 2003.

Fricke, W. "Friedrich Wilhelm Bessel (1784–1846)," *Astrophysics and Space Science: An International Journal of Cosmic Physics* 110, no. 1 (1985): 11–19.

Hamel, J. *Friedrich Wilhelm Bessel*. Leipzig: BSB B.G. Teubner, 1984.

Klein, F. *Development of Mathematics in the 19th Century*. Brookline, Mass.: Math Sci Press, 1979.

Lawrynowicz, K. *Friedrich Wilhelm Bessel, 1784–1846*. Basel: Birkhäuser Verlag, 1995.

Williams, H. *The Great Astronomers*. New York: Simon and Schuster, 1930.

⊠ Betti, Enrico
(1823–1892)
Italian
Topology, Algebra

Enrico Betti is known for his contributions to Galois theory (an abstract algebraic theory used to solve algebraic equations, developed by EVARISTE GALOIS) and the theory of elliptic functions. His work on the analysis of hyperspace was to later inspire JULES-HENRI POINCARÉ in the foundation of algebraic geometry.

Betti was born on October 21, 1823, in Pistoia, Italy, and his father died when he was quite young. As a result, his mother oversaw his education, and he later matriculated at the University of Pisa, receiving a degree in the physical and mathematical sciences. Afterward he became involved in the war for Italian independence, participating as a soldier in the battles of Curtatone and Montanara. His subsequent profession was as a high school mathematics teacher in Pistoia, though he continued his own researches into pure mathematics concurrently.

Much of Betti's work was in the field of algebra. The work of Evariste Galois, which received little recognition during its author's brief life, was largely summarized in a personal letter of 1832 that was later published by JOSEPH LIOUVILLE in 1846. Since that time, Betti furthered Galois's work on the solubility of algebraic equations by radicorational operations (the issue of determining which equations could have their solutions expressed in terms of radicals and rational numbers). By connecting Galois's work with the prior researches of NIELS HENRIK ABEL and Paolo Ruffini, Betti bridged the gap between the new methods of abstract algebra and the classical problems (such as the quintic) considered previously. Many at the time viewed the labors of Galois as irrelevant and sterile, but Betti's elaborations in two papers of 1852 and 1855 constitute an important step toward reversing those adverse opinions; today, Galois theory is seen as a fruitful and lovely component of abstract algebra.

He also investigated the theory of elliptic functions, a popular topic in the 19th century; Betti described this branch of mathematics by relating it to the construction of certain transcendental functions in 1861, and KARL WEIERSTRASS developed these ideas further in the ensuing years. Taking another, nonalgebraic look at the same subject, Betti investigated elliptic functions from the perspective of mathematical physics. Under the guidance of BERNHARD GEORG FRIEDRICH RIEMANN, whom Betti had met in Göttingen in 1858, Betti researched the procedures used in electricity and mathematical analysis.

In 1865 Betti accepted a professorship at the University of Pisa, which he retained for the remainder of his life. Later he became rector of the university and director of the teachers' college in Pisa. From 1862 he was a member of the Italian parliament, briefly served as undersecretary of state for public education in 1874, and became a senator in 1884. However, his principal interests were not in politics or administration, but in pure mathematical research; Betti desired only to have solitude for intellectual reflection, and animated intercourse with his close friends.

Betti's work in the area of theoretical physics led to a law of reciprocity in elasticity theory, known as Betti's theorem (1878). He first mastered GEORGE GREEN's methods for the integration of PIERRE-SIMON LAPLACE's equations in the theory of potentials, and utilized this methodology in the study of elasticity and heat. He also analyzed hyperspace in 1871; Poincaré would later draw inspiration from Betti to expand these preliminary investigations. The term *Betti numbers,* coined by Poincaré, would be commonly used as measurable characteristics of an algebraic variety (a high-dimensional surface that can be expressed as the locus of points satisfying an algebraic equation).

Betti was an excellent teacher, bringing his passion and extensive knowledge to the classroom, and he was an ardent proponent of a return to classical education. He regarded EUCLID OF ALEXANDRIA's *Elements* as a model text for instruction, and strongly advocated its return to the secondary schools. He influenced several generations of students at Pisa, guiding many toward the pursuit of scientific knowledge. He died on August 11, 1892, in Pisa.

Betti's impact on mathematics is still felt today. His early research into algebraic topology was fundamental, as the enduring importance of the Betti numbers to questions of classification testifies. Perhaps even more important was his development of Galois theory, which has become a huge component of modern studies in abstract algebra.

Further Reading

Weil, A. "Riemann, Betti and the Birth of Topology," *Archive for History of Exact Sciences* 20 (1979): 91–96.

⊠   **Bhaskara II**
     (1114–1185)
     Indian
     Trigonometry, Geometry, Algebra

Indian mathematicians contributed to the further development of the digital number system, and also supplemented the wealth of geometrical and arithmetical information then available. During the Dark Ages of Europe, mathematics was slowly progressing in the Middle East and India, and Bhaskara II was one of the best-known mathematicians of his time.

Bhaskara II is distinguished from Bhaskara I, an Indian from the seventh century well known for his exposition of ARYABHATA I's astronomy. Bhaskara II was recognized for his work in astronomy, but also for his efforts in pure mathematics. He was born in 1114 in India, but little is known of his life. Apparently, he came from a family of Brahmans known as the Sandilya gotra, and was born in the city of Vijayapura. Among his contemporaries, Bhaskara was famous for his scientific talents, as he had not only mastered the previous knowledge of BRAHMAGUPTA and others, but also expanded it through his own contributions.

Bhaskara was appointed head of the astronomical observatory at Ujjain, the foremost center of mathematical knowledge in India at that time. Due to this eminent position, Bhaskara represented the acme of mathematical knowledge in the world, since little of importance was transpiring in Europe in the 12th century. Bhaskara possessed a deep understanding of number systems and the solution of equations; as a successor to Brahmagupta, he grasped the concepts of zero and negative numbers. He studied numerous Diophantine problems—equations in one or more variables with integer coefficients—and often obtained solutions that were extremely large (this would have been impossible to achieve without an excellent number system facilitating such calculations).

There are at least six writings that can definitely be attributed to Bhaskara. The *Lilavati* (The beautiful), which is addressed to a woman of that name (perhaps his daughter or his wife), contains 13 chapters on mathematics, including such topics as arithmetic, plane geometry, solid geometry, algebra (called "the pulverizer"), the shadow of a gnomon, and combinations of digits. (A gnomon is a geometric shape that had fascinated the Greeks; it is the L shape remaining when one rectangle is removed from a larger one.) Bhaskara is careful to define his terms precisely, and discusses arithmetical and geometrical progressions of numbers. His discussion of the combination of digits, essentially a contribution to modern arithmetic, was perhaps of greatest importance. This was easily Bhaskara's most popular work, with almost three dozen commentaries and numerous translations.

Bhaskara easily manipulates the arithmetic of negative numbers, and knows how to multiply by zero. In addition, he avoided Brahmagupta's mistake of attempting division by zero, realizing the difficulty inherent in this operation; in the *Bijaganita* (Root extraction), Bhaskara writes that any number divided by zero is infinity, which is closer to the truth. His method of multiplication for large numbers is somewhat different from the modern technique, but amply effective. Bhaskara also demonstrates particular rules for squaring numbers, even though this is a special case of multiplication. He treats inverse proportion by discussing the rule of three, the rule of five, the rule of seven, and the rule of nine.

The *Bijaganita* treats algebra: positive and negative numbers (negative numbers were later "invented" by Fibonacci in Europe), zero, various types of equations (including the quadratic), and the multiplication of several unknowns. Again, there are several commentaries and translations.

Bhaskara's *Siddhantasiromani*, written in 1150, consists of two parts. The first section, called the *Ganitadhyaya*, treats mathematical astronomy, addressing the mean and true longitude of planets, diurnal motion, syzygies, lunar and solar eclipses, planetary latitudes, heliacal risings and settings of the planets, the lunar crescent, and planetary conjunctions. The second portion, called the *Goladhyaya*, deals with the sphere and is largely an explication of the former part: the nature of the sphere; cosmography; geography; planetary mean motion; eccentric-epicyclic model of planetary motion; construction of an armillary sphere; spherical trigonometry; calculations of the eclipse, visibility of the planets, and lunar crescent; astronomical instruments; description of the seasons; and the performance of astronomical computations. He also treats the sine function, expressing more interest in this function for its own sake, developing the well-known sum and product identities. The *Siddhantasiromani* also has more than a dozen commentaries and many translations.

Next, there is the *Vasanabhasya*, which is Bhaskara's own commentary on the *Siddhantasiromani*. The *Karanakutuhala* (Calculation of astronomical wonders), written in 1183, gives simpler rules than the *Siddhantasiromani* for solving problems in astronomy. It discusses the mean and true longitudes of planets, diurnal motion, lunar and solar eclipses, heliacal risings and settings, the lunar crescent, planetary conjunctions, and syzygies. Finally, Bhaskara's *Vivarana* has not been studied. Also, the *Bijopanaya*, written in 1151, has been attributed by some to Bhaskara, though this appears to be a later forgery.

Bhaskara's manifold achievements and superb talent placed him in a revered position among Indian intellectuals, and in 1207 an educational institution was endowed in order to study his writings. He certainly affected later Indian mathematicians, who were heavily influenced by his work on astronomy and mathematics.

Further Reading
Calinger, R. *Classics of Mathematics*. Upper Saddle River, N.J.: Prentice Hall, 1995.

Datta, B. "The Two Bhaskaras," *Indian Historical Quarterly* 6 (1930): 727–736.

Ifrah, G. *A Universal History of Numbers: From Prehistory to the Invention of the Computer*. New York: John Wiley, 2000.

Joseph, G. *The Crest of the Peacock: Non-European Roots of Mathematics*. London: Penguin Books, 1990.

Patwardhan, K., S. Naimpally, and S. Singh. *Lilavati of Bhaskaracarya*. Delhi, India: Motilal Banarsidass Publications, 2001.

⊠ Birkhoff, George David
(1884–1944)
American
Analysis, Geometry

There were few great American mathematicians until the 20th century; Europe had dominated mathematics for centuries. Birkhoff represents an important step in the reversal of this pattern; his brilliant discoveries in differential equations, geometry, and dynamics led to his recognition as one of the foremost mathematicians of America.

George Birkhoff, an early great American mathematician who studied the mathematical foundations of relativity *(Courtesy of the Library of Congress)*

George Birkhoff was born in Overisel, Michigan, on March 21, 1884. His father was a doctor, and Birkhoff received his early education at the Lewis Institute in Illinois. He spent a year at the University of Chicago before transferring to Harvard, graduating in 1905. He returned to the University of Chicago, completing his doctoral thesis two years later.

After Chicago, Birkhoff worked as a lecturer at the University of Wisconsin, during which time he married Margaret Elizabeth Grafius in 1908. He spent a few years at Princeton before becoming a professor at Harvard, later becoming the dean of the Faculty of Arts and Sciences from 1935 to 1939. Due to his professorship, he was able to devote most of his energy to mathematical research and the advising of graduate students.

Birkhoff's thesis dealt with boundary-value problems from the theory of differential equations, which he extended in later years. His early research treated linear differential equations, difference equations, and the generalized Riemann problem. This area of mathematics is relevant to mathematical physics, with applications to quantum mechanics. Birkhoff's research program proved to be ambitious: to construct a system of differential equations given a particular set of "singular points" (points of discontinuity in the solution). This effort has now evolved into an extensive field of research; Birkhoff took the first steps.

His major interest in the field of analysis was dynamical systems. Birkhoff attempted to extend the work of JULES-HENRI POINCARÉ on celestial mechanics, and he proved one of the latter's last conjectures involving the fixed points of continuous transformations of an annulus. Birkhoff introduced the concepts of wandering, central, and transitive motions, and investigated the topic of transitivity. The main corpus of modern dynamics emerged from Birkhoff's ideas, including ergodic theory and topological dynamics. His minimax principle and theorem on fixed points of transformations provided motivation in the areas of analysis and topology.

Birkhoff also thought deeply about the foundations of relativity and quantum mechanics, and he contributed some theoretical papers to these subjects. Although controversial among physicists, these works provide original critiques and a novel approach to relativity. Birkhoff also contributed to combinatorics, number theory, and functional analysis. His text on geometry has influenced American pedagogical trends in the teaching of high school geometry.

Birkhoff was highly regarded by his colleagues, and was viewed as one of the eminent mathematicians of America at that time. He was most influenced by Maxime Bôcher of Harvard and E. H. Moore of the University of Chicago, through whom he learned algebra and analysis. Birkhoff was president of the American Mathematical Society in 1925; he had many friends and collaborators in Europe, such as Jacques Hadamard, Tullio Levi-Civita, and Sir Edmund Whittaker. He died in Cambridge, Massachusetts, on November 12, 1944.

Birkhoff's main contributions lay in dynamical systems, but he also stimulated interest in topology and difference equations. Much of modern mathematics can trace a connection to the work of Birkhoff; he also represented the beginning of the trend away from European domination of mathematics.

Further Reading

Butler, L. "George David Birkhoff," *American National Biography 2*. New York: Oxford University Press, 1999.

Etherington, I. "Obituary: George David Birkhoff," *Edinburgh Mathematical Notes 1947* 36 (1947): 22–23.

Morse, M. "George David Birkhoff and His Mathematical Work," *American Mathematical Society. Bulletin. New Series*, 52 (1946): 357–391.

⊠   **Bolyai, János (Johann Bolyai)**
(1802–1860)
Hungarian
Geometry

One of the outstanding problems of Greek geometry was the proof of the fifth postulate of Euclid's *Elements* (often referred to as the parallel postulate) from the other, more intuitive axioms. It was equivalent to the statement that through any point separate from a given line, one could construct a unique parallel line; from this statement, one can deduce that the sum of the angles of any triangle is equal to two right angles. Many attempts over the centuries to establish this axiom rigorously had failed, with the latest and most notable attempt by Farkas Bolyai. His son János Bolyai would eventually construct a new, consistent geometry independent of the fifth axiom. Even though priority for this discovery is credited to CARL FRIEDRICH GAUSS, János Bolyai performed his research in ignorance of this, and so is often credited as a cofounder of non-Euclidean geometry.

János Bolyai was born on December 15, 1802, in Kolozsvár, Hungary, to Farkas Bolyai and Susanna von Árkos. The Bolyai family was descended from a long line of aristocrats, and Farkas Bolyai had farmed their estates before becoming a professor of mathematics, physics, and chemistry at the Evangelical-Reformed College at Marosvásárhely. He was also a close friend of Carl Friedrich Gauss. János Bolyai showed great talent in many areas, including mathematics and music, displaying proficiency in the violin at a young age. In 1815 he began study at his father's college, and in 1818 entered the imperial academy at Vienna in preparation for a military career, contrary to Farkas's desire for him to study in Göttingen under Gauss.

Young Bolyai graduated in 1822, but meanwhile his interest in geometry, especially the parallel postulate, had been awakened by his father's own lengthy obsession. Indeed, Farkas Bolyai had spent many years attempting the fifth axiom's deduction, without success; his correspondence with Gauss on this subject led to the latter's own discovery of non-Euclidean geometry, which his embarrassed conservatism never disclosed. Farkas Bolyai even warned his son emphatically against engaging his intellect with that problem in 1820, wishing to spare him many moments of anguish, confusion, and despair. However, the impetuous youth continued to contemplate the question.

After several years of vain labor, Bolyai turned in 1823 toward the construction of a geometry that did not require the fifth postulate—a geometry that in fact dispensed with that axiom altogether. Meanwhile, he graduated from the academy and began his first tour in Romania as a sublieutenant. He later visited his father in 1825, presenting his manuscript on his theory of absolute space—a space where through a given point not on a line, many distinct lines through the point could be constructed parallel to the given line, in direct refutation of the parallel postulate. Farkas Bolyai could not accept this new geometry, but he sent the manuscript to Gauss. The latter responded in 1832, astonished that János Bolyai had independently replicated his own work, and claiming his priority by more than three decades. Gauss directed János Bolyai to explore various questions, such as the volume of the tetrahedron in absolute space, but the young Hungarian was not encouraged. The assertion of Gauss's priority was first met with apprehension, and then with resentment.

Meanwhile, Bolyai finished his military career in Lvov in 1832: he was often sick with fever, so the army gave him a pension and dismissed him from service. Apparently, he had earned a reputation as a dashing officer with a predilection for duels. He came home to live with his father, and his manuscript was published as "Appendix Explaining the Absolutely True Science of Space" in Farkas's *Tentamen* in 1832, a systematic treatment of geometry, algebra, and analysis. However, this essay (as well as the book) received no response from mathematicians, and his discouragement over the situation with Gauss drove Bolyai into a reclusion both social and mathematical.

The relationship between father and son was also strained, mainly due to irritation over the unenthusiastic reception of their work. János Bolyai withdrew to the small family estate at Domáld, and in 1834 married Rosalie von Orbán, by whom he had three children. In 1837 both Bolyais attempted to retrieve their mathematical reputation through participation in a competition of the Jablonow Society. The topic treated the rigorous geometric construction of imaginary numbers, which was a subject of interest for many mathematicians, such as Gauss, SIR WILLIAM ROWAN HAMILTON, and AUGUSTIN-LOUIS CAUCHY. János Bolyai's solution resembled Hamilton's, but failed to gain the desired recognition, which only exacerbated his melancholic tendencies. He continued sporadic research in mathematics, of variable quality; his best results concerned absolute geometry, the relation of absolute trigonometry and spherical trigonometry, and the volume of the tetrahedron in absolute space. Some work by NIKOLAI LOBACHEVSKY on the same type of geometry reached him in 1848, and acted as an impetus to further his efforts. In his latter efforts, Bolyai became more concerned with the consistency of absolute space—whether logical contradictions might arise from his construction; these would not be resolved until later in the 19th century.

He continued work until 1856, the year that his father died, and his marriage with Rosalie broke up at the same time, increasing his isolation. Bolyai also worked on a theory of salvation, stressing the bond between individual and universal happiness. He died on January 27, 1860, after a protracted illness.

Bolyai made one solitary contribution to mathematics that was so outstanding in its creativity and importance as to merit him some fame, despite his status as a maverick. Along with Gauss and Lobachevsky, Bolyai is considered a cofounder of non-Euclidean geometry. These unusual geometries, initially scorned as ugly and useless, have found acceptance in the 20th century due to their great relevance to the curved space of our own universe.

Further Reading
Nemeth, L. "The Two Bolyais," *The New Hungarian Quarterly 1* (1960).

⊠ **Bolzano, Bernhard (Bernardus Placidus Johann Nepumuk Bolzano)**
(1781–1848)
Czechoslovakian
Analysis, Logic, Topology

An outstanding problem of the early 19th century, later to result in the radical developments of GEORG CANTOR, was to determine the foundations of the real number system. Such properties as the infinite divisibility of the real numbers and the density of rational numbers among irrationals had not been grasped, and as a result the basic theory of functions, including such topics as continuity and differentiability, were not well understood. Bernhard Bolzano, an active advocate of rigorous foundations for science and mathematics, made significant contributions to the knowledge of analysis; his emphasis on the necessity of a precise real-number system led to its development at the hands of RICHARD DEDEKIND, and his other researches were precursors to an arithmetic of the infinite and modern logic as well.

Bernardus Placidus Johann Nepumuk Bolzano was the fourth child of the pious Caecilia Maurer and a civic-minded art dealer named Bernhard Bolzano. He was born on October 5, 1781, in an ancient district of Prague, one of 12 children; his father was an Italian immigrant with an interest in social work who later established an orphanage. As a result of this environment, the younger Bolzano was concerned with ethics throughout his life, possessing an acute sensitivity to injustice.

In 1791 Bolzano entered the Piarist Gymnasium. He studied philosophy at the University of Prague in 1796. His interest in mathematics became stimulated through reading Kästner, who took great care to prove propositions that were commonly perceived to be evident. After 1800 Bolzano turned from philosophy to theology, though he had continuing doubts about the truth of Christianity. Instead, he turned toward moralism and away from supernatural religion, believing the supreme ethic to lie in the action that most benefited society. However, he reconciled this personal perspective with his commitment to Catholicism.

The emperor of Austria had decided to establish a chair in the philosophy of religion at every university, as part of the Catholic restoration movement against the Enlightenment. Much freethinking had spread through Bohemia, and the emperor feared the consequences of such radical ideas in view of the destruction wrought by the French Revolution. Bolzano was appointed to the chair at the University of Prague in 1805, despite his own Enlightenment sympathies. His lectures on religion were attended with enthusiasm, wherein he expounded his personal views without reserve.

Bolzano was respected by his colleagues, and became dean of the philosophical faculty in 1818. Meanwhile, Vienna brought a charge against him in 1816, since his Enlightenment views had made him unpopular with the conservative government; he was dismissed in 1819, forbidden to publish, and put under police supervision. Bolzano stubbornly refused to repent of his heresies, and the ordeal finally ceased in 1825 through the intercession of the nationalist leader Dobrovsky.

Although Bolzano was mainly concerned with social and religious issues, he was already attracted to the methodological precision of mathematics and logic. This led to some excellent contributions to mathematical analysis, although these accomplishments rarely met with any significant acknowledgment. Two unsolved problems—the proof of EUCLID OF ALEXANDRIA's parallel postulate and the foundation of analysis through clarification of infinitesimals—claimed Bolzano's attention. His 1804 *Betrachtungen über einige Gegenstände der Elementargeometrie* (Views on some articles of elementary geometry) attempted to describe a theory of triangles and parallels through a purely linear theory, which was never fully fleshed out. Ignorant of the work of NIKOLAI LOBACHEVSKY and JÁNOS BOLYAI on non-Euclidean geometry, Bolzano developed a methodological critique of Euclid's *Elements* in his manuscript *"Anti-Euklid."* For example, he required a proof of the statement that any closed curve divides the plane into two disjoint portions; this result later became known as the Jordan curve theorem, proved by CAMILLE JORDAN. Partially through the objections and questions raised by Bolzano, the field of mathematics known as topology came into existence in the late 19th century.

His *Rein analytischer Beweis* (Pure analytic proof) of 1817 obtained important results relevant to the foundation of mathematical analysis, later completed in his 1832–35 *Theorie der Reellen Zahlen* (Theory of real numbers). Many other mathematicians, such as JOSEPH-LOUIS LAGRANGE and JEAN LE ROND D'ALEMBERT, had attempted to liberate mathematics from the notion of the infinitesimal introduced by SIR ISAAC NEWTON and GOTTFRIED WILHELM VON LEIBNIZ in the 17th century, but Bolzano met with the first success in *Rein analytischer Beweis*. Here he gives the definition of a continuous function that is still in use today, and obtains a result on the property of assuming intermediate values. He also introduces the notion of a greatest lower bound of a set of real numbers having a given property, a concept that is a cornerstone in the theory of real numbers. Bolzano also discusses the "Cauchy convergence criterion," that a sequence of functions tends to some limit if the members of the sequence get closer to one another.

Although the proofs are incomplete, this was due to the present inadequacy of the concept of a real number. In his *Functionenlehre* (Functions model), a more complete theory of functions is presented, including several results later rediscovered by KARL WEIERSTRASS in the latter half of the 19th century. Bolzano showed that a continuous function over a closed interval must attain an extremal value, now called the Extreme Value Theorem in calculus; the proof requires the Bolzano-Weierstrass theorem about accumulation points of bounded sequences. He distinguishes between continuity and the property of assuming intermediate values as stronger and weaker features, respectively. He develops the connection between monotonicity and continuity and gives the construction of the Bolzano function, which was continuous but nowhere differentiable, significantly predating Weierstrass's own such example. The *Functionenlehre* contained many errors, including the false notion that the limit of a sequence of continuous functions must necessarily be continuous, and that term-wise integration of an infinite series is always possible.

His theory of quantities was completed in the *Theorie der Reelen Zahlen*, but this manuscript was not published and therefore failed to exert an influence on the subsequent development of analysis. Bolzano describes such real numbers as being capable of arbitrarily precise approximation by rational numbers. Also, his *Paradoxien des Unendlichen* (Paradoxes of infinity) contain many intriguing fragments of set theory, and he takes the subject to the boundary of cardinal arithmetic, the calculus of infinite sets. Bolzano observes that an infinite set can be put into one-to-one correspondence with a proper subset, and that this actually characterizes infinite sets. However, he does not take the next step in defining cardinals of infinity; Dedekind (1882) would later use this property of infinite sets to define infinity, and Cantor would develop a ranking of infinities.

From 1820 Bolzano worked on the treatise *Wissenschaftslehre* (Scientific model) of 1837, which was a theory of science grounded in logic. Its four volumes dealt with the proof of the existence of abstract truths, the theory of abstract ideas, the condition of the human faculty of judgment, the rules of human thought in the quest for truth, and the rules for dividing the sciences.

Although this work went largely unnoticed at the time, there is a close resemblance to modern logic, especially in Bolzano's notions of abstract proposition, idea, and derivability.

From 1823 Bolzano spent his summers at the estate of his friend Hoffmann in southern Bohemia. He later lived there for more than a decade. In 1842 he returned to Prague, where he continued his mathematical and philosophical studies until his death on December 18, 1848. Bolzano was an important mathematician of the 19th century, whose quest for truth led to excellent work on the foundations of the real number line. His name is found in many areas of analysis, such as the Bolzano-Weierstrass theorem and the Bolzano function; he is regarded as one of the founders of the modern theory of real analysis.

Further Reading

Berg, J. *Bolzano's Logic*. Stockholm: Almqvist and Wiksell, 1962.

George, R. "Bolzano's Concept of Consequence," *The Journal of Philosophy* 83, no. 10 (1986): 558–564.

———. "Bolzano's Consequence, Relevance, and Enthymemes," *Journal of Philosophical Logic* 12, no. 3 (1983): 299–318.

van Rootselaar, B. "Bolzano's Theory of Real Numbers," *Archive for History of Exact Sciences* 2 (1964/1965): 168–180.

George Boole constructed a viable, logical calculus in which philosophical arguments could be resolved. *(Courtesy of the AIP Emilio Segrè Visual Archives)*

⊠ Boole, George
(1815–1864)
British
Logic, Analysis

For much of history, the various fields of mathematics developed separately, or at least were seen as distinct areas of study. However, various mathematicians attempted to present a mathematical description of the foundations of logic, and to construct a logical arithmetic that would facilitate the resolution of abstruse philosophical arguments through verifiable computation. The first thinker to make significant progress toward these goals was George Boole, an Englishman noted for his contributions to logic as well as operator theory.

George Boole was born on November 2, 1815, in Lincoln, England, to a cobbler named John Boole. The latter's real interest lay in mathematics and the design of optical instruments, and his business consequently suffered from his distraction. George Boole was educated in the rudiments of mathematics by his father, but due to poverty was unable to pursue higher education. However, encouraged by his father, Boole advanced in his understanding of mathematics and soon acquired a familiarity with Latin, Greek, French, and German. Although his skill with literature was exemplary, his primary interest was mathematics.

At the age of 15 he started teaching in Lincoln. The Mechanics Institute was founded in 1834; Royal Society publications circulated through the school reading room, of which John Boole became curator, and George Boole devoted his remaining spare moments to the perusal of mathematical literature. In particular, he made his way through SIR ISAAC NEWTON's *Principia* with little assistance, and his local reputation led to a public speech marking the presentation of a Newton bust to the institute. By 1840 he contributed regularly to the *Cambridge Mathematical Journal* and the Royal Society; his talents were later recognized by award of a Royal Medal in 1844 and election to fellowship of the Royal Society in 1857.

Boole's scientific writings are comprised of some 50 papers on various topics, two textbooks summarizing his research, and two volumes on mathematical logic. The texts, on differential equations (1859) and finite differences (1860), were used for decades, and display Boole's keen intellect and fluid use of operators. The material on differential equations was original, using a difference and forward-shift operator to solve linear difference equations. Papers from 1841 and 1843 treated linear transformations, displaying an invariance principle for quadratic forms; the theory of invariants would be rapidly developed by other mathematicians in the latter half of the 19th century. Other work addressed differential equations, where Boole made much use of the differential operator D.

In 1849 Boole applied for the professorship of mathematics at the newly created Queen's College of Cork, and his appointment despite the absence of a formal university degree bore testimony to his widely recognized mathematical abilities. Though burdened with a heavy teaching load at Cork, Boole now inhabited an environment more conducive to research. He was a dedicated teacher, believing in the importance of

education—perhaps in consideration of his own lack. In 1855 he married Mary Everest, the niece of a professor of Greek in Queen's College.

After 1850 Boole mainly investigated the theory of probability, as this was related to his deep and abiding interest in the foundations of mathematical logic. His use of operators greatly furthered their power of applicability, but Boole was cautious about their indiscriminate use, and was always careful to verify the conditions of their implementation; he also stressed the necessity of clear definitions. As a result of these precise inquiries, Boole came to realize that a variable representing a nonnumerical quantity, such as a logical statement or other mathematical object, was not only mathematically valid but of great use in many enterprises.

A dispute had arisen between the philosopher Sir William Hamilton and the mathematician AUGUSTUS DE MORGAN over whether logic belonged to the domain of philosophy or mathematics. De Morgan, who was a friend of Boole, had made several contributions to logic through his laws on the theory of sets, but Hamilton was skeptical that mathematics could be of any benefit; Boole defended the validity of a mathematical approach to logic in *Mathematical Analysis of Logic* (1847), and laid an axiomatic framework for logic much like the foundation of classical geometry. History would later prove that Boole and De Morgan had won the argument, as mathematical logic has since evolved into a thriving (and surprisingly convoluted) discipline.

The attempt to reduce logic to a pure calculus had been previously attempted by GOTTFRIED WILHELM VON LEIBNIZ; the dream was to replace lengthy, quarrelsome philosophical debates with an algebraic system capable of resolving doubtful propositions through simple computations. Early efforts drew heavily on Euclidean arithmetic as an analogy for algebraic logic, but encountered thorny difficulties. Boole's construction was original and different, and essentially was a completely new algebra—different from arithmetic, and yet valid for its own purpose. The ideas seem to have originated from Boole's familiarity with operators: He would apply an operator with a defining property to some universe of elements, and thereby obtain all individuals or elements with that particular property. For example, an operator might be defined to select carrots from any universe of objects under discourse, such as the contents of one's garden. The successive application of operators to a universe, which was commutative, defined a multiplication for the algebra. From this starting point, Boole developed a notion of subtraction (which involved the complement of a set), addition (associated by Boole to the exclusive "or," though in modern times to the inclusive "or"), and even division. It is interesting that this was the first known idempotent algebra, which has the property that the square of any operator is equal to itself—since applying an operator twice in succession is equivalent to applying it just one time. This situation signals a clear and irrevocable departure from more familiar arithmetic, where the only idempotents are one and zero.

In *Investigation of the Laws of Thought*, Boole applies this calculus to the laws of probability. Using the symbol $P(A)$ for the probability of an event A, Boole describes the multiplication of probabilities in terms of the probability of the intersection of two independent events, the sum of probabilities as the probability of the mutually exclusive union of two events, and so forth. This symbolism allowed him to correct earlier work in probability. Boole's health began to decline in 1864, and when caught in the rain on the way to class, he gave his lecture in wet clothes. This event may have hastened his death, which occurred on December 8, 1864, in Ballintemple, Ireland.

Investigation of the Laws of Thought is certainly Boole's most important legacy; many others would later expand on his work in mathematical logic and so-called Boolean algebras. Even the flow of computer programs, which implement Boolean variables (a quantity that either takes the value of "true" or "false"), utilizes his theory. The design of electric circuits is particularly amenable to the use of a Boolean algebra, due to the binary system of on-off switches.

Further Reading

Barry, P. *George Boole: A Miscellany*. Cork, Ireland: Cork University Press, 1969.

Bell, E. *Men of Mathematics*. New York: Simon and Schuster, 1965.

Feys, R. "Boole as a Logician," *Proceedings of the Royal Irish Academy. Section A. Mathematical and Physical Sciences* 57 (1955): 97–106.

Kneale, W. "Boole and the Revival of Logic," *Mind* 57 (1948): 149–175.

MacHale, D. *George Boole: His Life and Work*. Dublin, Ireland: Boole Press, 1985.

Taylor, G. "George Boole, 1815–1864," *Proceedings of the Royal Irish Academy. Section A. Mathematical and Physical Sciences* 57 (1955): 66–73.

⊠   **Borel, Émile**
(1871–1956)
French
Analysis, Probability

Émile Borel is known as one of the founders of the modern theory of analysis. His development of measure theory and probability are perhaps the most important, as these ideas have led to a blossoming of research and activity in his wake; it is also noteworthy that he invented game theory a few decades before John Von Neumann took up that subject.

Born on January 7, 1871, Émile Borel was the son of a Protestant pastor in the village of Saint-Affrique. His mother, Émilie Teisié-Solier, was descended from a local merchant family. His father, Honoré Borel, had recognized his son's extraordinary talents, and in 1882 Émile Borel was sent to a nearby *lycée*. Later he obtained a scholarship to prepare for university in Paris, and there became attracted to the life of a mathematician; deciding upon this vocation, he put all his energy toward this goal, exercising great self-discipline. In his entrance exams Borel won first place to both the École Polytechnique and the École Normale Supérieur, but in 1889 he chose the latter institution.

In his first year the young mathematician published two papers and set his lifelong pattern of diligent study and determined focus. He had rejected the religion of his father, and took a rationalistic view toward human life and science. During his time as an undergraduate, he made many friendships, which would later facilitate his extensive cultural and political influence. Borel graduated in 1893 as first of his class, and immediately came to the University of Lille as a teacher, writing his thesis and 22 papers on various mathematical subjects within the next three years. Upon obtaining his degree from Lille, he returned to the École Normale Supérieur, where he continued his prodigious rate of research.

His early research focused on the solution of certain problems but, inspired by GEORG CANTOR in 1891, Borel's mind turned to the power of set theory. His 1894 thesis initiated the modern concept of measure (a precise and general mathematical formulation of the concept of measuring length, area, and volume), which has since proved to be fundamental in both the theory of real functions and probability. He also explored divergent series, nonanalytic continuation, denumerable probability (in between the finite and continuous probability theory), Diophantine approximation, and the distribution theory of analytic functions. These concepts are indebted to the genius of Cantor, in particular the notion of a denumerable set, that is, a set that can be put in one-to-one correspondence with the natural numbers. Two famous results are the Heine-Borel theorem, which concerns the compactness

of closed and bounded subsets of the real line, and the statement that any denumerable set has measure (length) zero. These nonintuitive facts display Borel's cunning intellect as well as his vision for pure mathematics.

Borel developed measure theory in the ensuing years, and his name is attached to many of the mathematical objects of that subject, such as sigma-algebras and the concept of measurability. He also saw that measure theory was an appropriate foundation for probability (1905), since probabilities of events can be viewed as measurements of the likelihood that a particular event occurs. As a result, Borel was able to introduce denumerable probabilities (1909), giving rise to many distributions so useful in the theory of statistics. However, Borel retained a cautious regard for the infinite, rejecting nonconstructive definitions as well as Cantor's hierarchies of infinity beyond the denumerable sets. Later, HENRI LEBESGUE and RENÉ-LOUIS BAIRE would push set theory and measure theory to levels of abstraction that Borel was unwilling to venture into.

Borel also influenced later mathematics through his simple proof of Picard's theorem in 1896, an outstanding problem that had defied solution for almost 20 years; his methods were instrumental to the subsequent maturation of complex function theory. His 1899 work on divergent series filled a notable gap in current knowledge of infinite series, and his work on monogenic functions (summarized in 1917) supplied a vital link between analytic and extremely discontinuous functions. With age, Borel turned toward physical and social problems that were amenable to mathematical techniques, despising generalization for its own sake.

For some time, Borel had been attracted to Marguerite Appell, and they were married in 1901; as a novelist and intellectual, she complemented her husband's varied activities. Childless, the pair adopted Fernand Lebeau, the orphaned son of Borel's sister. Marguerite and

Émile Borel launched *La revue du mois* (The monthly review) in 1906, a widely read periodical, though the post–World War I economic crisis would render its continued existence financially infeasible. Borel continued his remarkable profundity and wealth of publications, and as he aged his interests broadened from pure mathematics to applications and public affairs. He wrote texts, edited books, contributed to the daily press, played a leading role in university affairs, and maintained a diverse body of acquaintances. This heightened level of activity was possible due to intensity and efficiency; though generous of his time in the course of his responsibilities, he found social interruptions irritating, and would not tolerate those who wasted his time with peripheral matters.

In 1909 Borel obtained the chair of theory of functions at the Sorbonne, and commenced a 32-year tenure on the University Council as a representative of the faculty of science. The next year he concurrently served as vice director of the École Normale Supérieur, but this office was later terminated by the advent of World War I. Borel served in the military and later organized research in the War Office. As a result, his interests turned increasingly toward applications. After the war Borel moved to the chair of probability and mathematical physics at the Sorbonne, and he maintained mere honorary connections with the École Normale.

Most of Borel's more brilliant ideas had already been conceived by the start of World War I, and during this period of his life he continued their development through applications to science. However, between 1921 and 1927 he wrote several papers on game theory, which was entirely original and significantly predates Von Neumann's work in that area. Borel used games of strategy as models of military and economic situations, assuming the rationality of the competing "players." In this avenue he considered mixed strategies (which involve chance), symmetric games, and infinite games (those with infinitely many actions available), and proved the minimax theorem for three players.

During this time, Borel's political career advanced rapidly, as he moved through the offices of mayor of Saint-Affrique, councillor of the Aveyron district, Radical-Socialist member of the Chamber of Deputies, and minister of the navy. Through these opportunities, Borel was able to promote scientific legislation and found the Centre National de la Recherche Scientifique, as well as raise funds for the Institut Henri Poincaré. After retiring from politics in 1936 and from the Sorbonne in 1940, Borel continued to produce numerous books and papers; he also participated in the French Resistance. He was honored by numerous awards during his lifetime, and he died on February 3, 1956, shortly after a fall during the return from a conference of statistics in Brazil.

Borel made many great contributions to analysis. Most significant of all were his early discoveries of measure theory; the study of measures has since grown into a major discipline of modern mathematics, with numerous applications to the theory of probability. Borel must also be recognized as the first inventor of modern game theory, which since the development by John Von Neumann and John Nash has become a fruitful field of mathematics with numerous applications.

Further Reading

Collingwood, E. "Emile Borel," *Journal of the London Mathematical Society* 34 (1959): 488–512.

⊠ **Brahmagupta**
(ca. 598–665)
Indian
Algebra

Brahmagupta was another early Indian astronomer and mathematician who contributed to the advancement of mathematics. Born in

598, Brahmagupta was the son of Jisnugupta—the name "gupta" may indicate membership in the Vaisya caste. When he was 30 years old, Brahmagupta composed the *Brahmasphutasiddhanta*, a work on astronomy and mathematics. In this book he is called Bhillamalacarya, or the teacher from Bhillamala. His second work was the *Khandakhadyaka*, composed sometime after March 15, 665.

The *Brahmasphutasiddhanta* contains 24 chapters, treating the following topics: mean and true longitudes of planets, diurnal motion, lunar and solar eclipses, heliacal risings and settings, lunar crescent and shadow, planetary conjunctions, algebra, the gnomon, and the sphere. He also discusses measurements and instruments, including tables of values. The *Khandakhadyaka* deals mostly with astronomy, addressing the *arddharatrika* system: computation of the *tithis* and *naksatras*, longitudes of the planets, diurnal motion, lunar and solar eclipses, heliacal risings and settings, the lunar crescent, and planetary conjunctions. The appendix also discusses the projection of eclipses.

Brahmagupta's understanding of number systems represented significant progress beyond his contemporaries. The concept of zero was foreign to Indian mathematicians, and Brahmagupta defined it as the difference of a number with itself. He then derived its basic properties; he knew that zero was an additive identity, for example, but had difficulty defining division by zero, not realizing that this operation is impossible. Negative numbers are introduced by subtracting a (positive quantity) from zero, and are described as "debts"; Brahmagupta then demonstrates the arithmetic of positive and negative numbers, and shows, for instance, that a negative times a positive is a negative.

He also discusses extended multiplication of large numbers, utilizing a place-value number system quite similar to the modern method. Indeed, the current number system is derived, with some modifications, from the Indian mathematicians. Brahmagupta presents a procedure

for computing square roots that is actually equivalent to the iterative Newton-Raphson method. In order to solve certain quadratic equations, Brahmagupta introduced a symbolic algebraic notation and probably used the method of continued fractions. Some other topics of the *Brahmasphutasiddhanta* include rules for summing series—such as the sum of consecutive integers, squares, and cubes—and formulas for areas of quadrilaterals.

Brahmagupta believed in a stationary Earth, and he computed the length of the year, overestimating the true period slightly. His second work, the *Khandakhadyaka*, also gives an interpolation formula for the computation of sines.

Brahmagupta influenced later Indian mathematicians, such as BHASKARA II, who improved on the knowledge of negative numbers and the properties of zero. He died sometime after the publication of his second work, in 665. Considering his time period, he was quite advanced; at the time, no mathematics was being done in Europe. Perhaps he is most notable for his definition of the concept of zero, which has had an enormous impact on civilization ever since its inception.

Further Reading
Chatterjee, B. "Al-Biruni and Brahmagupta," *Indian Journal of History of Science* 10, no. 2 (1975): 161–165.

Datta, B. "Brahmagupta," *Bulletin of the Calcutta Mathematical Society* 22 (1930): 39–51.

Ifrah, G. *A Universal History of Numbers: From Prehistory to the Invention of the Computer.* New York: John Wiley, 2000.

Brouwer, Luitzen Egbertus Jan
(1881–1966)
Dutch
Logic, Topology

One of the hotly contested topics of 20th-century mathematics was the logical foundation of the discipline; specifically, certain mathematicians were laboring to show that the axiomatic formulation of mathematics was consistent (that any proposition could be proved to be either true or false, but not both). Brouwer represented an opposition to this agenda, putting forth his intuitionistic mathematics as a desirable alternative.

Luitzen Brouwer was born on February 27, 1881, in the town of Overschie in the Netherlands. He was intellectually precocious, completing his high school education at the age of 14; in 1897 he entered the University of Amsterdam, where he studied mathematics for the next seven years. Brouwer quickly mastered contemporary mathematics, and he obtained new results concerning continuous motions on manifolds.

Brouwer's interests were diverse. His mathematical activity included topology, mappings, and logic, as well as mystic philosophy. His personal view of mathematics as a free mental activity was constructivist and differed sharply from the formalistic approach espoused by DAVID HILBERT and BERTRAND RUSSELL. Brouwer participated in the debate over mathematics' foundations; he rejected the idea that logic should be the pillar of mathematics—rather, logic was just an expression of noted regularities and patterns in constructed systems. The bizarreness of this view became apparent when Brouwer attacked the law of the excluded middle, which states that either a given statement or its logical negation must be true (which is used in the "proof by contradiction" method).

Brouwer's doctoral thesis of 1907, *On the Foundations of Mathematics*, expresses his opinions. Out of these ideas was born "intuitionistic mathematics," which places an emphasis on the ability to construct mathematical objects. He rejected the law of the excluded middle in his system and criticized Hilbert's attempt to prove the consistency of arithmetic.

In the five years from 1907 to 1912, Brouwer discovered several valuable results. He studied Hilbert's fifth problem, the theory of continuous

groups, and in the process discovered the plane translation theorem and the "hairy ball theorem," which states that a smooth vector field on an even-dimensional sphere must vanish somewhere—or, in other words, every hairdo must have a cowlick.

Brouwer also studied various topological mappings, developing the technique of using so-called simplices to approximate the continuous maps. The associated degree led to the notion of homotopy class, which allowed the topological classification of many manifolds. As a result, the notion of dimension (in the topological sense) was put on a more rigorous footing.

In 1912 he was appointed as a professor of mathematics at the University of Amsterdam, and he soon resumed his research into the foundations of mathematics. In 1918 he published a different set theory, which did not rely on the law of the excluded middle, followed by similar notions of measure and function in the following years. As could be expected, the theorems he obtained are somewhat different (for example, real functions are always uniformly continuous). For these reasons, his results were not fully accepted, and many mathematicians have simply ignored his point of view. Proof by contradiction is a very powerful, commonly used method of proof; mathematicians are not willing to forsake the many theorems they can establish in order to embrace Brouwer's potentially more rigorous system.

From 1923 onward, Brouwer focused on his intuitionistic agenda, attempting to persuade mathematicians to reject the law of the excluded middle. In the late 1920s logicians began investigating the connection of Brouwer's logic to the classical logic; after KURT GÖDEL's incompleteness theorems annihilated David Hilbert's program, more people became interested in the intuitionistic approach to mathematics.

Brouwer gained international recognition from several societies and academies. He died in Blaricum, the Netherlands, on December 2,

1966. Although his efforts to persuade mathematicians toward his own point of view were mostly unsuccessful (again, this was due in part to the reluctance to give up the powerful tool of proof by contradiction, and also because the intuitionistic framework is rooted in mystic philosophy), Brouwer raised awareness about the limitations of any mathematical system and correctly predicted the demise of any attempt to establish the consistency and completeness of an axiomatic system. He is an important character in the history of mathematical logic, representing the antirationalistic countermovement of mysticism that arose in the 20th century.

Further Reading

van Dalen, D. *Mystic, Geometer, and Intuitionist: The Life of L. E. J. Brouwer.* Oxford: Clarendon Press, 1999.

Franchella, M. "L. E. J. Brouwer: Toward Intuitionistic Logic," *Historia Mathematica* 22, no. 3 (1995): 304–322.

Mancosu, P. *From Brouwer to Hilbert: The Debate on the Foundations of Mathematics in the 1920s.* New York: Oxford University Press, 1998.

van Stigt, W. "L. E. J. Brouwer: Intuitionism and Topology," *Proceedings, Bicentennial Congress Wiskundig Genootschap* (1979): 359–374.

———. "L. E. J. Brouwer 'Life, Art and Mysticism,'" *Notre Dame Journal of Formal Logic* 37, no. 3 (1996): 389–429.

C

⊠ Cantor, Georg
(1845–1918)
German
Logic, Analysis

Modern mathematics, in all of its branches, is founded upon set theory; that is, introductory material in such fields as probability and algebra invariably commences with a discussion of sets and logic. However, prior to the 20th century this was not the case, since mathematics was in earlier times conceived in less formal tones; mathematical truth was viewed as inseparably connected to metaphysical truth. Current results in set theory have demolished this idealism— witness the work of KURT GÖDEL on incompleteness and the independence of the continuum hypothesis. Georg Cantor was a pivotal figure in this transition, providing the first steps toward modern set theory and at the same time remaining as a final proponent of classical thought in mathematics before the flood of axiomatic formalism.

Georg Cantor was born on March 3, 1845, in St. Petersburg to German parents; his father, also named Georg Cantor, was a wealthy Protestant merchant, and his mother, Marie Böhm, was a Catholic from a line of renowned violinists. Religion would form an important component of Cantor's thought, as he tied his study of the mathematical infinite to the theological infinity of God.

Cantor attended the Gymnasium in Wiesbaden, and later the Realschule in Darmstadt, where his interest in mathematics was first aroused. His university studies in Zurich commenced in 1862 and resumed in Berlin in 1863 after his father's sudden death. KARL WEIERSTRASS was the leading mathematician of Berlin at the time, and attracted numerous students as disciples. Cantor studied different branches of mathematics, and even wrote a dissertation on number theory, but his main interest was the theory of real numbers and infinite series.

Throughout his life, Cantor had numerous friendships, some of which (such as his lengthy association with RICHARD DEDEKIND) were fueled by scientific correspondence and collaboration. He was president (1864–65) of the Mathematical Society, an organization that attempted to unify the work of diverse mathematicians, and later was an active promoter of scientific exchange. Later, he founded the Association of German Mathematicians (1890), becoming the president in 1893; the first international congress of mathematicians, a result of his endeavors, was held in Zurich in 1897.

In 1867 Cantor obtained his doctorate. He became a teacher at the University of Halle two years later. The position was poorly paid, but

Georg Cantor, founder of modern set theory, as well as the study of hierarchies of infinity and their arithmetic *(Courtesy of the Library of Congress)*

Cantor was able to survive due to the inheritance received from his father. He married Vally Guttmann in 1874, and together they built a happy home with five children—his wife's good humor contrasting with Cantor's melancholic tendencies. He attained full professorship in 1879 and continued his labors on set theory until his death; Cantor had hoped to obtain a more prestigious position in Berlin, but LEOPOLD KRONECKER continually blocked his efforts. Kronecker was one of Cantor's former teachers who disparaged the radical theory of sets.

Cantor's first significant work lies in the area of mathematical analysis. The basic concept of the real number system was still deficient in some respects, and Cantor's early labors in so-called

fundamental series (now called Cauchy sequences) bolstered the foundations. As a result, one could represent any real number as the limit of a sequence of rational numbers, though Cantor also described formulations involving infinite series and infinite products.

After an 1873 exchange with Dedekind, Cantor turned toward the question of whether the set of real numbers could be placed in one-to-one correspondence with the natural numbers (any such set would therefore be called "countable" or "denumerable"). It was already known that the rational numbers were countable, but no one had considered this new question; its solution in the negative was to initiate the modern theory of sets. Cantor's famous diagonalization argument shows the real numbers to be uncountable and, as a corollary, the existence of uncountably many transcendental numbers (those numbers that are not the solution to any integer coefficient algebraic equation, such as pi).

In 1874 Cantor turned to more difficult problems, such as establishing the impossibility of a one-to-one correspondence between a square and a line segment. After three years of effort, Cantor instead constructed a counterexample, giving an explicit invertible function that mapped the line into the square; this construction seemed to defy all intuitive concepts of dimension, and the result severely irritated many conservative mathematicians. Today, the topological concept of dimension is tied to continuous one-to-one correspondences (with continuous inverse) called homeomorphisms—Cantor's strange map was discontinuous.

The theory of point set topology is deeply indebted to Cantor's genius: He addressed such topics as point sets, closure, and density, and in many cases created the definitions himself. The notion of perfect set (one that is both closed and dense in itself) has a Cantorian genesis, and the most famous example of such is the "Cantor set" that is formed by removing successive middle thirds from a line segment iteratively. A century later, this same set would motivate the study of fractal geometry and the metric definition of dimension. The concept of *continuum*, a term of philosophical parlance in existence since medieval times, was given an exact mathematical definition by Cantor: A continuum was a continuous perfect set.

Much of his fundamental work can be found in *"Über eine Eigenschaft des Inbegriffes aller reellen algebraischen Zahlen"* ("About a characteristic of the essence of all real algebraic numbers") of 1874. Here he begins the delineation of the hierarchies of infinity: those sets that are countable versus those that have the "power" of the continuum (and are uncountable)—the latter type being a higher species of the infinite. For every set there is a higher power, obtained by taking the set of all subsets of a given set (called the power set). Cantor later proves that there can be no one-to-one correspondence between a set and its power set—the latter is always "larger." In this fashion, a kingdom of infinities can be constructed and studied; one outstanding question is whether there is an infinite set with cardinality (level of infinity) between the natural numbers and the continuum. The assertion that there is no such set is known as the continuum hypothesis, and Cantor was consumed with its proof, perhaps even contributing to his later lapse into madness. These cardinal numbers had their own transfinite arithmetic, in which such Trinitarian statements as "one plus one plus one equals one" held some validity.

Many of his peers mocked Cantor's theories, as they easily upset the classical intuition about how mathematical objects must behave. However, the work gained acceptance toward the beginning of the 20th century, and Cantor later became an honorary member of several mathematical societies. Since 1884 depression had afflicted him, perhaps brought on by his intense effort to solve various problems, such as the continuum hypothesis. He died on January 6, 1918, in the psychiatric clinic of Halle University.

Cantor's bold work in set theory opened up entire new vistas of mathematical thought, fueling 20th (and 21st) century research into fundamentals, set theory, real analysis, logic, and fractal geometry. The turn toward fundamentals resulted in the foundation of each branch of mathematics upon axiomatic set theory, and this in turn gave rise to the mathematical philosophy of formalism—the belief that mathematics consists of semantic rules that are carefully manipulated, as in a game, to arrive at new knowledge. This differs substantially from Cantor's Platonic thought, which conceived of the abstract existence of mathematical structures made concrete through various realizations in our own universe. For example, the atoms of the universe should be countable (according to Cantor), a concrete realization of the notion of denumerability. The absolute limit of the power operation resulted in an ultimate infinity, Cantor's vision of God, in which the concrete and the abstract were married. It is ironic that one who indirectly contributed to the advance of formalism should be one of the last great advocates of Platonic thought.

Further Reading

Dauben, J. *Georg Cantor: His Mathematics and Philosophy of the Infinite.* Cambridge, Mass.: Harvard University Press, 1979.

Grattan-Guinness, I. "Towards a Biography of Georg Cantor," *Annals of Science* 27 (1971): 345–391.

Hill, L. "Fraenkel's Biography of Georg Cantor," *Scripta Mathematica* 2 (1933): 41–47.

⊠ **Cardano, Girolamo**
(1501–1576)
Italian
Algebra, Probability

The Renaissance was a time of bold intellectual voyaging, where the man of learning might investigate all the branches of philosophy;

Girolamo Cardano developed an early notion of imaginary numbers and the rules of probability and published a method for solving the cubic equation. *(Courtesy of the Library of Congress)*

Girolamo Cardano epitomized this intrepid, proud, and inquisitive spirit. Cardano's name is somewhat infamous among mathematicians, due to his questionable dealings with the mathematician NICCOLÒ TARTAGLIA. However, his contributions to mathematics and science are numerous, including a vague preliminary formulation of imaginary numbers as well as the basic rules of probability. In his own age he was reputed as a great doctor, and his writings have influenced diverse areas of science such as geology and mechanics.

Girolamo Cardano was born on September 24, 1501, to an Italian jurist, Fazio Cardano, and a widow, Chiari Micheri. The boy was illegitimate, and his mother possessed a nasty temper;

Cardano's childhood was unpleasant, punctuated with illness. His father, a friend of LEONARDO DA VINCI, encouraged Cardano to study the classics, mathematics, and astrology, and he commenced his university studies in 1520 at Pavia. Six years later, Cardano had completed his studies in Padua with a doctorate in medicine.

Medicine was to be Cardano's foremost career; he would later acquire great fame for his remedies. He started his practice in Saccolongo, near Padua, where he remained for six years. Apparently Cardano had been unable to marry due to impotence, but upon obtaining release from this affliction he wed Lucia Bandareni in 1531, and she bore him two sons and a daughter. Three years later, Cardano became a teacher of mathematics in Milan thanks to the intervention and encouragement of his father's aristocratic friends. Simultaneously, Cardano continued to practice medicine, and he achieved a remarkable degree of success, such that his colleagues were stricken with envy; soon after 1536, when he published his first work *De malo recentiorum medicorum usu libellus* (A book concerning the bad practice of modern doctors), he was the foremost physician in Milan. In 1552 he even journeyed to Scotland in order to cure the archbishop of Edinburgh of asthma.

Cardano's 1539 *Practica arithmeticae et mensurandi singularis* (Practice of mathematics and individual measurements) was devoted to numerical calculation, and in this work he reveals his talent in the manipulation of algebraic expressions. He could solve some equations of third degree and higher (the solution of the quadratic was well known) before encountering Tartaglia. Cardano soon became acquainted with the latter mathematician, who had mastered the solution of the cubic (third degree equation) by a general method. After much importuning of Tartaglia, Cardano obtained the secret of the cubic's solution upon swearing an oath not to reveal it. However, Tartaglia was not the originator of this method, and he had learned it from

SCIPIONE DEL FERRO; when Cardano learned of del Ferro's prior discovery, he considered his oath to be irrelevant and subsequently published the method in his *Artis magnae sive de regulis algebraicis liber unus* (Book one of the great art or concerning the rules of algebra) of 1545. Of course, this action infuriated Tartaglia, who felt that he had been betrayed; his later publications accused Cardano of perjury, and Tartaglia continued to castigate his character.

The *Artis magnae sive de regulis algebraicis liber unus* presented many new ideas in the field of algebra. The so-called Cardano's rule provides the solution of cubic equations that lack a second-degree term, and Cardano also explained how to linearly transform an arbitrary cubic into this reduced form. He observes that an equation of degree more than one must have more than one root, and that knowing a root is tantamount to reducing the degree of the polynomial by one. These facts would later be formulated as part of the fundamental theorem of algebra, proved by CARL FRIEDRICH GAUSS in the 18th century. Cardano also discusses the solution of the quartic, or fourth degree, equation, attributed to his son-in-law LODOVICO FERRARI. Of course, the quintic, or fifth degree, polynomial did not admit of a method of solution, as would be proved by NIELS HENRIK ABEL and EVARISTE GALOIS centuries later.

Cardano also investigated the numerical approximation to the solution of an equation, using the method of proportional parts together with an iteration scheme. The idea of approximation (at least for equations) first appears with Cardano, and would much later be systematically developed through SIR ISAAC NEWTON's method and the subsequent theory of numerical analysis. He also observed the relationship between the roots of a polynomial and its coefficients, and is therefore considered the father of the theory of algebraic equations. In some situations he even used imaginary numbers, which would not be formally developed for centuries.

Besides this famous work in algebra, Cardano was also known for his passion for games of chance, such as dice, chess, and cards. His *Liber de ludo aleae* (Book on games of chance), completed in his old age, gives a first treatment of the theory of probability. This predates the pioneering work of BLAISE PASCAL and PIERRE DE FERMAT, although these two were unaware of Cardano's prior work and hence were not influenced by it. The important idea in this work is that even chance follows certain rules—the laws of probability. Probability as a numerical, measurable quantity is introduced as the ratio of outcomes in which an event can occur to all possible outcomes; today, this is known as the classical definition of probability, and has been replaced by a measure theoretic formulation, since Cardano's conception can only deal with equally likely outcomes. He enunciates the law of large numbers, as well as various other rules of probability, such as the multiplication law for independent events.

Meanwhile, Cardano advanced in his career as a physician, in 1543 accepting the chair of medicine at the University of Pavia, where he taught until 1560. In this year, his elder son was executed for poisoning his wife, and Cardano was meanwhile wearied by the public condemnation of his enemies as well as the dissolute life of his second son. As a result, Cardano left for the University of Bologna, where he obtained the chair of medicine in 1562.

His interests in astrology and magic led to an accusation of heresy, and the Inquisition in 1570 imprisoned Cardano; apparently he had cast the horoscope of Jesus Christ, attributing the Lord's eventful life to the influence of the stars. After a few months in prison, Cardano repented of his teaching, and obtained the favor of Pope Pius V. In Rome, during the last year of his life, Cardano wrote *De propria vita* (Book of my life), a thorough autobiography; he died on September 21, 1576.

Cardano authored some 200 works on medicine, mathematics, physics, religion, philosophy, and music, representing the typical Renaissance thinker in the diversity of his thought. Besides his mathematical writings, he published two encyclopedias of natural science, a compendium of knowledge, superstition, and the occult, contributed to mechanics and hydrodynamics, and developed early theories for the formation of mountains by the erosion of water, as well as conceiving the cycle of evaporation, condensation, and precipitation. He deduced the rising of the ocean floor from the presence of marine fossils on dry land, experimentally estimated the ratio of densities of air and water, and described numerous mechanical devices, including "Cardano's suspension." He noted that the trajectory of a projectile was similar to that of a parabolic curve, and he affirmed the impossibility of perpetual motion (excepting the celestial bodies). The numerous editions of his works bear testimony to his enduring and widespread influence on the next generation of thinkers.

Further Reading

Fierz, M. *Girolamo Cardano, 1501–1576: Physician, Natural Philosopher, Mathematician, Astrologer, and Interpreter of Dreams.* Boston: Birkhäuser, 1983.

Kenney, E. "Cardano: 'Arithmetic Subtlety' and Impossible Solutions," *Philosophia Mathematica II* (1989): 195–216.

Ore, O. *Cardano, the Gambling Scholar.* Princeton, N.J.: Princeton University Press, 1953.

⊠ Carnot, Lazare

(1753–1823)
French
Calculus

It is rare that a person achieves fame as both a politician and a scientist, but Lazare Carnot was renowned for both his mathematical and mechanical achievements, and known as the "Organizer of Victory" in the wars of the French

Lazare Carnot defined a machine abstractly and formulated the principle of continuous transfer of power. *(Courtesy of the National Library of Medicine)*

Revolution. His principle of continuity in the transmission of power is of great historical importance to mechanical engineering, and he made contributions to the foundations of analysis and calculus.

Born on May 13, 1753, in Nolay, France, Lazare Carnot was the son of a bourgeois lawyer of Burgundy. He was educated at the Oratorian College at Autun, and later at Paris, being groomed for a military career in the Corps of Engineers. He graduated after two years of attendance at the military school of Mézières; GASPARD MONGE was one of his professors, but they had little interaction. Carnot's approach to mathematics was slower, being more concerned with fundamentals. This attitude would later prove to have great relevancy for mechanics and physics.

After various posts, Carnot was assigned to Arras, and in 1787 he became acquainted with Robespierre. Meanwhile, Carnot had taken to writing on the topics of mechanics, mathematics, and military strategy, partly in order to ease his frustration over the slow progression of his career. The Académie des Sciences in Paris proposed a competition in 1777 over the topic of friction in simple machines; Carnot's submission failed to attain the prize, but he later developed his memoir into *Essai sur les machines en général* (Essay on general machines), published in 1783. Although it attracted little attention at the time, this work was an initial step in the French literature of engineering mechanics. Carnot also composed an essay on mathematics, in competition for a 1784 Berlin prize for justification of the infinitesimal calculus. He failed to win any award, but his paper later evolved into *Réflexions sur la métaphysique du calcul infinitesimal* (Reflections on the metaphysics of infinitesimal calculus) published in 1797.

Carnot achieved some literary fame for his writings on military strategy; his Éloge de Vauban, a tribute to Vauban (the founder of the Royal Corps of Engineers and an influential military theorist since the time of Louis XIV), won first prize in a 1784 competition. In this paper, Carnot affirms the importance of fortifying strategic locations and discusses war's proper use as the defense of civilization. This perspective clashed with the advocates of gallantry and movement. Ironically, Carnot would later abandon his conservative theories when commanding a largely undisciplined and untrained mass of soldiers.

His political career began in 1791 with his election to the Legislative Assembly, advocating career advancement for those with talent. In the ensuing year he came to distrust the monarchy, and adopted the republicanism common to his social class more out of civic commitment than political conviction. When war broke out in April 1792, Carnot was employed in military services, and he defeated the loyalists later that year. His integrity and organizational ability was evident, making him a valuable and trustworthy agent of the Republic. Next, he defended Belgium from attack, rallying the demoralized troops to their duty, and he was subsequently appointed to the Committee of Public Safety, although his main obligation was to the ongoing war. Perhaps because of his great skill in military matters, Carnot survived both the downfall of Robespierre in 1794 and the ensuing reaction, becoming a leading member of the Directory. Before being deposed by a leftist insurrection in 1797, Carnot had granted Napoleon control of the Italian army; the former fled to Switzerland and Germany, but in 1800 returned after Napoleon's seizure of power. As a result Carnot was named minister of war, an office that he soon resigned due to differences of opinion.

At this point Carnot returned to his former scientific interests, serving on various commissions to investigate French inventions of a mechanical and military nature. Always a committed patriot, Carnot volunteered to aid Napoleon during the latter's retreat from Moscow to the Rhine; Carnot received the government of Antwerp, which he successfully defended. During the Hundred Days, he again supported the emperor, and he was appointed minister of the interior. However, when the monarchy was subsequently reinvested, Carnot was forced to flee France once more; he lived out his remaining years in Magdeburg, dying on August 2, 1823.

Carnot's *Essai sur les machines en général* was a theoretical treatise on mechanical engineering. He gave an abstract definition of a machine, and developed the concept that power could be transmitted without perturbation or turbulence. His principle of perfect conversion said that motion could be smoothly translated without loss, that live force results in the moment of activity; or, in modern terms, input equals output.

His contributions to pure mathematics received public recognition, for his *Réflexions sur la métaphysique du calcul infinitesimal* was published in several languages and enjoyed a wide distribution. Carnot explains that the genius of calculus lay in the introduction of certain errors, which were later, through the procedures of the calculation, exactly compensated; hence, the results were exact, even though an approximation is initially introduced. AUGUSTIN-LOUIS CAUCHY, BERNHARD BOLZANO, and CARL FRIEDRICH GAUSS would later place calculus on a rigorous foundation, but this explanation was intended for the general public. Carnot's other geometric writings focused on negative and imaginary numbers, which he attempted to purge from mathematics, claiming that they were not reasonable quantities. He demonstrates the inadequacy of illustrating negative numbers as signed numbers, with a location on the left part of an axis; Carnot's approach is far from the formalism of the modern era, and he shunned the senseless shuffling of mathematical symbols. After several publications on his concept of geometric quantity, Carnot published a book on the science of geometric motion, an attempt to connect his mechanical and geometrical studies.

Further Reading

Boyer, C. "Carnot and the Concept of Deviation," *The American Mathematical Monthly* 61 (1954): 459–463.

Dupre, H. *Lazare Carnot, Republican Patriot*. Philadelphia: Porcupine Press, 1975.

⊠ Cartan, Élie
(1869–1951)
French
Geometry, Topology

A prominent theme of 20th-century mathematics was the study of differentiable manifolds (smooth high-dimensional surfaces). Cartan

exerted a profound influence over the development of this topic and contributed greatly to the shape of modern mathematics.

Élie Cartan was born in Dolomieu, France, on April 9, 1869, to a village blacksmith. Due to his poverty, it was unlikely that the young Cartan would ever study at a university, but his early talent in mathematics was recognized by a passing school inspector; as a result of this intervention, Cartan was able to study at the *lycée* in Lyons and later joined the École Normale Supérieure in Paris. After graduation, he commenced his research in the area of Lie groups, which are a special type of differentiable manifold. Cartan held various teaching positions until he secured a professorship at the University of Paris in 1912.

Cartan's doctoral thesis was concerned with providing a rigorous foundation to Wilhelm Killing's results on Lie algebras. Later, Cartan completed the classification of simple Lie algebras and determined their irreducible representations. For some three decades following his dissertation, Cartan was practically alone in his chosen field, as most French mathematicians were more interested in function theory. Due to his isolation, Cartan was forced to develop entirely original methods.

In 1913 Cartan discovered the spinors, a mathematical object of relevance in quantum mechanics. After 1925 he became more interested in topology, and started studying global properties of Lie groups, discovering several important results. His methods in differential systems were revolutionary, providing general solutions independent of a particular choice of variables. One of his chief tools, which he developed in the decade following his thesis, was the calculus of exterior differential forms. He then applied his technique masterfully to a series of problems from differential geometry, Lie groups, and general relativity.

Cartan also made substantial contributions to differential geometry, and it is said that he revitalized the subject after the initial work of GEORG FRIEDRICH BERNHARD RIEMANN. His concept of "moving frames" gave great power for establishing new theorems, and has become one of the most important techniques in modern mathematics. Cartan's concept of a connection helped define a more general type of geometry suitable to modeling the universe according to the precepts of general relativity. His connections were able to completely describe the symmetric Riemannian spaces, which play an important role in number theory.

It was a long time before Cartan obtained the recognition warranted by his genius and creativity. This was in part due to his humble nature, but also because the originality of his ideas eluded the grasp of his contemporaries. He taught at Paris until his retirement in 1940, and was elected to the French Academy of Sciences in 1931. He died on May 6, 1951, in Paris.

Cartan's mathematical achievements have had a great impact on the subsequent development of many areas of modern mathematics. After 1930 the younger generation of mathematicians became increasingly appreciative of his work, which they eagerly digested and supplemented. Now, the unified disciplines of Lie groups, differential systems, and differential geometry constitute a powerful tool and a central place in current mathematical research.

Further Reading

Chern, S., and C. Chevalley. "Elie Cartan," *American Mathematical Society. Bulletin. New Series* 58 (1952).

⊠   Cauchy, Augustin-Louis
(1789–1857)
French
Complex Analysis, Algebra, Differential Equations

Cauchy's profundity can be compared with that of CARL FRIEDRICH GAUSS, as to the quantity, quality, and variety of mathematical material

Augustin-Louis Cauchy made great advances in complex analysis, infinite series, calculus, algebra, and differential equations and developed an integral formula for the calculation of residues for complex integrals. *(Courtesy of the Library of Congress)*

considered. He made outstanding contributions to real analysis and calculus, complex function theory, differential equations, and algebra, as well as elasticity theory and celestial mechanics. His strange personality, alternately described as childishly naive and flamboyantly melodramatic, together with his profuse literary style combine to form a singular character in the history of mathematics. Indeed, the name of Cauchy is attached to more theorems and mathematical concepts than that of any other mathematician.

Augustin-Louis Cauchy was born on August 21, 1789, in Paris to Louis-François Cauchy, a powerful administrative official, and Marie-Madeleine Desestre. The couple had wed in 1787 and had four sons and two daughters. His father, who was an expert in classics, first educated

Augustin Cauchy, the eldest child. Later he met several leading scientists, such as PIERRE-SIMON LAPLACE. Cauchy next attended the École Central du Panthéon, and he was admitted to the École Polytechnique at the age of 16. A few years later he left school to become an engineer, and in 1810 he worked at the harbor of Cherbourg, where Napoleon was building up his naval operations against England. By 1813 Cauchy had returned to Paris.

Meanwhile, in 1811 Cauchy had solved a geometrical problem posed by JOSEPH-LOUIS LAGRANGE: the determination of the angles of a convex polyhedron from its faces. In 1812 he cracked a problem of PIERRE DE FERMAT—whether every number is the sum of n ngonal numbers. His 1814 treatise on definite integrals was submitted to the French Academy, and this essay would later become the foundation of the theory of complex functions. Two years later Cauchy won a prize contest of the French Academy on the topic of wave propagation on the surface of a liquid. By 1819 he had invented the method of characteristics used to solve partial differential equations, and in 1822 he laid the basis for elasticity theory.

These represent a small sample of Cauchy's extensive writings. He had obtained the position of adjoint professor of the École Polytechnique in 1815, and the next year was promoted to full professor and was appointed as a member of the Académie des Sciences; before 1830 he held chairs at both the Faculté des Sciences and the Collège de France. In the meantime he wrote many notable textbooks, which were remarkable for their precision.

In 1818 Cauchy married Aloïse de Bure, by whom he had two daughters; the family settled in nearby Sceaux. He was a devout Catholic, devoted to several charities throughout his life and helping to found the Institut Catholique. Cauchy served on a committee to promote sabbath observance, and apparently spent his entire salary on the poor of Sceaux. His personality has been described as bigoted, self-centered, and fanatical; others paint him as merely childish. For example, Cauchy wrote a defense of the Jesuits, contending that they were hated because of their virtue. His treatment of the memoirs of NIELS HENRIK ABEL and EVARISTE GALOIS has been cited as proof of his selfish egotism, though in general he recognized other persons' work and was careful in his referencing. Before presenting another's paper to the academy, Cauchy would often generalize and improve the author's results; it seems that his obsession with mathematics transgressed the boundaries of propriety, driving him to publish an idea as soon as it was developed. And Cauchy was prodigious: He produced at least seven books and more than 800 papers!

In the July revolution of 1830, the Bourbon monarchy was replaced by Louis-Philippe. A royalist, Cauchy refused to swear allegiance to the new king. As a result, he lost his chairs and went into self-imposed exile to Fribourg, Sardinia, and finally Prague, where he tutored the Bourbon crown prince and was later rewarded by being made a baron. In 1834 his wife and daughters joined him in Prague, but Cauchy returned to Paris in 1838, resuming his mathematical activity at the academy. Various friends attempted to procure a position for Cauchy, but his steadfast refusal to make the oath of allegiance rendered these efforts abortive. After the February Revolution of 1848, the republicans resumed power and Cauchy was permitted to take the chair at the Sorbonne. He continued publishing at an enormous rate until his death on May 22, 1857.

Cauchy had written a masterful calculus text in 1821, notable for its rigor and excellent style. This approach to mathematics was characteristic of him: He rejected the "generality of algebra," which was an illogical argument for treating infinitesimal quantities the same as finite ones. Cauchy distinguished between a convergent and divergent series (and refused to treat the latter type), laying specific conditions for convergence, such as the so-called Cauchy property for convergence of a sequence, as well as the root, ratio, and integral tests. Cauchy defined upper and lower limits for nonconvergent sequences, established the limit and series representations for the transcendental number e, and was the first to use the limit notation. He derived various rules for the manipulation of convergent series, and computed radii of convergence for power series, cautioning against rash use of Taylor's approximation. Cauchy proved a remainder theorem for series, invented the modern concept of continuity, and obtained a version of the intermediate value theorem—later proved by BERNHARD BOLZANO. Cauchy stressed the limit definition of both the derivative and the definite integral, as well as discussing indefinite and singular integrals. He made extensive use of the Fourier transform (discovered prior to JEAN-BAPTISTE-JOSEPH FOURIER) in differential equations, invented the so-called Jacobian (a special determinant), and gave a proof of the fundamental theorem of algebra.

In statistics, Cauchy treated regression theory using absolute errors, in contrast to Gauss's theory of least squares; one result of this investigation is the creation of the so-called Cauchy distribution. In algebra, Cauchy researched the inverse of a matrix, provided theorems on determinants, and investigated orthogonal transformations. He contrasted the geometric and algebraic construction of the complex number. He also laid the fundamentals of group theory, including the concepts of group, subgroup, conjugation, and order, and proved Cauchy's theorem for finite groups. He also unsuccessfully attempted the proof of Fermat's last theorem, which was proved only in 1994.

Cauchy's methods in the theory of differential equations include use of the Fourier transform and the method of characteristics. Cauchy stressed that not all such equations had solutions, and uniqueness could be stipulated only under important initial and boundary conditions; a well-specified partial differential equation with initial and boundary data is called the Cauchy problem. He also founded elasticity theory, generalizing it from the one-dimensional examples considered by 18th-century mathematicians; this was one of his most elegant and praiseworthy contributions to science. Cauchy also wrote on the topic of celestial mechanics, solving the Kepler equation and researching the perturbative function.

The theory of complex functions is, perhaps, most heavily indebted to Cauchy. He first justified limit and algebraic operations on complex numbers, and later developed Cauchy's integral formula and the calculus of residues. These tools have a remarkable breadth of application. It is interesting that Cauchy failed to deduce Liouville's theorem (that bounded regular functions must be constant), but he had no global, connecting perspective on the new science. However, his numerous contributions and insights greatly advanced the field of complex analysis.

Further Reading

Belhoste, B. *Augustin-Louis Cauchy: A Biography.* New York: Springer-Verlag, 1991.

Dubbey, J. "Cauchy's Contribution to the Establishment of the Calculus," *Annals of Science* 22 (1966): 61–67.

Fisher, G. "Cauchy's Variables and Orders of the Infinitely Small," *British Journal for the Philosophy of Science* 30, no. 3 (1979): 261–265.

Grabiner, J. *The Origins of Cauchy's Rigorous Calculus:* Cambridge, Mass.: MIT Press, 1981.

———. "Who Gave You the Epsilon? Cauchy and the Origins of Rigorous Calculus," *The American Mathematical Monthly* 90, no. 3 (1983): 185–194.

Grattan-Guinness, I. "Bolzano, Cauchy and the 'New Analysis' of the Early Nineteenth Century," *Archive for History of Exact Sciences* 6 (1970): 372–400.

Cavalieri, Bonaventura
(ca. 1598–1647)
Italian
Geometry, Calculus

Before SIR ISAAC NEWTON and GOTTFRIED WIL-
HELM VON LEIBNIZ systematically developed the
integral calculus, a few other mathematicians labored as predecessors, drawing on the ideas
hinted at by ARCHIMEDES OF SYRACUSE. The concept of indivisibles—those quantities so small
that they cannot be divided in half—had begun
to take hold, and Cavalieri was one of the first
proponents; his work on integration would later
inspire BLAISE PASCAL, Newton, and Leibniz.

The exact birth date of Bonaventura
Cavalieri is unknown, and nothing is known of
his family. He was born in Milan, Italy, and he
adopted the name Bonaventura upon entering
the Jesuit religious order as a boy, and he remained a monastic throughout his life. In 1616
he was transferred to the monastery at Pisa,
where he met Castelli, a Benedictine monk and
student of GALILEO GALILEI. At the time, Castelli
was lecturer in mathematics at Pisa, and he took
Cavalieri as his student. The boy quickly mastered EUCLID OF ALEXANDRIA, Archimedes, and
APOLLONIUS OF PERGA, and demonstrated a remarkable talent for geometry, sometimes acting
as substitute for Castelli. Later, Cavalieri was introduced to Galileo, with whom he exchanged
many letters over the years.

From 1620 to 1623 Cavalieri taught theology at Milan, having been ordained deacon to
Cardinal Borromeo. During this period he developed his first ideas on the method of indivisibles: One views a plane surface as the union of
infinitely many parallel lines (the indivisibles),
so that area is computed from the sum of all their
lengths. In the same fashion, a solid figure was
composed of infinitely many stacked surfaces, so
that volume could be computed by summing all
the areas. His next assignment was at Lodi, where
he stayed three years, and in 1626 he became

prior of the monastery in Parma; he sought a lectureship at Parma, but without success. Falling
ill in 1626 with gout, which plagued him
throughout his life, Cavalieri recovered in Milan
and soon announced to Galileo the completion
of his *Geometria Indivisibilibus Continuorum Nova
Quadam Ratione Promota* (A certain method for
the development of a new geometry of continuous indivisibles). Through the latter's assistance, Cavalieri obtained in 1629 the first chair
of mathematics at Bologna, which he held until his death on November 30, 1647.

It had become apparent to Cavalieri that
Archimedes was aware of a method for calculating areas and volumes that he was unwilling
to disclose—either out of competitive secrecy or
a desire to avoid derision from his conservative
colleagues. Cavalieri developed a rational system
of the so-called indivisibles and attempted to establish the validity of this approach. From his
principles, Cavalieri deduced several of the basic theorems of integral calculus, but without the
formalism of the integral itself. His method of
calculation, which involves the concept of congruence under translation, is shown to be valid
for parallelograms and plane figures lying between two parallel lines (and conglomerations
of such).

His contemporaries largely rejected Cavalieri's
methodology, unaware that Archimedes himself
had utilized similar techniques. Cavalieri obtained some basic formulas, such as the power
rule for integration of a polynomial, in 1639,
though it had been discovered three years earlier by PIERRE DE FERMAT and Gilles de Roberval.
He also discovered the volume of solids obtained
by rotating about an axis.

Also in *Geometria* there is an early formulation of the mean value theorem, which states
that between any two points on a curve can be
found a tangent line parallel to the chord connecting the two points. Cavalieri also investigated
logarithms, which had recently been invented
by JOHN NAPIER, as well as trigonometry with

applications to astronomy. His *Centuria di varii problemi* (A century of various problems) of 1639 treated the definition of cylindrical and conical surfaces, and also gave formulas for the volume of a barrel and the capacity of a vault. Among his other contributions to science are a theory of conics applied to optics and acoustics, the idea for the reflecting telescope (apparently prior to Newton), determination of the focal length of a lens, and explanations of Archimedes's burning glass.

Cavalieri's work was a first modern step toward calculus, and he should be seen as an essential link in the chain between Archimedes and the great 17th-century mathematicians who developed calculus—Pascal, Leibniz, and Newton, along with JOHN WALLIS and ISAAC BARROW.

Further Reading

Anderson, K. "Cavalieri's Method of Indivisibles," *Archive for History of Exact Sciences* 31, no. 4 (1985): 291–367.

Ariotti, P. "Bonaventura Cavalieri, Marin Mersenne, and the Reflecting Telescope," *Isis* 66 (1975): 303–321.

⊠ **Chebyshev, Pafnuty Lvovich**
(1821–1894)
Russian
Probability

Russian mathematics in the early 19th century was relatively inactive, especially in comparison to the abundant researches carried out by LEONHARD EULER in St. Petersburg. The primary impact of Chebyshev was to revive the pursuit of mathematical knowledge in Russia; the influence of the Petersburg mathematical school, founded by Chebyshev, extended beyond that town to Moscow and much of Europe as well.

Pafnuty Chebyshev was born to an aristocratic family on May 16, 1821, on the family estate in Okatovo, Russia. His father, Lev Pavlovich

Chebyshev, was a retired army officer who had fought against Napoleon; his mother, Agrafena Ivanovna Pozniakova Chebysheva, bore nine children. The family moved to Moscow in 1832, and Chebyshev received his early education from a famous tutor. In 1837 he enrolled in the mathematics and physics department of Moscow University, where he came under the influence of Brashman, who encouraged his students to pursue the most important problems of science and technology.

At this time Chebyshev wrote his first paper, which generalizes the Newton-Raphson method for finding the zeroes of a differentiable function; for this work he earned a silver medal in a departmental contest. In 1841 Chebyshev graduated with his bachelor's degree, and two years later he passed his master's examinations; meanwhile he published papers on the theory of multiple integrals and the convergence of Taylor series. His master's thesis, which he defended in 1846, was "An Essay on an Elementary Analysis of the Theory of Probability," and treated SIMÉON DENIS POISSON's law of large numbers. This early work characterizes Chebyshev's general approach: the precise calculation of bounds for a limit demonstrated with elementary techniques.

Chebyshev took an assistant professorship at St. Petersburg, where he worked toward completion of his doctoral thesis. His lectures at Petersburg University ranged from higher algebra to integral calculus and the theory of numbers; his teaching focused on particular topics of interest, and the special techniques that were relevant. While editing an edition of Euler's works, Chebyshev became increasingly interested in the theory of numbers. His monograph *Theory of Congruences* earned him his doctorate in mathematics in 1849 and a prize from the Academy of Sciences. One of the most important topics considered was the distribution of prime numbers; Chebyshev made substantial progress in finding precise asymptotics for the prime number function (given any integer, this function reports how many prime numbers are less than the given integer).

As a result of this work, which became quite well known in the scientific community, Chebyshev was promoted to extraordinary professor in 1850, and 10 years later attained full professor. During this decade Chebyshev investigated the theory of mechanisms, which led to his study of the best approximation of a given function. This topic involved the uniform approximation of a function by a polynomial. He had long possessed an interest in mechanics, which received additional stimulation from visiting several factories throughout Europe, and through 1856 Chebyshev delivered numerous lectures in practical mechanics. He also continued his research of the integration of algebraic functions, extending the achievements of NIELS HENRIK ABEL in the realm of elliptic integrals, and lectured on elliptic functions at the university.

For his work in practical mechanics and mathematics, Chebyshev was elected to the Petersburg Academy of Sciences in 1853, obtaining the chair of applied mathematics. In 1856 he became associated with the Artillery Committee, which was concerned with developing Russian ballistic technology; Chebyshev introduced mathematical solutions for artillery problems, and in 1867 he gave a formula for the trajectory of spherical missiles. Meanwhile, he actively contributed to the Ministry of Education, endeavoring to improve the teaching of science in secondary schools.

Chebyshev is recognized for his foundation of the Petersburg mathematical school, which consisted of an informal collection of his numerous pupils, including ANDREI MARKOV. The agenda of this community was directed toward the solution of pure and applied mathematical problems that arose from practical applications. Chebyshev was a proponent of finding practical solutions to problems, and he often tried to devise algorithms that would provide a numerical answer. Toward this end he advanced the use of inequalities, which allowed the construction of bounds and approximations simpler than an exact solution. The school pursued many branches of mathematics, but was connected in its development of thought from Euler, whose works had exercised a great influence upon Chebyshev.

From the 1850s a dominant aspect of Chebyshev's work was the theory of best approximation of functions, which led to research of orthogonal polynomials, limiting values of integrals, the theory of moments, interpolation, and methods of approximating quadratures; he also improved the methodology of continued fractions. Starting in the 1860s Chebyshev wrote several articles about technological inventions, and returned to the theory of probability. Two important works include his 1867 paper "On Mean Values," in which he generalizes the law of large numbers by implementing the so-called Chebyshev inequality, and an 1887 work, "On Two Theorems Concerning Probability," that generalized the central limit theorem. This latter achievement effectively extended the normal distribution's range of applicability in the field of statistics.

Many other problems of applied mathematics piqued his interest; Chebyshev investigated the problem of binding a surface with a cloth, giving rise to the "Chebyshev net," and he considered the equilibrium of a rotating liquid mass. Chebyshev built a calculating machine in the late 1870s that performed multiplication and division.

In 1882 he retired from Petersburg University, but he kept his academic salon active, supplying the new generation of intellectuals with ideas and encouragement. He continued working until his death on December 8, 1894. Chebyshev had been elected to numerous academic societies and had greatly influenced the development of Russian mathematics. The Petersburg school developed whole new areas of study, but was mainly characterized by Chebyshev's vision of the unity of theory and practice. His numerous contributions to diverse areas of mathematics, as well as his industrious mentorship, have served to propagate Chebyshev's ideas throughout modern mathematics.

Further Reading

Butzer, P., and F. Jongmans. "P. L. Chebyshev (1821–1894): A Guide to His Life and Work," *Journal of Approximation Theory* 96, no. 1 (1999): 111–138.

———. "P. L. Chebyshev (1821–1894) and His Contacts with Western European Scientists," *Historia Mathematica* 16 (1989): 46–68.

Stander, D. "Makers of Modern Mathematics: Pafnuty Liwowich Chebyshev," *Bulletin of the Institute of Mathematics and Its Application* 26, nos. 1–2 (1990): 18–19.

⊠ Ch'in Chiu-Shao
(ca. 1202–ca. 1261)
Chinese
Algebra

Mathematics in 13th-century China was mainly concerned with solutions of algebraic equations and determination of areas of certain shapes, with important applications to finance, commerce, agriculture, and astronomy. Ch'in Chiu-Shao worked on problems of this type, leaving behind some general methods for their solution. He was also an important influence on later Chinese mathematicians, such as CHU SHIH-CHIEH.

Ch'in Chiu-Shao was born around 1202 in the Szechuan province of China; his father was a civil servant, and Ch'in would follow his father's vocation. He was an ill-disciplined youth, and later became a vindictive, unprincipled adult. During one of his father's banquets, Ch'in recklessly hurled a stone into the midst of the assembled guests in a display of his archery skills; later in life, he would become known for poisoning his adversaries.

In 1219 Ch'in joined the army as the captain of a squad of volunteers, who helped suppress a local uprising. In 1224 and 1225 Ch'in followed his father to the capital city of Hangchow. There he studied astronomy under the tutelage of the official astronomers. He soon left the capital when his father was transferred to another position, and in 1233 it is known that Ch'in served as a sheriff.

In 1236 the Mongols invaded Szechuan, and Ch'in fled east, becoming a vice-administrator in Hupeh Province, and later governor of Ho-hsien in Anhwei Province. His next post was in Nanking in 1244, which he held briefly, and finally he came to Wu-hsing, where he wrote his *Mathematical Treatise* in 1247. According to his own account, Ch'in learned his mathematics from an unnamed mathematician.

Ch'in's manuscript, his only known mathematical writing, consisted of nine parts, each of which had two chapters. They deal with indeterminate analysis, astronomical calculations, land measurement, surveying via triangulation, land tax, money, structural works, military matters, and barter, respectively. Ch'in represented the height of Chinese attainment in the arena of indeterminate analysis, which had first appeared in the fourth century. One type of problem involved finding a number with various given remainders for given divisors; these types of problems now fall generally under the domain of the so-called Chinese remainder theorem. One could apply these results to calendar calculations and military logistics, among other things.

Ch'in's method for such remainder problems was general; he gave a formula for solving such questions that was not discovered in Europe until the 16th century. This technique was applicable when the various divisors were relatively prime (when they themselves had no common factors); but Ch'in also extended his method to the more general situation when the divisors were not relatively prime. This technique came to be known as "the Great Extension method of searching for unity." Of course, Ch'in did not use the modern notations of modular arithmetic, but introduced many technical terms of his own, such as celestial monads and operation numbers.

In solving algebraic equations, Ch'in used a counting board with rods arranged in certain formations to represent numbers and unknown quantities. In this way, he would calculate solutions to various equations, with degree as high as 10. His method, identical to that discovered by Paolo Ruffini in 1805, was labeled the "harmoniously alternating evolution"; it seems, however, that Ch'in was not the inventor of this technique, as his contemporaries were also familiar with it.

It is interesting that Ch'in's book gives various values for pi, such as 22/7 and square root of 10, as well as the old value of 3. He gives the areas of several geometric shapes, such as triangles (without the use of trigonometry), circular arcs, and quadrangles. He treats several simultaneous linear equations in several variables, and Ch'in also discusses the sum of certain series of numbers. Finally, he deals with problems involving finite differences, as these were of interest to calendar makers.

After this work Ch'in returned to the civil service in 1254, and he was appointed as governor of Hainan in 1258. He was dismissed three months later on charges of corruption, and he returned home with an immense fortune amassed from his acceptance of numerous bribes. He later became an assistant to his good friend Wu Ch'ien (of whom it is related that Ch'in cheated him out of a plot of land), and followed him to the provinces of Chekiang and Kwangtung. Shortly after receiving an appointment in Mei-hsien, Ch'in died. The year of his death is estimated to be 1261.

Ch'in was known as an expert poet, archer, fencer, equestrian, and musician, as well as being a foremost mathematician of his age and country.

The stories about him paint a disreputable picture; it is related that he punished a female member of his household by starvation. However, his mathematical talent is undisputed, and his mastery of indeterminate analysis reserves him a space in mathematical history.

Further Reading

Martzloff, J. *A History of Chinese Mathematics*. Berlin and Heidelberg: Springer-Verlag, 1997.

Mikami, Y. *The Development of Mathematics in China and Japan*. New York: Chelsea Publishing Company, 1974.

Shen, K. "Historical Development of the Chinese Remainder Theorem," *Archive for History of Exact Sciences* 38, no. 4 (1988): 285–305.

⊠   **Chu Shih-Chieh (Zhu Shijie)**
(ca. 1279–ca. 1303)
Chinese
Algebra

Much of Chinese mathematics focused on problems of algebra and the summation of series. Chu Shih-Chieh represented a significant advance in the knowledge of these areas, adding to the work of great 13th-century mathematicians such as CH'IN CHIU SHAO. He was certainly the greatest mathematician of his time and country.

Little is known of the personal life of Chu Shih-Chieh, but he was born sometime prior to 1280 and died after the publication of his second book in 1303. In the preface to this work, called the *Precious Mirror of the Four Elements*, the author claims to have spent 20 years journeying around China as a renowned mathematician. Afterward, he visited the city of Kuang-ling, where he attracted numerous pupils. It seems that Chu Shih-Chieh flourished in the latter part of the 13th century after the reunification of China through the Mongol conquest.

His first work, *Introduction to Mathematical Studies* of 1299, was a textbook for beginners.

The *Four Elements* contains the method of that name, evidently invented by Chu. This was the "method of the celestial element" extended to four variables; this prior method was apparently well known in China, though no record of it currently exists. Chu's method represents the four unknown quantities graphically, and he solved high-degree equations by using a transformation method. Chu does not describe this, but he was able to solve complicated quartic (fourth degree) equations. When exact solutions of such equations were not possible, Chu used an approximation. It is interesting that in finding square roots, Chu used a substitution technique known to Ch'in Chiu-Shao that is similar to modern methods.

In the same book, Chu has a drawing of Pascal's triangle, containing the coefficients of the expansion of a binomial. He gives an explanation of its use, and refers to this diagram as the "old method" (it was already known to 12th-century Chinese mathematicians). Considerable interest focused on the calculation of series, such as the sum of n consecutive integers. Chu's work represents an advance over previous knowledge of such sums, and he applied his results to cross-sections of pyramids and cones (for instance, the determination of how many balls are in a pyramidal stack of a given height). After Chu, Chinese mathematicians made little additional progress in the study of such higher series.

Chu also examined finite differences, which were important to Chinese astronomers in their formulas for celestial motion. Finite difference methods were known since the seventh century in China, but Chu applied them to several word problems.

Chu Shih-Chieh helped to advance Chinese mathematics through his techniques for solving algebraic equations and his computation of series. His works remained hidden for centuries, but when rediscovered they stimulated additional research in the 18th century.

Further Reading

Martzloff, J. *A History of Chinese Mathematics*. Berlin and Heidelberg: Springer-Verlag, 1997.

Mikami, Y. *The Development of Mathematics in China and Japan*. New York: Chelsea Publishing Company, 1974.

D

⊠ Dedekind, Richard
(1831–1916)
German
Analysis, Logic

Much of the mathematical work of the later 19th century was concerned with establishing rigorous foundations for previous mathematical topics, such as the concepts of function, infinity, and number. Dedekind worked in this latter area, being concerned with the definition of the real number and the concept of continuity.

Richard Dedekind was born in Brunswick, Germany, on October 6, 1831. His father, Julius Dedekind, was a professor of law at the Collegium Carolinum of Brunswick, and his mother, Caroline Emperius, was the daughter of another professor at the same institution. Richard Dedekind was the youngest of four children in this intellectual family; he lived with his second sister for most of his life. As a youth, Dedekind attended the local Gymnasium, where he eventually switched his focus from physics to mathematics, claiming that physics was too disordered. At the Collegium Carolinum, which CARL FRIEDRICH GAUSS had also attended, Dedekind mastered analytic geometry, differential and integral calculus, and higher mechanics.

In 1850 he entered the University of Göttingen, and he developed a close friendship with BERNHARD RIEMANN, while attending lectures by Moritz Stern, Wilhelm Weber, and Carl Gauss. Only two years later Dedekind obtained his doctorate under Gauss with a thesis on Eulerian integrals; he went on to Berlin to attend lectures by CARL JACOBI and GUSTAV PETER LEJEUNE DIRICHLET, filling in the rest of his education. In 1854 he obtained a lectureship at the University of Berlin, where he taught probability and geometry. Also at this time, Dedekind became friends with Dirichlet, who expanded his social and intellectual horizons. In 1858 Dedekind obtained an appointment at the Polytechnikum in Zurich, and four years later returned to his hometown, Brunswick, where he remained until his death.

Dedekind is well known among mathematicians for the so-called Dedekind cut, which was an element in his construction of the real numbers. He had already noticed the lack of a truly rigorous foundation of arithmetic; he successfully constructed a purely arithmetic definition of continuity, and exactly formulated the notion of an irrational number. In this connection, Dedekind's work builds on EUDOXUS OF CNIDUS's ancient theory of proportion as a foundation for the real numbers, although the two versions are not exactly identical; Dedekind established the fact that Euclidean postulates alone, devoid of a principle of continuity, could not establish a complete theory of real numbers. His concepts have had enduring significance for the field of mathematical analysis, especially through his use of order to understand the real numbers.

He published these ideas in an 1872 manuscript called *Stetigkeit und Irrationale Zahlen* (Continuity and irrational numbers), which established Dedekind as a leading researcher in the foundations of mathematics, along with GEORG CANTOR and BERNHARD BOLZANO. His 1888 book on numbers—*Was Sind und was Sollen die Zahlen* (*What Numbers Are and Should Be*)—delineated the logical theory of number, treating such topics as the continuity of space, the essence of arithmetic, and the role of numbers in geometry. One important discovery was the definition of infiniteness of a set through mappings, which was vital to Cantor's later research into set theory.

There are many similarities between Gauss and Dedekind, including their personalities: Like Gauss, Dedekind was an intense, disciplined worker who enjoyed a frugal lifestyle. He was a deep thinker who preferred mathematical notions to useful notations. Due to their close kinship, and the fact that Dedekind understood Gauss's work better than anyone else, he edited several of Gauss's unpublished manuscripts, and was able to comment cogently upon these works. This project led Dedekind toward examination of the complex numbers, and he gave the general definition of an algebraic ideal and established several classical results. This work in algebra, for which Dedekind is most famous, led to many fruitful developments by later mathematicians, such as EMMY NOETHER and DAVID HILBERT.

Dedekind was active at the Polytechnikum of Brunswick, of which he assumed the directorship from 1872 to 1875. He received many honorary doctorates during his life and had a wide number of correspondents. In 1894 he became an emeritus professor, and after his death on February 12, 1916, mathematicians in many countries mourned him.

Dedekind's contribution to mathematics might be measured through the quantity of ideas named after him—about a dozen. His contributions to the foundations of number allowed real analysis to progress, developing a deeper knowledge of the real numbers and the concept of continuity; his theorems in algebraic ideals have stimulated much additional activity in the 20th century.

Further Reading

Bell, E. *Men of Mathematics.* New York: Simon and Schuster, 1965.

Edwards, H. "Dedekind's Invention of Ideals," *Bulletin of the London Mathematical Society* 15, no. 1 (1983): 8–17.

Ferreirós, J. "On the Relations between Georg Cantor and Richard Dedekind," *Historia Mathematica* 20 (1993): 343–363.

Gillies, D. *Frege, Dedekind, and Peano on the Foundations of Arithmetic.* Assen, Netherlands: Van Gorcum, 1982.

⊠ Democritus of Abdera
(ca. 460 B.C.E.–ca. 404 B.C.E.)
Greek
Geometry

Democritus is numbered among the very early Greek mathematicians who influenced the later development of geometry. Although his mathematical works have not survived, it is clear that Democritus possessed an extensive interest in conics and other aspects of solid geometry. The great Greek geometers APOLLONIUS OF PERGA and ARCHIMEDES OF SYRACUSE came much later, but even they studied some of the problems investigated by Democritus.

Information on Democritus's life is distorted by several unverifiable accounts. One chronology places his birth after 500 B.C.E. and his death about 404 B.C.E., and represents him as the teacher of Protagoras of Abdera; another version

Democritus developed early ideas about the continuum. *(Courtesy of the National Library of Medicine)*

amusing. Although more than 60 of his works were contained in the library at Alexandria, none of these have survived intact, so knowledge of his writings comes completely from quotations and commentaries. Democritus's pupils propagated his doctrine, and one of them was a teacher of Epicurus. Hence it is thought that Epicureanism represents an elaboration of Democritus's physical theories.

The theory of atoms did not originate with Democritus—its roots have been traced back to the second millennium B.C.E.—but Democritus developed the idea extensively. Atoms were indivisible objects, the basic building blocks of both matter and soul; perceived differences in objects arise from the arrangement and position of atoms within the ambient void. Democritus's Earth was flat and long, with earthquakes caused by fluctuations in the quantity of water in underground cavities.

Democritus made use of the sphere in his natural philosophy, as both fire and soul consist of spherical atoms. He viewed the sphere as pure angle, by which he meant that it was uniformly bent. It is thought that Democritus conceived of the sphere as a polyhedron with minutely small faces, and therefore believed that a tangent makes contact with a circle over a distance rather than in a single point.

He discusses the question of whether the two contiguous surfaces produced when a cone is sliced horizontally are equal. If equal, it might seem that a cone is more like a cylinder; if unequal, the cone must have minute steps. These questions strike to the heart of divisibility and the concept of the continuum, which would become so intriguing for later Greeks and modern European mathematicians. Democritus's own opinion on the dilemma is unclear. Archimedes also records that Democritus examined the ratio of sizes between cylinders, pyramids, and prisms of the same base and height, but we are unaware of the extent of Democritus's knowledge.

frames his life much later, depicting him as a contemporary of Socrates, being born around 460 B.C.E. and dying in about 404 B.C.E. Most scholars accept the latter dates.

Democritus was born in Abdera, Thrace, and was fairly wealthy. He traveled widely, visiting Athens, and was known as the "laughing philosopher" since he found the follies of humankind

Democritus also explored the field of biology, and he derived a doctrine of the evolution of culture that represents the development from lesser to greater civilizations; this was contrary to the prevailing view that humankind had fallen from an original golden age.

Democritus commanded a significant sway over later thought in natural philosophy, and his atomism later influenced Epicureanism. It is difficult to gauge the extent of his mathematical accomplishments, but it is apparent that his researches and questions prompted the inquiries of following mathematicians.

Further Reading

Brumbaugh, R. *The Philosophers of Greece*. New York: Crowell, 1964.

Guthrie, W. *A History of Greek Philosophy*. Cambridge: Cambridge University Press, 1981.

Hahm, D. "Chrysippus' Solution to the Democritean Dilemma of the Cone," *Isis* 63, no. 217 (1972): 205–220.

Heath, T. *A History of Greek Mathematics*. Oxford: Clarendon Press, 1921.

Laertius, D. *Lives, Teachings, and Sayings of Famous Philosophers*. Cambridge, Mass.: Harvard University Press, 1959.

Russell, B. *History of Western Philosophy and Its Connection with Political and Social Circumstances from the Ancient Times to the Present Day*. London: Allen and Unwin, 1961.

⊠ De Morgan, Augustus
(1806–1871)
English
Logic

Aristotelian logic, for centuries the dominant mode of logical argument, was unable to evaluate logical statements which involved quantity. This inadequacy pointed to a general need to place logic on a mathematical foundation. This effort, which took place in the 19th and 20th centuries, was greatly assisted by Augustus De Morgan.

Augustus De Morgan was born in India on June 27, 1806. His father was an officer in the Indian colonial army, and his mother was the daughter of a pupil of ABRAHAM DE MOIVRE; this connection may account for De Morgan's later talent in mathematics. While he was still quite young, the family relocated to England, eventually settling in Taunton. De Morgan attended several private schools, gaining facility in Latin, Greek, and Hebrew, as well as a fervent interest in mathematics by age 14.

In 1823 he entered Trinity College. He later graduated fourth in his class. Upon the strong recommendation of his tutors, De Morgan obtained the chair of mathematics at University College in 1828. His life was characterized by strong convictions about Christianity; he wished to avoid even the appearance of hypocrisy, and as a result refused a fellowship at Cambridge that required his ordination. The college council dismissed a fellow professor in 1831 without grounds, and De Morgan immediately resigned on principle. He resumed the post in 1836 upon the death of his successor. Meanwhile, De Morgan became a fellow of the Astronomical Society in 1828, and later helped found the London Mathematical Society. In 1837 he married Sophia Elizabeth Frend.

He was interested in all branches of knowledge, and published prolifically—more than 850 articles and numerous textbooks on arithmetic, algebra, trigonometry, calculus, complex numbers, probability, and logic. These texts are known for their logical presentation and precision—as a teacher he endeavored to demonstrate principles rather than techniques. De Morgan's interests extended to the history of mathematics: he wrote a biography of SIR ISAAC NEWTON and composed one of the first significant works in the field of scientific bibliography.

De Morgan's mathematical contributions lay mainly in the fields of logic and analysis. In an 1838 article he invented the term *mathematical induction* as a technique of proof, formalizing a method that had long been used by mathematicians. His *Differential and Integral Calculus* (1842) gives a precise analytical formulation of AUGUSTIN-LOUIS CAUCHY's intuitive concept of a limit and a discussion of convergence rules for infinite series. This includes De Morgan's rule, a test for convergence involving the limit of the sequence of a series, which is useful when simpler tests are not informative. Elsewhere De Morgan describes a system that he created as "double algebra," which assisted in the geometrical interpretation of complex numbers, and suggested the idea of quaternions to SIR WILLIAM ROWAN HAMILTON.

Most important are his researches into logic. De Morgan was among the first to perceive the need for a better system than the Aristotelian, which could not handle statements involving quantity. Following the ideas of George Bentham, De Morgan invented algebraic notations for expressing logical statements, and his work later inspired GEORGE BOOLE's analytical formulation. Some of the basic rules of Boolean algebra are therefore called the De Morgan formulas. De Morgan was the first person to present a logical calculus of relations; he used an algebraic notation to express relations between objects, and went on to consider the composition of relations and the inverse of a relation.

De Morgan's other accomplishments include the promotion of a decimal monetary system, an almanac covering 4,000 years of lunar dates, and a probability text giving applications to life insurance. He died in London on March 18, 1871.

De Morgan is very important in the history of mathematics, as he substantially developed the algebraic foundation of logic (this would be further worked out by subsequent mathematicians such as Boole), and thus was an early advocate of the view that logic should be considered as a branch of mathematics, not a separate field of knowledge.

Further Reading

Halsted, G. "Biography: De Morgan," *The American Mathematical Monthly* 4 (1897): 1–5.

Rice, A. "Augustus De Morgan: Historian of Science," *History of Science* 34 (1996): 201–240.

———."Augustus De Morgan (1806–1871)," *The Mathematical Intelligencer* 18, no. 3 (1996): 40–43.

Richards, J. "Augustus De Morgan, the History of Mathematics, and the Foundations of Algebra," *Isis* 78, no. 291 (1987): 7–30.

Desargues, Girard
(1591–1661)
French
Geometry

In the late 16th century, mathematics was on the eve of a dramatic rebirth. It would emerge from the darkness of the medieval age, and the principal mathematicians of this time sought to recast and develop classical Greek mathematics. Concurrent with the powerful algebraic approach to geometry developed by RENÉ DESCARTES, Desargues advocated a unified graphical perspective. His ideas influenced such great thinkers as BLAISE PASCAL and SIR ISAAC NEWTON, even though they were inevitably overshadowed by the power of the Cartesian system.

Girard Desargues was born into a family of nine children on February 21, 1591, in Lyons. His father was an affluent tithe collector, and Girard's early studies took place in Lyons. However, little is known of his early years and education, and his first recorded scientific activity took place in 1626, when he proposed that the state construct machines to raise the water level of the Seine.

Around 1630 Desargues became friendly with several Paris mathematicians, such as Marin Mersenne and Gilles de Roberval; he regularly attended the meetings of the Académie Parisienne, in which the young Blaise Pascal would later participate. In 1636 Desargues published a work describing his so-called universal method of perspective. There he outlined a vast research program: to unify the various graphical techniques (such as those used by architects and draftsmen) via his "universal methods," while also incorporating projective geometry into the body of mathematical knowledge through the rigorous study of perspective. Projective geometry had few followers until the 19th century, and Desargues's work was greatly overlooked (and even ridiculed) during his own lifetime; its significance would be realized centuries later.

A competing work by Jean de Beaugrand evoked intellectual discussions on the topics of center of gravity, optics, and tangents, as well as other geometrical issues. Desargues was an avid participant in these disputations, distinguishing himself by his intent to understand the most general aspect of given problems. Although he alienated Beaugrand, he gained the esteem of Descartes and Mersenne. In contrast to Descartes's program to give geometry an algebraic foundation, Desargues wished to extend the influence of geometrical methods to graphical techniques via mechanics. His *Brouillon projet d'une atteinte aux événements des recontres du cône avec un plan* (Rough draft for an essay on the results of taking plane sections of a cone) of 1639 gave a description of conic sections from the perspective of projective geometry; this work was not popular, perhaps due to its divergence from the Cartesian approach. However, Blaise Pascal was able to appreciate the worth of Desargues's *Brouillon project*, and Pascal wrote his *Essay pour les coniques* (Essay on conic sections) as a tribute. Although this work influenced other great mathematicians, such as Newton, its full impact was not realized until the 19th century, when geometers acquired a renewed interest in projective geometry. This lack of popularity was surely the result of the increasing interest in the problems of infinitesimal calculus.

Beaugrand criticized Desargues's work vehemently, seemingly for personal rather than professional reasons. In 1640 Desargues published an essay concerning stonecutting, applying his techniques to practical graphing methods. However, his useful innovations were contrary to the established practice of the powerful trade guilds, and thus Desargues attracted the animosity of veteran artisans.

In 1641 Desargues became interested in the problem of determining various circular sections of cones having a conic base. His general solution relied solely on pure geometry. Roberval, Descartes, and Pascal became interested in this problem, and Desargues later generalized his technique.

Subsequently Desargues became involved in a dispute over the priority of his methods. He had worked to spread his graphical techniques among stonecutters, but in 1642 an anonymous publication plagiarized and distorted his work. The resulting debate injured Desargues's credibility and confidence. Desargues appointed the task of dissemination of his work to his disciple Abraham Bosse, an engraver, who later published two treatises discussing Desargues's method. A new dispute arose in 1644 with a stonecutter named Curabelle, with the apparent result that Desargues decided to forgo further publishing. However, Bosse continued to compose treatises on his master's method of perspective.

After 1644 Desargues's scientific activity declined. He started a new career as architect, fashioning some spectacular structures of a delicate figure. For example, Desargues used his mathematical knowledge to constuct curved staircases that were both functional and elegant. He implemented his techniques directly in practical applications, and in this way silenced the accusation of his enemies that his methods were purely theoretical. His engineering feats were extensive, including a system for raising water, which was installed near Paris. He died in Paris in October 1661.

Desargues must be credited as being one of the founders of projective geometry—the study of spaces of straight lines meeting infinitely far away from the observer. He also contributed to the knowledge of conics, introduced projective transformations, and furthered the development of graphical techniques useful in drawings. Sadly, his work was savagely contested in his own lifetime, and even among supportive mathematicians it received little circulation due to his cumbersome style of writing. His labors bore fruit only centuries after his death, when his papers were rediscovered by grateful 19th-century geometers.

Further Reading

Field, J. *The Invention of Infinity: Mathematics and Art in the Renaissance.* New York: Oxford University Press, 1997.

———. "Linear Perspective and the Projective Geometry of Girard Desargues," *Istituto e Museo di Storia della Scienza Firenze. Nuncivs. Annali di Storia della Scienza* 2, no. 2 (1987): 3–40.

———, and Gray, J. *The Geometrical Work of Girard Desargues.* New York: Springer-Verlag, 1987.

René Descartes, an outstanding French philosopher, introduced the idea of analytic geometry; namely, that geometric objects could be represented by equations that could be graphed on coordinate axes. *(Courtesy of the National Library of Medicine)*

⊠   **Descartes, René**
(1596–1650)
French
Geometry, Algebra

The 17th century was a time of heightened activity in science and mathematics, and René Descartes is one of the men who substantially affected the development of scientific knowledge and philosophy. His idealistic system attempted to explain all of human knowledge from a few basic principles. Although his program was overly optimistic, Descartes's influence was enormous, especially in mathematics. Perhaps his greatest contribution was his placement of geometry within the domain of algebra, allowing mathematicians to study curves and figures through analysis of algebraic equations.

René Descartes was born in La Haye, France, on March 31, 1596, to an aristocratic family. His father was a member of the parliament of Brittany, and his mother was a wealthy noblewoman. Descartes later inherited an estate in Poitou from her, which granted him financial independence and the leisure to pursue scientific studies. Descartes was educated by Jesuits, and became familiar with modern developments in mathematics and physics, including the recent researches of GALILEO GALILEI, as well as philosophy and classical literature.

He graduated with a law degree from the University of Poitiers and became a volunteer in the army of Prince Maurice of Nassau. On the night of November 10, 1619, Descartes reached two conclusions after a day of solitary thought: that a program of true knowledge must be carried out by himself, and that methodical doubt of current philosophical knowledge was the right way to begin such a task. He would look for self-evident principles as a starting point, from which one could deduce each of the sciences.

As a result of this epiphany, Descartes's later work was characterized by intensity, confidence, and a commitment to working alone. Later, Descartes would increasingly realize the importance of experimentation and empirical observation to the attainment of true knowledge. However, he did not immediately embark on this intellectual quest, but continued his travels in Europe until 1628. In this year, after a successful public debate on the topic of how to distinguish certain and probable knowledge, Descartes withdrew to a solitary life of scientific work in the Netherlands.

Descartes contributed many radical ideas to science. He treated animals and humans as mechanical objects and viewed the laws of motion as the ultimate laws of nature. In his opinion, science should not only demonstrate information, but it should explain as well. Some of his work on cosmology was merely qualitative, and his work suffered from a lack of empirical verification. However, Descartes spent an immense amount of time in experimentation in anatomy, chemistry, and optics.

As a mathematician, Descartes greatly advanced the discipline of algebra and laid the foundation for analytic geometry. Up to his time, few of the modern algebraic notations were employed. Descartes introduced the now familiar alphabetic symbols x, y, and z for unknown quantities, as well as superscripts for the powers of a variable. For example, x^2 was always interpreted as the area of a square on the line segment of length x; but Descartes abstracted the meaning of this symbol, so that one could manipulate x^2 without reference to any geometric construction.

Descartes's main goal in his *Géométrie* (Geometry), his masterpiece of 1637, was to apply algebra to geometry, providing a convenient notation for analyzing figures. He defined the six basic algebraic operations (addition, multiplication, raising to a power, and their inverses of subtraction, division, and taking a root), and defined an algebra of lines that extended the initial notions of the Greeks. But his most important idea was the graph of a function: Given a function, such as a polynomial $f(x)$, one could draw the correspondence between y and x via the equation $y = f(x)$ by using coordinate axes.

In another part of *Géométrie*, Descartes describes how to construct a normal line at any point of a curve by constructing an appropriate coordinate system and inscribing a circle that contacts the curve at one point. His method is similar to PIERRE DE FERMAT's method for finding extrema of a curve, and constitutes one of the first steps in the development of differential calculus. He also gives a purely algebraic theory of equations and states the fundamental theorem of algebra.

Although this work was an influential contribution to mathematics, it did not represent the total of Descartes's knowledge: His insistence on clear deduction from intuitive principles prevented him from stating or accepting more questionable ideas, such as the concept of the infinitesimal. After he completed the *Géométrie*, Descartes's mathematical studies were for the most part complete, and he spent the rest of his time on philosophy.

Descartes remained in the Netherlands until 1649, when he accepted a position as court philosopher to Christina, the queen of Sweden. Queen Christina interrupted his lifelong habit of sleeping through most of the morning, and Descartes died on February 11, 1650, from exposure to the cold morning air.

Descartes was an excellent scientist. He forms an interesting contrast with SIR ISAAC NEWTON, who emphasized the vital role of experimentation and observation. Descartes, however, was more concerned with carefully reasoned deduction from a few basic principles, and he was optimistic that induction (that is, knowledge obtained through experimentation) would eventually be unnecessary. In practice, Descartes found this goal impossible to obtain, and he was forced to experiment in order to attain the knowledge of natural phenomena that he desired. His rationalistic approach to science and philosophy is an enduring legacy for modern man. For mathematics, his development of algebraic methods for geometry revolutionized the study of curves and figures, giving a tremendous forward push to these disciplines.

Further Reading

Clarke, D. *Descartes' Philosophy of Science*. University Park: Pennsylvania State University Press, 1982.

Gaukroger, S. *Descartes: Philosophy, Mathematics, and Physics*. Sussex, U.K.: Harvester Press, 1980.

Haldane, E. *Descartes: His Life and Times*. London: J. Murray, 1905.

Pearl, L. *Descartes*. Boston: Twayne Publishers, 1977.

Scott, J. *The Scientific Work of René Descartes*. New York: Garland, 1987.

Shea, W. *The Magic of Numbers and Motion: The Scientific Career of René Descartes*. Canton, Mass.: Science History Publications, 1991.

Sorell, T. *Descartes*. New York: Oxford University Press, 1987.

⊠   Diophantus of Alexandria
(ca. 200–284)
Greek
Number Theory, Algebra

By the third century, Greek mathematics was already in decline. Diophantus represents a lone pinnacle of thought and activity (excepting the later ARCHIMEDES OF SYRACUSE), and is the founder of the field of indeterminate analysis (the solving of algebraic equations with more than one unknown). The number theory of

16th- and 17th-century Europe can trace much of its genesis to Diophantus's labors.

As with many ancient mathematicians, Diophantus's life is a mystery. We know that he lived in the third century in Alexandria, and he is thought to have married at age 33 and died at age 84. His four surviving writings are *Moriastica*, *Porismata* (Porisms), *Arithmetica* (Arithmetic), and a fragment of *On Polygonal Numbers*. The first is concerned with computations involving fractions, and the second is a collection of propositions cited in the *Arithmetica*. The fragment of *On Polygonal Numbers* uses geometric proofs for certain results on polygonal numbers that involve the number of vertices and sides of a given polygon.

The *Arithmetica* deals with practical, computational arithmetic; it is a collection of problems that Diophantus solves in a great variety of ways. Through his solutions he demonstrated his virtuosity as a mathematician, but presented no general technique or theory. Using certain tricks, Diophantus would commonly reduce the degree of the equation and the number of unknowns (as many as 10) to obtain a solution.

Six books of the *Arithmetica* have survived, in which Diophantus introduces the techniques of algebra and treats many specific problems. His notation differs substantially from the modern symbolism, and this must have hampered the development of general techniques for equations with multiple unknowns. There are 189 problems, ordered from simplest to most difficult, treating various determinate and indeterminate equations. Among the great diversity of material, Diophantus considers multiple equations of polynomials as well as the decomposition of numbers into parts (such as sums of squares).

In solving such problems, Diophantus is aware that multiple solutions are possible, although he discounts negative numbers, as these did not yet exist. Rational number solutions were acceptable, but irrationals such as square roots were excluded. For determinate linear and quadratic equations, Diophantus used balancing and completion. He would typically reduce the number of unknowns and the degree through the method of "false position" and by making substitutions; and he made approximations utilizing algebraic inequalities when direct methods were not possible. It is noteworthy that Diophantus's solutions are remarkably free from error.

Through his writings, Diophantus demonstrates himself to be a first-rate mathematician and ingenious problem-solver. He probably drew upon current Greek knowledge of procedures for solving linear and quadratic problems, though Diophantus made great advances over his predecessors. His work influenced later Arabic mathematicians, who absorbed the corpus of Greek mathematical thought. When European mathematicians such as FRANÇOIS VIÈTE and PIERRE DE FERMAT rediscovered him in the 17th century, the so-called Diophantine problems became a cornerstone of number theory.

Further Reading

Heath, T. *Diophantus of Alexandria: A Study in the History of Greek Algebra*. New York: Dover Publications, 1964.

———. *A History of Greek Mathematics*. Oxford: Clarendon Press, 1921.

Klein, J. *Greek Mathematical Thought and the Origin of Algebra*. Cambridge, Mass.: MIT Press, 1968.

Sesiano, J. *Books IV to VII of Diophantus' 'Arithmetica' in the Arabic Translation Attributed to Qusta ibn Luqa*. New York: Springer-Verlag, 1982.

Swift, J. "Diophantus of Alexandria," *The American Mathematical Monthly* 63 (1956): 163–170.

⊠ **Dirichlet, Gustav Peter Lejeune**
(1805–1859)
German
Number Theory, Analysis, Differential Equations

In the beginning of the 19th century in Germany, CARL FRIEDRICH GAUSS had already made outstanding discoveries in the theory of numbers. Of his many successors, Dirichlet is memorable as a mathematician of great ability who significantly extended the knowledge of number theory.

Gustav Dirichlet was born in Düren in 1805. His father was a postmaster, and Gustav was educated at a public school. Before age 12, he expressed a zealous interest in mathematics, even spending his spare money on mathematical books. In 1817 he entered the Gymnasium in Bonn, and he progressed rapidly in his studies. Two years later Dirichlet was transferred to a Jesuit college in Cologne, where he completed his major examinations by age 16. Although his parents desired Dirichlet to study law, he instead chose to follow his passion—mathematics—and traveled to Paris in 1822 to pursue further studies with the great French mathematicians.

In Paris, after surviving a bout of smallpox, Dirichlet attended the lectures at the Collège de France, and in 1823 secured an attractive position as tutor to the children of a famous French general. Through this situation, Dirichlet was introduced to French intellectual life. Among his mathematical acquaintances, he was especially drawn to JEAN-BAPTISTE-JOSEPH FOURIER, who would continue to exert a significant influence on Dirichlet's later work.

His first interest was number theory, and this continued to be Dirichlet's major area of contribution to mathematics. In 1825 he presented his first paper on so-called Diophantine equations of degree five (equations in more than two variables involving fifth powers, and requiring integer solutions). The results of this work in algebraic number theory led to additional progress on Fermat's last theorem, a famous unsolved conjecture (proved in 1994 by Andrew Wiles) in number theory.

In 1825 Dirichlet's employer died, and he returned to Germany. Although he did not have a doctoral degree, he obtained a position at the

University of Breslau; Dirichlet subsequently earned his spurs with a thesis concerning the prime divisors of certain polynomials. He also contributed the law of biquadratic reciprocity, building on Gauss's own pioneering work. The atmosphere in Breslau was not conducive to research, and so Dirichlet moved to Berlin in 1828, becoming a lecturer at the military academy there. In 1831 he married Rebecca Mendelsohn-Bartholdy, and also became a member of the Berlin Academy of Sciences.

Dirichlet spent almost three decades as a professor in Berlin, and during this time he exerted a profound influence on the development of German mathematics. He trained many students and continued to author papers of the highest quality and relevance. Dirichlet was shy and retiring, expressing a modest reluctance to make public appearances. During these years, Dirichlet communicated with KARL GUSTAV JACOB JACOBI, another great German mathematician.

Dirichlet's early work in number theory delved into topics that Gauss had sketched in his *Disquisitiones Arithmeticae* (Arithmetic Investigations) of 1801—topics such as quadratic forms, the quadratic and biquadratic laws of reciprocity, and the number theory of Gaussian integers. At an 1837 meeting of the Academy of Sciences, Dirichlet presented his first work on analytic number theory, in which he established that any arithmetical progression must contain an infinite number of primes. Some follow-up papers worked out the convergence of so-called Dirichlet series, as well as determining the class number for quadratic forms. In this literature one first encounters Dirichlet's "pigeon-hole principle," used in many mathematical proofs, which states that if more than n objects are placed in n holes, at least one hole must have more than one object contained inside it. Dirichlet was searching for a general algebraic number theory that would be valid for fields of arbitrary degree. His techniques included a generalization of

quadratic forms, and he founded the algebraic theory of units.

Meanwhile, Dirichlet was researching mathematical analysis, and was especially interested in Fourier series. These power series could approximate both continuous and discontinuous functions, and had been utilized by DANIEL BERNOULLI and LEONHARD EULER to model the vibrations of strings. Dirichlet's method of proving convergence of a trigonometric series differed from AUGUSTIN-LOUIS CAUCHY's prior approach, and his approach later became standard. In an 1837 paper Dirichlet formulates the modern notion of a function as a special correspondence between a pair of variables.

Dirichlet is also known for his contributions to mechanics, where he develops a method to evaluate integrals via a discontinuity factor. The Laplace partial differential equation with a constraint on the boundary values of the solution is now known as the Dirichlet problem; an 1850 paper by Dirichlet deals with this equation, which has applications to heat, magnetism, and electricity. An 1852 paper treats hydrodynamics, giving the first exact integration for the hydrodynamic equations.

After Gauss's death in 1855, the University of Göttingen solicited Dirichlet as a replacement for the deceased prince of mathematics, and Dirichlet spent his remaining few years in the superior research environment of Göttingen. He continued his work in mechanics until he suffered a heart attack, from which he later died on May 5, 1859.

Dirichlet should be viewed as a successor to Gauss in his work in number theory. However, his accomplishments in analysis, mechanics, and differential equations are also quite noteworthy. Through his extensive tutelage, Dirichlet also passed on his passion and knowledge for mathematics to a new generation of pupils, who included RICHARD DEDEKIND and LEOPOLD KRONECKER.

Further Reading

Butzer, P. "Dirichlet and His Role in the Founding of Mathematical Physics," *Archives Internationales d'Histoire des Sciences* 37, no. 118 (1987): 49–82.

Fischer, H. "Dirichlet's Contribution to Mathematical Probability Theory," *Historia Mathematica* 21 (1994): 39–63.

Koch, H. "Gustav Peter Lejeune Dirichlet," in *Mathematics in Berlin*. Boston: Birkhäuser Verlag, 1998.

Rowe, D. "Gauss, Dirichlet and the Law of Biquadratic Reciprocity," *The Mathematical Intelligencer* 10 (1988): 13–26.

E

Eratosthenes of Cyrene
(ca. 276 B.C.E.–ca. 195 B.C.E.)
Greek
Geometry, Number Theory

In ancient Greece it was well known that the Earth was a sphere, and Eratosthenes first calculated its circumference to a surprising degree of accuracy. Although principally known as a geographer, he was actually one of the foremost mathematicians of his time, having accomplished important work in geometry and number theory.

The most likely account of Eratosthenes' life informs us that he was born around 276 B.C.E. to Aglaos in the town of Cyrene. In his early manhood he studied in Athens, where he became associated with the members of the Academy. Around 235 B.C.E., he was invited to Alexandria by King Ptolemy III to serve in the library there, and five years later he became its head. He became tutor to the king's son, and remained in favor with the royal family until his death in 195 B.C.E.

Eratosthenes was well known among his contemporaries as being an extraordinary scholar, having produced works in mathematics, geography, philosophy, literary criticism, grammar, and poetry. Laboring in so many fields, he was foremost in none, and therefore was known as "Beta" (the second letter of the Greek alphabet). However, his great accomplishments in mathematics clearly demonstrate that he was no second-rate mathematician. Indeed, even ARCHIMEDES OF SYRACUSE dedicated a treatise to Eratosthenes.

Eratosthenes' *Geography* long remained an authority, and he was the first to give the field a mathematical foundation. He considered the entire terrestrial globe, which was divided into zones, and he attempted to estimate distances along vaguely defined parallels. His new world map replaced the traditional Ionian depiction of the known world; he had much information at his disposal, as the library in Alexandria was the greatest repository of ancient records.

Eratosthenes' famous estimate of the Earth's circumference was based on some simple principles of similar triangles; due to errors in certain estimates, he arrived at 250,000 stades (about 29,000 miles), which is fairly close to the true value of about 25,000 miles. His depictions of other geographical distances also suffer from inaccuracies, largely due to errors in the recorded estimates of travelers. Eratosthenes divided the globe into five latitudinal zones: two frigid, two temperate, and one torrid (tropical). He calculated the radius of each latitude that separates the various zones, using his computation of the Earth's circumference.

Besides his geographical calculations, Eratosthenes contributed to mathematics in his work *Platonicus* (Platonic), which treats proportion, progression, and musical scales. He gives his solution to the famous problem of doubling the cube, which involves constructing a large cube from a given cube that has exactly twice the volume of the original. Eratosthenes reduced the mathematical problem to a geometrical one of finding two mean proportionals in continuous proportion between two straight lines. He even described a mechanical apparatus for finding these so-called mean proportionals.

He is also famous for his method of finding prime numbers, known as the sieve of Eratosthenes. This involves writing out all odd integers and successively crossing out multiples of three, five, seven, and so forth, so that the remaining numbers must be the primes. Although this method is slow, it is guaranteed to locate all the primes less than a given threshold.

Eratosthenes is ranked among the great Greek mathematicians for his many contributions. He was the first to accurately estimate the circumference of the Earth, using only mathematical principles and a few measurements. The doubling of the cube was an outstanding problem that had long defied solution, and Eratosthenes' genius is evident in his solution.

Further Reading

Fowler, D. *The Mathematics of Plato's Academy: A New Reconstruction*. Oxford: Clarendon Press, 1999.

Goldstein, B. "Eratosthenes on the 'Measurement' of the Earth," *Historia Mathematica* 11, no. 4 (1984): 411–416.

Heath, T. *A History of Greek Mathematics*. Oxford: Clarendon Press, 1921.

Rawlins, D. "Eratosthenes' Geodest Unraveled: Was There a High-Accuracy Hellenistic Astronomy," *Isis* 73 (1982): 259–265.

⊠ Euclid of Alexandria
(ca. 325 B.C.E.–ca. 265 B.C.E.)
Greek
Geometry

The mathematical activity of ancient Greece was not so organized as in modern times, as there was little uniformity of notation or effort. Euclid of Alexandria is credited for organizing the vast material of known but incoherent theorems and collecting them in the single work known as the *Elements*. Although he made some contributions of his own, Euclid is mainly distinguished for gathering the great quantity of geometric information.

We know only that Euclid lived in Alexandria during the early part of that city's life, being active in the years between 325 B.C.E. and 265 B.C.E. He worked after the time of Plato's disciples, but before the rise of ARCHIMEDES OF SYRACUSE. He dwelt in Alexandria during the reign of the first Ptolemy, and founded a thriving school of mathematics in that city.

Euclid may have been a Platonist, as he was friendly with Plato's associates EUDOXUS OF CNIDUS and Theaetetus. When asked by a student about the use of geometry, Euclid responded by giving him three obols (the coins of that time), since "he must need make gain out of what he learns." Euclid is described as a fair man, not given to vaunting. It is probable that he attended the Academy at Athens as a young man, where he would have studied mathematics, and was later invited to Alexandria during the foundation of its famous library.

Besides the *Elements*, Euclid wrote some minor mathematical works: *Data, On Divisions of Figures, Porisms, Surface Loci,* and *Book of Fallacies*. These treat a variety of topics, such as magnitudes, analysis, divisions of circles, conic sections, and locus theorems. The *Elements*, written in 13 books, constitute a work that has greatly influenced human thought for more than two millennia. The work is mainly concerned with certain geometrical problems, and it sets out to solve them in a series of propositions with proofs. Euclid's method always proceeds from what is known to the unknown through carefully reasoned steps. The various propositions are placed in a majestic order, so that previous results are used in subsequent proofs, in a sort of mathematical progression. The books also contain various essential definitions as well as certain postulates and axioms, which were assumptions to be taken for granted. For example, he takes the existence of points, lines, and circles for granted (as well as the ability to construct them), and from here shows how many other figures can be drawn.

It is interesting to note that from his first three postulates one can deduce that the space of Euclid's geometry is infinite and continuous, embracing both the infinitely large and the infinitely small. The fifth postulate has drawn much attention, especially in the last two centuries, and essentially states that parallel lines never meet. Many mathematicians subsequently attempted to deduce this fifth postulate from the other four, thus making it redundant; their failure (see JÁNOS BOLYAI and CARL FRIEDRICH GAUSS) has resulted in the so-called non-Euclidean geometries.

Book I treats the geometry of points, lines, triangles, squares, and parallelograms; this includes proposition 47, more well known as the Pythagorean theorem. Book II develops the transformation of areas, and Book III deals with the intersections of circles. Book IV is concerned with the inscribing of rectilinear figures in circles, with applications to astronomy. Next, Euclid develops a general theory of proportion, which has been praised by mathematicians for its elegance and accuracy. His definition of proportion in Book V has never been superseded as a formulation of the concept of proportion, and is recognized as a wonderful contribution to mathematics.

Next, Book VI treats the general theory of proportion applied to similar figures, illustrating the importance of the previously discussed definition of proportion. The next three books deal with arithmetic; these present more of an outmoded approach to the study of numbers, which Euclid probably included out of deference to traditional doctrines. The topics include prime numbers and least common multiples, as well as geometric progressions of numbers. Book X treats irrational magnitudes, as Euclid sets out the "method of exhaustion" used to calculate areas and volumes. His final three books treat solid geometry, such as parallelepipeds, pyramids, cones, and spheres. Euclid ends with consideration of the five Platonic figures, called the pyramid, cube, octahedron, dodecahedron, and icosahedron, which had been objects of fervent study for the Greeks. Not only does he determine their angles, but also he determines that these are the only possible regular solids.

Of this huge body of work, Euclid is mainly credited with organizing the known material and providing simplified proofs in some cases. The theory of proportion and method of exhaustion is attributed to Eudoxus, and the knowledge of irrational quantities is due to Theaetetus. However, Euclid was the inventor of the parallel postulate, giving an insightful definition to the concept of a parallel line. The *Elements* introduced new standards of rigor into mathematical thinking, and also moved mathematics further into the arena of geometry. Euclid's influence, for both these reasons, was profound and long lasting; numerous later mathematicians, such as SIR ISAAC NEWTON, would also cast their mathematical ideas in the rigorous geometrical mold that Euclid set forth so long ago.

Further Reading

Archibald, R. "The First Translation of Euclid's Elements into English and Its Source," *The American Mathematical Monthly* 57 (1950): 443–452.

Berggren, J., and Thomas, R. *Euclid's "Phaenomena": A Translation and Study of a Hellenistic Treatise in*

Spherical Astronomy. New York: Garland Publishing, 1996.

Busard, H. *The Latin Translation of the Arabic Version of Euclid's "Elements" Commonly Ascribed to Gerard of Cremona*. Leiden, the Netherlands: Brill, 1984.

Fraser, P. *Ptolemaic Alexandria*. Oxford: Clarendon Press, 1972.

Heath, T. A *History of Greek Mathematics*. Oxford: Clarendon Press, 1921.

———. *The Thirteen Books of Euclid's Elements*. New York: Dover Publications, 1956.

Knorr, W. "What Euclid Meant: On the Use of Evidence in Studying Ancient Mathematics," in *Science and Philosophy in Classical Greece*. New York: Garland, 1991.

⊠ Eudoxus of Cnidus

(408 B.C.E.–355 B.C.E.)
Greek
Analysis, Geometry

Our modern theory of real numbers is essential to the solution of algebraic equations and all of mathematical analysis; and yet, for many of the Greeks, there was no concept of an irrational number—it did not exist. Eudoxus, who created a rigorous mathematical foundation for real numbers through his theory of proportions, removed this conceptual block. As a result, Greek mathematics was able to continue advancing.

Eudoxus was born in Cnidus in 408 B.C.E., the son of Aischines. While still a young man, he studied geometry with Archytas of Tarentum, and his philosophical inquiries may well have been inspired by Plato, whose lectures he attended while studying in Athens. After returning to his native city, Eudoxus went on a trip to Egypt, spending some of his time with the priests of Heliopolis. He there composed his eight-year calendric cycle, which probably included the risings and settings of constellations. After a year

in Egypt, he settled in Cyzicus and founded a school (probably dealing with mathematics and philosophy), and later made a second visit to Athens. It seems that he had some additional interaction with Plato at this time, although Plato did not exert much influence upon Eudoxus's philosophy. He returned to Cnidus, where he lectured, wrote textbooks, and provided laws for the citizens.

Eudoxus's mathematical thinking lies behind much of the material of Books V, VI, and VII of EUCLID OF ALEXANDRIA's *Elements*. Since none of Eudoxus's written works are extant, we can rely only on Euclid's account. Eudoxus researched mathematical proportion, for the first time giving a sensible, rigorous definition of the concept (which is still in use today). He also investigated the method of exhaustion (a protocalculus idea, used to compute areas and volumes), and was interested in the axiomatic development of mathematics (this approach greatly influenced Euclid, who carefully laid out various postulates and axioms of geometry in the *Elements*). Eudoxus may have been the first to approach mathematics in this systematic fashion.

Before Eudoxus's theory of proportion, Greek mathematics was immobilized by the irrational numbers—the Pythagoreans had already discovered square roots, but to their way of thinking these quantities did not really exist. Only rational numbers (ratios of integers) existed for these earlier Greeks. In order to make progress in number theory and the solutions of equations (and also geometry), it was necessary to include irrational numbers; Eudoxus's theory of proportions gave a rigorous definition of the real numbers, which in particular showed the existence of irrational quantities. It is interesting that modern definitions of the real numbers, such as those propounded by RICHARD DEDEKIND and KARL WEIERSTRASS, are virtually identical with Eudoxus's ancient formulation.

Eudoxus worked on the old "Delian problem" of duplicating the cube (see ERATOSTHENES

OF CYRENE). According to Archimedes, Eudoxus proved that the volume of a pyramid is one-third the volume of the prism containing it, with similar results for the cone. Though DEMOCRITUS OF ABDERA already knew these facts, Eudoxus was the first to prove them. It seems that he also discovered formulas for the area and volume of circles and spheres, respectively. These propositions are given in Book XII of the *Elements*, which reflects much of Eudoxus's work in this arena.

Another important aspect of his work was the application of spherical geometry to astronomy. Eudoxus, in his work *On Speeds*, expounds a geocentric astronomical system involving rotating spheres. Although the model was highly idealized, having a poor fit to the known observational data, Aristotle took the idea quite literally and popularized it through his own work. Eudoxus had his own observatory and carefully watched the heavens as part of his own studies; he published his results in the *Enoptron* and the *Phaenomena*, which were well-used references for two centuries. Eudoxus was also known as a great geographer, and his *Tour of the Earth* gave a systematic description of the known world, including political, historical, and ethnographical information.

Eudoxus was certainly one of the greatest intellectuals of his time, though his work is known today only through secondhand accounts. His contribution to mathematics through the formulation of the real number system cannot be overemphasized; this work allowed the further development of Greek mathematics through such persons as Archimedes and Eratosthenes.

Further Reading

Heath, T. A *History of Greek Mathematics*. Oxford: Clarendon Press, 1921.

———. *The Thirteen Books of Euclid's Elements*. New York: Dover Publications, 1956.

Huxley, G. "Eudoxian Topics," *Greek, Roman and Byzantine Studies* 4 (1963): 83–96.

Stein, H. "Eudoxos and Dedekind: On the Ancient Greek Theory of Ratios and Its Relation to Modern Mathematics," *Synthese* 84, no. 2 (1990): 163–211.

Euler, Leonhard
(1707–1783)
Swiss
Number Theory, Mechanics, Analysis

The 18th century witnessed the development of various 17th-century mathematical ideas—calculus was one important example. Leonhard Euler was exceptional among his peers for not only the breadth and profusion of his work but also his great originality; he largely founded number theory, defined the modern concept of

Leonhard Euler was a great Swiss mathematician who worked principally in number theory and differential equations. For his profundity the 18th century was often known as the "Era of Euler." (*Courtesy of the Library of Congress*)

a function, and formulated a general theory for the calculus of variations. His renown and virtuosity were such that the 18th century was sometimes referred to as the "Era of Euler."

Leonhard Euler was born in Basel on April 15, 1707. His father, Paul Euler, was a Protestant minister, and his mother, Margarete Brucker, was a minister's daughter; this religious background remained with Euler throughout his life. Euler's father, who was interested in mathematics himself, having attended JAKOB BERNOULLI's lectures at the University of Basel, educated his son in his early years. Because his Gymnasium did not teach mathematics, Euler studied privately with an amateur mathematician, and he displayed remarkable talent for one his age. In 1720 he entered the University of Basel and soon came under the guidance of JOHANN BERNOULLI. In 1722 he received his bachelor of arts degree, and a year later his master's in philosophy; at age 16, he joined the theology department.

However, Euler's strength lay in mathematics, and he soon gave up the ambition to be a minister. About this time he began his own research in mathematics and published an article on algebraic reciprocal trajectories. There were few opportunities in Switzerland for young mathematicians, so Euler accepted an offer to join the new St. Petersburg Academy of Sciences in 1727. His official appointment was as an adjunct of physiology, although he was permitted to work in mathematics. Euler became professor of physics in 1731 and professor of mathematics in 1733; the atmosphere at the young academy was stimulating for Euler, who interacted with Jakob Hermann, DANIEL BERNOULLI, and CHRISTIAN GOLDBACH.

Euler's life was marked by his remarkable diligence and activity. His mathematical research was reported in the sessions of the academy; meanwhile, he was involved in the training of Russian scientists, as well as the study of Russian territory (Euler assisted in the construction of geographical maps) and development of new technology (Euler studied problems in shipbuilding and navigation). But his contributions to mathematics were prolific—Euler prepared more than 80 works in his first 14 years at St. Petersburg.

Many of his best ideas were formulated in his youth, even while at Basel, and were fleshed out much later. Due to his voluminous correspondence with other scientists, Euler's discoveries were often made public before they were even published; this brought him no small amount of fame. In 1733 he married Katharina Gsell, and he soon had two sons. His quiet life was marred only by the blinding of his right eye in 1738; according to Euler, this was due to overstrain from his cartographic work. However, in 1740 the political situation in Russia became unstable, and Euler accepted an offer to work at the Berlin Society of the Sciences.

Euler stayed in Berlin for 25 years, during which time he was blessed with many additional children. During this period, he worked in both the Berlin and St. Petersburg academies. He was director of the Berlin Society of the Sciences, which he largely transformed. Besides the numerous administrative duties, he dealt with several practical problems, such as correcting the level of the Finow Canal. He consulted with the government on problems of insurance, pensions, and hydraulics, and even organized a few state lotteries. Meanwhile, Euler received a pension from the St. Petersburg Academy, and in return he edited the academy's journal, apprised it of new scientific ideas, and oversaw competitions. Euler received 12 prizes from the Paris Académie des Sciences from 1738 to 1772.

The Berlin period was fruitful, as Euler produced more than 380 works—some of which were lengthy books—on topics such as the calculus of variations, the calculation of orbits, ballistics, analysis, lunar motion, and differential calculus. His famous *Lettres à une princesse d'Allemagne sur divers sujets de physique et de philosophie* (Letters to a German princess on diverse topics of physics and philosophy) were written in a popular manner and became a great success in Europe. Euler participated in many academic debates on such topics as the religion of pure reason espoused by GOTTFRIED WILHELM VON LEIBNIZ, and the principle of least action.

After 1759, Euler's relationship with King Frederick of Prussia deteriorated, and he eventually returned to St. Petersburg in 1766. Soon after his return, a brief illness left him completely blind; this hampered his ability to do research, but with the help of assistants he was able to dictate his thoughts, and so continue his work. The only change seems to be that his articles became more concise, and half of his total works were produced after 1765. His memory (he could recite Virgil's *Aeneid* verbatim) remained flawless, and he continued to have original ideas. Euler's activity in the academy was unabated when he died on September 18, 1783, of a brain hemorrhage.

Euler was one of the most important mathematicians since SIR ISAAC NEWTON. He was deeply interested in applications, but would develop the pertinent mathematics to deep levels of abstraction and generality. His foremost subject was analysis, contributing to the calculus of variations, the theory of differential equations, functions of a complex variable, and the theory of special functions. Many modern conventions and notations are due to him, such as the symbol $f(x)$ for the value of a function and i for the square root of -1.

In number theory Euler was concerned with the theory of divisibility, introducing the so-called Euler's function, which tallies the quantity of divisors of a given integer. These studies led him to the discovery of the law of quadratic reciprocity, whose complete proof was later established by CARL FRIEDRICH GAUSS. Euler investigated decompositions of prime numbers as linear combinations of squares, and worked on Diophantine analysis via continued fractions. His methods were algebraic, but Euler was the first to introduce analytic methods into number theory—in particular, he deduced a famous identity relating sums of reciprocal squares to a product of prime numbers, which was a first step in the study of the Riemann zeta-function. Euler studied mathematical constants, such as e and pi, as well as Euler's constant (which comes up in the study of the divergent harmonic series).

Euler stated the theorem that an algebraic polynomial of degree n had n roots of the form $a + bi$, which is now known as the fundamental theorem of algebra. His 1751 proof had some omissions, which were later corrected by Gauss. Euler also attempted to derive an exact formula for the roots of the fifth degree polynomial, and his failures led him to approximation methods of numerical analysis.

Although many mathematicians had studied infinite series, Euler was unusually successful in their calculation, deriving simple formulas for sums of reciprocal even powers of integers. Through these studies, Euler studied special functions (such as the Bessel functions) and discovered Euler's constant for the approximation of the harmonic series. He made great use of power series, and introduced trigonometric series before JEAN-BAPTISTE-JOSEPH FOURIER as an analytic tool. Euler believed that divergent series could be useful, and this effort would come to fruition much later, in the 20th century.

Euler presented the idea that mathematical analysis is the study of functions; to this end, he more clearly defined the concept of a function, which closely approximates the modern notion. Through consideration of the logarithm of negative numbers, Euler came to an understanding of the exponentiation of imaginary numbers, deriving many crucial elementary facts. He advanced the knowledge of complex numbers, discovering the differential equations that relate the real and imaginary parts of an analytic function. Euler applied his techniques to the computation of real integrals.

He also made numerous discoveries in differential and integral calculus, deriving substitution rules, validating the interchange of partial derivatives, and founding the concept of multiple integrals. As a result of the many special cases and techniques of integration he employed, the beta and gamma functions were discovered, which are useful in physics. Euler made great contributions to the field of differential equations, including the method of variation of constants as well as the use of characteristic curves. Some of the applications of this work include vibrating string problems, hydrodynamics, and the motion of air in pipes.

His studies in the calculus of variations led him to the Eulerian differential equation, and his exposition of the subject became classical. Euler was the first to formulate the principal problems of this subject and the main methods of solution. In geometry, Euler investigated spherical trigonometry and founded a theory of lines on a surface—one of the initial steps toward the modern subject of differential geometry. He analyzed the curvature of a surface in terms of the curvature of embedded principal curves, and introduced Gaussian coordinates, which were extensively used in the 19th century.

Euler was also the first author in topology, solving the famous riddle of seven bridges of Königsberg; he studied polyhedra, deriving what later became known as the Euler characteristic—a formula relating the number of edges, faces, and vertices.

Besides these contributions to pure mathematics, Euler labored in mechanics, astronomy, and optics. Euler systematized mechanics, introducing analytical methods that greatly simplified the subject. He studied celestial mechanics and elasticity, deriving the famous Euler buckling formula, used to determine the strength of columns. In fluid mechanics, he studied equilibrium positions and presented three classic works discussing the motion of incompressible fluids; Euler also improved the design of the hydraulic turbine.

In astronomy, Euler was interested in the determination of orbits of comets and planets, the theory of refraction, and the physical nature of comets. He presented an extensive lunar theory, which enabled a more precise calculation of a ship's longitudinal position at sea. Euler assisted physics by mathematizing it (that is, by introducing many techniques of analysis to better understand certain problems). Indeed, he is credited as founding mathematical physics. He studied optics as well, constructing a nonparticle theory of light that viewed illumination as the product of certain oscillations in the ambient ether.

Euler was a humble man, but also one of the greatest scientists and mathematicians of all time, and especially the 18th century; he was recognized by his peers as an outstanding genius. His mathematical research has stimulated an enormous amount of subsequent activity, and many of his ideas were ahead of their time.

Further Reading

Ayoub, R. "Euler and the Zeta Function," *The American Mathematical Monthly* 81 (1974): 1067–1086.

Deakin, M. "Euler's Invention of Integral Transforms," *Archive for History of Exact Sciences* 33, no. 4 (1985): 307–319.

Dunham, W. *Euler: The Master of Us All.* Washington, D.C.: The Mathematical Association of America, 1999.

Edwards, H. "Euler and Quadratic Reciprocity," *Mathematics Magazine* 56, no. 5 (1983): 285–291.

Ewing, J. "Leonhard Euler," *The Mathematical Intelligencer* 5, no. 3 (1983): 5–6.

Finkel, B. "Biography. Leonard Euler," *The American Mathematical Monthly* 4 (1897): 297–302.

Weil, A. "Euler," *The American Mathematical Monthly* 91, no. 9 (1984): 537–542.

F

Fatou, Pierre-Joseph-Louis
(1878–1929)
French
Analysis

The theory of integration was an intensely researched topic in the late 19th century, and Pierre Fatou contributed to certain basic aspects of HENRI-LOUIS LEBESGUE's theory of integration. His results, later developed by Caratheodory and FRIGYES RIESZ, were fundamental in the young theory of integration.

Fatou was born in Lorient, France, on February 28, 1878. He attended the École Normale Supérieure from 1898 to 1901, where he studied mathematics. Since there were few positions for mathematicians, Fatou accepted a position at the Paris observatory, where he continued to work until his death on August 10, 1929. While working there, he obtained his doctorate in 1907 and was appointed titular astronomer in 1928.

One of the applied mathematical problems that fascinated Fatou was the calculation of the perturbation of a planet due to the movements of a second planet. CARL FRIEDRICH GAUSS had formulated some intuitive results, but Fatou was able to give these a rigorous mathematical foundation through the study of differential equations. Fatou also investigated the movement of a planet through a resistant medium, which was based on the supposition that stellar atmospheres were more extensive in the past.

In pure mathematics, Fatou contributed to the theory of Taylor series, and was particularly interested in the circle of convergence. His researches in this direction led him to formulate the so-called Fatou's lemma, which gives a sufficient condition for convergence of a series of functions. He formulated his results under the umbrella of Lebesgue integration theory, and his theorem is also a key result toward determining the validity of swapping limit and integral. Fatou also studied rational functions of a complex variable and determined how the coefficients of a Taylor series affect the singularities of the resulting function.

Lebesgue integration theory later became an extremely important part of real analysis, and Fatou's researches in this field have had an enduring significance.

Further Reading

Alexander, D. *A History of Complex Dynamics: From Schröder to Fatou and Julia*. Braunschweig/ Wiesbaden: Friedrich Vieweg and Sohn, 1994.

Fermat, Pierre de
(1601–1665)
French
Number Theory, Calculus, Probability

Pierre de Fermat is known as one of the greatest mathematicians of the 16th century, having made contributions to the foundations of calculus, probability, and number theory. In the last-named subject he is particularly renowned, for his research into divisibility and the properties of prime numbers would later fuel much 19th- and 20th-century investigation.

Pierre de Fermat was born in Beaumont-Lomagne, France, on August 20, 1601. His father, Dominique Fermat, was a prosperous merchant, while his mother, Claire de Long, was a noblewoman. As a result of his mother's pedigree,

Pierre de Fermat formulated the famous "Fermat's Last Theorem," which remained unproved for 300 years. He also contributed to number theory and probability. *(University of Rochester, courtesy of AIP Emilio Segrè Visual Archives)*

Fermat enjoyed a high social status and later chose the profession of law. He received a classical secondary education, and probably studied at the University of Toulouse. In any event, he certainly lived in Bordeaux in the late 1620s, and at this time he first began his mathematical investigations.

Fermat received the degree of bachelor of civil laws from the University of Orleans in 1631, and embarked on his legal career in the local *parlement*. The same year, Fermat married his cousin Louise de Long, by whom he had five children. It seems that Fermat enjoyed financial prosperity, and he was allowed the privilege, as a member of the aristocracy, to append "de" to his last name. However, his performance in his office was unsatisfactory, and Fermat advanced only through the death of his professional colleagues. In 1642 he ascended to the highest councils of the *parlement*, later serving as president of the Chambre de l'Édit, which had jurisdiction over legal suits between Huguenots and Catholics. Fermat was a devoted Catholic throughout his life.

Fermat enjoyed some fame as a mathematician during his own life, though his unwillingness to publish kept him from the renown he might have obtained. He was also reputed as a classical scholar, being fluent in several languages. He enjoyed good health, surviving an attack of plague in 1652, and died in Castres on January 12, 1665.

Fermat's development as a mathematician may have commenced during his Bordeaux period, at which time he became familiar with the works of FRANÇOIS VIÈTE. From Viète Fermat acquired the new symbolic algebra, as well as the conception of algebra as a tool useful for geometric problems. Fermat sought to build on Viète's concepts, including the ability to solve and construct determinate equations; his method often involved reducing a given problem to a known class of problems (much like an inverse type of induction). At first, Fermat heavily relied on the ancient Greeks for ideas on mathematical analysis, but he often generalized the original problems considered, using reduction analysis and his natural genius to arrive at general solutions.

By spring 1636, Fermat had already completed his *Ad locos planos et solidos isagoge* (Introduction to planes and solids), a work setting forth an analytic geometry that was extremely similar to RENÉ DESCARTES's *Géométrie* (Geometry) of 1637. Although these works were virtually identical in their use of algebraic equations to describe geometric curves, the issue of priority is unresolved, as each mathematician was working independently. Fermat started from the works of PAPPUS OF ALEXANDRIA and APOLLONIUS OF PERGA, realizing that the loci of points discussed by the latter could all be described by algebraic equations in two unknowns. He then employed a single axis with origin and moving ordinate (similar to Descartes's graphical method, which did not involve coordinates) to describe a given curve. Fermat then considered the general second-degree equation by reducing it into seven irreducible forms (or special cases), which included lines, hyperbolas, ellipses, parabolas, and circles. Fermat's presentation differed substantially from that of Descartes, who passed over the issue of construction and focused on an advanced theory of equations. Pursuing the implications of his research after 1636, Fermat demonstrated the graphical solution of determinate algebraic equations. In 1643 he tried to extend his methods to solids of revolution (those solids obtained by revolving a curve about a fixed axis). This latter effort was not successful, as Fermat did not yet have the tools of a three-dimensional coordinate system, although he laid the correct algebraic foundation for such a system of solid geometry. Fermat established the connection between dimension and the number of unknowns, an important conceptual contribution to 17th century mathematics.

Fermat also developed a method of computing maxima and minima of curves, which essentially involved a calculation of the derivative of a polynomial. However, Fermat did not use any infinitesimals in his method, and thus his work was peripheral to the foundation of calculus. Using his technique, Fermat could determine the centers of gravity for geometrical figures, as well as the formation of tangent lines to a given curve. This work became a pivotal point in a 1638 debate with Descartes, who criticized Fermat's work because it rivaled his own mathematics set forth in *Géométrie*. Although they eventually made peace when Descartes admitted that his critique of Fermat's work was invalid, the two men remained at strife; the reputation of Fermat, who adamantly refused to publish his work, suffered as a result.

The quadrature of curves (that is, the computation of the area under a curve by means of approximating it by rectangles) was also studied by Fermat, who expanded on ARCHIMEDES OF SYRACUSE's labors on the spiral. Fermat was able to approximate a given area with arbitrary accuracy (through the number of rectangles chosen), and thus calculate the area beneath certain simple polynomials. At first his style was geometrical, relying on carefully drawn figures, but later he adopted a more algebraic approach. His various results on quadrature eventually circulated in 1679, by which time they were obsolete, in view of the more comprehensive work of SIR ISAAC NEWTON and GOTTFRIED WILHELM VON LEIBNIZ. It seems that Fermat did not realize that the method of tangents and quadrature were inverse to one another, and this work exerted little influence on later mathematics.

Fermat is best known for his work in number theory, which was largely neglected by his 17th-century colleagues. His labors went completely unappreciated until LEONHARD EULER revived interest in number; finally, in the 19th century CARL FRIEDRICH GAUSS and others proved many of the important results and established number theory as a modern field of mathematical inquiry. Fermat was interested in integer solutions of algebraic equations, and his early research centered on divisibility and the study of the prime numbers. His methods are not known, because most of his results were written in letters to friends or in the margins of other books; apparently, Fermat used the sieve of ERATOSTHENES OF CYRENE as a criterion for primeness. He derived several important theorems (without proof), investigating the decomposition of primes as sums of squares. In this connection, Fermat was interested in integer solutions to x^n 1 y^n 5 z^n where n is at least two. The fact (proved only recently, by Andrew Wiles in 1994) that there are no solutions for n larger than two is known as Fermat's last theorem; he jotted this conjecture in the margin of one of his books.

One technique that Fermat applied repeatedly was the method of infinite descent: He would argue by contradiction, constructing an infinite sequence of decreasing (positive) integers, which could not exist. The main importance of Fermat's work in number theory is the stimulus that it gave to research in the late 18th and 19th centuries.

Fermat also contributed to the study of optics (over which subject he also debated with Descartes, objecting to his a priori reasoning), and is credited, along with BLAISE PASCAL, as being the founder of the theory of probability. Through a series of letters written during 1654, these two mathematicians corresponded on a variety of probability questions, such as how to fairly divide the stakes of an interrupted game. Though their methods differed somewhat (Fermat made direct calculations rather than deriving general formulas), they both used the concept of "expected winnings," defined through the mathematical expectation.

The later years of Fermat's life saw little interaction with other mathematicians, as he increasingly devoted his spare time to number theory. Although his work, especially his efforts in number theory, deserved the acknowledgment of his colleagues, Fermat fell into increasing obscurity due to his reluctance to publish. After the 17th century he was completely forgotten, until rediscovered by Euler and others in the 19th century, when the renewed interest in number theory drew inspiration from his intellect.

Further Reading

Edwards, H. *Fermat's Last Theorem, a Genetic Introduction to Algebraic Number Theory.* New York: Springer-Verlag, 1977.

Indorato, L., and P. Nastasi. "The 1740 Resolution of the Fermat-Descartes Controversy," *Historia Mathematica* 16, no. 2 (1989): 137–148.

Singh, S. *Fermat's Last Theorem: The Story of a Riddle That Confounded the World's Greatest Minds for 358 Years.* London: Fourth Estate, 1998.

⊠ Ferrari, Ludovico
(1522–1565)
Italian
Algebra

One of the hot mathematical problems of the 16th century was the solution of the cubic (or third degree) polynomial; mathematicians searched for a general formula, in terms of the coefficients, that would instantly produce the answer. Some of the famous characters in this intellectual quest were GIROLAMO CARDANO, NICCOLO TARTAGLIA, SCIPIONE DEL FERRO, and Ludovico Ferrari. Ferrari probably made the most substantial contribution of that time toward solving the cubic and quartic equations.

Ludovico Ferrari was born in Bologna, Italy, on February 2, 1522. His father, Alessandro Ferrari, was a refugee from Milan, and when he died Ludovico went to live with his uncle. In 1536 he traveled to Milan to serve in the household of Girolamo Cardano, where he could receive an education. Ferrari was very intelligent, and he quickly absorbed Latin, Greek, and mathematics.

In 1540 Ferrari was appointed as a public lecturer in Milan, and soon defeated a competing mathematician in a public disputation. He collaborated with Cardano on his research into the cubic and quartic equations, and the results were published in the *Artis magnae sive de regulis algebraicis liber unus* (also known as *Ars magna* [Great art]) in 1545. Because Cardano had published information that Tartaglia had revealed to him under an oath of secrecy, Tartaglia became enraged at the betrayal, and as a result a feud erupted. Cardano claimed that Tartaglia's secret method for solving a certain cubic was already known to Scipione del Ferro, and hence was essentially public knowledge. Tartaglia maintained that Cardano had stolen his research. Ferrari vigorously defended his mentor, and refuted Tartaglia's public defense through a series of letters (which were rife with personal attacks), and eventually through a public disputation in 1548. This debate, over which the governor of Milan presided, seems to have been won by Ferrari, who was probably a superior mathematician to Tartaglia.

Ferrari's method for solving a certain type of quartic (or fourth degree polynomial) involved introducing a second variable, which had to satisfy certain constraints. This second variable's constraints led to a cubic equation. With this ingenious method, Ferrari could first solve the derived cubic and then go back to solve the original quartic.

As can be surmised from his letters, Ferrari's character was both loyal and pugnacious. His handling of Tartaglia was belligerent, but this may have been due to his personal bond with his former master Cardano. As a result of Ferrari's success in the debate with Tartaglia, he received many offers of employment, and he agreed to become the tutor to the son of the cardinal of Mantua. He carried out a survey of the province of Milan, and after eight years he retired to Bologna due to ill health. In 1564 he obtained a post at the University of Bologna, which he held until his death on October 5, 1565, in Bologna, Italy.

Of the mathematicians of that time, Ferrari was probably the best at solving polynomial equations. His work would constitute some of the early steps in the grand effort to solve fourth and fifth degree polynomials; these problems would be definitively answered by NIELS HENRIK ABEL and EVARISTE GALOIS in the 19th century.

⊠ Ferro, Scipione del
(1465–1526)
Italian
Algebra

In mid-16th-century Italy, there was much interest and debate over the solution of the cubic, or third degree, polynomial. Before the publication in about 1545 of GIROLAMO CARDANO's controversial book *Artis magnae sive de regulis algebraicis liber unus* (also known as *Ars magna* [Great Art]), Scipione del Ferro had already discovered the general solution of certain cubic equations some decades earlier.

Scipione del Ferro was born on February 6, 1465, in Bologna, Italy. His father was Floriana Ferro, a papermaker, and his mother was named Filippa. Of his early education nothing is known, but del Ferro became a lecturer in arithmetic and geometry at the University of Bologna, where he remained from 1496 to 1526. Del Ferro was active as a businessman in the years 1517 to 1523. He died on November 5, 1526, in Bologna.

He left no writings behind him, but other sources declare him to be a great algebraist and arithmetician. Of all his accomplishments, the most renowned is his solution of the cubic of the form $x^3 1 ax 5 b$. The discovery of a formula for the solutions of such an equation had eluded mathematicians since antiquity; the Greeks were fascinated by this problem. In the 15th century, despite much effort after the time of LEONARDO FIBONACCI, it was thought to be impossible. Del Ferro's path to discovery can only be surmised, but he probably relied on Fibonacci's *Liber abbaci* (Book of the abacus). It seems that his achievement took place within the first two decades of the 16th century, but del Ferro did not give any printed account. Rather, he passed his technique on orally to certain individuals.

One of these heirs, Antonio Maria Fior, became involved in a dispute in 1535 with NICCOLO TARTAGLIA, in which Fior used his knowledge of the solution of the cubic to advantage. The latter was then prompted to make his own discovery of the solution to the cubic, although unbeknownst to Tartaglia, del Ferro had priority. In 1542 Annibale dalla Nave—the successor of del Ferro—revealed the method to Cardano, who subsequently included it in his 1545 *Ars magna*.

Del Ferro also contributed to the knowledge of algebra through the study of fractions with irrational denominators. The problem of rationalizing the denominator goes back to EUCLID OF ALEXANDRIA, who considered square roots, but del Ferro was the first to consider more complicated irrational numbers, such as those involving cube roots. From the testimony of LUDOVICO FERRARI, it is known that del Ferro also investigated the geometry of the compass, although it is unclear what contributions he made.

Del Ferro was certainly one of the most accomplished algebraists of his time, although all modern knowledge of him is secondhand. His solution of the cubic was the first successful step in a long progression of mathematical interest; interest in related questions would eventually give rise to the elegant Galois theory of number fields.

Further Reading

Crossley, J. *The Emergence of Number*. Victoria, Australia: Upside Down A Book Company, 1980.

Rose, P. *The Italian Renaissance of Mathematics: Studies on Humanists and Mathematicians from Petrarch to Galileo*. Geneva: Droz, 1975.

⊠ Fibonacci, Leonardo (Leonardo of Pisa)
(ca. 1170–ca. 1240)
Italian
Arithmetic

After the blaze of light in Greece during the classical era, a great intellectual and cultural darkness consumed Europe; Leonardo Fibonacci rekindled that light during the first stirrings of the Italian Renaissance, and that illumination was destined to wax greater into the brilliant radiance of current mathematical achievement. Certainly, others made important contributions in earlier centuries in other parts of the world, but Fibonacci was the first great mathematician of the Christian West. As a Renaissance character, he revived interest in classical literature and values and, in particular, renewed the appreciation for mathematical knowledge.

Leonardo Fibonacci was a member of the Bonacci family, born in Pisa, Italy, to Guglielmo Bonacci. We only have an estimate of the date of his birth, 1170, since there are few records of the details of his life—one of the main sources is his own book, *Liber abbaci* (Book of the abacus). He was nicknamed Bigollo, a term that designates a loafer, which may have been an epithet hurled by those who thought lightly of the value of mathematical work. His father was an official in the Republic of Pisa, and in 1192 he received a commission to direct a Pisan trading colony in Algeria. The young Fibonacci accompanied his father, who hoped to school his son in the arts of calculation so that he could one day become a merchant. Fibonacci far exceeded his father's expectations.

The instruction in Africa from an Arab master was quite good, probably much better than in Europe, and Fibonacci encountered the "new" Indian numerals. These numbers were symbolically quite similar to modern digits, and consisted of 10 distinct numerals, which could describe any quantity merely through their proper arrangement (the same as the modern numeric system). At the time in Europe, most merchants still used Roman numerals, for which the calculations of addition and multiplication are far more difficult. Fibonacci quickly mastered this superior number system. In the ensuing years, he traveled widely, including Egypt, Greece, Sicily, Syria, and Provence, in pursuit of his mercantile vocation, and in all the cities he would communicate with local scholars on their methods of calculation. Through these disputations, Fibonnaci came to see that these other learned men, who did not understand the Indian system, were at a great mathematical disadvantage, and were often in error.

These experiences were crucial for Fibonacci's development. In 1200 he returned to his native city and worked for the next 25 years on calculation with Indian numerals. Due to his background in business, he was driven by practical concerns, and thus his investigations were motivated by a desire to apply them to commercial matters; however, he also did considerable theoretical work in algebra and geometry.

In 1202 Fibonacci's *Liber abbaci* was completed; like the abacus it was named after, this work focused on computation. New material was added in a second version in 1228. The first section dealt with Roman numerals and finger calculations, then Indian numerals were introduced, along with the fraction bar. The next portion was mainly relevant to merchants, resembling an almanac—there was information on the price of goods, the calculation of interest and wages, measurement of quantities, and exchange of currencies. The third section contained puzzles and mathematical riddles, and rules for the summation of series (for instance, there was a formula for the sum of a geometric series). One famous problem is stated as follows: Given a pair of rabbits, which take a month to mature and then produce a pair of offspring every month, how does the population increase? Assuming that the offspring mature in the same fashion as their parents, the monthly population follows the sequence *1, 1, 2, 3, 5, 8, . . .* These numbers, now known as the Fibonacci sequence, are one of the first examples of recursion, since each term is equal to the sum of the two preceding terms. Recursion, the concept that a thing's definition depends on itself (or at least its past self), is a powerful concept in modern mathematics, computer science, and philosophy.

Even more important for the history of mathematics is Fibonacci's introduction of negative numbers. Prior to this time, merchants had a concept of subtraction, as a way of keeping track of their inventory. But since it was impossible to have negative inventory, the concept of a negative number was nonsensical to them. For example, they would say that the equation (though they would not write it this way) x 1 2 5 1 has no solution. However, Fibonacci used negative numbers, thought of as debits or debts, in order to solve equations, and it seems that he was the first to do so. Others who came after him would formalize the notion of a negative number and construct the integers. It is interesting to note that some mathematical concepts now taken for granted, like negative numbers, were once very mysterious, and it required genius and creativity to arrive at the new idea. Certainly, Fibonacci's peers caught on slowly.

The fourth section of this book dealt with the calculation of radicals, using formulas of arithmetic from EUCLID OF ALEXANDRIA's *Elements*, and contained examples of the ancient method of approximation. For example, to approximate pi, the ancients would find two fractions, one a bit smaller (such as 223/71) and the other a bit larger (such as 220/70) than pi, which could be easily calculated. In general, the *Liber abbaci* is remarkable for the richness of its examples and the rigor of proof. Fibonacci was a master of his art, and he would present several different methods of solution, including algebraic and geometric approaches.

Fibonacci also wrote *Practica Geometriae* (Practice of geometry) in 1220 or 1221, which focuses on geometry. Appealing to Euclid's *Elements*, he solves square and cube root problems, and gives various calculations of segments and surfaces of plane figures. An approximation of pi is given by inscribing a 96-gon. There are also some practical directions for the field surveyor; for example, he gives directions for the use of the "archipendulum," a geodetic instrument used to find horizontal projections of straight lines lying on an inclined hill.

Fibonacci also made great progress in indeterminate analysis, the study of several equations in several unknowns. In *Flos* (Flower) (1225) and *Liber Quadratorum* (Book of square numbers) (1225) he demonstrates his facility with number theory, posing and solving various ancient problems in indeterminate analysis. In 1225 he was presented to Emperor Frederick II, and his latter writings were in response to questions posed by the imperial philosopher Theodorus. The last record of Fibonacci is in 1240, when he was awarded an annual salary by his city for his advice about accounting practices.

Certainly Fibonacci played a pivotal role in the rebirth of mathematics in western Europe. His systematic presentation of new and ancient knowledge, moving fluidly from easier to harder problems, assisted the dissemination of mathematical ideas. Most important, through Fibonacci a new concept of number emerged in the West. His endorsement of the Indian numeral was crucial to advance the science of calculation, but he was the first to recognize negative quantities, and zero as well, as genuine numbers. In addition, his use of a symbol or letter as an abbreviated representation of a generic number was an important step toward modern algebra, which is abstract and totally symbolic. Fibonacci was familiar with Arabic texts, which had preserved the flower of Greek mathematical endeavor; in transmitting and systematizing this material, Fibonacci revived interest in the classics. In the ensuing years, European mathematicians would make wondrous advances from the Greek foundation.

Further Reading

Chong, P. "The Life and Work of Leonardo of Pisa," *Menemui Matematik. Discovering Mathematics* 4, no. 2 (1982): 60–66.

Gies, J., and F. Gies. *Leonard of Pisa and the New Mathematics of the Middle Ages.* New York: Crowell, 1969.

Hooper, A. *Makers of Mathematics.* New York: Random House, 1958.

⊠   **Fisher, Sir Ronald Aylmer**
       (1890–1962)
       British
       Statistics

Ronald Aylmer Fisher was born into a large family of ordinary origins; before his death he would be bestowed with numerous honors, and would receive knighthood. This talented man, whom many would describe as a genius, made several important contributions to the theory of statistics. Indeed, the theories of hypothesis testing, analysis of variance, experimental design, and estimation are much indebted to his labors.

Twin sons were born on February 17, 1890, in London, England, to Fisher's father, a British auctioneer. One of them soon died, and Ronald was the survivor. In the following years he developed his mathematical gifts, directing all his energy in this direction. He studied at Cambridge from 1909 to 1912, concentrating on mathematics and theoretical physics. After graduation Fisher took up diverse employments unrelated to mathematics, and in 1917 he married Ruth Eileen Guiness, who bore him eight children. Fisher was eccentric, and with his eloquent

Sir Ronald Aylmer Fisher laid the mathematical foundations for modern statistics. *(Courtesy of the Library of Congress)*

tongue made a strong impression on most people he encountered. However, despite being amiable toward his own following, he could be quite abrasive toward his rivals. In fact, Fisher created many enemies through his unveiled hostility toward dissenters, expressed through scathing personal remarks.

Fisher started his mathematical career when he joined Rothamsted Experimental Station in 1919, with the task of sorting and analyzing numerous field data. Through his time at Rothamsted, Fisher would establish himself as a leading statistician; later he would become a professor of eugenics at University College and a

professor of genetics at Cambridge. His first contribution to mathematics was the discovery of the sampling distributions of various statistics, such as the correlation coefficient. The sampling distribution is important, since it tells the practitioner how unlikely an extreme value of a statistic, computed on a data set, would be. Fisher developed WILLIAM GOSSET's work on *t* statistics, constructing a complete theory of hypothesis testing for small samples. Hypothesis testing is now a huge component of statistical theory, and is basically a mathematical formulation of the methods by which Western civilization has pursued empirical science.

Subsequently, Fisher developed an extension of the *t* test to multiple groups called the ANOVA (analysis of variance)—now one of the most widely used statistical procedures by medical and industrial researchers. Given several groups of data, each separated by a factor (such as males and females or blood type), the ANOVA procedure assesses whether there are any significant differences between the groups. Fisher further pointed out that the consideration of several factors simultaneously (so, for example, one might vary gender and blood type concurrently) was not only possible but was also crucial for determining whether factors affect each other. These contributions to experimental design are viewed by many as the most important of all that Fisher has done—and indeed, these ideas and procedures are very widely used throughout science.

In terms of theory, Fisher desired to place statistics on a firm mathematical foundation. In the paper "On the Mathematical Foundation of Theoretical Statistics" (1922) he developed a sensible theory of estimation. The central issue was the following: Given a collection of numerical data, how can one summarize—with one number or statistic—a particular feature of the measurements in the "best" possible way? Fisher formulated the following criteria for a "good" statistic: it should be consistent (increased accuracy with larger sample size), efficient (precise), and sufficient (all relevant information has been utilized). He made the concept of "information" quantitative, which gave a method for measuring the amount of order within data.

Besides making the theory of estimation more rigorous and structured, Fisher developed the concept of standard error mathematically. Typically, estimates would be accompanied by a "plus or minus" band of values, which would form an interval around the estimate. Fisher would associate a probability to each interval; if the interval was widened, the probability would increase toward one. The probability was the likelihood of capturing the desired parameter within the interval. In this way, one could rigorously quantify "how good" an interval was. Because this procedure would involve the probable location of a parameter—which was supposed to be fixed and unknown—a controversy arose between Fisher's school of thought and his opponents. Debate still continues today, between Bayesian statisticians, who view unknown parameters as being themselves random, and Frequentists, who hold to the orthodox view.

Ronald Fisher also labored extensively in the field of genetics, and was particularly interested in the theory of natural selection. He formulated a "fundamental theorem of natural selection," which stated, "The rate of increase in fitness of any organism at any time is equal to its genetic variance in fitness at that time." His work, typically, was a blend of theory and practice, and he conducted some breeding experiments in his own home.

Later in life, Fisher was bestowed with many honors: In 1929 he was elected to fellowship of the Royal Society, and in 1952 he received knighthood. In 1959 he retired from his position at Cambridge and moved to Australia. There he spent his last three years working on mathematical statistics at the Commonwealth Scientific and Industrial Research Organization. He died in Adelaide, Australia, on July 29, 1962.

Fisher is famous among modern statisticians for his work on the mathematical foundations of statistics. He is also well known for his research into genetics. Many statistical objects, such as the Fisher Information Criterion, can be attributed to his genius, and the modern field of mathematical statistics is founded on much of his work.

Further Reading

Box, J. R. A. *Fisher, the Life of a Scientist.* New York: John Wiley, 1978.

Gower, J. "Ronald Aylmer Fisher 1890–1962," *Mathematical Spectrum* 23 (1990–91): 76–86.

⊠ **Fourier, Jean-Baptiste-Joseph**
(1768–1830)
French
Analysis

Jean-Baptiste-Joseph Fourier was the son of a tailor. He was born on March 21, 1768, in the town of Auxerre, France. By age nine he had lost both his parents, Joseph and Edmée. The archbishop placed him in the local military school, where he developed a strong inclination toward mathematics. Before the end of his life, Fourier would go on to found the theory of trigonometric series and make great advances in the understanding of the dynamics of heat.

Fourier was born in a tranquil period of France's history, which was soon to erupt into the chaos of the French Revolution. Initially, the young man wished to join the artillery or engineers, but was instead sent to a Benedictine school in St.-Benoît-sur-Loire. When the revolution began in 1789, he returned to Auxerre as a teacher in his former military school. He became prominent in local affairs, and defied the government through his brave defense of the victims of the Terror. In 1794 he was arrested, but was released after Robespierre's execution and briefly attended the École Normale. Though

Joseph Fourier studied the theory of heat and developed trigonometric series as representations of functions. He invented harmonic analysis. (*J. Boilly Del., Geille Scup., Deutsches Museum München, courtesy AIP Emilio Segrè Visual Archives*)

this school only existed for a year, it seems that Fourier made a strong impression on the faculty, and he was appointed as an assistant lecturer in 1795 at the École Polytechnique. There he fell afoul of the reaction to the previous regime (which he had actually struggled against) and was imprisoned, but his colleagues managed to procure his release. In 1798 he was chosen to accompany Napoleon on his Egyptian campaign, where he became secretary of the Institut d'Égypte and conducted various diplomatic missions. Despite these duties, Fourier found time to pursue his mathematical interests.

In 1801 Fourier returned to France, but his desire to return to his post at the École Polytechnique was not realized—Napoleon, having ascertained Fourier's administrative talent,

appointed him as prefect of the department of Isére. He was successful in this appointment, and was made a baron in 1808 by Napoleon. At this time he wrote the historical preface of the *Description de l'Égypte*, completed in 1809, which was a record of the work of the Institut d'Égypte. When Napoleon was defeated in 1814, the party escorting him to Elba planned to pass through Grenoble, where Fourier was installed as prefect. Fourier negotiated a detour for the group in order to save Napoleon from an embarrassing encounter. On Napoleon's return from Elba in 1815, Fourier fulfilled his duties as prefect by organizing a token resistance at Lyons. Later, the two friends met up in Bourgoin, and Napoleon reestablished his trust in the mathematician by making him a count and the prefect of the Rhône.

However, the new regime was brutal, and before the end of Napoleon's brief restoration, Fourier had resigned his commission, and he came to Paris to pursue his research without distraction. Things were difficult for Fourier, since he was unemployed with a poor political reputation. Soon an old friend secured him a position as director of the Bureau of Statistics in the department of the Seine, which provided for his needs while leaving sufficient time for him to progress in his mathematical studies.

Fourier's main achievements lie in the area of heat diffusion. Much of the work was completed during his tenure at Grenoble, though his interests in heat go back to his sojourn in Egypt. In 1807 he presented a lengthy paper on heat diffusion in special continuous bodies to the Academy; the content was based on the diffusion (or heat) equation in three variables. Due to the use of so-called Fourier series in the paper, one of the reviewers, JOSEPH-LOUIS LAGRANGE, prevented the work's publication—Lagrange felt that trigonometric series were of little use. In 1810 a revised version of the paper was submitted in competition for a proffered prize, and the update contained new material on heat diffusion in infinite bodies. The latter sections of the paper dealt with the physical aspects of heat, such as radiation, which would occupy Fourier increasingly in later years. This excellent work won the prize, and later it was expanded into the book *Théorie analytique de la chaleur* (Analytic theory of heat).

The importance of Fourier's contributions can be seen in two aspects: first, the formulation of the physical problem as a boundary-value problem in the theory of linear partial differential equations; and second, the powerful mathematical tools for the solution of these problems. These tools would become vastly influential to the development of later mathematics, leaving numerous descendants behind.

Early notions on the mechanics of heat involved the notion that some type of shuttle transferred heat between discrete particles. Eventually, Fourier was able to discover a differential equation that smoothly described the dynamics of heat—this was the so-called diffusion equation. The domain for this equation was a "semi-infinite" strip—essentially the positive part of the x-axis—that was uniformly hot at one end and uniformly cold on the sides. This configuration of the problem was both simple and physically meaningful. In this context, Fourier constructed a series solution to the problem that involved trigonometric terms. He was aware of the convergence difficulties involved with this type of approach, and he handled these issues quite effectively. The surprising thing about his work was that he demonstrated that for many generic functions one could construct trigonometric series that were identical with the function on an interval. For nonperiodic functions, it seems strange that one can express them as a sum of sines and cosines.

Fourier then generalized his solutions to three dimensions and to other configurations, such as a cylinder. Some of his last creative work came in 1817 and 1818, wherein he developed a relation between integral-transform solutions and operational calculus. The so-called Fourier transform of a function, so useful for the solution of differential equations, came out of these labors.

In many ways Fourier was very practical in his approach to mathematics: Every statement had to possess physical meaning, and he was guided in his investigations by his excellent physical intuition. He developed a coherent pathway through a jumble of ad hoc techniques for solving differential equations, and a gift for interpreting the asymptotic properties of his solutions for physical meaning. When possible, he would test his results against the outcome of experimentation. His mathematical legacy is enormous, with such giants as BERNHARD RIEMANN, GEORG CANTOR, and HENRI-LÉON LEBESGUE following his work in mathematical analysis.

In 1817 Fourier was elected to the reconstituted Académie des Sciences after some political troubles. Gradually he advanced in his career, despite the enmity of SIMÉON-DENIS POISSON and the opposition of royalists. His later honors include election to the Académie Française in 1827 and election as a foreign member of the Royal Society. Throughout his life, he won the support of many friends through his unselfish support and encouragement, and he aided many mathematicians and scientists in his later years.

While in Egypt, he had developed some illness, possibly myxedema, so that increasingly he was confined to his own heated quarters. On May 4, 1830, he had an attack while descending some stairs in his Paris home. He died 12 days later. He is certainly one of the greatest of all mathematicians, as Fourier analysis is an enormously successful method in engineering and statistics; its applications to differential equations, called harmonic analysis, is a lovely and thriving branch of mathematics.

Further Reading

Arago, F. "Joseph Fourier," in *Biographies of Distinguished Scientific Men.* Boston: Ticknor and Fields, 1859.

Bose, A. "Fourier, His Life and Work," *Bulletin of the Calcutta Mathematical Society* 7 (1915–16): 33–48.

———. "Fourier Series and Its Influence on Some of the Developments of Mathematical Analysis," *Bulletin of the Calcutta Mathematical Society* 9 (1917–18): 71–84.

Grattan-Guinness, I. *Joseph Fourier, 1768–1830: A Survey of His Life and Work.* Cambridge, Mass.: MIT Press, 1972.

Herivel, J. *Joseph Fourier: The Man and the Physicist.* Oxford: Clarendon Press, 1975.

———."The Influence of Fourier on British Mathematics," *Centaurus* 17, no. 1 (1972): 40–57.

⊠ **Fréchet, René-Maurice**
(1878–1973)
French
Analysis

Functional analysis arose in the 20th century through the genius of several mathematicians. René-Maurice Fréchet was one of these important individuals. Fréchet was the first to present a notion of topology (the study of continuous functions and their effects on high-dimensional surfaces) for the new function spaces, and his abstract ideas became fundamental to the later development of this field.

Fréchet was born on September 10, 1878, in Maligny, France. He was the fourth of six children, and his parents were middle-class Protestants. His father, Jacques Fréchet, was the director of an orphanage, but later became a schoolteacher when the family moved to Paris. Fréchet's mother, Zoé, ran a boardinghouse for foreigners. At the Lycée Buffon in Paris, Fréchet learned mathematics from Jacques Hadamard, who recognized the youngster's budding talent.

Fréchet entered the École Normale Supérieure in 1900, and graduated three years later. During this time he made the acquaintance of ÉMILE BOREL, and this developed into a lifelong friendship. Fréchet continued his studies under the tutelage of Hadamard, and completed his dissertation in 1906 on the topic of functional calculus. The study of functionals (or numerically valued functions of ordinary functions) was a new topic, and Fréchet introduced topological notions into the space of functionals in several novel ways. In particular, Fréchet was able to define the notions of continuity and limit for these functionals. Generalizing the work of GEORG CANTOR to function spaces, Fréchet was able to define the notions of compactness, separability, and completeness that are encountered in point spaces. These early ideas later became pivotal elements of the modern theory of functional analysis. Today, functional analysis is used in a wide variety of engineering and statistical applications, and is largely responsible for the rapid advance of many technologies (for instance, mediating the effect of wind turbulence on aircraft flight) of the present day.

Fréchet eventually obtained a professorship at the University of Poitiers in 1910. During World War I, he served as an interpreter to the British army. After the war he headed the Institute of Mathematics at the University of Strasbourg in 1919. He married Suzanne Carrive in 1908, and they had four children.

Meanwhile, Fréchet continued his research into functional analysis, establishing the representation theorem for continuous linear functionals in 1907. FRIGYES RIESZ independently discovered this important result. Fréchet generalized the notion of derivative from ordinary calculus to operators in function spaces and also extended the integration ideas of Johann Radon and HENRI-LOUIS LEBESGUE to spaces without a topology. He also developed some of the first abstract topological spaces from certain set axioms. These results are now classical in the field of functional analysis and point-set topology.

Fréchet moved to the University of Paris in 1928, where he taught mathematics until his

1949 retirement. During this period he focused on probability and statistics, using functional analysis as a tool to solve several concrete problems in probability and statistics. However, this work was not equal in originality to his first contributions to the topology of function spaces. He died in Paris on June 4, 1973.

Fréchet's work received accolades from his colleagues in America, and he received several honors during his lifetime, being made a fellow of the Royal Society of Edinburgh and an Honorary Fellow of the Edinburgh Mathematical Society. Hadamard, in a 1934 report to the Academy of Sciences, announced that Fréchet's work in functional analysis, in terms of abstraction and generality, could be compared with the pioneering labors of EVARISTE GALOIS in algebraic field theory. Certainly, Fréchet's results gave a firm topological foundation to functional analysis, which has proved to be one of the most useful tools of modern mathematics, with manifold applications to statistics and engineering.

Further Reading

Kendall, D. "Obituary: Maurice Fréchet, 1878–1973," *Journal of the Royal Statistical Society. Series A. Statistics in Society* 140, no. 4 (1977): 566.

Taylor, A. "A Study of Maurice Fréchet I," *Archive for History of Exact Sciences* 27 (1982): 233–295.

———. "A Study of Maurice Fréchet II," *Archive for History of Exact Sciences* 34 (1985): 279–380.

———. "A Study of Maurice Fréchet III," *Archive for History of Exact Sciences* 37 (1987): 25–76.

⊠   Fredholm, Ivar
(1866–1927)
Swedish
Analysis

The theory of integral equations, which is concerned with finding an unknown function that satisfies an equation involving its integral, has wide applications to mathematical physics, and has become a field of interest in its own right. Ivar Fredholm made a few significant contributions to this field, and his work has attained classical importance to this branch of mathematics.

Ivar Fredholm was born in Stockholm, Sweden, on April 7, 1866, the son of an upper-class family. His father was a wealthy merchant, and his mother came from the elite of Sweden; as a result, Fredholm received the best education. He displayed his brilliance at an early age, passing his baccalaureate in 1885. A year at the Polytechnic Institute of Sweden fostered an enduring interest in applied mathematics and practical mechanics. He enrolled in the University of Uppsala the next year, obtained his bachelor of science degree in 1888 and his doctorate in 1898. Fredholm also took classes at the University of Stockholm, studying under the renowned Magnus Mittag-Leffler, and he received an appointment there in 1898; in 1906 he became a professor of mathematical physics. He died on August 17, 1927, in Stockholm.

Fredholm's thesis treated a topic in the theory of partial differential equations, which had applications to the study of deformations of objects subjected to interior or exterior forces. A decade later, Fredholm completely generalized his work to solving the general elliptic (a particular type of differential equation) partial differential equation.

Fredholm acquired fame for his solution of the so-called Fredholm integral equation, which has wide applications in physics—for example, these equations arise in the study of the vibrating membrane. Many mathematicians, such as NIELS HENRIK ABEL and VITO VOLTERRA, had already attacked this problem with only partial success. Fredholm presented a complete solution in 1903 after recognizing a fundamental analogy between the Fredholm equation and an equation of matrices; this observation would later become a cornerstone in functional analysis—namely, that integration against a kernel function was a linear operator similar to matrix multiplication. By examining the analogy of the matrix determinant for the integral operator, Fredholm was able to formulate precise conditions under which the equation was even solvable, and to give a formula for the solution when it existed.

This work certainly constitutes a milestone in functional analysis and the theory of integral equations. When these advances were communicated to DAVID HILBERT, he was inspired to further the study of these equations; soon afterward, Hilbert invented a theory of eigenvalues for integral operators, in analogy with matrices, and constructed Hilbert spaces. Thus, Fredholm inspired the construction of some of the most valuable tools of functional analysis.

Further Reading

Garding, L. *Mathematics and Mathematicians: Mathematics in Sweden before 1950.* Providence, R.I.: American Mathematical Society, 1998.

⊠   Frege, Friedrich Ludwig Gottlob
(1848–1925)
German
Logic

Gottlob Frege performed substantial work on mathematical logic in the 19th century; indeed, he is viewed by many as the father of modern mathematical logic. The language that he created in order to rigorously analyze arithmetic would later develop into the syntax and notation of modern proof theory.

Gottlob Frege was born on November 8, 1848, in Wismar, Germany, to Alexander Frege and Auguste Bialloblotzky. His father was the principal of a girls' high school in Wismar, and Gottlob attended the Gymnasium there. From 1869 to 1871 he was a student at Jena, and after this period matriculated at the University of Göttingen, where he took courses in mathematics, physics, chemistry, and philosophy. Two

years later he had earned his doctorate in philosophy with the thesis *Über eine geometrische Darstellung der imaginaren Gebilde in der Ebene* (Over a geometrical representation of imaginary things in the plane). His 1874 dissertation was concerned with certain groups of functions, and Frege's ambition was to give a definition of quantity that would greatly extend the applicability of the resulting arithmetic. At about this time he began work on the project of providing a rigorous foundation for arithmetic. Frege wished to define number and quantity in a satisfactory manner, and he turned to logic as an appropriate vehicle.

At this period of history there was little in the way of a coherent treatment of mathematical logic. Since Frege wanted to be precise in his development of the theory of numbers, he decided to construct a language of logic in which to formulate his ideas. The tools for analyzing mathematical proofs were published in *Begriffschrift* (Concept script) in 1879, and some of the ideas from his Jena dissertation entered into his concept of quantity. In the same year, he was appointed extraordinary professor in Jena, and was made an honorary professor in 1896. His diligent work toward the logical construction of arithmetic over the years resulted in his two-volume *Grundgesetze der Arithmetik* (Basic laws of arithmetic) (1893–1903). In 1902 BERTRAND RUSSELL pointed out a contradiction in Frege's system of arithmetic; this comment proved to be disastrous, as Frege could find no way of remedying the problem. Indeed, as later work by KURT FRIEDRICH GÖDEL would demonstrate, any efforts to construct complete and consistent number theories were doomed to failure.

The *Begriffschrift* should be viewed as a formal language as a vehicle for pure thought. This language consisted of various symbols (such as letters) that could be combined together according to certain rules (the grammar) to form statements. As with arithmetic, after which Frege's language was modeled, one could then perform calculations whose result would be a logical calculation rather than a numeric quantity. The idea of a logical calculus goes back at least to GOTTFRIED WILHELM VON LEIBNIZ, who supposed that one day all philosophical debate could be reduced to logical calculations. Frege's calculus could be used to formalize the notion of a mathematical proof, so that one could, essentially, compute the conclusion.

The basic components of Frege's calculus are an assertion symbol (represented by a vertical stroke), a conditional symbol (for instance, A implies B), and a deduction rule, which states the following: If we assert A, and A implies B, then we may assert B. Frege also developed notation for negation, and demonstrated that logical *and* and *or* could be expressed in terms of the conditional and negation symbols. On top of these basic notions he added a theory of quantity, rigorously defining such notions as *for all* and *there exists*.

There is a school of mathematics called formalism, whose adherents believe that there is no true or inherent meaning to mathematics, but that mathematics is purely a formal language with which other ideas may be expressed, and mathematical truth can be arrived at only by playing according to the rules of the game. Frege was not a formalist and was not interested in applying his system to questions pertaining to a formalist agenda. Ironically, his work was quite suitable as a foundation for formal logic.

Frege's work *Grundlagen der Arithmetik* (Foundations of arithmetic) (1884) defines the notion of number and relies upon the language introduced in *Begriffschrift*. Here he gives a criticism to the previous theories of number, pointing out their inadequacies; he argues that equality of number is an essential component to the notion of number. The *Grundgesetze* incorporates and refines his previous work, including improvements based on several papers. Many of these ideas had great influence on subsequent philosophical discussion, in particular influencing the philosophy of Wittgenstein.

After 1903 Frege's powers of thought were in decline; he seemed unable to keep up with an increasingly modern and alien mathematical culture. In this latter period, he spent his energy reacting against various new developments in mathematics, and especially came into conflict with DAVID HILBERT and his program for the axiomatization of mathematics. In 1917 Frege retired, and after this produced *Logische Untersuchungen* (*Logical investigations*) as an extension of previous work. He died in Bad Kleinen, Germany, on July 26, 1925.

Frege is principally remembered for his work on mathematical logic, which led to modern proof theory. Other great logicians such as Russell and Gödel continued his work. Although Frege's effort to construct a complete, consistent number theory was doomed to failure, the ideas that he formulated in the course of his research greatly influenced later generations of mathematicians.

Further Reading

Angelelli, I. *Studies on Gottlob Frege and Traditional Philosophy*. Dordrecht, the Netherlands: Kluwer Academic Publishers Group, 1967.

Dummett, M. *Frege: Philosophy of Language*. Cambridge, Mass.: Harvard University Press, 1981.

———. *Frege: Philosophy of Mathematics*. London: Ducksworth, 1991.

———. *The Interpretation of Frege's Philosophy*. Cambridge, Mass.: Harvard University Press, 1981.

Kenny, A. *Frege*. London: Penguin Books, 1995.

Weiner, J. *Frege*. New York: Oxford University Press, 1999.

Wright, C. *Frege's Conception of Numbers as Objects*. Aberdeen, U.K.: Aberdeen University Press, 1983.

⊠ **Fubini, Guido**
(1879–1943)
Italian
Analysis, Geometry

Guido Fubini was one of Italy's most productive mathematicians, opening up new areas of research in several areas of analysis, geometry, and mathematical physics. His unfailing intuition, together with his mastery of the techniques of calculation, made him a formidable mathematician. His accomplishments earned him the royal prize of Lincei in 1919, and he was a member of several Italian scientific academies.

On January 19, 1879, in Venice, Guido Fubini was born to Lazarro Fubini and Zoraide Torre. Lazarro Fubini taught mathematics in Venice, and the son followed in his father's footsteps. He quickly completed his secondary studies in Venice, and entered the Scuola Normale Superiore di Pisa at age 17. A few years later, in 1900, Fubini defended a thesis on Clifford's parallelism in elliptic spaces, a topic in differential geometry. This subject studies smooth surfaces and solids (and their higher-dimensional analogs), and Fubini's contribution came to have great importance for this area of mathematics after the thesis was included in a 1902 edition of Luigi Bianchi's treatise on differential geometry.

Fubini had already made great progress for one so young, and he remained at Pisa for another year to obtain the diploma, a higher degree that would allow him to teach at the university level. The memoir that he wrote for his diploma investigates the theory of harmonic functions in spaces of constant curvature—a topic quite different from that explored in his doctoral thesis.

It is said that Guido Fubini was a man of great cultivation and kindness; his affability and wit made him a pleasant companion. As a teacher, Fubini was possessed of great talents, and over many years as a professor he was able to influence many young mathematicians. He was a small man, but had a vigorous voice. Family was quite important to Fubini, and he took a serious interest in his sons' engineering studies. Luigi Bianchi, one of his teachers from Pisa, was a role model for him, and Fubini was grateful for Bianchi's assistance and guidance.

In 1901 Fubini was placed in charge of a course at the University of Catania, and was soon nominated to the position of full professor. From Catania he went to the University of Genoa, and in 1908 again transferred, to the Politecno in Turin. At the Politecno and University of Turin, Fubini taught mathematical analysis.

In the subject of analysis Fubini did much of his best work, focusing on linear differential equations, partial differential equations, analytic functions of several complex variables, and monotonic functions. Within the calculus of variations, he studied various problems involving integration, such as nonlinear integral equations with asymmetric kernels. He also examined discontinuous groups, in particular studying motion on Riemannian surfaces. For non-Euclidean spaces, he introduced sliding parameters, which made possible a transposition of results from ordinary differential geometry to elliptical geometry.

Differential projective geometry was the branch of mathematics to which Fubini made his most significant contributions. He developed general procedures, which still bear his name. Projective geometry is the study of spaces of lines, and arose out of medieval artistic studies of perspective. To this difficult subject, Fubini brought the tools of differential calculus and group theory.

Fubini also made contributions to mathematical physics. During World War I he made theoretical studies on the accuracy of artillery fire, and later examined problems in acoustics and electricity. The mathematical aspects of engineering interested him, and a posthumous work on engineering mathematics appeared in 1954.

Fubini continued for many years at Turin, and in 1928, upon the death of Bianchi, he became coeditor of the *Annali di matematica pura ed applicata* (Annals of pure and applied mathematics). He held this position for 10 years, but in 1938 faced forced retirement due to new racial laws instituted by the Fascist government. He was concerned for the future of his two sons, and the following year he received and accepted an offer from the Institute for Advanced Study in Princeton, New Jersey. In the United States he was made welcome, and his voluntary exile proved to be wise due to the unfolding events in Europe.

At this point his health was poor, but he continued to teach at New York University until he died of a heart ailment on June 6, 1943, in New York City. Fubini left a great legacy in mathematics: He had stimulated many branches, opening up new areas of inquiry and providing innovative techniques. His textbooks have been widely employed for courses in analysis, with collections of problems used by many generations of students. Indeed, his labors were varied, yet with great influence on the future of mathematics.

Further Reading

Papini, P. "Guido Fubini 1879–1943," *European Mathematical Society Newsletter* 9 (1993) 10.

G

⊠ **Galilei, Galileo**
(1564–1642)
Italian
Mechanics, Geometry

Galileo Galilei is one of the best-known names in the history of science. This man lived in a time when speculative philosophy was gradually supplanted by mathematics and experimental evidence, and indeed he contributed, perhaps more than any of his contemporaries, to this paradigm shift. Galileo's research into mathematics, mechanics, physics, and astronomy completely altered the way that people pursued knowledge of the natural world, and started an avalanche of scientific inquiry throughout Europe.

Galileo was born on February 15, 1564, in Pisa, Italy. His father, Vincenzio Galilei, was a musician and member of an old patrician family. Vincenzio married Giulia Ammannati of Pescia in 1562, and Galileo was born two years later. He would be one of seven children. He was first tutored in Pisa, but the family returned to Florence in 1575. He studied at the monastery of Santa Maria at Vallombrosa until 1581, when he was enrolled at the University of Pisa as a medical student. Galileo had little interest in medicine, but preferred mathematics, in which he progressed rapidly despite his father's disapproval. In 1585 he left school without a degree

and pursued the study of EUCLID OF ALEXANDRIA and ARCHIMEDES OF SYRACUSE privately.

During the next four years, Galileo gave private mathematics lessons in Florence, while composing some minor works on mechanics and geometry. It was at this time that Galileo's father became engaged in a musical controversy. Vincenzio Galilei resolved the dispute through experimental investigations, and this approach proved to have a great influence on his son. Galileo would mature into a great experimentalist, testing mathematical theories with physical evidence.

In 1589 Galileo obtained the mathematics chair at Pisa, where he performed some of his first experiments on falling bodies. At about this time, Galileo embarked on a lifelong campaign to discredit Aristotelian physics, the official view of the world espoused by the Roman Catholic Church, which, among other things, declared that the denser objects fall faster. Galileo infuriated many of his fellow professors by publicly demonstrating that bodies of different weight fall at the same speed—by dropping such objects out of the Leaning Tower of Pisa. His treatise on these topics was *De motu* (On motion), and it relied on some ideas from Archimedes.

His father died in 1591, creating an uncertain financial situation for Galileo. Due to the animosity that he had aroused, his position at

Galileo Galilei studied mechanics and derived the square law for free fall. He also advanced the separation of science and theology. *(Courtesy of the Library of Congress)*

Pisa was not renewed; however, his friends assisted him in obtaining an appointment at Padua, where the community was less conservative. He lectured on Euclid, CLAUDIUS PTOLEMY, and mechanics, but did not become interested in astronomy until much later. In 1597 Galileo expressed his sympathies to the Copernican system to Johannes Kepler, but he did not publicly advance the anti-Aristotelian astronomy at this point. In the same year he manufactured an instrument (the proportional compass) for sale, over which a controversy later arose in which Galileo obtained the priority of its invention.

While in Padua, Galileo took a mistress named Marina Gamba, who later bore him two daughters and a son. His eldest daughter, Virginia, would be a great solace to him in later years of strife and conflict. In 1602 he became interested in the motions of pendulums and the acceleration of falling bodies, and he derived the square law for free fall correctly in 1604, though with an incorrect assumption. In the same year, a supernova led to dispute over the Aristotelian notion of the incorruptibility of the heavens, and Galileo delivered several public lectures on this topic. He was soon to become increasingly interested in the study of the skies.

In 1609 Galileo learned of the invention of a telescope by Hans Lipperhey, a Dutch lens grinder, and the Paduan professor set about constructing his own version, which was eventually 30 times more powerful than the original. This device, so useful for navigation, won him a lifetime appointment at Padua, and he set about using it to view the heavens. He soon discovered that the Moon had mountains and that the Milky Way consisted of many separate stars. Galileo published many additional discoveries in *Sidereus nuncios* (The siderial messenger) (1610). His resulting fame gained him the post of mathematician and philosopher to the grand duke of Tuscany, where he could focus on his research without having to teach.

The book created a furor in Europe, and many claimed that it was a fraud, though Kepler endorsed it. In the satellites of Jupiter, Galileo now saw decisive evidence against the Aristotelian conception that all heavenly bodies revolved around the Earth. In 1611 he journeyed to Rome, where he was honored by the Jesuits of the Roman College and admitted to the Lincean Academy.

After this time, Galileo turned back to physics and became embroiled in more controversies in Florence. The dispute concerned the behavior of bodies floating in water, and Galileo supported the theories of Archimedes against those of Aristotle; he was able, using the concepts of moment and velocity, to extend Archimedes's ideas beyond hydrostatic situations.

In 1613 Galileo published *Letters on Sunspots,* which spoke out decisively for the Copernican system for the first time in print. Certain Catholics did not favorably regard this document, and the opposition grew over the next few years. In Galileo's opinion, theology should not interfere with purely scientific questions—those that could be resolved experimentally; this opinion later came before the Inquisition, and in 1615 Galileo went to Rome to fight the suppression of Copernicanism. Pope Paul V, annoyed by questions of theological authority, appointed a commission to determine the Earth's motion: in 1616 the commission ruled against the Copernican system, and Galileo was prohibited from advocating that view.

Returning to Florence, Galileo turned to the problem of determining longitudes at sea. He also took up mechanics again, correctly defining uniform acceleration and putting forth many of his kinematic principles. But Galileo had a feisty personality, and he was soon drawn into a new controversy regarding the motion of three comets that appeared in 1618. In a highly celebrated polemic of science, *Il saggiatore* (The assayer), Galileo set forth a general scientific approach to the investigation of celestial phenomena without direct reference to the Copernican system. In this essay, Galileo repudiates any authority that contradicts direct investigation, and thus puts forth empirical science as a sole foundation of knowledge of the universe. This work was published in 1623 and dedicated to Pope Urban VIII on his installation. Galileo secured his old friend's permission to write a book that would impartially discuss the Copernican and Ptolemaic systems, called *Dialogue Concerning the Two Chief World Systems.*

This work, which occupied Galileo for the next six years, consisted of a dialogue between two advocates—for the Copernican and Ptolemaic systems, respectively—attempting to win a layman over to their side. Galileo remains officially uncommitted, except in the preface; the important concepts include the relativity and conservation of motion. Sunspots and ocean tides were presented as pro-Copernican arguments, as they could not be explained without terrestrial motion. The book was printed in Florence in 1632, and soon its author was commanded to come before the Inquisition in Rome.

The pope, though once a friend of Galileo, had become convinced by Galileo's enemies that the Aristotelian perspective was deliberately made to look foolish by the author. The trial was prosecuted with vindictiveness, and Galileo was sentenced to life imprisonment after abjuring the Copernican heresy. Under house arrest, he spent his remaining years completing his unfinished work on mechanics. By 1638 *Discourses and Mathematical Demonstrations Concerning Two New Sciences* had appeared in France (he could not publish in Italy, as his works were banned). The content deals with the engineering science of materials and the mathematical science of kinematics, and underlies much of modern physics. Both the pendulum and the inclined plane play a large role in *Two New Sciences,* and Galileo deduces the parabolic motion of trajectories.

In the last four years of his life Galileo was blind, and before his death he was denied the request to attend Easter services or consult doctors. Finally, on January 8, 1642, in Arcetri, Italy, he passed away. He was certainly one of the greatest scientists of all time, and an able mathematician as well. Not only did he make great contributions to science, but also advanced a new epistemology—that knowledge of the natural world (including mathematical knowledge) should be acquired through reason and experiment.

Further Reading

Campanella, T. *A Defense of Galileo, the Mathematician from Florence.* Notre Dame, Ind.: University of Notre Dame Press, 1994.

Drake, S. *Galileo at Work: His Scientific Biography.* Chicago: University of Chicago Press, 1978.

———. *Galileo Studies: Personality, Tradition, and Revolution.* Ann Arbor: University of Michigan Press, 1970.

———. *Galileo.* New York: Hill and Wang, 1980.

———. *Galileo: Pioneer Scientist.* Toronto, Ont.: University of Toronto Press, 1990.

Fantoli, A. *Galileo: for Copernicanism and for the Church.* Vatican City: Vatican Observatory Publications, 1994.

Geymonat, L. *Galileo Galilei.* Turin: Piccola Biblioteca Einaudi, 1969.

Redondi, P. *Galileo Heretic.* Princeton, N.J.: Princeton University Press, 1987.

Ronan, C. *Galileo.* New York: Putnam, 1974.

Shea, W. *Galileo's Intellectual Revolution: Middle Period, 1610–1632.* New York: Science History Publications, 1977.

⊠ Galois, Evariste
(1811–1832)
French
Algebra

The French mathematician Evariste Galois led a meteoric life, notable for its short duration and mathematical profundity. Aside from his involvement in politics as a demagogue, Galois in his work focused on the solution of algebraic equations and the foundation of modern group theory. It seems that he condensed a lifespan of deep mathematical work into just a few years of troubled existence, accomplishing more in his brief time than many achieve through decades of labor. His writings, though despised and unrecognized in his own lifetime, later proved to be the fruit of a great genius, and his work in the theory of groups and fields is now a pillar of the modern discipline of algebra. Even his writings on mathematical epistemology demonstrated remarkable insight, outlining an uncannily accurate prediction of the course of modern mathematics.

Evariste Galois was born on October 25, 1811, in Bourg-la-Reine, France. He was the son of Nicolas-Gabriel Galois, a liberal town mayor, and Adelaïde-Marie Demante, an eccentric woman who determined to raise her son in the principles of stoic morality and austere religion. However, the young Galois had a happy childhood and a good education. In October 1823 he continued his studies at College Louis-le-Grand in Paris. His discipline problems there, perhaps in response to a royalist establishment, would prove to be an enduring characteristic of his personality.

In 1827 Galois entered his first mathematics courses, and was so deeply impressed that he began reading the original works on his own initiative. When he continued into more advanced instruction, he was at the same time pursuing his own personal investigations. Through 1828 he studied recent literature on the theory of equations, number theory, and the theory of elliptic functions (these are a class of functions, related to the cubic, which have many interesting properties), and in March 1829 he started to publish his results.

For centuries, mathematicians had been doing work on quadratic, cubic, and quartic equations, attempting to provide general formulas for the solutions. But an outstanding problem that remained impregnable to attack was the solution of the quintic, or fifth degree, polynomial with integer coefficients. In 1828 Galois believed that he had solved this problem, unaware that NIELS HENRIK ABEL had previously shown that this was impossible; however, he soon realized his error, and instead set forth to investigate solubility more generally. The methods he used involved group theory, which at the time was not very advanced; in the course of his labor, Galois would precisely formulate this theory, and introduce vital, original ideas to it. A mathematical group is a set with certain prescribed arithmetic operations—examples include the integers under addition, or the rotational and reflective symmetries of a polygon. The so-called Galois theory studies the various groups that are related to a particular equation. In May 1829, he communicated his results to the Academy of Sciences via AUGUSTIN-LOUIS CAUCHY.

However, what seemed to be a promising career for the young Galois would evaporate through a series of frustrating circumstances, some of which were due to his volatile character. In July 1829 his father committed suicide, despondent over persecution for his liberal views; Evariste, who was of the same liberal political disposition (liberalism at this time meant antimonarchical republicanism) seemed doomed to suffer his father's fate. Shortly afterward, in February 1830, Galois prepared a memoir containing his new results for the Academy of Sciences, hoping to win that year's grand prize. However, JEAN-BAPTISTE-JOSEPH FOURIER lost the manuscript, and Galois was ejected from the competition. Suspecting this to be additional persecution, Galois became increasingly alienated from the scientific community. This memoir commemorated the death of Abel, another mathematician who had done work in the same area, and the work established that Galois had made significant progress beyond Abel, although there remained some obstacles to obtaining a general answer to the question of the quintic's solvability.

The next major event was the July revolution of 1830, in which Galois was politically involved. In December of that year, Galois was expelled from the École Normale Supérieure for writing an antiauthoritarian letter, and he subsequently devoted himself to writing political propaganda, even participating in the Paris riots. In May he was arrested and imprisoned for making a "regicide toast," but was released a month later.

Meanwhile, Galois published some work on analysis, and presented an updated version of the previous memoir, in which he demonstrates how the former difficulties were overcome. The editor of the journal, SIMÉON-DENIS POISSON, disparaged the work and returned it to Galois. As a result, Galois's frustration grew such that he came to despise his fellow scientists.

In July 1831 Galois was again arrested, and he continued his mathematics while incarcerated. Later, in March 1832, he was transferred to a nursing home, where he wrote some essays on science and philosophy. The circumstances of his death are cluttered, and there are competing theories as to the cause; however, it seems that he had some premonition of it. After a love affair that ended unhappily, he set about writing all his main results down. On May 30, 1832, he was mortally wounded in a duel, and he died in Paris on May 31.

Despite his contemporaries' inability to recognize the value of his work, it has since proved to be of profound influence in the creation of modern algebra. Not only did Galois theory provide a complete answer to the question of the quintic, but it could be applied to many other problems as well; for example, one can prove the impossibility of trisecting an angle with ruler and compass. Perhaps Galois went unnoticed in his day due to the profundity of his thought, being too far beyond his peers to be properly appreciated; or it may have been due to his irascible temperament and inability to get along with his fellows. Fifteen years after his death, his celebrated memoir was finally published, and mathematicians, by this time more receptive, came to greatly appreciate his influence and thought. His intuition about the direction of future mathematics was remarkable, sketching in a few sentences the main highways of modern research, and his importance for modern algebra cannot be overstated.

Further Reading
Ng, L. "Evariste Galois," *Mathematical Medley* 22, no. 1 (1995): 32–33.

Ritagelli, L. *Evariste Galois (1811–1832)*. Boston: Springer-Verlag, 1996.

⊗ Gauss, Carl Friedrich
(1777–1855)
German
*Statistics, Geometry, Analysis,
Complex Analysis, Number Theory,
Probability, Algebra*

Known as the "prince of mathematicians," Carl Gauss is often ranked with SIR ISAAC NEWTON and ARCHIMEDES OF SYRACUSE as the foremost of thinkers; certainly, among his contemporaries he had no rivals, as even they acknowledged. Conservative, cold, introspective, brilliant, prolific, tragic, and ambitious—Gauss's life represents that of the ideal or archetypal mathematician in many respects. His work extended through pure mathematics, including arithmetic and number theory, geometry, algebra, and analysis, to applied mathematics—probability and statistics, mechanics, and physics—to the sciences of astronomy, geodesy, magnetism, and dioptrics, to industrial labors in actuarial science and financial securities. Gauss was an active field researcher, empiricist, data analyst and statistician, theorist, and inventor, with more than 300 publications and more than 400 original ideas throughout a long lifetime of intense and sustained effort. His genius flourished in a time of little mathematical activity in Germany, and is the more remarkable for his solitary and reclusive style.

Carl Friedrich Gauss was born on April 30, 1777, in Brunswick, Germany, to lower-class parents. Gauss's mother was highly intelligent but semiliterate, and was a devoted supporter of her son throughout her long life. His father worked various professions in an attempt to extricate his family from poverty; of a practical bent, he never appreciated his son's extraordinary gifts, which were manifested at a young age. Before he could talk, Carl had learned to calculate, and at age three he had corrected mistakes in his father's wage calculations! In his eighth year, while in his first arithmetic class, Gauss found a formula

Carl Gauss, greatest of mathematicians, dominated algebra, geometry, complex analysis, number theory, and statistics and invented the principle of least squares in regression. *(Courtesy of AIP Emilio Segrè Visual Archives, Brittle Book Collection)*

for the sum of the first *n* consecutive numbers. His teacher, suitably impressed, supplied the boy with literature to encourage his intellectual development.

In 1788, at age 11, the prodigy entered the Gymnasium, where he made rapid progress in all his studies, especially classics and mathematics. Through the benevolence of his teachers, the duke of Brunswick appointed Gauss a stipend, effectively making him independent; he was 16 at the time. In 1792 he entered the Collegium Carolinum, already possessed of a thorough scientific education. His extensive calculations and empirical investigations had led him to deep familiarity with numbers and their properties; he had already independently discovered Bode's law of planetary motion and the binomial theorem for rational exponents.

While at the Collegium, Gauss continued his investigations in empirical arithmetic and formulated the principle of least squares used in statistics. In 1795 he entered the University of Göttingen, and by this time he had rediscovered the law of quadratic reciprocity, related the arithmetic-geometric mean to infinite series expansions, conjectured the prime number theorem, and found some early results in non-Euclidean geometry. Gauss read Newton, but most mathematical classics were unavailable; as a result, he nearly became a philologist. However, in 1796 he made the significant discovery that the regular 17-gon could be constructed by ruler and compass, an outstanding problem that had been unsolved for 2,000 years. This success encouraged him to pursue mathematics.

His fate as a mathematician was set, and the years until 1800 were marked by a remarkable profusion of ideas. In style, Gauss adopted the rigor of Greek geometry, although he thought algebraically and numerically. He pursued intense empirical researches, followed by the construction of rigorously laid theories. This approach to science ensured that there was a close connection between theory and practice.

In 1798, finished with the university, Gauss returned to Brunswick, where he lived alone and worked assiduously. The next year he presented the proof of the fundamental theorem of algebra, which states that any degree n polynomial has exactly n roots in the complex numbers; with this result, the first of four proofs he would write for this theorem, he earned his doctorate from the University of Helmstedt. The year 1801 signaled two great achievements for Gauss: the *Disquisitiones arithmeticae* (Arithmetical investigations) and the calculation of the orbit of the newly discovered planet Ceres. The former was a systematic summary of previous work in number theory, in which he solved most of the difficult outstanding questions and formulated concepts that would influence future research for two centuries. He introduced the concept of modular congruence, proved the law of quadratic reciprocity, developed the theory of quadratic forms, and analyzed the cyclotomic equation. This book won Gauss fame and recognition among mathematicians as their "prince," but his austere style ensured that his readership was small. As for Ceres, it was a new planet that had been observed by Giuseppe Piazzi and subsequently was lost. Gauss, equipped with his computational talents, took on the task of locating the truant celestial body. With a more accurate orbit theory, which used an elliptical rather than circular orbit, and his least squares numerical methods, he was able to predict Ceres' location. Because he did not disclose his methods, the feat seemed superhuman, and established Gauss as a first-class scientific genius.

During the next decade, Gauss exploited the scientific ideas of the previous 10 years. He transitioned from pure mathematician to astronomer and physical scientist. Although he was treated well by the duke of Brunswick, who still supported him with a stipend, Gauss decided on astronomy as a stable career in which he could pursue research without the burden of teaching; in 1807 he accepted the directorship of the Göttingen observatory. He made some contacts among other scientists that sprouted into collaborations, but had little interaction with other mathematicians—he exchanged a few letters with SOPHIE GERMAIN and later had GUSTAV PETER LEJEUNE DIRICHLET and BERNHARD RIEMANN as students, but he did not work closely with any of these persons. This seems to be due to ingrained introspection, a consequence of his underappreciated childhood talents, and a driving ambition that made him unwilling to share discovery with others. Much of Gauss's work went unpublished, ostensibly because he thought it unworthy of dissemination; the real reason seems to be his possessive secretiveness that fostered a reluctance to reveal his methods.

In this time period, Gauss's political views were fixed: A staunch conservative, he was disconcerted by the chaos of revolution and was skeptical of democracy. In philosophy he was an empiricist, rejecting the idealism of Immanuel Kant and Georg Hegel. He also experienced some personal happiness in this time; in 1805 he married Johanna Osthoff, by whom he begot a daughter and son. But in 1809 she died in childbirth, and Gauss was plunged into loneliness. Though he soon remarried, to Minna Waldeck, this marriage was less happy, as she was often sick. Gauss dominated his daughters and quarreled with his sons, who left Germany for the United States.

In his early years at Göttingen, Gauss had another surge of mathematical ideas on hypergeometric functions, the approximation of integration, and the analysis of the efficiency of statistical estimators. His astronomical duties devoured much of his time, but he continued with mathematical investigations in his spare moments. At this time he developed many of the notions of non-Euclidean geometry, worked out from his early years in Göttingen as a student. However, his conservatism made him reluctant to accept the truth of his discoveries, and he was unwilling to face the public ridicule attendant on such novel mathematics. This led to later arguments over priority with JÁNOS BOLYAI, who independently developed non-Euclidean geometry despite Gauss's negative influence.

Gauss's endeavors in science were also considerable, but we shall pass over them briefly, and focus on their mathematical aspects. In 1817 Gauss became interested in geodesy, the measurement of the Earth. He completed, after many administrative obstacles, the triangulation of Hannover 30 years later. As a result of his arduous fieldwork, he invented the heliotrope, a device that could act as a beacon even in the daytime by reflecting sunlight. His work in geodesy inspired the early mathematics of potential theory, and the mapping of one surface to another,

an important concept in differential geometry. He was also stimulated to continue his research in mathematical statistics, and his *Disquisitiones generales circa superficies curves* (General investigations of curved surfaces) in 1828 would fuel more than a century of activity in differential geometry. By 1825 Gauss had new results on biquadratic reciprocity and was working on non-Euclidean geometry and elliptic functions. Slowing down due to age, Gauss turned toward physics and magnetism for fresh inspiration. In 1829 he stated the law of least constraint, and in 1830 he contributed to the topic of capillarity and the calculus of variations. The year 1830–31 was quite difficult, as Gauss was afflicted by a heart condition and his wife soon died from tuberculosis. At this time Gauss began collaboration with Wilhelm Weber in magnetism, and they invented the first telegraph in 1834. Gauss's 1839 work based on worldwide magnetic observatory data expressed the magnetic potential on the Earth's surface by an infinite series of spherical functions. His fruitful collaboration with Weber had already ended with the latter's exile for political reasons. In 1840 Gauss gave a systematic treatment of potential theory as a mathematical topic, and in 1841 he analyzed the path of light through a system of lenses.

From the early 1840s Gauss's productivity gradually decreased. He had more liking for teaching, and Dedekind and Riemann were among his most gifted students. Working in actuarial science, he collected many statistics from periodicals; this data aided him in his financial speculations, which made him quite wealthy. His health gradually failed, until he died in his sleep on February 23, 1855, in Göttingen.

Gauss was one of the greatest mathematicians of all time. Later mathematicians, unaware that Gauss had already gone before them, replicated many of his discoveries. His name is associated with many diverse areas of mathematics, and his impact cannot be overestimated.

Further Reading

Bühler, W. *Gauss: A Biographical Study.* New York: Springer-Verlag, 1981.

Coxeter, H. "Gauss as a Geometer," *Historia Mathematica* 4, no. 4 (1977): 379–396.

Dunnington, G. *Carl Friedrich Gauss, Titan of Science.* New York: Hafner, 1955.

Forbes, E. "The Astronomical Work of Carl Friedrich Gauss (1777–1855)," *Historia Mathematica* 5, no. 2 (1978): 167–181.

———. "Gauss and the Discovery of Ceres," *Journal for the History of Astronomy* 2, no. 3 (1971): 195–199.

Hall, T. *Carl Friedrich Gauss: A Biography.* Cambridge, Mass.: MIT Press, 1970.

Plackett, R. "The Influence of Laplace and Gauss in Britain," *Bulletin de l'Institut International de Statistique* 53, no. 1 (1989): 163–176.

Sheynin, O. "C. F. Gauss and the Theory of Errors," *Archive for History of Exact Sciences* 20, no. 1 (1979): 21–72.

Sprott, D. "Gauss's Contributions to Statistics," *Historia Mathematica* 5, no. 2 (1978): 183–203.

Stigler, S. "Gauss and the Invention of Least Squares," *The Annals of Statistics* 9, no. 3 (1981): 465–474.

⊠ Germain, Sophie
(1776–1831)
French
Number Theory, Geometry

Sophie Germain is known as one of France's greatest mathematicians. She made important contributions to number theory, partial differential equations, and differential geometry. Germain was able to accomplish much despite a lack of formal education and her parents' opposition.

Born the daughter of Ambroise-François Germain and Marie-Madeleine Gruguelu on April 1, 1776, in Paris, Sophie Germain lived in an affluent household during turbulent times. Her father was a deputy to the States-General, and was by profession a merchant; later he became a director of the Bank of France. Under this comfortable situation, Germain grew up with her father's extensive library at her disposal. At a time when women did not regularly receive educations, Germain supplied the lack herself by reading at home. At age 13, she read an account of the death of ARCHIMEDES OF SYRACUSE by a careless soldier, and the Sicilian mathematician became a heroic symbol for her. At this young age, she decided to be a mathematician. Although her parents were opposed to this direction of her energies, she first mastered Latin and Greek, and then started to read SIR ISAAC NEWTON and EUCLID OF ALEXANDRIA.

Eventually, the library at home became insufficient for Germain's intellectual needs, and at age 18 she sought a better situation. She was able to obtain lecture notes of courses taught at the École Polytechnique, and was particularly interested in JOSEPH-LOUIS LAGRANGE's lectures on analysis. Although not registered, Germain pretended to be a student, taking the pseudonym Le Blanc, and submitted a term paper on analysis to Lagrange. Lagrange was duly impressed by its originality, and he sought out its author. On discovering that the writer was actually Germain, Lagrange became her sponsor and mathematical adviser.

Germain obtained higher education purely through correspondence with the great scholars of Europe; by this means she became well versed in mathematics, literature, biology, and philosophy. She became interested in certain problems of number theory after reading ADRIEN-MARIE LEGENDRE's 1798 *Théorie des nombres* (Theory of numbers), and a voluminous correspondence between the two soon arose. In the course of these communications they collaborated on mathematical results, and some of Sophie's discoveries were included in the second edition of the *Théorie*.

Also at this time she read CARL FRIEDRICH GAUSS's *Disquisitiones arithmeticae* (Arithmetical investigations), and entered into a correspondence with him under the pseudonym of Le Blanc. In 1807, when French troops were occupying Hannover, she feared for Gauss's safety in Göttingen. Hoping there would be no repeat of Archimedes's death in the person of Gauss, she communicated to the French commander there, who was a friend of her family. In this fashion, Gauss came to know her true identity.

Among her work on number theory, Germain worked on the famous problem called Fermat's last theorem, which was solved by Andrew Wiles in 1994. The theorem is a conjecture by PIERRE DE FERMAT, which states that there are no integer solutions x, y, z to the equation $x^n 1 y^n 5 z^n$ if n is an integer greater than two. Germain was able to show that no positive integer solutions exist if x, y, and z are relatively prime (have no common divisors) to one another and to n, where n is any prime less than 100.

Germain was interested in mathematics other than number theory; indeed, she made contributions to applied mathematics and philosophy. In 1808 the German physicist Ernst Chladni visited Paris and conducted experiments in acoustics and elasticity. He would take a horizontal plate of metal or glass, sprinkle sand uniformly on top of it, and then cause vibrations in the plate by rubbing the edge with a violin bow. The resulting oscillations would move the particles of sand into certain stable clusters, called Chladni figures. In 1811 the Académie des Sciences offered a prize for the best explanation of the phenomenon; the challenge was to formulate a mathematical theory of elastic surfaces that would agree with the Chladni figures.

Germain attempted to solve the problem, and after a series of revisions and subsequent contests, she won the prize in 1816 with a paper bearing her own name. Her work treated the vibrations of curved and plane elastic surfaces in generality. In 1821 she produced an enhanced version of her prize paper, in which she stated that the law for the general vibrating elastic surface is given by a fourth order partial differential equation. One of the concepts playing a role in this work was the notion of mean curvature, which was an average of the principal curvatures, that is the curvatures of a surface in two perpendicular directions.

In later work Germain expanded on the physics of vibrating curved elastic surfaces, considering the effect of variable thickness. She also contributed to philosophy, developing the concept of unity of thought—that science and the humanities would always be unified with respect to their motivation, methodology, and cultural importance. She died on June 27, 1831, in Paris.

Germain's work has not received a great following, and this may be partly due to her gender. Her work on number theory and differential equations was of the highest quality, and she contributed to the development of differential geometry through her notion of mean curvature.

Further Reading

Bucciarelli, L. Sophie Germain: An Essay in the History of the Theory of Elasticity. Boston: Kluwer, 1980.

Dalmedico, A. "Sophie Germain," Scientific American 265 (1991): 117–122.

Grinstein, L., and P. Campbell. Women of Mathematics. New York: Greenwood Press, 1987.

⊠ Gibbs, Josiah Willard
(1839–1903)
American
Mechanics, Geometry

In the 19th century physicists were tremendously interested in several topics of thermodynamics (the theory of heat); even the basic axioms of the discipline were not universally agreed upon. Josiah Gibbs made important mathematical and physical contributions to this project, laying the foundations for the modern theory of statistical mechanics.

Josiah Willard Gibbs studied the theory of heat and promoted the spread of vector analysis. *(Courtesy of AIP Emilio Segrè Visual Archives)*

Josiah Gibbs was born in New Haven, Connecticut, on February 11, 1839, to an affluent family. His father, of the same name, was a well-known professor of sacred literature at Yale, and Gibbs's mother, Mary Anna Van Cleve Gibbs, raised four daughters in addition to Josiah. The boy grew up in New Haven and attended Yale, winning several prizes in Latin and mathematics and graduating in 1858. Gibbs continued his studies in the graduate engineering school, obtaining his Ph.D. in 1863, two years after his father's death.

He spent the next three years as a Latin tutor, and after the death of his mother and two sisters, Gibbs traveled to Europe to further his studies. He visited the universities of Paris, Berlin, and Heidelberg, remaining a year in each city, and greatly extended his knowledge of both mathematics and physics. This study abroad laid the foundation for his subsequent accomplishments in theoretical physics.

Gibbs returned to America in 1869, and was able to live, along with his two sisters, off his inheritance, residing in his childhood home close to Yale. Two years later he was appointed professor of mathematical physics at Yale, a position he held without salary for nine years. At this time Gibbs wrote his memoirs on thermodynamics, which undoubtably constitute his greatest contribution to science and mathematics.

His first published paper, "Graphical Methods in the Thermodynamics of Fluids," displayed an admirable mastery of thermodynamics. Gibbs assumed that entropy—the tendency for heat to dissipate—was as important as energy, temperature, pressure, and volume toward understanding the properties of heat flow, and he formulated a differential equation that relates these quantities elegantly. A second paper extended his results to three dimensions; characteristic of Gibbs's talent was his emphasis on a geometrical approach (as opposed to the algebraic approach). Through his analysis, Gibbs was able to demonstrate how various phases (solid, liquid, gas) of a substance could coexist.

Although these initial articles had a narrow readership in their respective journals, Gibbs sent copies of his work to various leading European physicists, including James Maxwell, and in this way gained wider recognition. Soon afterward, Gibbs completed his memoir *On the Equilibrium of Heterogeneous Substances*, which generalized his previous work and greatly extended the domain of thermodynamics to chemical, elastic, electromagnetic, and electrochemical phenomena. Generally, Gibbs stressed the importance of characterizing equilibrium as the state where entropy is maximized. This is equivalent to the minimum energy principle of mechanics. In this way, Gibbs's thought greatly impacted chemistry.

Gibbs's work reached continental scientists such as Max Planck, where it eventually exerted a substantial influence. Meanwhile, Gibbs was turning toward optics and the electromagnetic theory of light; he defended the electromagnetic theory of light against purely mechanical theories based on elastic ethers. In the realm of pure mathematics, Gibbs rejected the use of quaternions in the study of theoretical physics, and so he developed his own theory of vector analysis. A textbook based on his lectures was published on this topic in 1901.

In 1902 Gibbs produced a book on statistical mechanics that takes a statistical approach to physical systems by representing the coordinates and momenta of particles with probability distributions. The main theme of his work was the analogy between the average behavior of such statistical mechanical systems and the behavior produced by the laws of thermodynamics. Thus, his theory of statistical mechanics laid a mathematical foundation for the physics of heat flow. Although incomplete, Gibbs's work was a useful contribution to rational mechanics. Indeed, Gibbs's labors greatly advanced physics, and later came to dominate the whole field of thermodynamics.

Gibbs never married, and continued teaching at Yale until his death on April 28, 1903. Although he had made some contributions to engineering, such as the design of a new governor for steam engines, it is for his insightful analysis of thermodynamics—the importance of entropy, the relationship of entropy to equilibrium, and his statistical mechanical formulation of the field—that Gibbs is known.

Further Reading

Bumstead, H. "Josiah Willard Gibbs," *American Journal of Science* 4, no. 16 (September 1903).
Crowther, J. *Famous American Men of Science.* Freeport, N.Y.: Books for Libraries Press, 1969.
Rukeyser, M. *Willard Gibbs.* Garden City, N.Y.: Doubleday, Doran and Company, 1942.
Seeger, R. J. *Willard Gibbs, American Mathematical Physicist par Excellence.* Oxford: Pergamon Press, 1974.
Smith, P. "Josiah Willard Gibbs," *American Mathematical Society. Bulletin. New Series* 10 (1903).
Wheeler, L. *Josiah Willard Gibbs, the History of a Great Mind.* New Haven, Conn.: Yale University Press, 1962.

⊠   **Gödel, Kurt Friedrich**
(1906–1978)
Austrian
Logic

In the beginning of the 20th century, three schools of thought held sway over mathematical logic: formalism, intuitionism, and logicism. Formalism taught that mathematics was primarily a syntax into which meaning is introduced, intuitionism stressed the role of intuition over pure reason, and logicism viewed mathematics as part of logic. Kurt Gödel established a new mode of thought—namely, that mathematical logic was a branch of mathematics, that had only indirect ramifications on philosophy. His theorems, especially his incompleteness theorem, have earned him considerable fame as a first-rate mathematician, since his work is extremely relevant to epistemological questions (questions relating to the foundations of knowledge).

Kurt Gödel was born on April 28, 1906, in Brno, the Czech Republic, which at the time was part of the Austrian Empire. Rudolf Gödel, his father, was a weaver who eventually attained a significant amount of property. Marianne Handschuh, his mother, had a liberal education, and the household in which Gödel and his older brother Rudolf grew up was upper class. Gödel had a happy childhood, and was called "Mr. Why" by his family, due to his numerous questions. He was baptized as a Lutheran, and remained a theist (a believer in a personal God) throughout his life.

Gödel advanced rapidly through school, excelling in mathematics, languages, and religion at a German high school in Brno. He also be-

Kurt Gödel was a great logician famous for the incompleteness theory, which is concerned with the foundations of mathematics. *(Photograph by Richard Arens, courtesy of AIP Emilio Segrè Visual Archives)*

came interested in philosophy after 1920, and the famous philosopher Immanuel Kant was influential throughout Gödel's life. When he graduated in 1924, Gödel had already mastered much of university mathematics, and thus he was very well prepared to enter the University of Vienna. Initially he considered taking a degree in physics, but after some classes on number theory Gödel switched to mathematics. From 1926 to 1928 he was involved in the Vienna Circle, a group of logical positivists interested in epistemology. Gradually, Gödel fell away from these philosophers due to his own Platonic position. Platonism, as applied to the philosophy of mathematics, espouses a belief in the true abstract reality of mathematical objects (such as numbers), which attain concrete particular realizations in the world.

In 1929 Gödel's father died, and in the same year Gödel completed his dissertation. He received his doctorate in mathematics in 1930. This paper provided the completeness theorem for first-order logic, which showed that every valid formula in first-order logic was provable. The term *completeness* refers to the issue of whether every true mathematical theorem has a proof; thus, incomplete systems are somewhat mystical, in that they contain true statements that cannot be established through reason and logic alone. Later in 1930 Gödel announced his famous incompleteness theorem: There are true propositions of number theory for which no proof exists. This result had enormous ramifications in mathematics, since it effectively destroyed the efforts of mathematicians to construct a logical calculus that would prove all true statements; it also influenced philosophy and epistemology. The philosophical version of the theorem says that in any system of thought, one cannot produce a proof for every true statement, as long as one is restricted to that system.

In the following years Gödel published numerous articles on logic and worked as a lecturer at the University of Vienna. While extreme shyness made him a poor public speaker, the content of his lectures included the most recent research in the foundations of mathematics. In 1933 he visited the Institute for Advanced Study at Princeton (a mathematical think tank affiliated with Princeton University), where he would spend increasing amounts of time as the political situation in Europe deteriorated. Gödel also suffered from mental depression, and he stayed at a sanatorium in Europe in 1934 after a nervous breakdown. In 1935 he returned to America and continued his important new work in set theory, obtaining a significant breakthrough concerning the axiom of choice. Soon afterward he resigned, suffering from overwork and depression, and returned to Austria. His work from this time period showed that the axiom of choice and the continuum hypothesis, two important postulates of set theory, were relatively consistent (consistency means that a given postulate does not contradict the other axioms of the system).

In 1938 Gödel married Adele Porkert Nimbersky, a nightclub dancer. They were soon forced to flee back to the United States due to the Nazi persecution in Austria—Gödel's association with Jews and liberals made him a target for discrimination. He was prevented from continuing his lectureship at Vienna, and was even attacked by right-wing students. As a result, Gödel and his wife moved back to Princeton in 1940, escaping Austria to the east via the Trans-Siberian Railway.

At Princeton the introverted Gödel had a quiet social life; however, he did develop some close friendships with his colleagues, including Albert Einstein. Out of this relationship, Gödel became increasingly interested in the theory of relativity—later, after 1947, he contributed to cosmology by presenting mathematical models in which time travel was logically possible. In 1943 Gödel turned increasingly toward philosophical research, where he expressed his

Platonist views and criticized BERTRAND RUSSELL's logicism.

In the later portion of his life, Gödel received numerous honors and awards, such as the Einstein Award in 1951 and the National Medal of Science in 1974. It is interesting that he steadfastly refused to receive any honors from the Austrian academic institutions because of their previous treatment of him. In 1953 he became a full professor at the institute, continued his work on logic and cosmology, and in 1976 retired as an emeritus professor. He died on January 14, 1978, in Princeton, after suffering from depression, paranoia, and malnutrition—believing that his food was being poisoned, Gödel refused to eat and starved to death.

Kurt Gödel made extraordinary discoveries in mathematical logic and set theory. His work in cosmology and philosophy is also noteworthy. Gödel essentially established the framework for modern investigations. Since he showed that number theory was incomplete, the project of DAVID HILBERT and previous logicians to mechanize the proof making of mathematics became impractical. Instead, logicians began to focus on the completeness and consistency questions of various types of logical systems. This paradigm shift was due to Gödel's epochal incompleteness theorem. His results on the axiom of choice and continuum hypothesis emphasized the relative nature of any answer to these questions; here also, a rich new field of set theoretical research was spawned by Gödel's initial discoveries. In a broader sense, Gödel's ideas have influenced countless philosophers and computer scientists, with ramifications in epistemology and artificial intelligence.

Further Reading

Dawson, J. "Kurt Gödel in Sharper Focus," *The Mathematical Intelligencer* 6, no. 4 (1984): 9–17.
Hofstadter, D. *Gödel, Escher, Bach: An Eternal Golden Braid*. New York: Basic Books, 1999.

Wang, H. "Kurt Gödel's Intellectual Development," *The Mathematical Intelligencer* 1, no. 3 (1978): 182–185.

———. *Reflections on Kurt Gödel*. Cambridge, Mass.: MIT Press, 1987.

———. "Some Facts about Kurt Gödel," *Journal of Symbolic Logic* 46, no. 3 (1981): 653–659.

⊠ **Goldbach, Christian**
(1690–1764)
German
Number Theory, Analysis

Christian Goldbach was an amateur mathematician, possessing no formal training. Nevertheless, he corresponded with many scientists and mathematicians around Europe, and was one of the few persons who understood the works of PIERRE DE FERMAT and LEONHARD EULER. His contributions to mathematics were sporadic with flashes of brilliance. There were also surprising gaps in his knowledge. However, through his mathematical communications, he was able to participate in the mathematical inquiries of his time and stimulate others toward fundamental results.

Christian Goldbach was born in Königsberg, Prussia, on March 18, 1690. His father was a minister, and Goldbach received a good education, studying mathematics and medicine at the University of Königsberg. Around 1710 he began traveling about Europe, and made the acquaintance of several leading mathematicians, such as GOTTFRIED WILHELM VON LEIBNIZ, ABRAHAM DE MOIVRE, and DANIEL BERNOULLI. Sometime after 1725 Goldbach received a position as professor of mathematics as the Imperial Academy of Russia.

Goldbach was a skilled politician, and he advanced quickly in political circles to the detriment of his mathematical research. In 1728 he moved to Moscow to become tutor to the king's son Peter II; he returned to St. Petersburg in 1732 and quickly rose to a powerful position in the Imperial Academy. In 1737 he had administration of the academy, but was simultaneously rising in government circles. In 1742 he severed his ties with the academy, and eventually rose to the rank of privy councilor in 1760, overseeing the education of the royal family.

Goldbach's knowledge of advanced mathematics was acquired informally through discussions with mathematicians rather than through consistent reading. He became intrigued with infinite series in 1712 after meeting Nikolaus Bernoulli, and this date probably marks the beginning of his own research into that subject. Of his various papers, some of which repeat material already published by others, two show genuine originality: One treats the manipulation of infinite series, and the other concerns a theory of equations. Goldbach developed a method for transforming one series into another by adding and subtracting certain terms successively. These new terms were allowed to be divergent, so long as the end result was convergent. Second, Goldbach applies some results from number theory to test whether a given algebraic equation has a rational root. This method developed from a correspondence with Leonhard Euler, with whom Goldbach began communicating in 1729.

Besides these original contributions to mathematics, Goldbach kept abreast of current developments and entered into the dialogue of mathematicians regarding new results. For example, Goldbach communicated one of Fermat's conjectures on prime numbers to Euler, who was able to construct a counterexample. He is also famous for the Goldbach conjecture that every even integer could be expressed as the sum of two prime numbers. This conjecture remains unproved today.

Goldbach died on November 20, 1764, in Moscow. Although Goldbach undoubtably possessed considerable mathematical talent, this was not developed due to his success in civic affairs. However, Goldbach was able to stimulate research into mathematical ideas in his own time, and also in the modern era through his mysterious conjecture.

Further Reading

Yuan, W. *Goldbach Conjecture.* Singapore: World Scientific, 1984.

⊠   **Gosset, William**
(1876–1937)
British
Statistics

William Gosset, known informally as "Student," his common pseudonym, was an important figure in the development of mathematical statistics. Because he was not a professor at a university, his perspective on data analysis was practical, and his research addressed tangible, real-world statistical problems. Perhaps Gosset's most vital contribution to statistics was the realization that the "sampling" distribution is critical for inference. His work has had enduring relevance and influence on modern statistical procedures commonly used in science and medicine today.

William Sealy Gosset was born on June 13, 1876, in Canterbury, England, the eldest son of Colonel Frederic Gosset and Agnes Sealy. As a young man he studied mathematics and chemistry at Winchester College and New College at Oxford, where in 1899 he obtained a degree in the natural sciences. Soon afterward he joined the brewing company Arthur Guinness & Sons, which was located in Dublin, being employed as a chemist. In 1906 Gosset married Marjory Surtees, and later had two children.

In the course of his work on quality control, it became necessary to analyze the brewing process statistically. Eventually, in 1906 Gosset came to University College, London, to work under the statistician Karl Pearson. Previous work in statistics, much of it due to the efforts of CARL FRIEDRICH GAUSS, emphasized the importance of large samples and asymptotic distributions. The term *sample* refers to the data set, usually a collection of numbers, that represents repeated measurements of a phenomenon. The older work in statistics used approximations that relied upon large samples (roughly speaking, 30 or more data points), whereas the data available to Gosset came in a much smaller size. Since the present theory was inadequate to handle this situation, Gosset was forced to develop new methods applicable to small samples.

Over the next several years, Gosset contributed to statistical theory under the pseudonym "Student," and corresponded with a variety of statisticians, including SIR RONALD AYLMER FISHER, Jerzy Neyman, and Karl Pearson. Gosset's most famous paper, entitled *The Probable Error of a Mean,* analyzed the ubiquitous sample mean statistic from a small sample perspective and derived its distributional properties without relying upon a large sample approximation. The distribution of the scale-normalized sample mean statistic that Gosset discovered came to be known as Student's t distribution, and there is a corresponding statistical test, which is called Student's t test. This work, accomplished through a combination of mathematical analysis and Monte Carlo simulation, was later found to be optimal in statistical testing theory, and its importance is demonstrated through its continued use today, along with its descendant, the ANOVA (analysis of variance) procedure.

Gosset stayed with Guinness, obtaining an assistant in 1922, and gradually built up a modest statistics department there until 1934. In 1935 he moved to London to head the new Guinness brewery there. He continued his statistical work until his death on October 16, 1937, in Beaconsfield, England.

Gosset's contribution to mathematics was somewhat untraditional, for at that time most of the important research was taking place in the various universities. However, in the field of statistics more than other branches of mathematics, it is crucial for investigations to be motivated by practical problems; thus, it seems that Gosset was well situated. His emphasis on and development of small sample theory was pivotal for the evolution of mathematical statistics; most important, perhaps, was the attention he drew toward the sampling distribution of a statistic.

Further Reading

Pearson, E. *Student—A Statistical Biography of William Sealey Gosset*. Oxford, U.K.: Oxford University Press, 1990.

———. "Student as a Statistician," *Biometrika* 30 (1939): 210–250.

———. "Some Reflections on Continuity in the Development of Mathematical Statistics 1840–1894," *Biometrika* 54 (1967): 341–355.

⊠ **Grassmann, Hermann Günter**
(1809–1877)
German
Geometry, Algebra

Hermann Grassmann made substantial contributions to algebra and geometry during the 19th century. His ideas were so advanced that many of his colleagues failed to recognize their merit, but later generations quickly gravitated toward Grassmann's highly abstract and beautiful work.

Hermann Günter Grassmann was born on April 15, 1809, in Stettin, a town in Prussia, though now it lies in Poland. Grassmann taught at the high school in Stettin for most of his life; he began teaching in 1831 and continued until his death, except for a brief period (1834–36) at Berlin. While teaching, he was able to devote some of his time to personal research into algebra and geometry.

Grassmann is well known for his development of vector calculus, but his most important work was his 1844 *Die lineale Ausdehnungslehre* (The theory of linear extension). This book developed an abstract algebra—a set with certain rules of arithmetic operations that define how the symbols in the set interact—in which the symbols were geometric objects such as points, lines, and planes. His algebra gave certain rules for the interactions of these things. Grassmann also studied the subspaces of a given geometric space and developed a certain type of algebraic manifold (a high-dimensional surface given as the solution of an algebraic equation) that was later called the Grassmannian.

Grassmann also invented the concept of an exterior algebra—another algebra with a special product called the exterior product. This abstract structure was related to the quaternions of SIR WILLIAM ROWAN HAMILTON, and was later developed by William Clifford into a tool that has been quite useful in quantum mechanics. The exterior algebra is an important object of study in modern differential geometry. Grassmann's ideas were quite advanced for his time, and they were accepted slowly; this led to frustration for Grassmann, who in his later years turned away from mathematics to the study of Sanskrit. (His Sanskrit dictionary is still used today.) Besides his mathematical work, Grassmann also contributed to the literature of acoustics, electricity, and botany.

Grassmann died on September 26, 1877, in Stettin. Although disappointed by the underacceptance of his brilliant ideas, Grassmann achieved fame later on. At the end of the 19th century, more geometers began to discover his work; ÉLIE CARTAN was inspired to study differential forms (an example of the exterior product), which are important to differential geometry. Today, Grassmann is viewed as an early contributor to the budding field of algebraic geometry.

Further Reading

Fearnley-Sander, D. "Hermann Grassmann and the Creation of Linear Algebra," *The American Mathematical Monthly* 86, no. 10 (1979): 809–817.

———. "Hermann Grassmann and the Prehistory of Universal Algebra," *The American Mathematical Monthly* 89, no. 3 (1982): 161–166.

Heath, A. "Hermann Grassmann: The Neglect of His Work," *Monist* 27 (1917): 1–56.

⊠ **Green, George**
(1793–1841)
British
Calculus, Differential Equations

One of the most remarkable scientific theories of the 19th century—the mathematical theory of electricity—was largely developed by a self-taught miller, George Green. His contributions were outstanding, but Green little realized their importance, and much of his life is shrouded in obscurity.

George Green was born in July 1793 in Sneinton, England. His exact birthday is not known, but he was baptized on July 14, 1793. He was named after his father, a prosperous baker. Green's mother was Sarah Butler, who helped Green's father to buy his own bakery in Nottingham. Green had one sister, Ann, who was two years younger.

Green received very little education. When he was nine years old, he was sent to Robert Goodacre's school for two years, where he first became interested in mathematics. It is unknown how Green became interested in mathematics, but he applied himself to the subject vigorously, until he surpassed Goodacre. Throughout his life, Green continued to study mathematics in his spare moments.

In 1802 Green left school to work in his father's business, which became quite successful over the years. Green's father bought a piece of land in 1807, and there built a mill; this was destined to become Green's private study. In 1817 a house was built beside the mill, and Green's family moved there. Green continued his own mathematical investigations in his spare moments away from work.

Green had little access to current mathematics and could not stay abreast of the French developments. However, he nevertheless displayed a familiarity with contemporary mathematics in his later works, and it is hypothesized that the Cambridge graduate John Toplis tutored him. In any event, Green acquired great familiarity with British and French mathematics, and he mastered calculus and differential equations. Meanwhile, Green had several children by Jane Smith, the daughter of the mill's manager; he met Smith sometime before 1823. In this year he also gained access to the transactions of the Royal Society, which increased his resources.

The next years were difficult: His parents died, and two daughters were born. Despite the numerous disturbances, Green managed to study mathematics in the top floor of the mill, and in 1828 published *An Essay on the Application of Mathematical Analysis to the Theories of Electricity and Magnetism*. This was certainly one of the most important mathematical works ever, since it gave a mathematical theory for electricity—his work introduced the potential function, demonstrated the relationship between surface area integrals and volume integrals (known as Green's formula), and defined the important "Green's function" that is ubiquitous in the theory of differential equations. This monumental work was little appreciated by its provincial audience, but one reader named Sir Edward Bromhead encouraged Green to pursue his mathematical gifts.

As a result of Bromhead's friendship, Green was introduced to several mathematicians, including CHARLES BABBAGE. From 1830 Green published three additional papers of great worth, treating the topics of electricity and hydrodynamics. Upon Bromhead's advice, Green left his mill in 1833 to enroll at Cambridge as an undergraduate. There Green excelled at mathematics, but had difficulty in his other subjects due to his poor education. Nevertheless he graduated fourth in his class in 1837, and afterward stayed on at Cambridge, conducting his own research. He obtained a Perse fellowship in 1839 despite the requirement necessitating bachelorhood, since Green was legally unmarried. However, he had seven children by Jane Smith.

Green produced papers on hydrodynamics, optics, and the refraction of sound, such as *Mathematical Investigations Concerning the Laws of the Equilibrium of Fluids Analagous to the Electric Fluid* (1833) and *On the Determination of the Interior and Exterior Attractions of Ellipsoids of Varying Densities* (1835). In 1840 he fell ill, and returned to Nottingham to recuperate. Green made out his will (his estate went to his family) and died on May 31, 1841, in Nottingham.

The importance of Green's work was hardly realized (neither by him nor by his contemporaries) during his own lifetime. A few years later, in 1850, Green's works were republished by William Thomson, an event of great interest to JOSEPH LIOUVILLE. Through James Clerk Maxwell (a great scientist who worked on electricity, magnetism, and heat) and others, Green's theory of electricity would be fully developed by the turn of the 20th century. Thus, Green's work became greatly influential to science. But Green is best known today for Green's theorem and Green's function, which are both highly significant in the theory of differential equations.

Further Reading

Cannell, D. *George Green: Mathematician and Physicist 1793–1841: The Background to His Life and Work.* London: Athlone Press, 1993.

Cannell, D., and N. Lord. "George Green, Mathematician and Physicist 1793–1841," *Mathematical Gazette* 66 (1993): 26–51.

Edge, D. "The Omission of George Green from 'British Mathematics (1800–1830),'" *Bulletin of the Institute of Mathematics and Its Applications* 16, no. 2–3 (1980): 37.

⊠ Gregory, James
(1638–1675)
British
Calculus, Geometry, Algebra

James Gregory, one of the greatest mathematicians of the 17th century, was also one of the least known, largely due to his own isolation. Indeed, his work on the foundations of calculus, conducted independently of and contemporaneously with SIR ISAAC NEWTON, were not recognized until centuries after his death; and in many other areas of mathematics, such as number theory, algebraic equations, integration, and differential equations, Gregory significantly

James Gregory, a little-known mathematician who made many early discoveries in calculus *(Courtesy of the Library of Congress)*

anticipated the discoveries of later mathematicians.

James Gregory was born in November 1638 in Drumoak, Scotland, to John Gregory, a cleric learned in theology, and Janet Anderson, whose brother was a pupil of FRANÇOIS VIÈTE. Gregory was the youngest child of his parents, having two older brothers, Alexander and David. His mother, who was intellectually gifted, educated Gregory. After his father's death in 1651, his brother David oversaw his mathematical instruction. This involved reading EUCLID OF ALEXANDRIA's *Elements*, which James found quite easy.

Gregory pursued higher education at Marischal College in Aberdeen. His health was poor, and he suffered from quartan fever while still a youth. While in school, Gregory became interested in telescopes and completed his first book, *Optica Promota* (The advance of optics). This work described a reflecting telescope—a novel invention that increased the telescope's power—and the mathematical equations of reflection. The book covers mathematical astronomy through several postulates and theorems. In 1663 Gregory traveled to London, and was able to get his book published; his telescope was constructed by Robert Hooke some 10 years later.

In 1664 Gregory traveled to Italy to continue his mathematical studies. He spent much of his time at the University of Padua with the mathematician Stefano Angeli; there Gregory applied infinite series to the calculation of the areas of the circle and the hyperbola. Gregory also learned the method of tangents (the predecessor of the theory of differentiation), and made such discoveries in early calculus to earn him the right of discovery. Indeed, his early work on calculus mirrored the labors of Newton, although neither mathematician was aware of the other's work. Certainly, Gregory received no credit for his discoveries during his own lifetime, since he was reclusive and unwilling to disseminate his knowledge. For example, in *Vera circuli et hyperbolae quadratura* (The true squaring of the circle and the hyperbola) (1667), Gregory lays the foundations for infinitesimal geometry. The thesis of this document was that the numbers pi and *e* are transcendental—a concept that few mathematicians of the time even grasped. Although flawed, Gregory's arguments included an amazing breadth of ideas, such as convergence, algebraic functions, and iterations.

His *Geometriae pars universalis* (The universal part of geometry) (1668), a first attempt at a calculus textbook, clearly showed that differentiation and integration are inverse operations. After concluding his work at Padua, Gregory returned to London in 1668 and became involved in a dispute with CHRISTIAAN HUYGENS. The latter had received Gregory's *Geometriae pars universalis* for review, and accused Gregory of having stolen some of his own ideas. In retrospect, this was impossible, but it nevertheless soured relations between the two mathematicians and fostered Gregory's reluctance to publish.

During the summer of this year, Gregory obtained the infinite series expansions for the trigonometric functions and found the antiderivative of the secant function, solving a problem in navigation. At meetings of the Royal Society—to which he was elected a fellow in 1668—Gregory discussed scientific topics such as astronomy, gravitation, and mechanics. Through the intervention of another fellow, Charles II was persuaded to create the Regius chair at St. Andrews University for Gregory, in order to facilitate his continuing mathematical research.

Gregory took up the post, and in 1669 was married to Mary Jamesome; they had two daughters. Gregory's teaching was not well received, partly because the students were inadequately prepared. The educational style of St. Andrews focused on the classics and placed little emphasis on current developments in science and mathematics. Later, the faculty rebelled against him, claiming that his mathematical teachings had a negative impact on their own courses; his salary was even withheld.

Meanwhile, Gregory continued his own research. On learning of ISAAC BARROW's work, he was able to extend it and greatly develop the foundations of calculus—for example, he discovered Taylor's theorem long before Brook Taylor did. When Gregory became aware of the work Newton was doing on calculus, he deferred his own publications in order to avoid another nasty dispute. He also discovered the refraction of light, but did not pursue further research on this topic, again in deference to Newton. Gregory was also involved in astronomy, and actually took up a collection personally in order to build an observatory at St. Andrews in 1673. Relations with the St. Andrews faculty had become so odious that he left for the University of Edinburgh in 1674, taking up the chair of mathematics there.

Gregory held his post for only one year before dying of a stroke in October 1675 in Edinburgh. He was only 36 years old. His last year was especially productive, as Gregory made inroads into Diophantine equations. Before many other mathematicians, he began to realize that the quintic equation did not admit rational solutions; NIELS HENRIK ABEL would prove this more than a century later. Gregory is a fascinating character, since his tremendous contributions to science and mathematics had gone largely unnoticed until the early 20th century when his true contributions were revealed. Besides being a codiscoverer of calculus and infinitesimal geometry, Gregory developed tests for convergence (such as AUGUSTIN-LOUIS CAUCHY's ratio test), defined the Riemann integral, developed a theory of differential equations that allowed for singularities, and attempted to establish the transcendence of pi. Thus, Gregory was far ahead of most of his contemporaries; however, his influence was negligible due to the obscurity of his life and his reluctance to publish.

Further Reading

Dehn, M., and E. Hellinger. "Certain Mathematical Achievements of James Gregory," *The American Mathematical Monthly* 50 (1943): 149–163.

H

Hamilton, Sir William Rowan
(1805–1865)
Irish
Complex Analysis, Algebra, Mechanics

In the 19th century the concept of the complex number was further developed, and it was found to be a useful tool for understanding other branches of mathematics. A similar type of number relevant to quantum mechanics is the so-called quaternion, which was discovered by the prodigy Sir William Rowan Hamilton. Although he made contributions to optics, mechanics, and general algebra, he is most famous for the quaternions and his acceptance of noncommutativity in algebraic systems.

William Rowan Hamilton was born in Dublin, Ireland, on August 4, 1805, and from an early age he displayed a remarkable genius for languages. Hamilton was educated by his uncle, and the boy had mastered Greek, Hebrew, and Latin by age five. He also possessed mathematical talent, being capable of rapid calculation; around 1820 Hamilton read through SIR ISAAC NEWTON's works and began his own astronomical observations through his telescope.

Around 1822 Hamilton's interest in mathematics reached a new phase, and he began his own research. He investigated the properties of curves and surfaces, which eventually led to his *Theory of Systems of Rays* of 1827. Meanwhile, he had entered Trinity College, having achieved the top score on his entrance examinations; he continued to win special honors in classics and science throughout his college career.

Upon graduation in 1827, Hamilton was appointed astronomer royal at Dunsink Observatory, and also became a professor of astronomy at Trinity. However, he did little actual observation, focusing his energy on pure mathematics. His first work on optics introduced his notion of the "characteristic function," which described the mathematical portion of optics completely. His theory was independent of whether one viewed light as particle or wave, and thus Hamilton largely freed himself from this contentious debate.

Next Hamilton applied his characteristic function to celestial mechanics in his 1833 paper *On a General Method of Expressing the Paths of Light and of the Planets by the Coefficients of a Characteristic Function*. Later in 1834 he applied the same principles to dynamics in *On a General Method in Dynamics*. These papers were hard to read, owing to Hamilton's terse style, and thus they did not enjoy much popularity. He introduced the so-called Hamilton equation for the energy of a conservative system, which is ubiquitous in modern mechanics. Although the Hamiltonian formulation of mechanics had

Sir William Rowan Hamilton worked in the field of algebra, and developed a number system for four-dimensional spaces, known as quaternions, which is used in physics. *(Courtesy of the Library of Congress)*

little practical advantage over the prior Lagrangian approach, it did carry over easily into the quantum mechanical situation. Hamilton's theory also maintained a close affinity between optics and mechanics.

His research led him to the discovery of general methods in the calculus of variations. More important, Hamilton discovered the quaternions in 1843. He had earlier become interested in a geometric explanation of the complex numbers, and in 1835 he presented a *Preliminary and Elementary Essay on Algebra as the Science of Pure Time*, which describes the complex numbers as points in the plane with a special rule for addition and multiplication. The intriguing title reveals

Hamilton's Kantian philosophy—geometry was the science of pure space, and algebra was the science of pure time. From this standpoint, Hamilton attempted to construct an analogous algebra for three-dimensional space. This was subsequently proved to be impossible, and Hamilton eventually formulated his new algebra in four dimensions. The resulting quadruples were called quaternions; they could be added, multiplied, and divided into each other according to certain rules. The resulting algebra was a first example of a noncommutative system; part of Hamilton's genius lay in recognizing that there was nothing innately illogical about this situation. More than a century later, quaternions and other noncommutative algebras exert a profound influence on quantum mechanics and quantum computers.

The story is related that Hamilton's sudden discovery occurred on a bridge across the Royal Canal in Dublin, on October 16, 1843; he scratched the relevant formula into the stones of the bridge. The quaternions were not immediately accepted, as the vector analysis of JOSIAH WILLARD GIBBS was more popular; Hamilton's difficult treatise, the *Elements of Quaternions* (published in 1867 after his death), was inaccessible to most of his contemporaries.

Hamilton received many honors during his life, and served as the president of the Royal Irish Academy from 1837 to 1845. The lord lieutenant of Ireland knighted him in 1835 for his work as a scientist. Hamilton was thwarted in love as a young man, but in 1833 he married Helen Bayly, by whom he had two sons and a daughter. Hamilton was an avid poet, but his friend William Wordsworth encouraged him to concentrate on mathematics, where his true gifts lay. He was full of energy and had many literary friends, including Ellen de Vere and Samuel Coleridge. After the death of his first love, Catherine Disney, in 1853, Hamilton fell into alcoholism; he died in Dublin on September 2, 1865.

Given the early genius of his childhood, Hamilton may have expected more of himself mathematically. However, he left his mark on the field of mechanics through his use of the principle of least action, the derivation of the characteristic function, and the Hamiltonian equation for the energy of a system. He also profoundly influenced the development of abstract algebra through his discovery of the quaternions. The applications of these strange numbers are still being explored today.

Further Reading

Arunachalam, P. "W. R. Hamilton and His Quaternions," *Mathematical Education* 6, no. 4 (1990): 261–266.

Graves, R. *Life of Sir William Rowan Hamilton*. New York: Arno Press, 1975.

Hankins, L. *Sir William Rowan Hamilton*. Baltimore, Md.: Johns Hopkins University Press, 1980.

MacDuffee, C. "Algebra's Debt to Hamilton." *Scripta Mathematica* 10 (1944): 25–35.

Synge, J. "The Life and Early Work of Sir William Rowan Hamilton," *Scripta Mathematica* 10 (1944): 13–24.

⊠   **Hardy, Godfrey Harold**
(1877–1947)
British
Number Theory, Analysis

One of the most famous mathematical collaborations of the 20th century was between Godfrey Hardy and John Littlewood. Their research into modern number theory, together with the genius of SRINIVASA RAMANUJAN, greatly advanced the field. During his lifetime, Hardy was recognized as the leading British mathematician in pure mathematics.

Godfrey Harold Hardy was born in Cranleigh, England, on February 7, 1877. His parents were both intellectuals with an interest in mathematics; his father, Isaac Hardy, was a master at Cranleigh School. Thus, the young Hardy and his two sisters received an excellent education, in which they were encouraged to ask questions.

From a young age, Hardy was good with numbers; at age 13 he attended Winchester College on a scholarship, and in 1896 came to Trinity College in Cambridge. Hardy was successful at several competitions involving the rapid calculation of problems, earning a Smith's Prize in 1901. He developed an affinity for mathematical analysis after reading CAMILLE JORDAN's *Cours d'analyse* (Course in analysis) at the instigation of one of his professors. In the next 10 years Hardy attacked a series of research problems concerning the convergence of infinite series and integrals. His 1908 text *A Course on Pure Mathematics* became a classic, effectively transforming undergraduate mathematics education through its clear exposition of number, function, and limit.

Hardy was a lecturer at Trinity College until 1919, when he became a professor of geometry at Oxford. During this time, he had begun his fruitful collaboration with Littlewood, which resulted in about 100 joint papers on Diophantine approximation, the additive and multiplicative theory of numbers, the Riemann zeta function, and infinite series.

In 1913 Hardy received a manuscript from the amateur Indian mathematician Srinivasa Ramanujan. He quickly discerned the genius of the author, who had been able to obtain advanced mathematical results in number theory without formal training, and arranged for Ramanujan to come to England in 1914. For the next three years, the two worked intensively on a series of mathematical results—Hardy's experience with analysis and Ramanujan's intuitive genius with numbers led to many great achievements, including an asymptotic formula for the number of partitions of a given integer. Sadly, Ramanujan fell ill in 1917, and he returned to India two years later, dying in 1920.

Hardy founded a flourishing school of research at Oxford, and returned to Cambridge in 1931 as a professor of pure mathematics. He never married, but dwelt with his devoted sister. Hardy's main passion was mathematics, although he was also interested in cricket and was a confirmed atheist. His mastery of the English language increased the popularity of his literature, and he was known to be lively and enthusiastic. He died in Cambridge on December 1, 1947.

Hardy's research into analytic number theory advanced the field. His work with Ramanujan and Littlewood led to fundamental results in the study of number, and he stimulated and encouraged many younger mathematicians during his life.

Further Reading

Chan, L. "Godfrey Harold Hardy (1877–1947)—the Man and the Mathematician," *Menemui Mathematik. Discovering Mathematics* 1, no. 3 (1979): 1–13.

Fletcher, C. "G. H. Hardy—Applied Mathematician," *Bulletin of the Institute of Mathematics and Its Applications* 16, nos. 2–3 (1980): 61–67.

Milne, E. "Obituary: Godfrey Harold Hardy," *Royal Astronomical Society. Monthly Notices* 108 (1948): 44–46.

Newman, M. "Godfrey Harold Hardy, 1877–1947," *The Mathematical Gazette* 32 (1948): 50–51.

Snow, C. "Foreword," in *A Mathematician's Apology* by G. H. Hardy. Cambridge, U.K.: Cambridge University Press, 1967.

⊠ al-Haytham, Abu Ali (Alhazen)
(ca. 965–ca. 1040)
Arabian
Geometry

The Arabic mathematician and natural philosopher Abu Ali al-Haytham, also known as Alhazen, played an important role in preserving and transmitting the classical knowledge of the Greeks. He made numerous contributions to optics and astronomy, investigating light, vision, refraction, sundials, and the height of the stars. In mathematics, he is known for his treatment of "Alhazen's problem," where he builds on the knowledge of his Greek and Arabic predecessors.

Little is known of al-Haytham's early life, and many of the accounts of his middle years are conflicting. Apparently, he left Iraq during the reign of the Egyptian caliph al-Hakim, who had founded a famous library in Cairo. Al-Haytham, already a famous mathematician, had made the claim that he could regulate the flow of waters on the Nile through certain constructions; the Egyptian caliph then invited him to Egypt to carry out his boast. Al-Haytham had based his claim on the assumption that the upper Nile entered Egypt through high ground, and he soon discovered that his project would be impossible due to the unexpectedly different terrain. Ashamed and afraid of reprisal, he confessed his failure to the caliph, who put him in charge of a government office. There, al-Haytham pretended to be insane, fearing the anger of the capricious caliph, and was confined in his house until al-Hakim's death. Then al-Haytham revealed his sanity, and he spent the rest of his life writing scientific texts and teaching students.

Another account relates that al-Haytham first occupied the office of minister at Basra, but in order to devote himself purely to the pursuit of science and learning, he feigned madness to escape his official duties. Afterward he journeyed to Egypt, where he spent his life at the Azhar Mosque, making copies of EUCLID OF ALEXANDRIA's *Elements* about once a year. He died around 1040 in Cairo.

In his autobiography al-Haytham reflected on his doubts regarding various religious sects and became convinced that there could be only one truth. He turned toward the philosophical sciences of mathematics, physics, and metaphysics as subjects in which truth could be more easily obtained by rational inquiry after the manner of Aristotle. Al-Haytham wrote on many subjects, including logic, ethics, politics, poetry, music, and theology. He achieved fame in mathematics for his treatment of "Alhazen's problem," which concerns the reflection of light from a surface. If one takes any two points on the reflecting surface, be it flat or curved, the problem is to find a third position on the surface where light from one point will be reflected to the other. CLAUDIUS PTOLEMY had shown that there exists a unique point for concave spherical mirrors. Al-Haytham set out to solve the problem for all spherical, cylindrical, and conical surfaces, whether convex or concave. Although he was not always successful, he did demonstrate his great facility with higher Greek mathematics. His general solution is based on six geometrical lemmas, or steps; he would apply these lemmas in succession to various kinds of surfaces. These solutions are included in his *Optics*.

About 20 other writings of al-Haytham deal entirely with mathematics. Some of them deal with the solution of difficulties arising from certain parts of Euclid's *Elements*. His *Solution of the Difficulties in Euclid's Elements* attempts to treat most of the problems arising from Euclid, giving alternative constructions in certain cases and replacing indirect proofs with direct proofs. It seems that al-Haytham intended this, along with another work, to form a commentary on Euclid. In the axioms of Euclid, he attempts to replace the troublesome fifth postulate—which states that parallel lines never intersect—with a postulate involving equidistance. There had been many Islamic attempts to prove the fifth postulate, and al-Haytham was able to deduce the parallel postulate from his postulate on equidistance, though he used the concept of motion in his proof, which is somewhat foreign to Greek geometry.

Al-Haytham also composed two works on the quadrature of lunes—crescent-shaped figures. These contain various propositions on the geometry of lunes, and the subject is related to the topic of squaring the circle (the construction of a square with area equal to that of a specified circle). In another tract al-Haytham demonstrates the possibility of squaring the circle, without providing an explicit construction. In *On Analysis* he discusses the principles of analysis (breaking down) and synthesis (putting together) used in the discovery and proof of mathematical theorems and constructions. He illustrates these principles through applying them to arithmetic, geometry, astronomy, and music, which at that time were considered to be the four mathematical disciplines. He stresses the role of "scientific intuition," when a certain property is yet to be proved, and can be conjectured only from evidence. Such conjectures, led by the intuition, must be made before the process of analysis and synthesis can be made. This seems to be related to more modern notions of scientific investigation.

Further Reading

Hogendijk, J. *Ibn al-Haytham's "Completion of the Conics."* New York: Springer-Verlag, 1985.

Langermann, Y. *Ibn al-Haytham's "On the Configuration of the World."* New York: Garland, 1990.

Rashed, R. *The Development of Arabic Mathematics: Between Arithmetic and Algebra.* Boston: Kluwer Academic Press, 1994.

Sabra, A. *The Optics of ibn al-Haytham.* London: Warburg Institute, University of London, 1989.

Heaviside, Oliver
(1850–1925)
British
Mechanics

Oliver Heaviside is known for his use of mathematical techniques and ideas in the fields of electrical engineering and physics, and in this sense anticipated the use of Laplace and Fourier transforms, which became ubiquitous later on.

In his own day he acquired some fame due to his innovations in electrical engineering, and he influenced the development of mathematical physics.

Heaviside was the youngest of four sons born to Thomas Heaviside, an artist, and his wife Rachel Elizabeth West. He was born on May 18, 1850, in London. He was entirely self-taught and acquired a level of understanding that eventually earned him an honorary doctorate from the University of Göttingen. While a teenager, Heaviside engaged in electrical experimentation, and he published his first technical article at age 22. From 1870 to 1874 he was a telegraph operator at Newcastle-on-Tyne. After this time he lived privately (with narrow means) through the assistance of his brother.

Starting in 1873 Heaviside published several papers on electrical engineering that made telegraphy practical, despite the opposition of several powerful engineers who disagreed with Heaviside's correct theories. Heaviside claimed that additional coils added to a long-distance cable would improve performance, and this was later shown to be correct. The slow acceptance of Heaviside's ideas was due not only to his lack of reputation and credentials, but also to his utilization of sophisticated mathematical tools to formulate and express his theories.

Heaviside saw the benefit of operational calculus to the investigation of transients, foreseeing the use of Laplace and Fourier transforms in electrical engineering. He also developed a vector notation for performing calculations in three-dimensional system, which was along the lines of JOSIAH WILLARD GIBBS's system and in contrast to SIR WILLIAM ROWAN HAMILTON's quaternionic formulation. Heaviside was the first to write the "telegrapher's equation," which is a differential equation involving voltage and resistance. This equation also depends on constants representing capacitance and inductance, terms that Heaviside invented. This equation has numerous applications to dynamical systems.

Besides these mathematical contributions, Heaviside introduced a new system of electromagnetic units, correctly predicted the existence of a reflecting ionized region surrounding the Earth, and proposed a theory of motion for an electric charge. His fame spread during his life, resulting in his election to the Royal Society in 1891. Although he was extremely generous to others who needed his scientific help, his financial situation inhibited his continued research; various professional societies and his friends later supported him. He died in his seaside cottage in Paignton on February 3, 1925.

Heaviside introduced useful mathematics into physics and electrical engineering. The former subject was, of course, already mathematically oriented, but neither took full advantage of current mathematical techniques. In this way, Heaviside set a pattern for 20th-century engineering, as mathematical ideas have been increasingly instrumental for designing new technologies.

Further Reading

Nahin, P. *Oliver Heaviside, Sage in Solitude: The Life, Work, and Times of an Electrical Genius of the Victorian Age.* New York: IEEE Press, 1988.

Yavetz, I. *From Obscurity to Enigma: The Work of Oliver Heaviside, 1872–1889.* Boston: Birkäuser Verlag, 1995.

⊠ **Hermite, Charles**
(1822–1901)
French
Algebra, Analysis

After the deaths of CARL FRIEDRICH GAUSS, AUGUSTIN-LOUIS CAUCHY, CARL JACOBI, and GUSTAV PETER LEJEUNE DIRICHLET in the 1850s, Europe was deprived of its best mathematicians. In the areas of arithmetic and analysis, Charles Hermite became the sole successor to these giants, retaining his position of glory for many years. Not only was he exceedingly influential in his own time, but Hermite also laid important groundwork for 20th-century research as well.

Charles Hermite was born in Dieuze, France, on December 24, 1822, the sixth child of seven. His mother was Madeleine Lallemand and his father was Ferdinand Hermite, an artist and engineer. In 1829 the family moved to Nancy, where Charles attended the Collège de Nancy. He continued his studies in Paris at the Collège Henri IV and the Collège Louis-le-Grand, but his performance was not spectacular. Hermite focused on reading the works of LEONHARD EULER, Gauss, and JOSEPH-LOUIS LAGRANGE instead of preparing for his examinations.

From 1840 to 1841, while at Louis-le-Grand, Hermite published his first two papers, wherein he attempted to prove the impossibility of solving the quintic by radicals—he was unaware of NIELS HENRIK ABEL's results. Despite scoring poorly on his entrance examinations, Hermite was admitted to the École Polytechnique in 1842. He was refused further study due to lameness in his right foot that forced him to use a cane; he was allowed to resume his studies due to the intervention of certain influential persons. At about this time Hermite entered the social circle of Joseph Bertrand—he would later marry Bertrand's sister.

Hermite began serious work on Jacobi's famous inversion problem for hyperelliptic integrals, and in 1843 he succeeded in generalizing Abel's work on elliptic functions to hyperelliptic functions. He communicated his result to Jacobi, which initiated a six-year correspondence and gained him renown in the mathematical community.

Hermite became an admissions examiner at the École Polytechnique in 1848, and he acquired a more permanent position in 1862, eventually becoming professor of analysis in 1869. During these years he was enormously productive, and corresponded heavily with many mathematicians.

From 1843 to 1847 he focused on elliptic function. One of the most intriguing problems of the time was the inversion of integrals of algebraic functions, and Hermite made progress on this question by introducing theta functions.

Next, in 1847 Hermite turned to number theory, generalizing some of Gauss's results on quadratic forms. From here he further extended his results to algebraic numbers (which included square roots), deriving some of their fundamental properties. In 1854 he studied the theory of invariants, discovering the reciprocity law, which gave a correspondence between binary forms. Hermite then applied the theory of invariants to abelian functions in 1855, and his results became a foundation for CAMILLE JORDAN's theory of "abelian groups." From 1858 to 1864 he researched the quintic equation and class number relations, and in 1873 he turned to the approximation of functions. It is noteworthy that Hermite proved the transcendence of the number e in 1873; his methods would later be extended to establish the transcendence of pi. His work covered Legendre functions, series for elliptic integrals, continued fractions, Bessel functions, Laplace integrals, and special differential equations.

Hermite was known as a cheerful man who was unselfish in sharing his discoveries with others. He fell ill with smallpox in 1856, and later became a devout Catholic under Cauchy's influence. During his life he received many honors, being awarded membership at several learned societies. He died in Paris on January 14, 1901.

Hermite is chiefly remembered as an algebraist and analyst. He invented the so-called Hermitian forms, which are a complex generalization of quadratic forms, as well as the Hermitian polynomials, which are of use in the approximation of functions. His work has been absorbed into more general structures, and in this sense his thought lives on in the more abstract mathematics of the 20th century.

Further Reading

Stander, D. "Makers of Modern Mathematics: Charles Hermite," *Bulletin of the Institute of Mathematics and Its Applications* 24, no. 7–8 (1988): 120–121.

⊠   **Hilbert, David**
(1862–1943)
German
Logic, Algebra, Analysis, Geometry

David Hilbert is probably best known for his list of 23 outstanding mathematical problems, which guided much of 20th-century research. However, much more important were his contributions to the theory of algebraic invariants, algebraic number theory, and the foundations of mathematics. Few mathematicians have had so profound an impact on subsequent research as Hilbert. His foresight into the future of mathematics was uncannily accurate, even bordering on the prophetic.

Hilbert's family consisted of German Protestants living in East Prussia. His father, Otto Hilbert, was a judge in Königsberg, where David Hilbert was born on January 23, 1862. It is said that he inherited his mathematical talents from his mother. The young Hilbert attended the Friedrichskolleg in Königsberg beginning in 1870, and he studied at the University of Königsberg from 1880 to 1884, obtaining his Ph.D. in 1885. After some traveling, Hilbert obtained a position at the University of Königsberg in 1892, and in the same year he married Käthe Jerosch. In 1895 he was appointed to a chair at the University of Göttingen, where he remained until his retirement in 1930.

Hilbert's first research, in the period up to 1893, was on algebraic forms. He studied the theory of algebraic invariants, approaching the subject from a revolutionary symbolic standpoint and dispensing with the algorithmic methods of the past. It is noteworthy that the modern approach to algebra follows Hilbert's abstract path.

David Hilbert was a versatile mathematician who contributed to logic, functional analysis, and algebra. Hilbert spaces were a powerful generalization of flat Euclidean space. *(Aufnahme von A. Schmidt, Göttingen, courtesy of AIP Emilio Segrè Visual Archives)*

He was the first to propose these new techniques, which later became classical. Mention should be made of his famous *Nullstellensatz* (zero position principle), which gives a condition for a polynomial to be included in a special set of functions called an ideal.

From 1894 to 1899 Hilbert turned to number theory, taking an algebraic perspective to the subject. His *Der Zahlbericht* (Commentary on numbers) of 1897 was a summary of all current knowledge, organized from a contemporaneous viewpoint. It proved to be a crucial guidebook for the next half-century of research into algebraic number theory. Hilbert's contributions to algebraic number theory were so profound and extensive, it almost seems that he began the topic. His work focused on the reciprocity law and the notion of the class field. Although his brilliant work provided stimulating ideas for decades to come, Hilbert moved on to the foundations of geometry, leaving the further details to his students and successors.

From 1899 to 1903 Hilbert emphasized the axiomatic character of geometry. His *Grundlagen der Geometrie* (Foundations of geometry) (1899) attempted to establish the consistency of geometric axioms and to determine which theorems were independent of certain axioms. For example, non-Euclidean geometry had already been invented, and was a geometrical system that was independent of EUCLID OF ALEXANDRIA's parallel postulate. Hilbert brought algebra to bear on geometry to obtain results concerning consistency and independence. His work in this area would lead to future ideas of field and topological space.

Although the Dirichlet principle for solving the boundary value problem in the theory of partial differential equations had been discredited by KARL WEIERSTRASS, Hilbert succeeded in giving a rigorous proof. His technique of diagonalization later became classic in abstract analysis. From 1904 to 1909 Hilbert labored on the calculus of variations and integral equations. Hilbert focused on homogeneous equations, arriving at the notion of a function space with an inner product (later these would be called Hilbert spaces, and are of great practical use in functional analysis and statistics), and defined the spectrum of an operator. The term *spectrum* was prophetic, as physicists some two decades later would connect the spectra of operators to optical spectra. FRIGYES RIESZ and John Von

Neumann would later follow up Hilbert's first clumsy steps in the new field of operator theory.

Next, Hilbert turned to mathematical physics, feeling that the subject was too important to be left to the physicists. He obtained results on kinetic gas theory and relativity, but this work was not as influential as his previous success in algebra and analysis. After 1918 Hilbert was heavily involved in the foundations of mathematics. He was eager to demonstrate the consistency of number theory in particular. Although some of his concepts, such as the transfinite function, were quite brilliant, ultimately the program was doomed to failure. Essentially, Hilbert was obsessed with proving that mathematical proof was valid—thus he was engaged in "metamathematics" (that is, the study of mathematical thought processes, including the structure of proofs). KURT FRIEDRICH GÖDEL dealt a death blow to the prospect of establishing the consistency of number theory in 1931. From this time is dated the genesis of the modern studies in the foundations of mathematics.

Hilbert fell ill from anemia in 1925, and he made only a partial recovery due to new treatments. His list of 23 problems, set as tasks for the 20th century and delivered at a 1900 address at the International Congress of Mathematicians, has proved to be of enduring importance. It treats a wide breadth of problems, including the cardinality of the continuum, the consistency of arithmetic, the axiomatization of physics, the Riemann hypothesis, and the study of general boundary value problems. Some of these have been completely or partially solved, others are unsolved, and still others have been shown to be unsolvable (or dependent on a choice of axiom). In any event, they have provided an enormous stimulus for mathematicians. The topics enumerated in the 23 problems have for the most part been major areas of research into pure mathematics.

Hilbert died on February 14, 1943, in Göttingen. He was known for his intense personality and mathematical boldness. HERMANN MINKOWSKI was both a close friend and a significant influence, as they studied together in Königsberg. One of his most important mentors was LEOPOLD KRONECKER. Hilbert had many famous students, including HERMANN WEYL. His impact on 20th-century mathematics has been tremendous.

Further Reading

Bernays, P. "David Hilbert," *Encyclopedia of Philosophy III*. New York: Macmillan, 1967.

Lewis, D. "David Hilbert and the Theory of Algebraic Invariants," *Irish Mathematical Society Bulletin* 33 (1994): 42–54.

Reid, C. *Hilbert-Courant*. New York: Springer-Verlag, 1986.

Rowe, D. "David Hilbert on Poincaré, Klein, and the World of Mathematics," *The Mathematical Intelligencer* 8, no. 1 (1986): 75–77.

Weyl, H. "David Hilbert and His Mathematical Work," *American Mathematical Society. Bulletin. New Series* 50 (1944): 612–654.

⊠ Hipparchus of Rhodes
(ca. 190 B.C.E.–ca. 120 B.C.E.)
Greek
Trigonometry

Hipparchus of Rhodes was one of the greatest astronomers of antiquity, and was also well known for the mathematical techniques that he imported into the study of the stars. Many of the astronomical calculations were made accessible through the trigonometric formulas of Hipparchus; he may also have been the first to use spherical trigonometry and stereographic projection.

Hipparchus of Rhodes was not born in Rhodes, though he spent much of his later career at that island. He was born in Nicaea, in the northwestern portion of Turkey, sometime in the first quarter of the second century B.C.E. He was most active between 147 B.C.E. and 127 B.C.E., which are known to be the dates of his first and last astronomical observations.

Little is known of Hipparchus's early life, but it is probable that he began his scientific career in Nicaea and moved to Rhodes before 141 B.C.E. He was quite famous and respected during his lifetime, but later fell into obscurity due to the small circulation of his published works. CLAUDIUS PTOLEMY wrote the *Almagest*, which drew heavily on the previous writings of Hipparchus, and it is from this source that scholars' scanty knowledge of Hipparchus is drawn.

In order to calculate the position of heavenly bodies, it was necessary for the Greeks to solve certain trigonometric problems. Hipparchus wrote a work (its name is unknown and its existence is known only indirectly) on the chords of a circle, and produced a chord table, which was basically an early table of sines. He constructed the table by computing the values directly at intervals of 7½ degrees, and then by linearly interpolating between these values. Although Indian astronomers later used this chord table, Ptolemy's superior chord table superseded it. Nevertheless, Hipparchus was the first to construct such a table, and this tool allowed him to solve many trigonometric problems relevant to astronomy. In this sense, Hipparchus can be regarded as the founder of trigonometry; he also transformed astronomy into a quantitative science.

Many of the astronomical calculations performed by Hipparchus involved spherical trigonometry (the measurement of triangles located on a sphere), but many scholars think that he was able to solve these problems without an explicit knowledge of spherical trigonometry. There is also evidence that Hipparchus used stereographic projection, which is a method of mapping the sphere (minus the North Pole) onto a plane through the equator, thus providing a way of translating coordinates.

Besides these mathematical accomplishments, Hipparchus was most famous for his numerous contributions to astronomy. It is interesting that he drew upon Babylonian lunar data for some of his theories; he was able to calculate the size of the Moon and Sun (the latter calculation was inaccurate). He composed works on geography and astrology, as well as a book on optics.

Hipparchus's main achievement was the transformation of astronomy from a qualitative to a quantitative science; he successfully employed mathematical formulas to calculate distances and angles of various celestial bodies. His own observational data, along with the transmission of Babylonian astronomical data, were both important to the development of astronomy. Hipparchus was known to be open-minded, critical, and empirical—he tested scientific theories against observations. His own writings were highly specialized, but it seems that Hipparchus had conceived of a complete astronomical system. Ptolemy fleshed this out. Mathematically, Hipparchus deserves fame for founding the discipline of trigonometry and constructing the first trigonometric table.

Further Reading

Dicks, D. *The Geographical Fragments of Hipparchus*. London: University of London, Athlone Press, 1960.

Dreyer, J. *A History of Astronomy from Thales to Kepler*. New York: Dover Publications, 1953.

Grasshoff, G. *The History of Ptolemy's Star Catalogue*. New York: Springer-Verlag, 1990.

Heath, T. *A History of Greek Mathematics*. Oxford: Clarendon Press, 1921.

Neugebauer, O. *A History of Ancient Mathematical Astronomy*. New York: Springer-Verlag, 1975.

Sarton, G. *A History of Science*. Cambridge, Mass.: Harvard University Press, 1959.

⊠ Hippocrates of Chios
(ca. 470 B.C.E.–ca. 410 B.C.E.)
Greek
Geometry, Analysis

Hippocrates of Chios was an early Greek mathematician who made contributions toward the problem of duplicating the cube, the quadrature of lunes, and the elements of geometry. In fact, he was the first to compose an *Elements of Geometry*, although Hippocrates' version did not achieve the fame and renown of EUCLID OF ALEXANDRIA's work of the same name.

As with most persons of antiquity, the specific dates of his birth and death are unknown, although scholars have been able to pinpoint his activity to the latter portion of the fifth century B.C.E. Not to be confused with the physician Hippocrates of Cos, this Hippocrates was born on the island of Chios in the Aegean Sea. Reportedly, Hippocrates of Chios was a merchant whose wealth was ruined by pirates. He then pursued his enemies to Athens, where he spent much of his remaining life.

In Athens Hippocrates attended lectures, becoming proficient in geometry and analysis. It is probable that Hippocrates already possessed some mathematical education, since there was a flourishing school in Chios; it is possible that early in his life Hippocrates came under the influence of the Pythagoreans, who were based in nearby Samos. Three mathematical problems—the duplication of the cube, the squaring of the circle, and the trisection of an angle—held the attention of the Athenians, and Hippocrates studied the first two.

The method of analysis refers to the process of reducing a problem into smaller parts that may be easier to solve. Hippocrates applied the method of analysis to the duplication of the cube. This famous problem amounted to finding a geometric construction for the cube root of 2; Hippocrates reduced this to the task of finding two mean proportionals x and y between the numbers *a* and *2a*, where *a* is the given side of the cube. In other words, one needed to solve the ratio *a*/*x* 5 *y*/*2a*. ERATOSTHENES OF CYRENE later completed the solution by demonstrating how to solve this ratio geometrically.

Lunes are shapes similar to a crescent moon. Greek mathematicians attempted to find the area within a given lune by inscribing and circumscribing various shapes with known areas—a method known as quadrature. Hippocrates was successful in squaring the lune (that is, he was able to construct a rectangular figure with area equal to that contained within certain given lunes), although he was unable to square the circle (it is impossible, since the number pi cannot be expressed in terms of algebraic numbers). Some ancient commentators mistakenly attributed the latter claim—that he was able to square the circle—to Hippocrates, but Hippocrates was a talented mathematician, and it is unlikely that he could have made such a fallacy. He also gave the first known example of the Greek construction of "verging," which is used in establishing the quadrature of a lune.

Hippocrates was aware of several properties of triangles, such as the Pythagorean theorem and various relationships between the angles. It is probable that Hippocrates' *Elements of Geometry* contained such knowledge, covering much of the first two books of Euclid's *Elements*. Hippocrates was also familiar with the geometry of the circle. For example, he knew how to circumscribe a circle about a given triangle, and was familiar with the angles within the circle. It is conjectured that Hippocrates' *Elements* contained some solid geometry as well, although he was unaware of the theory of proportion encountered in Book V of Euclid's *Elements*.

Hippocrates was probably the first to articulate the theorem relating a circle's radius to its circumference, although this was not proved until later. Besides these mathematical works, he contributed to astronomy through his speculations on the nature of the comet.

The work of Hippocrates has been lost due to the ravages of time, and his accomplishments have been pieced together from secondary sources. From these it is clear that Hippocrates was not only a foremost intellectual of his time and one of the greatest mathematicians of Athens, helping to make that city a center of learning, but he was also a contributor to Greek mathematics whose enduring work stimulated his successors.

Further Reading

Aaboe, A. *Episodes from the Early History of Mathematics*. Washington, D.C.: Mathematical Association of America, 1964.

Amir-Moéz, A., and J. Hamilton. "Hippocrates," *Journal of Recreational Mathematics* 7, no. 2 (1974): 105–107.

Heath, T. A *History of Greek Mathematics*. Oxford: Clarendon Press, 1921.

Hughes, B. "Hippocrates and Archytas Double the Cube: A Heuristic Interpretation," *The College Mathematics Journal* 20, no. 1 (1989): 42–48.

⊠ **Hopf, Heinz**
(1894–1971)
German
Topology

Topology, the study of the form of mathematical sets, became an increasingly popular discipline in the 20th century. Powerful new tools such as homology and algebraic ring theory were brought to bear on important problems, and much progress was made in the project of topological classification. Heinz Hopf was a key player in these developments.

Heinz Hopf was born in Breslau, Germany, on November 19, 1894. He studied mathematics at the university in his hometown, but World War I interrupted his career. After a long period of service, Hopf was able to attend a set theory course at the University of Breslau in 1917; he became fascinated with the topological work of

LUITZEN EGBERTUS JAN BROUWER and pursued further studies in Berlin. In 1925, Hopf received a Ph.D. in mathematics. Later he received a fellowship to study at Princeton University in 1927. In 1931 Hopf was appointed full professor of mathematics at the Eidgenössische Technische Hochschule in Zurich, Switzerland.

Although Hopf published only a small number of papers, such as *Fundamentalgruppe und Zweite Bettische Gruppe* (Fundamental groups and second Betti groups), he was tremendously influential in the field of topology, due to the breadth and originality of his ideas. He built on Brouwer's methods, developing the concepts of mapping degree and homotopy class—these were mathematical tools that brought algebraic group theory into play to assist in the classification of continuous manifolds. Hopf had an excellent geometric intuition, but his arguments became increasingly algebraic under the influence of EMMY NOETHER.

Some of Hopf's most important work focused on mappings of high-dimensional spheres, vector fields, and fixed point theorems. He defined the inverse homomorphism, which became a powerful tool in the study of manifolds. In 1931 Hopf identified an infinite number of relationships between the three-dimensional sphere and the two-dimensional sphere, and made conjectures about the so-called Hopf fiber map. After World War II, Hopf's early research in these areas developed into a thriving field of study.

In the area of vector fields, Hopf studied bilinear forms, almost complex manifolds, and the homology of group manifolds. His main tool in these researches was homology, which refers to classes of embeddings of simple objects (like triangles and tetrahedrons) into a given manifold. Other work by Hopf in the 1940s led to the development of cohomological algebra, a vigorous new field of pure mathematics.

Besides all this excellent work in algebraic topology, Hopf also explored differential geometry. For example, he investigated complete surfaces, congruency of convex surfaces, and isometry; he also wrote about the tangent of a closed plane curve. Heinz Hopf was energetic and cheerful, and he gave clear, stimulating lectures. With his wife, Anja Hopf—whom he married in October 1928—he was a gracious host to colleagues and political exiles. During World War II, he provided refuge for his German friends in Switzerland, where they would be safe from Nazi persecution. He died on June 3, 1971, in Zollikon, Switzerland. He earned several honorary doctorates from such institutions as Princeton, Freiburg, and the Sorbonne, and was president of the International Mathematical Union from 1955 to 1958.

Heinz Hopf was enormously influential in the area of topology: He developed homology into one of the most widely used tools of algebraic topology, and obtained several important results, especially in the study of high-dimensional spheres. The origins of cohomology can be traced back to Hopf, as can the concept of homotopy groups.

Further Reading

Behnke, H., and F. Hirzebruch. "In Memoriam Heinz Hopf," *Mathematische Annalen* 196 (1972): 1–7.

Cartan, H. "Heinz Hopf (1894–1971)," *International Mathematical Union* (1972): 1–7.

Frei, G., and U. Stammbach. "Heinz Hopf," in *History of Topology*. Amsterdam: Elsevier Science B.V., 1999.

⊠   **Huygens, Christiaan (Christian Huyghens)**
(1629–1695)
Dutch
Mechanics, Geometry, Analysis, Probability

Between the time of RENÉ DESCARTES and SIR ISAAC NEWTON, it is said that Christiaan Huygens (sometimes referred to as Christian Huyghens) was Europe's greatest mathematician. He made substantial contributions to mechanics, astronomy, the measurement of time, the theory of light, and geometry. His work demonstrated the efficacy of a mathematical approach to the study of nature, and Huygens developed many sophisticated mathematical tools.

Christiaan Huygens was born in The Hague, the Netherlands, on April 14, 1629. His family was prominent, having a long history of diplomatic service to the royal house. Christiaan's father, Constantijn Huygens, educated both his sons personally, covering music, ancient languages, mathematics, and mechanics. Christiaan Huygens displayed his considerable intellectual talents at a young age, and he had a gift for applying theory to actual constructions—at age 13 he constructed a lathe.

In 1645 Huygens attended the University of Leiden, where he studied law and mathematics. During his two years there, he became familiar with the recent works of FRANÇOIS VIÈTE, PIERRE DE FERMAT, and Descartes. Huygens began to research the mechanics of falling bodies, and began a correspondence with Mersenne. After completing his university studies, he matriculated at the College of Orange from 1647 to 1649, where he pursued law. However, Huygens did not pursue a career in diplomacy, but rather chose to be a scientist.

Huygens lived at home until 1666, receiving financial support from his father that enabled him to focus on his scientific research. He first investigated mathematics, considering quadratures of curves as well as algebraic problems. Huygens's mathematical contributions are important, in that he improved on existing methods, and was successful in his application of these to natural phenomena. He also developed the new theory of evolutes and was one of the founders of the theory of probability.

In 1651 Huygens produced a manuscript that refuted Gregory of St. Vincent's quadrature of the circle. In the same work, he derived a connection between the quadrature and the

Christiaan Huygens contributed to mechanics, geometry, and probability, and invented the pendulum clock. *(Courtesy of the Library of Congress)*

center of gravity for circles, ellipses, and hyperbolas. His next publication, in 1654, approximates the center of gravity of any arc of a circle and thus obtains an approximate quadrature. A similar technique, developed more than a decade later, produced a quick method for calculating logarithms.

Upon learning of BLAISE PASCAL's work in probability, Huygens began studying gambling problems in 1656, such as the fair division of stakes for an interrupted game. He invented the concept of the mathematical expectation, which represents the long-term winnings of a game of chance. This idea, expressed by Huygens in a primitive form, is now of central importance to the modern theory of probability.

In 1657 Huygens related the arc length of the parabola to the quadrature of the hyperbola, and he used this property to find the surface area of a paraboloid of revolution. A year later, he discovered a vital theorem of modern calculus—that the calculation of the surface area of a surface of revolution could be reduced to find the quadrature of the normal curve.

His theory of evolutes, which concerns the geometry of cords dangling from a convex surface, was developed in 1659 as a component of his research into pendulum clocks. His method of evolutes essentially determines the radius of curvature of a given algebraic curve. Huygens also studied logarithms, starting in 1661, and in this connection introduced the natural exponential function.

Huygens also contributed to areas of science. He completed a manuscript on hydrostatics in 1650, in which he derived the law of ARCHIMEDES OF SYRACUSE from a basic axiom. In 1652 he formulated the rules of elastic collision and commenced his study of optics. Later in 1655, together with his brother, he turned to lens grinding and the construction of telescopes and microscopes. He built some of the best telescopes of his time, and was able to detect the rings of Saturn. Huygens also observed bacteria and other microscopic objects.

In 1656 Huygens invented the pendulum clock as a tool for the measurement of time. It had become increasingly important to accurately measure time, since this technology was necessary to astronomy and navigation; Huygens's invention had much success. In his theoretical investigation of pendulum swing, Huygens discovered that the period could be made independent of the amplitude if the pendulum's path was a cycloid. He then constructed the pendulum clock such that the bob of the pendulum would be induced to have a cycloidal path. This so-called tautochronism of the cycloid is one of Huygens's most famous discoveries.

Next, Huygens began studying centrifugal force and the center of oscillation in 1659, obtaining several fundamental results. He rigorously derived the laws of descent along inclined planes

and curves and derived the value for the acceleration due to gravity on the Earth, which is about 9.8 meters per second squared. Huygens turned to fall through resisting media (such as air) in 1668, and conceived of the resistance (or friction) as proportional to the object's velocity. Huygens also investigated the wave theory of light; he explained reflection and refraction in 1676 by his conception of light as a series of fast-moving shock waves.

It is interesting that Huygens did not accept the Newtonian concept of force, and he was able to circumvent it completely. He was also critical of GOTTFRIED WILHELM VON LEIBNIZ's concept of force, although he agreed with the principle of conservation in mechanical systems. In his natural philosophy, he agreed with Descartes, attempting to arrive at a mechanistic explanation of the world. One of his most popular works speculated on the existence of intelligent life on other planets, which Huygens thought was highly probable.

During the period 1650–66, Huygens met many French scientists and mathematicians, and he visited Paris several times. In 1666 Huygens accepted membership in the newly founded Académie Royale des Sciences and moved to Paris, where he remained until 1681. He was the most prominent member of the academy, and received a generous stipend. He spent this time developing a scientific program for the study of nature, observing the heavens, and expounding his theories of gravity and light.

Huygens suffered from ill health, and several times was forced to return to the Hague. In 1681 he again left due to illness and, due to political and religious tensions, was not invited to come back to France. Huygens had never married, but was able to live off the family estate. In the last decade of his life he returned to mathematics, having become convinced of the fruitfulness of Leibniz's differential calculus. However, Huygens's mathematical conservatism led him to employ his old geometrical methods, and this somewhat inhibited his progress and understanding of calculus. Nevertheless, Huygens was able to solve several mathematical problems posed publicly, such as Leibniz's isochrone, the tractrix, and the catenary.

Huygens finally succumbed to his ill constitution, and he died on July 8, 1695. He was the most preeminent scientist and mathematician of his time (at least before Newton and Leibniz became active), and he made brilliant contributions to diverse areas of science. However, Huygens's reluctance to publish theories that were insufficiently developed limited his influence in the 18th century; neither did he have any pupils to carry on his thought. His work in mechanics opened up new frontiers of research, but his mathematical work mostly extended older techniques rather than opening up new vistas for exploration. Nevertheless, Huygens was a master at applying mathematical methods to scientific problems, as his work in the measurement of time eminently demonstrates.

Further Reading

Barth, M. "Huygens at Work: Annotations in His Rediscovered Personal Copy of Hooke's 'Micrographia,'" *Annals of Science* 52, no. 6 (1995): 601–613.

Bell, A. *Christian Huygnes* [sic] *and the Development of Science in the Seventeenth Century*. London: E. Arnold, 1950.

Dijksterhuis, E. "Christiaan Huygens," *Centaurus* 2 (1953): 265–282.

Yoder, J. *Unrolling Time: Christiaan Huygens and the Mathematization of Nature*. New York: Cambridge University Press, 1988.

I

Ibrahim ibn Sinan (Ibrahim Ibn Sinan Ibn Thabit Ibn Qurra)
(908–946)
Arabian
Geometry

The Arabs inherited the works of famous Greek mathematicians, such as EUCLID OF ALEXANDRIA, APOLLONIUS OF PERGA, and ARCHIMEDES OF SYRACUSE. Once they had mastered the ideas therein, several of them were able to extend the methods. Ibrahim ibn Sinan was one Arab who employed great originality in his study of mathematics, and he represents a high point in Arabian scientific knowledge.

Ibrahim ibn Sinan was born in 908, probably in Baghdad, into a family of famous scholars. His father, Sinan ibn Thabit, was a physician, astronomer, and mathematician. Ibrahim led a brief life, dying at age 38 in Baghdad, but he accomplished a significant amount of scientific activity. Besides his labor in mathematics, Ibrahim examined the apparent motions of the Sun, studied the optics of shadows, and investigated astronomical instruments such as the astrolabe.

In mathematics proper, Ibrahim's written works cover the tangents of circles and geometry in general. His quadrature of the parabola (determination of the area enclosed by a given parabola) involves an expansion of Archimedes'

method. Ibrahim's grandfather Thabit ibn Qurra had already generalized Archimedes' technique, which was equivalent to summing definite integrals, but his exposition was quite lengthy. In contrast, Ibrahim's analysis is simple and elegant. He decomposes the area of the parabola into an approximating collection of inscribed triangles, and he proves an elementary relation between the areas of the inscribed polygons. As a result, the desired area is four-thirds of the first inscribed triangle. Ibrahim's genius is evident in his graceful solution to this problem.

He also sought to revive classic geometry, which had been neglected by his contemporaries. Ibrahim desired to both provide a practical method for solving geometrical problems and to categorize problems according to their difficulty and method. Following the epistemology of the ancient Greeks, Ibrahim argued for the dual importance of synthesis and analysis. The work of Ibrahim ibn Sinan exerted a deep influence on the mathematical philosophy of subsequent Arabic mathematicians.

Further Reading

al'Daffa, A. *The Muslim Contribution to Mathematics.* London; Prometheus Books, 1977.

Rashed, R. *The Development of Arabic Mathematics: Between Arithmetic and Algebra.* Boston: Kluwer Academic, 1994.

J

Jacobi, Carl (Carl Gustav Jacob Jacobi)
(1804–1851)
German
Analysis, Number Theory, Mathematical Physics

In early 19th-century Germany, Carl Jacobi ranked among the foremost mathematical successors of CARL FRIEDRICH GAUSS. Jacobi distinguished himself by his numerous contributions to analysis, especially in the area of elliptic integrals; for the diversity of his activity and the breadth of his intellect, he has been compared to LEONHARD EULER.

Born on December 10, 1804, in Potsdam, Germany, Jacobi was the second son of Simon Jacobi, a wealthy Jewish banker, and he received an excellent education from his uncle. Jacobi had an older brother, Moritz, who became a physicist in St. Petersburg, and a younger brother and sister. Jacobi was intellectually advanced as a young boy, and he entered the high school in Potsdam in 1816. He was soon promoted to the highest class despite his youth; when he graduated in 1821, Jacobi had mastered Greek, Latin, and history and possessed an extensive knowledge of mathematics, already having attempted the solution of the quintic equation.

Jacobi went on to the University of Berlin, where he concentrated on mathematics. Working privately, he soon mastered the works of Euler, JOSEPH-LOUIS LAGRANGE, and several other leading mathematicians. In 1824 he passed his preliminary exams, and soon submitted a Ph.D. thesis. Having converted to Christianity, he was allowed to commence his academic career at the University of Berlin at the young age of 20.

Jacobi's lectures were stimulating, since he described his current research to his audience. His first lecture in 1825 dealt with the analytic theory of curves and surfaces. This was Jacobi's most prolific period, and he established contact with fellow mathematicians such as Gauss, ADRIEN-MARIE LEGENDRE, and NIELS HENDRIK ABEL. Much of Jacobi's research built upon and developed Gauss's explorations. Legendre was the first to study elliptic integrals in a systematic fashion, and both Abel and Jacobi became his intellectual heirs, competing in their investigations of transcendental functions.

Jacobi relocated to the University of Königsberg in 1826, as there were more opportunities for advancement there. Through interactions with FRIEDRICH WILHELM BESSEL, Jacobi became increasingly interested in applied problems. Jacobi's publications enjoyed a wide popularity, and he soon advanced to associate professor in 1827 and full professor in 1832. During his 18 years at Königsberg, Jacobi produced amazing results on the theory of elliptic functions, analysis, number theory, geometry, and mechanics. Many of his papers were published in Crelle's *Journal for Pure and Applied Mathematics*, and Jacobi was partly responsible for its rise to international repute. Although he energetically pursued his research, Jacobi also lectured about 10 hours a week, often discussing the most recent advances in knowledge. Jacobi developed the research seminar—essentially a collection of advanced students—and also encouraged the research-oriented approach to university teaching.

Jacobi married Marie Schwinck in 1831, and had five sons and three daughters with her. He traveled to Paris in 1829 in order to meet the leading French mathematicians, and visited Legendre, JEAN-BAPTISTE-JOSEPH FOURIER, and SIMÉON-DENIS POISSON. Later, he attended a mathematical conference in Britain in 1842. In 1843 Jacobi became quite ill with diabetes, and he traveled through Italy in the hope that the milder climate would improve his health; on his return, Jacobi moved back to Berlin, and he occasionally lectured at the University of Berlin.

Up to this time, Jacobi's research was mainly concerned with elliptic functions. A summary of his initial results was published in *Fundamenta nova theoriae functionum ellipticarum* (New foundations of the theory of elliptic functions) in 1829; herein, Jacobi discussed the transformation and representation of elliptic functions, revealing many of the most important properties. One of Jacobi's important ideas (which was independently developed by Abel and Gauss) was the inversion of an elliptic integral, and this led to several important formulas. Along with Abel, Jacobi also introduced imaginary numbers into the theory of elliptic functions and discovered their double periodicity. Throughout his competition with Abel, Jacobi remained generous

and good-willed, advocating the term *abelian* for certain results on transcendental functions. Later in the same work, Jacobi expressed these integrals as infinite products, and was able to apply his results to number theory—for example, he was able to prove that any integer can be represented as the sum of at most four squares, which had been previously conjectured by PIERRE DE FERMAT.

This work continued through the 1830s, with additional results on the theta function. In number theory, Jacobi studied the theory of residues, quadratic forms, and the representations of integers as sums of squares and cubes. Jacobi also contributed to partial differential equations (into which field he introduced elliptic functions), mathematical physics (Jacobi studied the configurations of rotating liquid masses), and the theory of determinants. Jacobi gave a systematic presentation of determinants in 1841, and he introduced the "Jacobian," the determinant used in change of variable calculations in integral calculus. Besides these labors in mathematics, Jacobi lectured on the history of mathematics, and even started the immense project of producing a volume of Euler's complete works.

Jacobi took an interest in Euler as a kindred spirit, since their view of mathematics was similar. Jacobi, like Euler, was a good calculator, and enjoyed an algorithmic perspective on solving problems; Jacobi was versatile in many areas of mathematics, and he wrote prolifically.

He committed some political blunders in 1848, alienating himself from the Prussian monarchy. As a result his salary was cut, and he was forced to sell his house in Berlin. In 1849 he received an offer from Vienna, and Prussia restored his salary—evidently, they were loath to lose such an eminent mathematician. In 1851 Jacobi contracted influenza, followed by smallpox, which proved fatal. He died on February 18, 1851, in Berlin. His good friend GUSTAVE-PETER-LEJEUNE DIRICHLET gave a eulogy in 1852, describing Jacobi as the greatest mathematician in the Berlin Academy since Lagrange.

Jacobi's work spanned several fields, but his work on elliptic functions and integrals is the most significant. In his own time he was recognized, along with Dirichlet, as one of the greatest German mathematicians. Yet even after his death, his work continued to prove influential; he left behind a school of mathematicians and an impressive body of mathematical ideas.

Further Reading

Hawkins, T. "Jacobi and the Birth of Lie's Theory of Groups," *Archive for History of Exact Sciences* 42, no. 3 (1991): 187–278.

Pieper, H. "Carl Gustav Jacob Jacobi," in *Mathematics in Berlin*. Berlin: Birkhäuser Verlag, 1998.

Jordan, Camille
(1838–1921)
French
Algebra, Analysis, Topology

In the latter portion of the 19th century, considerable mathematical activity focused on the development of group theory, flowering from the brilliant research of EVARISTE GALOIS. Among the many talented algebraists, Camille Jordan was notable for his virtuosity and leadership of the subject. He also made substantial contributions to other areas of mathematics, such as combinatorial topology and analysis.

Camille Jordan was born on January 5, 1838, in Lyons, France. His father was an engineer, and many members of his family were well known (his cousin Alexis Jordan was a famous botanist). Camille Jordan was successful in mathematics from a young age, and he entered the École Polytechnique at age 17. His nominal career as an engineer lasted until 1885, during which time he wrote more than 100 papers.

Jordan was an excellent all-around mathematician, publishing noteworthy papers in all fields of study. He investigated the symmetries of polyhedrons from a purely combinatorial viewpoint, which was original. Jordan's conception of rigor in analysis exceeded that of his peers, and his text *Cours d'analyse* (Course in analysis) became a popular classic. Jordan was active in the first developments of measure theory, constructing the notion of exterior measure, inventing the concept of a function of bounded variation, and proving that any such function could be decomposed as the difference of two increasing functions. This profound result paved the way for later advanced results concerning the decomposition of positive and signed measures. In topology, he realized that it was possible to decompose a plane into two regions via a simple closed curve (this intuitive concept was already known to many, but Jordan was the first to suggest some ways to prove it).

Jordan's chief mathematical fame is derived from his talent as an algebraist. He was the first to systematically develop finite group theory, with the applications of Galois theory in mind. One of his most famous results was part of the Jordan-Hölder theorem concerned with the invariance of certain compositions of groups. Jordan researched the general linear group (the group of invertible matrices), and applied his results to geometric problems.

Jordan was interested in the "solvability" of finite groups (the characterization of the finite groups by certain numerical invariants). He set up a recursive machinery in an attempt to resolve this problem, and in the process discovered many new algebraic techniques and concepts, such as the orthogonal groups over a field of characteristic two. In 1870 Jordan produced his *Traité des substitutions et des équations algébriques* (Treatise on substitutions and algebraic equations), a valuable summary of all his previous results on permutation groups. This work heavily influenced algebraic research for the next three decades.

As a result of his outstanding and innovative work, Jordan's fame spread, attracting numerous foreign students, including FELIX KLEIN and SOPHUS LIE. From 1873 to 1912 he taught (while still working as an engineer) at the École Polytechnique and the Collège de France. Jordan's most profound results are his "finiteness theorems," which provide bounds on the number of subgroups of a given mathematical group. These results and others have now become classical in the study of abstract algebra.

Jordan died on January 22, 1921, in Paris. He was honored during his lifetime, having been elected to the Academy of Sciences in 1881. He was the undisputed master of group theory during the time he was active, and his work greatly influenced the subsequent evolution of the modern study of algebra.

Further Reading

Johnson, D. "The Correspondence of Camille Jordan," *Historia Mathematica* 4 (1977): 210.

K

al-Karaji, Abu (al-Karaji, Abu Bakr Ibn Muhammad Ibn Al-Husayn; al-Karkhi)
(ca. 953–ca. 1029)
Arabian
Algebra

Al-Karaji made great contributions to algebra by first treating numbers independently of geometry. In this respect he differed from the Greeks and from his Arabic predecessors. He was then able to develop many of the basic algebraic properties of rational and irrational numbers, and therefore represents an important step in the evolution of algebraic calculus. Al-Karaji is known as the first author of the algebra of polynomials.

There is much dispute among scholars about the spelling of this man's name. From earlier translations he was known as al-Karkhi, but this was later disputed, and the name al-Karaji was put forth. The latter name has stuck. The controversy is of some pertinence, since the name al-Karkhi would indicate Karkh, a suburb of Baghdad, whereas al-Karaji is indicative of an Iranian city. In any event, al-Karaji dwelled in Baghdad, where he produced most of his mathematical work, and his books were written from the end of the 10th century through the beginning of the 11th century. Some scholars believe

he was born on April 13, 953. After this period, he apparently departed for the "mountain countries" in order to write works on engineering.

His treatise on algebra, called *al-Fakhri fi'-ljabr wa'l-muqabala* (Glorious on algebra), offers the first theory of algebraic calculus developed by the Arabs. Al-Karaji built upon the techniques of previous Arab mathematicians, such as ABU AL-KHWARIZMI, but his approach was completely new. He sought to separate algebraic operations from the geometric representation given them by the Greeks. The *Arithmetica* of DIOPHANTUS OF ALEXANDRIA influenced al-Karaji and played a part in al-Karaji's arithmetization of algebra.

In the *al-Fakhri*, al-Karaji first studies the arithmetic of exponents—multiplication and division of monomials translates into addition and subtraction of their exponents. His successors were able to apply these rules toward the extraction of square roots. Al-Karaji took a bold step in producing algebraic rules for real numbers, independent of any geometrical interpretation. For one thing, algebraic operations (such as addition and multiplication) and their basic rules (such as associativity and commutativity) were known to be true for rational numbers, but no theory had been developed for irrational numbers (such as square roots). Al-Karaji defined the notion of irrational numbers from Book

X of EUCLID OF ALEXANDRIA's *Elements*. For Euclid this theory of incommensurability applied only to geometrical quantities, not to numbers. Thus, al-Karaji extended this concept of irrationality to numbers in a leap of faith, and extended the algebraic operations to this class. Modern mathematicians would later rigorously develop an algebra of real numbers that was purely arithmetical.

One consequence of this conceptual leap was that Euclid's *Elements* would no longer be considered as a purely geometrical book. Al-Karaji went on to develop the calculus of radicals, deriving rules that allowed the calculation of simple expressions involving square roots. In a similar vein, al-Karaji gave formulas for the expansion of binomials. In his proof of the so-called binomial theorem, the beginnings of mathematical induction can be seen. Al-Karaji also derived formulas for the sum of consecutive integers and consecutive squares.

Al-Karaji was interested in applying these methods to the solution of polynomial equations. He considered linear, quadratic, and certain special higher-degree equations—in this area the influence of Diophantus on al-Karaji is evident. In the area of indeterminate analysis, al-Karaji was able to clarify and extend Diophantus's work, and considered problems involving three nonlinear equations in three unknowns. Diophantus was known for his ingenuity in deriving special tricks for individual problems. In contrast, al-Karaji strove to develop general methods that could handle even more cases.

Little is known of the conclusion of Al-Karaji's life, but some scholars believe that he died in 1029. Al-Karaji produced a fresh perspective on algebra. Under his guidance, algebra was made independent of geometry and more closely linked to analysis. This attitude diverged significantly from Greek thought and became normative for later Arab mathematicians. His transformation of algebra later had an impact on

Europe through LEONARDO FIBONACCI, who imported Arabic ideas and methods to Italy in the 12th century.

Further Reading
Crossley, J. *The Emergence of Number*. Victoria, Australia: Upside Down A Book Company, 1980.

Neugebauer, O. *The Exact Sciences in Antiquity*. Providence, R.I.: Brown University Press, 1957.

Parshall, K. "The Art of Algebra from al-Khwarizmi to Viète: A Study in the Natural Selection of Ideas," *History of Science* 26, no. 72, 2 (1988): 129–164.

Rashed, R. *The Development of Arabic Mathematics: Between Arithmetic and Algebra*. Boston: Kluwer Academic, 1994.

⊠   **al-Khwarizmi, Abu (Abu Ja'far Muhammad Ibn Musa al-Khwarizmi)**
(ca. 780–850)
Arabian
Algebra

Al-Khwarizmi is an important Arab in the history of Middle Eastern mathematics, since he played a role in the transmission of Hindu knowledge to Arabia, from whence it made its way to Europe. His development of algebra, even though rudimentary, was an important foundation for later mathematicians such as ABU AL-KARAJI.

The life of al-Khwarizmi is fairly obscure, but he was probably born sometime before 800 in Qutrubbull, a district between the Tigris and Euphrates Rivers near Baghdad. Under the reign of the Caliph al-Mamun from 813 to 833, al-Khwarizmi became a member of the House of Wisdom, an academy of scientists in Baghdad. Al-Khwarizmi wrote books that treated astronomy, algebra, Hindu numerals, the Jewish calendar, geography, and history.

His *Algebra* was an elementary work, designed to provide practical help with common calculations used in commerce. The first part is concerned with the solution of actual algebraic equations, while the second and third sections treat measurement and applications. Al-Khwarizmi gives six basic types of equations that include linear and quadratic equations in one variable. At this stage there is no notion of zero or negative number, and a substantial portion of the techniques is concerned with removing negative quantities. In fact, the word *algebra* comes from *al-jabr*, which means "restoration." This refers to the operation of adding a positive quantity to both sides of an equation to remove a negative quantity. A similar operation called balancing is also used. The full name of the book is *The Compendious Book on Calculation by Completion and Balancing*. Besides these basic rules, the author provided information on how to find the area of various plane figures, such as triangles and circles, as well as the volume of solids such as the cone and pyramid.

Al-Khwarizmi's *Algebra* is believed to be the first Arabic work on the topic of algebra. There is some dispute among scholars over whether he derived his information from Greek or Hindu sources. His use of diagrams indicates that he may have been familiar with EUCLID OF ALEXANDRIA's *Elements*.

Al-Khwarizmi's treatise on Hindu numerals is also quite important for the history of mathematics, since it is one of the earliest works to expound the superior numerical system of the Hindus. This is essentially the modern system, which involves 10 numerical symbols in a place-value system. They are mistakenly referred to as "Arabic numerals," since they came to Europeans via the Arabs. It is likely that the Hindu numeric system had already been introduced to the Arabs, but al-Khwarizmi was the first to present a systematic exposition.

Besides these mathematical labors, al-Khwarizmi composed a work on astronomy that derived from the knowledge of the Hindus. His *Geography* was an improvement over Ptolemy's,

as it included the greater knowledge of the Arabs.

Al-Khwarizmi died sometime in the ninth century, perhaps around 850. Al-Khwarizmi's *Algebra* was used widely in both Arabia and Europe after the 12th century. More important, perhaps, is the impact of his treatise on Hindu numerals, which facilitated the explosion of European mathematics following the 12th century.

Further Reading

Crossley, J. *The Emergence of Number*. Victoria, Australia: Upside Down A Book Company, 1980.

Hogendijk, J. "Al-Khwarizmi's Table of the 'Sine of the Hours' and the Underlying Sine Table," *Historia Scientiarum. Second Series. International Journal of the History of Science Society of Japan* 42 (1991): 1–12.

Kennedy, A., and W. Ukashah. "Al-Khwarizmi's Planetary Latitude Tables," *Centaurus* 14 (1969): 86–96.

Kennedy, E. "Al-Khwarizmi on the Jewish Calendar," *Scripta Mathematica* 27 (1964): 55–59.

⊠ Klein, Felix (Christian Felix Klein)
(1849–1925)
German
Algebra, Analysis, Geometry

Felix Klein was an important character in the development of 19th century mathematics: he advanced current knowledge of group theory and Riemann surfaces, contributed to hyperbolic and projective geometry, and developed the theory of automorphic functions. His work gave direction and impetus to the next generation of mathematicians in Europe.

Christian Felix Klein was born in Düsseldorf, Germany, on April 25, 1849. After graduating from the local high school, he began studying mathematics and physics at the University of Bonn, obtaining his doctorate in 1868. Initially he wanted to be a physicist, but

Felix Klein, a geometer and algebraist who made connections between mathematical groups and certain classes of surfaces *(Aufnahme von Fr. Struckmeyer, Göttingen, courtesy of AIP Emilio Segrè Visual Archives, Landé Collection)*

under the influence of his teacher Julius Plücker, he switched to mathematics. His dissertation dealt with topics in line geometry (also known as projective geometry).

Next, Klein pursued further education in Göttingen, Berlin, and Paris, with a brief interruption due to the Franco-Prussian War. In 1871 he obtained a lectureship at Göttingen, and the following year he became a professor at the University of Erlangen. During this time, Klein studied certain special surfaces and curves and provided important models for the new hyperbolic and elliptic geometries previously discovered by NIKOLAI LOBACHEVSKY and JÁNOS BOLYAI. His examples were based on projective geometry, and he was the first to give such constructions; one of his important papers from this time was *On the So-Called Non-Euclidean Geometry*, which put non-Euclidean geometry on a solid footing. Next, Klein identified the groups that are naturally associated with various types of geometries. Later he connected these theoretical results to physics through the theory of relativity.

Klein held professorships at Munich, Leipzig, and finally Göttingen in 1886. In 1875 he married Anne Hegel, and they had one son and three daughters. Besides his early work in projective geometry and group theory, Klein made contributions to function theory—he considered this to be his most important work. Klein was able to successfully relate Riemann surfaces, a class of surfaces encountered in complex analysis, to number theory, algebra, differential equations, and the theory of automorphic functions. Klein's excellent spatial intuition enabled him to trace remarkable relationships. He diverged from the school of thought led by KARL WEIERSTRASS, which took an arithmetic approach. In 1913, HERMANN WEYL gave a rigorous foundation to many of Klein's important ideas.

Klein was also interested in the solution of the quintic, since the theory that had developed involved algebra, group theory, geometry, differential equations, and function theory. He derived a complete theory for the quintic through stereographic projection of the group symmetries of the icosahedron, and consequently discovered the elliptic modular functions. After studying their properties, he went on to investigate automorphic functions and algebraic function fields. All of this research stimulated further exploration by his own students, and the ideas have continuing relevance for many areas of modern mathematics.

Although Klein did most of his work in pure mathematics, he was very concerned with applications. In the 1890s he turned to physics and engineering. He even helped to found the Göttingen Institute for Aeronautical and Hydrodynamical Research, and attempted to encourage engineers to a greater appreciation of mathematics. He retired in 1913 due to poor health, and he died on June 22, 1925, in Göttingen.

Klein was a versatile mathematician, contributing to several branches of mathematics, and he helped to establish Göttingen as a center of mathematical activity in Germany. Through his many pupils and his extensive research, Klein exerted a great influence on the development of mathematics from the 19th to the 20th century.

Further Reading

Halsted, G. "Biography. Professor Felix Klein," *The American Mathematical Monthly* 1 (1894): 416–420.

Rowe, D. "The Early Geometrical Works of Sophus Lie and Felix Klein," in *The History of Modern Mathematics*. Boston: Academic Press, 1989.

———. "Klein, Hilbert, and the Göttingen Mathematical Tradition," *Osiris* 2, no. 5 (1989): 186–213.

———. "The Philosophical Views of Klein and Hilbert, The Intersection of History and Mathematics," *Science Networks. Historical Studies* 15 (1994): 187–202.

Yaglom, I. *Felix Klein and Sophus Lie: Evolution of the Idea of Symmetry in the Nineteenth Century.* Boston: Birkhäuser, 1988.

⊠ **Kovalevskaya, Sonya (Sofia Kovalevskaya, Sofya Kovalevskaya)**
(1850–1891)
Russian
Differential Equations, Analysis

In the opinion of some historians, Sonya Kovalevskaya was the greatest female mathematician prior to the 20th century. She made outstanding contributions to the theory of partial differential equations and also advanced the study of elliptic functions.

Born on January 15, 1850, in Moscow, she was the daughter of Vasily Korvin-Kukovsky, a Russian nobleman and officer, and Yelizaveta Shubert, also an aristocrat. Sonya was educated by an English governess, and participated in a sophisticated social circle after the family moved to St. Petersburg. Around age 14 she became interested in mathematics, apparently stimulated by the wallpaper of her father's country estate, which consisted of lithographs of his notes on differential and integral calculus. Sonya showed great potential while taking an 1867 course at the naval academy of St. Petersburg.

Sonya and her sister Anyuta subscribed to the radical ideology of the late 19th century, and both were unwilling to accept the traditional lifestyle that Russian society advocated. Therefore Sonya contracted a marriage with Vladimir Kovalevsky, a young paleontologist, which made feasible her desire to study mathematics at a foreign university. In 1869 the couple moved to Heidelberg, and later, in 1871, Sonya came to Berlin, where she studied under KARL WEIERSTRASS. Since she was a woman, she was not allowed to attend lectures; instead, she received private instruction from Weierstrass. By 1874 Kovalevskaya had already completed three research papers on partial differential equations and abelian integrals. As a result of this work, she qualified for a doctorate at the University of Göttingen.

Despite Kovalevskaya's impressive mathematical talent, she was unable to obtain an academic position in Europe, and so she returned to Russia to live with her husband. They had one daughter, born in 1878. The couple worked odd jobs for several years, but separated in 1881. During this time Kovalevskaya's husband became involved with a disreputable company, resulting in his disgrace and suicide in 1883. Appealing to

Weierstrass for assistance, Kovalevskaya obtained an appointment at the University of Stockholm. In Sweden Kovalevskaya continued her research into differential equations, which is discussed below. In 1889 she was elected to the Russian Academy of Sciences; at the height of her career she fell ill from pneumonia, and died on February 10, 1891, in Stockholm.

Kovalevskaya is most famous for her work in partial differential equations. She expanded on the work of AUGUSTIN-LOUIS CAUCHY and formulated the existence and uniqueness of solutions in a precise and general manner, introducing the important boundary and initial conditions to the problem. The resulting Cauchy-Kovalevskaya theorem gave necessary and sufficient conditions for a solution of a given partial differential equation to exist.

Kovalevskaya also contributed to the important field of abelian integrals, explaining how to express some of these integrals in terms of simpler ones. She won a prize for her memoir *On the Rotation of a Solid Body about a Fixed Point* (1888), which generalized the previous work of LEONHARD EULER and JOSEPH-LOUIS LAGRANGE. She also studied the motion of Saturn's rings, which earned her the epithet "Muse of the Heavens." Parallel to her career as a mathematician, Kovalevskaya also wrote several works of literature that were favorably received.

In a period when it was exceedingly difficult for women to enter academics, Sonya Kovalevskaya was rare in her ability to enter the field of mathematics and make significant discoveries with far-reaching impact. However, independent of her gender, she certainly ranks as one of the most talented and influential mathematicians of the 19th century. Her work on partial differential equations has become emblematic of modern approaches to the subject—namely, to focus on questions of existence and uniqueness of solutions through specification of certain boundary conditions. In this way, Kovalevskaya's work had guided the development of the theory of differential equations, which has numerous applications to science and engineering today.

Further Reading

Cooke, R. *The Mathematics of Sonya Kovalevskaya.* New York: Springer-Verlag, 1984.

Grinstein, L., and P. Campbell. *Women of Mathematics.* New York: Greenwood Press, 1987.

Kennedy, D. *Little Sparrow: A Portrait of Sophia Kovalevsky.* Athens: Ohio University Press, 1983.

Koblitz, A. *A Convergence of Lives: Sofia Kovalevskaia: Scientist, Writer, Revolutionary.* Boston: Birkhäuser, 1983.

⊠ Kronecker, Leopold
(1823–1891)
German
Number Theory, Algebra

Leopold Kronecker was an eminent German mathematician in the late 19th century who was known for his ability to unite separate areas of mathematics. However, his puritanical outlook, which struck out against the current trends in analysis, tended to inhibit the growth of new mathematics.

Leopold Kronecker was born on December 7, 1823, in Liegnitz, Germany, to Isidor Kronecker and Johanna Prausnitzer. They were a wealthy Jewish family, and their son received private tutoring at home. At the high school, Kronecker was taught by ERNST KUMMER, who encouraged the boy's natural mathematical talent.

In 1841 Kronecker went on to the University of Berlin, where he attended mathematics lectures by GUSTAV PETER LEJEUNE DIRICHLET. He was initially interested in philology and philosophy, and later studied astronomy at the University of Bonn. However, he focused his energies on mathematics and completed his doctorate in 1845 with a dissertation on complex numbers. Dirichlet, who was one of Kronecker's examiners and remained a lifelong friend, was impressed by Kronecker's penetration and knowledge of mathematics.

Kronecker returned to his hometown of Liegnitz on family business. During this time he pursued mathematics in his spare time as an amateur, and continued his correspondences with leading mathematicians while managing his family affairs. He married his cousin Fanny Prausnitzer in 1848, and his financial situation improved so much over the years that he was able to return to Berlin as a private scholar in 1855. The following year, KARL WEIERSTRASS came to Berlin and became friends with Kronecker and Kummer.

At about this time, Kronecker's mathematical productivity increased greatly. He wrote about number theory, elliptic functions, and algebra. He also related the various branches of mathematics to one another. As a result of his work, he was elected to the Berlin Academy in 1861. Exercising his right as a member, Kronecker gave a series of lectures at the University of Berlin on the topics of algebraic equations, number theory, determinants, and multiple integrals. Kronecker did not attract many students, but his ideas were nevertheless quite influential within the academy.

During the 1870s Kronecker's relationship with Weierstrass gradually disintegrated. This was primarily due to a divergence in their approach to analysis. Weierstrass emphasized the importance of irrational numbers and more modern methods, while Kronecker believed that most of mathematics—including algebra and analysis—should be studied under the category of arithmetic. In particular, he dispensed with irrational numbers completely; he uttered the well-known saying "God Himself made the whole numbers—everything else is the work of men." These views, which now seem antiquated and preposterous, rubbed shoulders with the tide of new ideas in analysis. Eventually, Weierstrass and Kronecker ceased all communication.

Kronecker's orthodoxy prevented him from appreciating the value of GEORG CANTOR's new set theoretic results on infinity. Because he was influential, he actually prohibited the development of new ideas.

Nevertheless, Kronecker was able to advance mathematics through his talent at unifying and connecting the different branches of arithmetic, analysis, and algebra. His theorems on boundary formulas, cyclotomic theory, and the convergence of infinite series are particularly noteworthy. His paper *"Über den Zahlbegriff"* (About the concept of number) of 1887 outlined his program to study only mathematical objects that could be constructed in a finite number of steps. Out of his dissertation came the theory of units for an algebraic number field, which would later become an important topic in modern algebra. As a mathematician, Kronecker stressed the utility of the algorithm as a means of calculation rather than as a worthy idea in itself.

Kronecker continued at Berlin, while still feuding with Weierstrass. In 1891 Kronecker's wife died, and Kronecker himself died soon afterward, on December 29, 1891, in Berlin. Although of Jewish heritage, he converted to Christianity in the last year of his life.

Kronecker represents an orthodoxy of 19th-century thought, which resisted the new wave of ideas ushered in by younger mathematicians, like Cantor. The very movement he sought to combat later became the mainstream of modern mathematics, and thus Kronecker seems, in retrospect, to be merely an obstacle to progress. The old school of mathematics still clung to a more intuitive conception of mathematics, which the increasingly abstract and formalistic mathematics of the late 19th century ignored. On the positive side, Kronecker was successful in his attempts to unify the different branches of mathematics. One can also view Kronecker's stress on finitely constructed mathematics as anticipatory of the later 20th-century movement of intuitionism, spearheaded by LUITZEN EGBERTUS VAN BROUWER and HENRI-JULES POINCARÉ.

Further Reading

Edwards, H. "An Appreciation of Kronecker," *The Mathematical Intelligencer* 9 (1987): 28–35.

———. "Kronecker's Place in History," in *History and Philosophy of Modern Mathematics*. Minneapolis: University of Minnesota Press, 1988.

———."On the Kronecker Nachlass," *Historia Mathematica* 5, no. 4 (1978): 419–426.

⊠   **Kummer, Ernst (Ernst Eduard Kummer)**
(1810–1893)
German
Algebra

Ernst Kummer was one of the great creative mathematicians of the 19th century, contributing to function theory, algebra, and geometry. Several mathematical techniques and ideas are attributed to him, and his efforts helped to advance modern mathematics.

Ernst Kummer was born on January 29, 1810, in Sorau, Germany, to Carl Gotthelf Kummer, a physician who died in 1813, and Frederike Sophie Rothe. Kummer entered the Sorau high school in 1819, and pursued Protestant theology at the University of Halle in 1828. However, he soon turned to mathematics, at first as a preparation for philosophy. In 1831 he received his doctorate, and he taught mathematics and physics at the Gymnasium in Liegnitz from 1832 to 1842. During this time, LEOPOLD KRONECKER was one of his students, and Kummer was able to encourage his natural talent.

His research at this time focused on the hypergeometric series introduced by CARL FRIEDRICH GAUSS. Kummer probed deeper than anyone else, obtaining several remarkable discoveries. The failed attempts to prove Fermat's last theorem led Kummer to study the factorization of integers and

develop the theory of ideals. He also discovered the Kummer surface, a four-dimensional manifold with 16 conical double points and 16 singular tangent planes. A gifted teacher, he succeeded in inspiring several students to carry out independent investigations. He had previously sent some of his work on function theory to CARL JACOBI, who helped procure a professorship for Kummer at the University of Breslau in 1842. In 1840 Kummer married Ottilie Mendelssohn, a cousin of GUSTAV PETER LEJEUNE DIRICHLET's wife. He held his position at Breslau until 1855, and there he did his important work on number theory and algebra. Kummer introduced ideal numbers and ideal prime factors in order to prove a great theorem of PIERRE DE FERMAT. In later years, Kronecker and RICHARD DEDEKIND further developed his initial results.

In 1855 Dirichlet left the University of Berlin to succeed Gauss at Göttingen, and Kummer was named as Dirichlet's replacement. By 1856 both KARL WEIERSTRASS and Kronecker had also come to Berlin, ushering in a period of mathematical productivity at the university. Kummer and Weierstrass constructed the first German seminar in pure mathematics in 1861, which attracted many young students. Kummer's lectures, which covered topics such as analytic geometry, mechanics, and number theory, were heavily attended due to his excellent exposition.

Kummer was blessed with an immense amount of energy. He simultaneously taught at the Kriegsschule from 1855 to 1874, was secretary of the mathematical section of the Berlin Academy from 1863 to 1878, and served several times as dean and rector of the University of Berlin. During this last phase of his career, Kummer focused on geometry, with applications to ray systems and ballistics. His study of ray systems followed the work of SIR WILLIAM ROWAN HAMILTON, although Kummer took an algebraic perspective. In the course of this research he discovered the so-called Kummer surface. Numerous mathematical concepts have been named after him.

When Kronecker and Weierstrass parted ways in the 1870s, Kummer may also have been estranged from Weierstrass. Certainly, Kummer was politically and mathematically conservative, shying away from many of the new developments. For example, Kummer rejected non-Euclidean geometry as pointless. He also considered mathematics a pure science, and believed that the appeal of mathematics lay in its dearth of applications. It is noteworthy that this has probably been the view of mathematicians for most of history, and only in the modern era has the opinion emerged that mathematics is valuable only if it can contribute to technology and societal improvement.

In 1882 Kummer retired from his position, claiming that his memory had been weakening. He died on May 14, 1893, in Berlin. Both Gauss and Dirichlet exerted a great influence over Kummer's development as a mathematician, and he had a great respect for them both. Despite his conservatism, Kummer was able to affect the evolution of mathematics through his numerous pupils and his raw creativity. His work in algebra on the arithmetization of mathematics was perhaps the most important.

Further Reading

Calinger, R. "The Mathematics Seminar at the University of Berlin: Origins, Founding, and the Kummer-Weierstrass Years," in *Vita Mathematica.* Washington, D.C.: Mathematical Association of America, 1996.

Edwards, H. "Mathematical Ideas, Ideals, and Ideology," *The Mathematical Intelligencer* 14 (1992): 6–18.

Ribenboim, P. "Kummer's Ideas on Fermat's Last Theorem," *L'Enseignement Mathématique. Revue Internationale. Deuxième Série* (2) 29, nos. 1–2 (1983): 165–177.

L

Lagrange, Joseph-Louis (Giuseppe Lodovico Lagrangia)
(1736–1813)
Italian
Mechanics, Analysis, Algebra, Differential Equations

Joseph Lagrange has been described as the last great mathematician of the 18th century. His mathematical ideas were highly original and influential, paving the way for the more abstract studies of the 19th century. Perhaps his most important contribution lies in his mechanistic formulation of the universe, giving exact mathematical formulas for the laws governing motion and mechanics.

Joseph-Louis Lagrange was born on January 25, 1736, in Turin, Italy. His name at birth was Giuseppe Lodovico Lagrangia, but later in life he adopted the French formulation Joseph-Louis Lagrange. Lagrange's father was Giuseppe Francesco Lodovico Lagrangia, and his mother was Teresa Grosso. His family was mostly of French descent, although Lagrange's mother was the only daughter of a Turin physician. Lagrange was the eldest of 11 children, most of whom died during childhood. Lagrange's father held the post of treasurer of the Office of Public Works and Fortifications at Turin. Despite this prestigious position, the family lived modestly.

Lagrange was originally intended for a career in law, but once he began studying physics, Lagrange recognized his own talent for the mathematical sciences. At first he developed an interest in geometry, but by age 17 was turning toward analysis. His first paper (1754) developed a formal calculus, which he later realized was already known to GOTTFRIED WILHELM VON LEIBNIZ. Subsequently, he began work on the problem of the tautochrone and began the development of his calculus of variations. This was essentially an application of the ideas of calculus to bundles of functions, rather than a single function.

In 1755 Lagrange sent his early results on this new calculus of variations to LEONHARD EULER. Lagrange developed this original and highly useful piece of mathematics when he was only 19. At the end of his life, he considered it to be his most important contribution. Euler expressed his interest in the novel method for solving optimization problems and, as a result of his growing renown, Lagrange was named professor at the Royal Artillery School in Turin in 1755. This position was poorly paid, and Lagrange felt underappreciated by his fellow citizens, which led him to later leave Italy.

The next year Lagrange applied his method to mechanics. He was able to describe the trajectory of an object subject to certain forces as the solution to an optimization problem in the

Joseph-Louis Lagrange developed a mechanistic mathematical formulation of the universe known as Lagrangian mechanics. *(Courtesy of AIP Emilio Segrè Visual Archives, E. Scott Bar Collection)*

calculus of variations. This elegant mathematical formulation of mechanics would revolutionize the study of dynamical systems.

Meanwhile, the Royal Academy of Sciences at Turin was founded, to which Lagrange made numerous fundamental contributions over the next decade. His works from the time period up to around 1770 include material on the calculus of variations, differential equations, the calculus of probabilities, celestial mechanics, and fluid motion. He developed the technique of integration by parts, so familiar to calculus students, and won several prizes offered by the Academy of Sciences in Paris, for his outstanding work on the motions of the Moon and other celestial bodies. Lagrange's system of mechanics made the principle of least action—that a particle chooses

the trajectory that minimizes energy—the foundation of dynamics. Many French mathematicians, including JEAN D'ALEMBERT and PIERRE-SIMON LAPLACE, recognized the excellent quality of his work.

In 1763 Lagrange was invited to Paris, where he was heartily received by the mathematical community there. D'Alembert attempted to secure Lagrange a superior position in Turin, but the promises of the royal court failed to materialize. As a result, Lagrange accepted an offer to fill Euler's vacant position in Berlin in 1766, which initiated the second scientific period of Lagrange's life.

Lagrange made friends with Johann Lambert and JOHANN BERNOULLI, and was named director of the Berlin Academy of Sciences. He had no teaching duties, which allowed him to focus on his mathematical research. Lagrange wed his cousin, Vittoria Conti, in 1767, and they were married—though childless—for 16 years, until Vittoria's health declined and she died in 1783 after a protracted illness.

While in Berlin Lagrange enjoyed continued participation and success in the Paris competitions, making outstanding contributions to the three-body problem. Besides these public contests, Lagrange developed his own personal work on celestial mechanics, publishing several important papers from 1782 onward. Meanwhile, he had already begun to investigate certain problems in algebra, completely solving a celebrated indeterminate equation posed by PIERRE DE FERMAT in 1768. Building on Euler's previous work, Lagrange proved that every integer can be expressed as the sum of, at most, four perfect squares (1770); he characterized prime numbers through a divisibility criterion, and further developed the theory of quadratic forms (1775), opening avenues of future research for CARL FRIEDRICH GAUSS and ADRIEN-MARIE LEGENDRE. He gave an exposition of the method of infinite descent, inspired by Fermat, and utilized the method of continued fractions.

He made one particularly important contribution to analysis in 1770, when he gave a series expansion involving the roots of a given equation, which had useful scientific applications. Lagrange's formula proved to be of enduring interest to mathematicians, as most of the great analysts of the 19th century, including AUGUSTIN-LOUIS CAUCHY, studied the consequences of this idea. This work, in conjunction with that of Alexandre Vandermonde, reveals the concept of the permutation group, which would later be developed precisely by Galois.

Lagrange also contributed to fluid mechanics in the 1780s, imaginary roots of algebraic equations in the 1770s, and infinitesimal analysis from 1768 to 1787. His work on the integration of differential equations, expanding on the ideas of Euler, represents an early step in the theory of elliptic functions, which would attract much interest in the 19th century. His work on partial differential equations must also be mentioned, as he brought integration powerfully to bear on several problems. His work in probability is of lesser significance.

Lagrange's considerable contributions to mechanics were scattered among several publications, and he summarized them in a 1788 treatise. Around this time, Lagrange had settled in Paris. Although Turin had attempted to lure Lagrange to return to his native city, he was not eager to leave Berlin until the death of his wife in 1783. But the French mathematicians, who aggressively solicited his presence, were successful in attracting Lagrange. In 1787 he became a pensioned member of the Academy of Sciences, where he weathered the chaotic political turmoil of the succeeding decades.

In 1792 Lagrange married Renée-Françoise-Adélaïde Le Monnier, with whom he also had a happy marriage. During the beginning of the Parisian phase of his career, Lagrange's activity abated somewhat. He was active in the 1790 Constituent Assembly on the standardization of weights and measures, and later taught analysis

at the newly founded École Polytechnique until 1799. After Napoleon rose to power Lagrange was appointed a grand officer of the Legion of Honor and in 1808 a count of the Empire. He died on the morning of April 11, 1813, in Paris. Universities throughout Europe observed his death, and Laplace gave his funeral oration.

Lagrange made extensive contributions to many areas of mathematics; these labors often opened up new areas of inquiry (such as elliptic functions, quadratic forms, and the calculus of variations). Most significant was his formulation of mechanics, sometimes called Lagrangian mechanics, which essentially mechanized the understanding of the physical universe. This proved to be a powerful and influential mode of describing the known world, and continues to affect mathematical inquiry today.

Further Reading

Baltus, C. "Continued Fractions and the Pell Equations: The Work of Euler and Lagrange," *Communications in the Analytic Theory of Continued Fractions* 3 (1994): 4–31.

Fraser, C. "Isoperimetric Problems in the Variational Calculus of Euler and Lagrange," *Historia Mathematica* 19, no. 1 (1992): 4–23.

Koetsier, T. "Joseph Louis Lagrange (1736–1813): His Life, His Work and His Personality," *Nieuw Archief voor Wiskunde* 4, no. 4 (3) (1986): 191–205.

Sarton, G. "Lagrange's Personality (1736–1813)," *Proceedings of the American Philosophical Society* 88 (1944): 457–496.

⊠   **Laplace, Pierre-Simon**
(1749–1827)
French
Probability, Mechanics, Differential Equations

Pierre-Simon Laplace was certainly one of the most eminent scientists and mathematicians of

Pierre-Simon Laplace studied the heat equation, where the Laplace operator appears, and developed many first results of probability. *(Courtesy of AIP Emilio Segrè Visual Archives)*

the late 18th century in Paris, and may be regarded as one of the principal founders of the theory of probability. His scientific theories, remarkable for their modernity and sophistication, held sway for many years and profoundly influenced the later evolution of thought. Laplace was remarkably talented as a mathematician, and he was a prominent intellectual in France during his lifetime.

Pierre-Simon Laplace was born on March 23, 1749, in Beaumont-en-Auge, in the province of Normandy, France, to Pierre Laplace, a prosperous cider trader, and Marie-Anne Sochon, who came of a wealthy family of landowners. Although Laplace's family was comfortable financially, they did not possess an intellectual pedigree. In his early years Laplace attended a Benedectine priory, his father intending him for a career in the church. At age 16 Laplace enrolled at Caen University, where he studied theology; however, some of his professors recognized his exceptional mathematical talent, and stimulated him to pursue his innate gifts at Paris.

So it was that at age 19, Laplace departed from Caen without a degree and arrived at Paris, with a letter of introduction to the eminent JEAN D'ALEMBERT. D'Alembert warmly accepted Laplace, and would fill the role of a mentor to the brilliant young mathematician. D'Alembert also procured a position for Laplace as professor at the École Militaire. This position afforded Laplace little intellectual stimulus, but it enabled him to remain in Paris, where he was able to interact with the Parisian mathematical community and produce his first papers. These works, read before the Academy of Sciences in 1770, built upon the work of JOSEPH-LOUIS LAGRANGE on the extrema of curves and difference equations.

Laplace was an ambitious young man who was well aware of his own talent, and he made this fact apparent to his inferior colleagues. This arrogance alienated many, while they were at the same time forced to admit his brilliance. Laplace was indignant at being passed over for election to the Academy of Sciences due to his youth, but by 1773 he was made an adjoint of that institution after having read 13 papers before the community within three years. Laplace's early work was of high quality on a variety of topics, including differential equations, difference equations, integral calculus, mathematical astronomy, and probability. These latter two topics would form a recurring theme in Laplace's lifetime work.

In the 1770s Laplace built up his reputation as a mathematician and scientist, and in the 1780s he made his most important contributions. Laplace demonstrated that respiration was a form of combustion, studied the impact of moons upon their planets' orbits, and formulated the classical mathematical theory of heat. The Laplace operator (referred to as the "Laplacian" by mathematicians) forms an important role in the basic differential equation for heat. His work in astronomy at this time laid the groundwork for his later seminal masterpiece on the structure and dynamics of the solar system.

In 1784 Laplace became an examiner of the Royal Artillery Corps, and served on various scientific committees. He used his expertise in probability to compare mortality rates among hospitals—one of the first exercises in survival analysis. In 1785 Laplace was promoted to a senior position in the Academy of Sciences, and soon afterward Lagrange joined the same institution. The proximity of both these eminent scientists led to an explosion of scientific activity in Paris.

On May 15, 1788, Laplace married Marie-Charlotte de Courty de Romanges, who was 20 years younger; they had two children. Laplace became involved in a committee to standardize weights and measures in 1790 that advocated the metric system. By this time the French Revolution had already commenced, and Laplace posed as a republican and antimonarchist to avoid political persecution. He was somewhat of an opportunist, strategically altering his political opinions throughout the Revolution in order to escape attack. In 1793 he fled the Reign of Terror, but was later consulted by the government on the new French calendar; although this calendar was incompatible with astronomical data, Laplace refrained from criticism to protect himself.

Laplace taught probability at the École Normale, but his abstraction made his lectures inaccessible to the students there. These lectures were later published as a collection of essays on probability in 1814, giving basic definitions as well as a wealth of applications to mortality rates, games of chance, natural philosophy, and judicial decisions. In 1795 the Academy of Sciences, which had been shut down by the revolutionaries, was reopened, and Laplace became a founding member of the Bureau des Longitudes and head of the Paris Observatory. However, in the latter capacity Laplace proved to be too theoretical, as he was more concerned with developing his planetary theory for the dynamics of the solar system than with astronomical observation. In 1796 Laplace presented his famous nebular hypothesis in his *Exposition du système du monde* (The system of the world), which delineated the genesis of the solar system from a flattened, rotating cloud of cooling gas into its present form. In five books Laplace described the motion of celestial bodies, the tides of the sea, universal gravitation, the mechanical concepts of force and momentum, and a history of the solar system. Much of his material is remarkably modern in its description of the world, which is a testimony to the enduring legacy of his scientific thought.

This important work was followed up by the *Traité du Mécanique Céleste* (Treatise on celestial mechanics), which gave a more mathematical account of his nebular hypothesis. Here Laplace formulates and solves the differential equations that describe the motions of celestial bodies, and more generally applies mechanics to astronomical problems. Herein appears the Laplace equation, which features the Laplacian, although this differential equation was known previously. Characteristically, Laplace failed to give credit to his intellectual progenitors. However, it is clear that Laplace was heavily influenced by Lagrange and ADRIEN-MARIE LEGENDRE.

Laplace received a variety of honors under the empire of Bonaparte, including the Legion of Honor in 1805; he was chancellor of the senate and briefly served as minister of the interior. In 1806 he became a count, and after the restoration became a marquis in 1817. In 1812 he published his *Théorie Analytique des Probabilités* (Analytic theory of probability), which summarized his contributions to probability. Therein Laplace detailed Bayes's theorem (see THOMAS BAYES), the concept of mathematical expectation, and the principle of least squares (simultaneously invented by CARL FRIEDRICH GAUSS); these three ideas have had a momentous impact on science and statistics. He applied his techniques to a wide variety of topics, such as life expectancy and legal matters. Although others (such as BLAISE PASCAL) had contributed to probability previously, Laplace gave a more systematic treatment, and clearly demonstrated its utility in practical problems.

Laplace's scientific ideas were profound. He sought to reduce the study of physics to the interactions between individual molecules, acting at a distance. This singularly modern formulation was revolutionary in its wide range of applications, including the study of pressure, density, refraction, and gravity. His work is also distinguished from previous molecular theories in its precise mathematical formulation. In the first decades of the 19th century, Laplace went on to apply his principles to a variety of scientific problems, such as the velocity of sound, the shape of the Earth, and the theory of heat. He also founded the Société d'Arcueil in 1805, in which SIMÉON DENIS POISSON was also active; this group actively advocated a prominent role of mathematics in scientific exploration. After 1812 this group's energy waned, and Laplace's ideas came under attack as newer paradigms were advanced. For example, Laplace held to the fluid theories of heat and light, and these fell out of favor with the advance of JEAN-BAPTISTE-JOSEPH FOURIER's ideas.

The wane of Laplace's scientific hegemony was also accompanied by increasing social isolation, as his colleagues became disgusted with his political infidelity. In later life he supported the restoration of the Bourbons, and was forced to flee Paris during the return of Bonaparte. He died on March 5, 1827, in Paris, France. The Academy of Sciences, in honor of his passing, canceled its meeting and left his position vacant for several months.

Laplace contributed to the wave of scientific thought in Paris in the late 18th century. Although many of his ideas were soon discarded, others have endured to modern times; even his outdated theories were influential on the next generation of scientists. More notable was his advocacy of a stronger role of mathematics in scientific enterprise, and his precise formulation of mathematical laws for scientific phenomena. His mathematical work has proved to be more enduring; in particular, his efforts in differential equations, probability, and mechanics have become classical in these disciplines. Of particular note is the mathematical theory of heat and his fundamental work on basic probability.

Further Reading

Bell, E. *Men of Mathematics*. New York: Simon and Schuster, 1965.

Crosland, M. *The Society of Arcueil: A View of French Science at the Time of Napoleon I*. Cambridge, Mass.: Harvard University Press, 1967.

Gillispie, C. *Pierre-Simon Laplace, 1749–1827: A Life in Exact Science*. Princeton, N.J.: Princeton University Press, 1997.

Stigler, S. "Laplace's Early Work: Chronology and Citations," *Isis* 69, no. 247 (1978): 234–254.

———. "Studies in the History of Probability and Statistics XXXII: Laplace, Fisher, and the Discovery of the Concept of Sufficiency," *Biometrika* 60 (1973): 439–445.

Lebesgue, Henri-Léon
(1875–1941)
French
Analysis

Henri Lebesgue played an important role in the development of integration theory as one of the most active branches of 20th-century mathematics. The so-called Lebesgue integral is now classic in integration theory and has been a cornerstone for continuing research as well as an aid in applications.

Henri Lebesgue was born on June 28, 1875, in Beauvais, France. As a young man, Lebesgue studied at the École Normale Supérieure from 1894 to 1897. After graduation, Lebesgue spent the next two years working in his school's library, where he became acquainted with the work of RENÉ-LOUIS BAIRE on discontinuous functions. Lebesgue taught at the Lycée Centrale in Nancy from 1899 to 1902 while completing his doctoral thesis for the Sorbonne. He set out to develop a more general notion of integration that would allow for the discontinuous functions discovered by Baire.

In the process of working on his thesis, Lebesgue became acquainted with the work of CAMILLE JORDAN and ÉMILE BOREL on measurability and integration; since the time of BERNHARD RIEMANN's integral, mathematicians had gradually introduced concepts from measure theory. Lebesgue's early work expanded Borel's efforts, and he successfully constructed a definition of integration that was more general than Riemann's. More significantly, Lebesgue was able to apply his integral to several problems of analysis, including the validity of term-by-term integration of an infinite series. Also, the fundamental theorem of calculus, which relates integration and differentiation, was not able to handle nonintegrable functions with bounded derivative. Lebesgue's new integral resolved this difficulty. He also worked on curve rectification (computing the length of a curve).

After submitting his thesis, Lebesgue was given a position at the University of Rennes, which lasted until 1906. He was at the University of Poitiers from 1906 to 1910, and then was appointed as a professor at the Sorbonne from 1910 to 1919. Lebesgue continued his research on the structure of continuous functions and integration;

he took the first steps toward a theory of double integrals, which was later completed by GUIDO FUBINI. A wave of research followed in the wake of Lebesgue's work, and this effort included such mathematicians as PIERRE FATOU. Through FRIGYES RIESZ, the Lebesgue integral became an invaluable tool in the theory of integral equations and function spaces. His other research included the structure of sets and functions, the calculus of variations, and the theory of dimension.

Lebesgue received many honors, such as the Prix Santour in 1917 and election to the French Academy of Sciences in 1922. During the last two decades of his life, his interests shifted increasingly to pedagogical issues and elementary geometry. He died on July 26, 1941, in Paris. Besides his own pivotal contributions, Lebesgue was an active proponent of abstract theories of measure, and thus is largely responsible for the important position of measure theory in modern mathematics. His essential improvement on the basic Riemann integral resolved many outstanding mathematical questions and opened up a new vista for future exploration.

Further Reading

Burkill, J. "Henri Lebesgue," *Journal of the London Mathematical Society* 19 (1944): 56–64.

———."Obituary: Henri Lebesgue. 1875–1941," *Obituary Notices of Fellows of the Royal Society of London* 4 (1944): 483–490.

May, K. "Biographical Sketch of Henri Lebesgue," in *Measure and the Integral* by Henri Lebesgue. San Francisco: Holden-Day, 1966.

⊠ **Legendre, Adrien-Marie**
(1752–1833)
French
Number Theory, Analysis, Geometry

Legendre was an important figure in the transition from 18th- to 19th-century mathematics.

His contributions to number theory and analysis raised many significant questions that future mathematicians would pursue. He was also one of the founders of the central theory of elliptic functions.

Adrien-Marie Legendre was born on September 18, 1752, in Paris, France. His family was affluent, and Legendre received an excellent scientific education at the schools of Paris. In 1770 Legendre defended his theses on mathematics and physics at the Collège Mazarin.

Legendre possessed a modest fortune, which gave him the liberty to pursue mathematical research in his leisure time. Nevertheless, he taught mathematics at the École Militaire in Paris from 1775 to 1780. Legendre won a 1782 prize from the Berlin Academy, with a paper concerning the trajectory of cannonballs and bombs, taking air friction into account. Over the next few years he increased his scientific output, attempting to gain more renown among the French scientists; he studied the mutual attractions of planetary bodies, indeterminate equations of the second degree, continued fractions, probability, and the rotation of accelerating bodies. Throughout his life, Legendre's favorite areas of research were celestial mechanics, number theory, and elliptic functions.

In 1786 Legendre published *Traité des fonctions elliptiques* (Treatise on elliptic functions) that outlined methods for discriminating between maxima and minima in the calculus of variations, and the so-called Legendre conditions gave rise to an extensive literature. He also studied integration by means of elliptic arcs, which was really a first step in the theory of elliptic functions. Around this time Legendre was promoted in the Academy of Sciences, and contributed to some geodetic problems, bringing his expertise with spherical trigonometry to bear.

Legendre next studied partial differential equations, expressing the so-called Legendre transformation. He self-published his 1792 work on elliptic transcendentals, since the French government suppressed the academies. This was a strenuous time for Legendre. He married a young girl, Marguerite Couhin, while the French Revolution destroyed his personal fortune. His young wife was able to give him emotional stability while he continued writing new scientific works.

In 1794 Legendre received a new post concerned with weights and measures. In the meantime, he published his *Elements of Geometry,* which would dominate elementary instruction in geometry for the next century. During the next decade he directed the calculation of new, highly accurate trigonometric tables; they were based on the newer mathematical techniques of the calculus of variations.

Legendre published his *Essay on the Theory of Numbers* in 1798, which expanded on his previous work of 1785, with material on indeterminate equations, the law of reciprocity of quadratic residues, the decomposition of numbers into three squares, and arithmetical progressions. His 1806 work on the orbits of comets gave the first public exposition of the method of least squares. However, Legendre was infuriated to learn that CARL FRIEDRICH GAUSS had been using the method in private since 1795.

In the succeeding decades Legendre expanded on the theory of elliptic functions, indeterminate equations, and spherical trigonometry. His work in number theory was noteworthy for the law of quadratic reciprocity. Legendre gave an imperfect demonstration of this law in 1785, and Gauss proved it rigorously in 1801. Legendre contributed to the knowledge of Fermat's last theorem, establishing the result in a special case, and was a precursor of analytic number theory—he studied the distribution of prime numbers, stating their asymptotics in 1798. His best achievements lie in the theory of elliptic functions; expanding on the work of LEONHARD EULER and JOSEPH-LOUIS LAGRANGE, Legendre essentially founded this theory in

1786 by expressing elliptic integrals in terms of certain more basic types called transcendentals. A master calculator, Legendre developed extensive tables for the values of these elliptic functions. NIELS HENRIK ABEL and KARL JACOBI substantially developed his early work in the following years. Legendre succeeded PIERRE-SIMON LAPLACE in 1799 as the examiner of mathematics at the school of artillery, and resigned in 1815, succeeding Lagrange at the Bureau de Longitudes in 1813. He received several honors, including membership in the Legion of Honor. On January 9, 1833, he died in Paris after a painful illness.

Legendre's approach to mathematics was typical of the 18th century. Many of his arguments lacked rigor, and he was highly skeptical of innovations such as non-Euclidean geometry. He was, in many respects, a disciple of Euler and Lagrange, whose view on mathematics influenced him greatly. But Legendre's contributions to number theory and elliptic functions led to whole new arenas of inquiry, and it is here that his impact was so pronounced.

Further Reading

Grattan-Guinness, I. *The Development of the Foundations of Mathematical Analysis from Euler to Riemann.* Cambridge, Mass.: MIT Press, 1970.

Hellman, C. "Legendre and the French Reform of Weights and Measures," *Osiris* 1 (1936): 314–340.

Pintz, J. "On Legendre's Prime Number Formula," *The American Mathematical Monthly* 87, no. 9 (1980): 733–735.

Gottfried Leibniz, recognized as cofounder of calculus, formulated the notion of limit, which is crucial to real analysis. *(Joh. Gottfr. Auerbach ad viv. Delin Viennae 1714. Joh. Elias Haid sc. 1781. Aug. Vind., AIP Emilio Segrè Visual Archives)*

⊠   Leibniz, Gottfried Wilhelm von
(1646–1716)
German
Calculus, Logic, Differential Equations

One of the most hotly debated issues in the history of mathematics was the question of priority in the discovery of infinitesimal calculus. SIR ISAAC NEWTON and Gottfried Leibniz had each made remarkable discoveries in differential calculus, and each man's followers fostered an ugly argument over who should be credited with the original discovery. Whatever the truth may be, there is no doubt that Leibniz was one of the greatest mathematicians of his time, which is apparent not only from the breadth and depth of his original ideas, but also from his ability to organize others' thoughts more efficiently.

Gottfried Wilhelm von Leibniz was born on July 1, 1646, in Leipzig, Germany, to Friedrich Leibniz, a professor at the University of Leipzig, and Katherina Schmuck. The family was of Slavonic descent, but had been dwelling in

Germany for several generations. Leibniz was a precocious student, and his teachers initially attempted to restrain his curious nature. After his father died in 1652, he was allowed access to his father's library. In this manner Leibniz educated himself, so that when he entered the University of Leipzig at age 15, he had already mastered the classics. His voracious appetite for reading remained with him throughout his life, and Leibniz was able to digest a great variety of scholarly subjects.

Leipzig held to the unscientific Aristotelian tradition, first learning Euclidean geometry at the University of Jena, where he briefly studied after 1663. He completed his doctorate at Altdorf in 1666, and soon entered the service of a nobleman of the Holy Roman Empire. Leibniz initiated a correspondence with many scientific societies, and he began work on a calculating machine that was finally completed in 1674. In 1671 he journeyed to Paris on a diplomatic mission designed to forestall the French monarch's invasion of the Rhineland. This project was unsuccessful, but while in Paris Leibniz developed a lifelong friendship with CHRISTIAAN HUYGENS.

During these years, Leibniz expanded on his earlier instruction in mathematics, developing calculation rules for finite differences. Continued peace negotiations led him to London in 1673, where he was admitted to the Royal Society and became familiar with the works of ISAAC BARROW. At this time Leibniz received hints of Newton's work on infinitesimal calculus, and he soon developed his own computational techniques and notation. By 1674 Leibniz effected the arithmetical quadrature of the circle.

Leibniz's previous patron had died, and in 1676 he took on a new position in Hannover, acting as librarian and engineer. A few years later he became a court councilor and was busily engaged in genealogical research for the duke. Meanwhile, Leibniz had started researching

algebra, and had obtained several important results by 1675, such as the determination of symmetric functions and an algorithm for the solution of higher-degree algebraic equations. He conjectured that the sum of complex conjugate numbers is always a real number. ABRAHAM DE MOIVRE later proved this result. Leibniz also investigated progressions of primes and arithmetic series, such as the sum of reciprocal squares. He learned of the transcendence of the logarithmic and trigonometric functions and their basic properties, and investigated some problems in probability.

But his greatest discovery came late in 1675, when he introduced the notion of the limit to infinitesimal calculus. This method, and his corresponding notation, facilitated the further spread and understanding of the new mathematics. Newton disparaged his work, as it did not solve any new problems; but the strength of Leibniz's system was its clarity and abstraction of the general principles of calculus. Leibniz did proceed to solve several important differential equations with his techniques. Many of his discoveries of this time were written only as notes and ideas in letters, and were not systematically developed or published until 1682. In the next few years he presented a few papers to the public that treated arithmetical quadrature, the law of refraction, algebraic integrations, and differential calculus.

In 1687 Leibniz traveled around Germany to continue his genealogical research. He also visited Italy, and finally completed his project in 1690—his efforts helped raise the duchy of Hannover to electoral status in 1692. Leibniz attracted attention from the scientific community through his attack on Cartesian dynamics in 1686. Out of this controversy, several dynamical questions were posed and solved by Leibniz, Huygens, and JAKOB BERNOULLI, including the famous problems of the catenary (1691) and the brachistochrone (1697). Characteristically, Leibniz disclosed only his results and not his methods. In fact, his papers were often written hastily. Despite some errors, his work was noteworthy for the originality of his ideas, some of which were precursors to EVARISTE GALOIS's work on the solubility of equations. Leibniz defined the center of curvature, developed the method of undetermined coefficients in the theory of differential equations, and constructed the power series for exponential and trigonometric functions.

In the later years of the 17th century, much of Leibniz's time was taken up in the controversy with Newton over the discovery of calculus. The followers of Newton contended that Leibniz had plagiarized his ideas directly from Newton and Barrow. Leibniz defended himself in 1700, stressing that he had already published his material on differential calculus in 1684. The ugly public debate raged back and forth, egged on by nationalistic considerations, until the Royal Society held a biased investigation, which ruled in favor of Newton in 1712. This verdict was accepted without question for about 140 years. Now it is thought that Leibniz developed his methods independently of Newton.

Leibniz journeyed to Berlin in 1700 and founded the Berlin Academy, becoming president for life. He labored to make certain political and religious reforms and was appointed a councilor to Russia in 1712. He spent the last few years of his life attempting to complete the history of the house of Brunswick while plagued by gout. He died on November 14, 1716. Besides his remarkable contributions to mathematics, Leibniz researched physics, logic, and philosophy. He wrote on topics as diverse as religious dogma (theodicy) and planetary motion, and developed a logical calculus that would allow for the certainty of deductions through an algebraic system. In this aspect, Leibniz was a forefather of numerous other formal logicians such as GEORGE BOOLE and FRIEDRICH LUDWIG GOTTLOB FREGE.

His greatest talent as a mathematician was his ability to penetrate the thoughts of other scientists and present them in a coherent fashion suitable for computation. The notation that he developed for differential calculus is the quintessential example of this power—he assiduously perceived that the notion of limit was crucial to the study of infinitesimal calculus. The details, for Leibniz, were not so important as the underlying abstract concepts. His legacy in mathematics continues to this day.

Further Reading

Broad, C., and C. Lewy. *Leibniz: An Introduction.* London: Cambridge University Press, 1975.

Hostler, J. *Leibniz's Moral Philosophy.* London: Duckworth, 1975.

Ishiguro, H. *Leibniz's Philosophy of Logic and Language.* New York: Cambridge University Press, 1990.

Merz, J. *Leibniz.* Edinburgh: Blackwood, 1884.

Rescher, N. *Leibniz: An Introduction to His Philosophy.* Oxford: Blackwell, 1979.

Ross, G. *Leibniz.* New York: Oxford University Press, 1984.

Rutherford, D. *Leibniz and the Rational Order of Nature.* New York: Cambridge University Press, 1995.

⊠ Leonardo da Vinci
(1452–1519)
Italian
Geometry

Leonardo da Vinci is one of the most famous persons of the medieval period. An artist, engineer, and scientist, he was both diverse and prophetic. He made substantial contributions to art, anatomy, technology, mechanics, geology, and mathematics.

Leonardo da Vinci was born on April 15, 1452, in Empolia, Italy. He was the illegitimate

Leonardo da Vinci held mathematics to be the key to all the other sciences and studied curvilinear surfaces. *(Courtesy of the Library of Congress)*

son of Piero da Vinci, a Florentine citizen. His mother was a peasant girl named Caterina. Leonardo's father was soon married to a respectable Italian woman, Albiera di Giovanni Amadori. Leonardo received a rudimentary education, and he displayed his talents for music and art at a young age. In 1467 he was apprenticed to Andrea del Verrocchio, with whom he studied painting, sculpture, and mechanics.

Leonardo completed some of his early paintings during this time, including *Baptism of Christ*. In 1482 he departed in order to work for the duke of Milan; by this time he was already accomplished in architecture, painting, and sculpture, as well as military engineering. He remained in Milan until 1499, during which time he became

more interested in physics and mechanics and in the properties of light. He also augmented his meager education in mathematics, studying Latin and geometry concurrently.

Leonardo formulated his theory of the supremacy of painting on carefully laid mathematical principles of proportion and perspective. His interest in proportion led him to conduct further research in physics and mathematics. Some of his early work in mathematics was quite erroneous, as he did not have an adequate grasp of arithmetical computation—one example is his claim that the fraction 2/2 is the square root of 2, since he falsely asserts that 2/2 times 2/2 is 4/2.

His other projects during the time in Milan include the physics of light, the physics of vision, and the problem of mechanical flight. He collaborated with the mathematician Pacioli on the *Divina proportione* (Divine proportion). It is probable that Leonardo had read EUCLID OF ALEXANDRIA's *Elements* before making the drawings in this book. Leonardo's notebooks contain proofs of various propositions in the *Elements*, and it is likely that his friend Pacioli encouraged and assisted him in his study of Euclid.

Leonardo departed for Venice after the French captured the duke of Milan, and later he returned to Florence. He briefly served under Cesare Borgia as a military engineer, and later completed his famous *Mona Lisa*. From 1500 to 1506 he pursued research into human anatomy, and more of his time was occupied with mathematics and mechanics. After completing his study of Euclid—Leonardo was especially interested in the treatment of proportion in Book X of the *Elements*—he began his own research on equiparation. He was mainly interested in the squaring of curvilinear surfaces (transforming these curved regions into squares with the same area), although his method of proof was often mechanical rather than strictly geometrical.

Leonardo proposed several methods for squaring the circle; he was familiar with ARCHIMEDES OF SYRACUSE's method, but rejected the latter's approximation of pi by 22/7. He attempted to improve the approximation by inscribing a 96-sided polygon in the circle.

Encouraged by his supposed discovery of the quadrature of the circle on November 30, 1504, he pursued similar research on doubling squares and quadrupling circles. He also became interested in the doubling of the cube (which had already been solved by ERATOSTHENES OF CYRENE centuries ago), dissatisfied by a recent solution given by Valla. Eventually, Leonardo conceived of a solution that eliminated the need for a mechanical apparatus, and he was thereby able to obtain extremely accurate approximations for the cube root of two. However, he was unable to provide a rigorous proof for his method.

Many of his mathematical writings are included in the *Codex Atlanticus* (Atlantic codex). Leonardo continued to investigate the properties of curvilinear surfaces, such as the portions left between a circle and an inscribed square or hexagon. He also explored the possibility of human flight by studying the anatomy of birds, as well as the movement of water. In 1506 he returned to Milan, where he served under the French governor. In this latter period of his life, he produced some of his best anatomical drawings, and his scientific efforts spread to hydrology, geology, meteorology, biology, and human physiology. In all these areas, he felt that mathematics held the keys of knowledge, and he attempted to formulate geometrical laws for these disciplines. The French were expelled in 1513, and Leonardo departed for Rome, hoping to find work with Pope Leo X; this failed to materialize, and he returned to the service of France in 1516, working under Francis I. He suffered a stroke in Amboise, and died on May 2, 1519.

Leonardo's approach to the study of nature cannot be called scientific in the modern sense.

He did believe in the importance of empirical investigation, but many of his ideas were purely speculative, without solid reasoning behind them. Of course, many of his concepts were brilliant contributions as well. In mathematics, he seems to have been an amateur. He certainly made some worthwhile discoveries, and he deeply respected the role of mathematics in the investigation of nature. But many of his works were deeply flawed, and his approach to proofs was more typical of his identity as an artist. In addition, his mathematical works have not influenced the subsequent progress of mathematical thought. His geometrical research on curvilinear areas did develop an aspect of Euclid's work, but his writings were not well known in his own time, and thus did not exert an influence on other mathematical thinkers.

Further Reading

Clark, K. *Leonardo da Vinci.* London: Viking, 1975.

Kemp, M. *Leonardo da Vinci, the Marvelous Works of Nature and Man.* London: J.M. Dent, 1981.

McLanathan, R. *Images of the Universe; Leonardo da Vinci: The Artist as Scientist.* Garden City, N.Y.: Doubleday, 1966.

Moody, D., and M. Clagett. *The Medieval Science of Weights.* Madison: University of Wisconsin Press, 1960.

Zubov, V. *Leonardo da Vinci.* Cambridge, Mass.: Harvard University Press, 1968.

Lévy, Paul-Pierre
(1886–1971)
French
Probability, Analysis, Differential Equations

In the early 20th century, the field of probability lacked unity and cohesion. Paul Lévy made fundamental contributions to this area, forming it into one of the major divisions of modern mathematics. He also developed the theory of partial differential equations and functional analysis, propelling these fields of thought forward.

Paul Lévy was born on September 15, 1886, in Paris, France. He belonged to a family of mathematicians, including his father and grandfather. His father, Lucien Lévy, was an examiner at the École Polytechnique. Paul Lévy was an outstanding student, attending the Lycée Saint Louis in Paris, where he won prizes in mathematics and science. In his entrance examinations to college, he scored first place for the École Normale Supérieur and second place for the École Polytechnique.

He chose to attend the latter institution and began publishing papers while still an undergraduate. His first paper (1905) studied semiconvergent series. Lévy later graduated in first place and spent a year in the military before joining the École des Mines in 1907. While there, Lévy also attended lectures by Charles Picard and Jacques Hadamard. The latter greatly influenced Lévy's research, encouraging him to pursue functional analysis.

In 1910 Lévy started to research functional analysis, and Picard, JULES-HENRI POINCARÉ, and Hadamard examined his thesis the following year. He obtained his doctorate in 1912. Lévy became professor at the École des Mines in 1913 and, in 1920, became professor of analysis at the École Polytechnique. During World War I Lévy served in the French military and worked on mathematical ballistics problems to aid the war effort.

His work on functional analysis extended the calculus of variations to function spaces, and followed the same lines of thought as those of VITO VOLTERRA. But his greatest work lay in probability, where he labored extensively for many years. Lévy borrowed many techniques from analysis to attack probability problems, and also initiated the development of probability into a mature field of mathematics, capable of being applied to other disciplines. In particular, he worked on limit laws, the theory of martingales, and the properties of Brownian motion. The latter two areas form two large branches of the theory of stochastic processes, which are widely used in engineering, statistics, and the sciences to model and solve a variety of practical problems.

Beyond these advances in probability, Lévy also studied the theory of partial differential equations and geometry. In the former area, Lévy extended Laplace transforms and generalized the notion of functional derivatives. He produced several texts that have been widely used by students of mathematics. Lévy died on December 15, 1971, in Paris, France.

Lévy made important contributions to probability and functional analysis, which have been two of the most important areas of mathematics for modeling real scientific problems in the 20th century. He was a deep thinker with an appreciation for mathematical beauty and utility.

Further Reading

Doob, J. "Obituary: Paul Lévy," *Journal of Applied Probability* 9 (1972): 870–872.

Kendall, D. "Obituary: Paul Lévy," *Journal of the Royal Statistical Society. Series A. Statistics in Society* 137 (1974): 259–260.

⊠ **Li Chih** (Li Yeh)
(1192–1279)
Chinese
Algebra

Li Chih, also known as Li Yeh, was one of the greatest Chinese mathematicians. He is known for developing methods to solve algebraic equations. The method of the celestial element, which Li Chih helped to propagate, has exerted an enduring influence on Chinese and Japanese mathematics up to present times.

Li Chih was born in 1192 in Beijing, China. His father was Li Yü, an official in the northern government. Li Chih received his education in his father's native province of Hopeh. In 1230 he passed his civil service examination and was appointed as a registrar in Shensi Province. Before he started this post, he became the governor of Chün-chou in Honan Province. In 1232 the Mongols captured this city, and Li Chih fled for safety.

By 1234 the kingdom of the Jurchen had fallen to the Mongol invaders, and Li Chih devoted his energies to private studies in mathematics. During this time, he frequently lived in poverty, but he managed to complete his most important work, *Sea Mirror of the Circle Measurements*, which is discussed below. By 1251 his circumstances had improved, and he settled in Feng-lung, in Hopeh Province. Although he still lived in isolation, he made friends with two other famous men, Chang Te-hui and Yuan Yü. The trio became known as "the Three Friends of Lung Mountain."

In 1257 Kublai Khan consulted Li Chih on certain matters of government and the reasons for earthquakes. Shortly, Li Chih completed a second mathematical work: *New Steps in Computation* in 1259. When Kublai Khan ascended the throne in 1260, he offered Li Chih a government post, which he refused due to his age. In 1264 the Mongolian emperor created the Han-lin Academy, designed to record the official history of the Liao and Jurchen kingdoms, and Li Chih was recruited to join this body. He soon resigned, again claiming old age, and retreated to Feng-lung, where he attracted a group of pupils.

Li Chih later changed his name to Li Yeh, in order to avoid having the same name as the third Tang emperor. Before his death in 1279, he instructed his son to burn all his writings except *Sea Mirror of the Circle Measurements*, as this alone seemed—to him—to be of benefit to posterity.

New Steps in Computation also survived conflagration, as did some other nonscientific works.

Sea Mirror of the Circle Measurements was completed in 1248. Li Chih therein introduced an algebraic process known as the "method of celestial elements" and the "coefficient array method." This method exerted much influence through China and Japan, even though it was not well understood. Li Chih was not the method's inventor, having learned it from the mathematician P'eng Che, of whom little is known. The method is used to solve algebraic equations of high degree by arranging the coefficients in vertical columns, ascending with the power of the unknown. The absolute term, which refers to the additive constant in the equation, occupies a middle place, and reciprocal powers of the unknown descend beneath it. It is interesting that Li Chih was able to denote both negative quantities and zero.

Li Chih would display equations of up to the sixth degree, but he did not describe the process used to solve them. Scholars have therefore concluded that the method of solution was common knowledge in China at that time. He was largely responsible for standardizing the terminology used to describe the various coefficients. The term *celestial element* refers to the unknown variable. In the book, Li Chih considers some 170 problems concerned with circles inscribed in or circumscribed around triangles, and then he applies the solutions to a variety of word problems, such as finding the diameter of a circular city wall given certain conditions.

The *New Steps in Computation* is a much simpler text. Perhaps Li Chih realized that many people had trouble understanding his first book. It contains 64 problems, some of which treat the quadratic equation, and some that deal with relationships between circles and squares. Toward the end, he provides three values for *pi*: the old value of 3, as well as 3.14 and 22/7.

Li Chih was significant in his dissemination of the method of the celestial element, and was certainly one of the most talented mathematicians of his time. Although CH'IN CHIU-SHAO was a contemporary, they were probably ignorant of one another due to their distant geographical locations. Essentially, scholars categorize Li Chih as an algebraist, since he was more concerned with the algebraic formulation of equations than with the exposition of their solution.

Further Reading

Martzloff, J. *A History of Chinese Mathematics.* Berlin/Heidelberg: Springer-Verlag, 1997.

⊠ **Lie, Sophus (Marius Sophus Lie)**
(1842–1899)
Norwegian
Geometry, Differential Equations, Algebra

One of the most popular and elegant branches of mathematics in the 20th century has been the theory of Lie groups. This discipline combines ideas from algebra, geometry, and analysis, and is relevant to theoretical physics. Sophus Lie first discovered these objects, and thus founded a fruitful arena for future research.

Marius Sophus Lie, commonly known as Sophus Lie, was born on December 17, 1842, in Nordfjordeide, Norway. He was the sixth and youngest child of Johann Lie, a Lutheran pastor. He attended a local school, and from 1857 to 1859 studied at Nissen's Private Latin School in Oslo. From 1859 to 1865 he continued his education at Christiania University in Oslo. Originally he showed little interest in mathematics, and he focused on the sciences. After his examination in 1865, Lie gave private lessons, and he became interested in astronomy.

Lie's life acquired new direction after his discovery in 1868 of some geometrical papers by the mathematicians JEAN-VICTOR PONCELET and Julius Plücker. The idea that space could be made up of lines instead of points had a profound impact on Lie's conception of geometry. He obtained a scholarship abroad, living in Berlin in winter 1869, where he became acquainted with FELIX KLEIN. Both men's scientific endeavors benefited greatly from the friendship that ensued. Klein was an algebraist intrigued by particular problems, whereas Lie was a geometer and analyst interested in generalizing concepts.

They spent summer 1870 in Paris, where they came in contact with CAMILLE JORDAN and GASPARD MONGE as well as other French mathematicians. Lie discovered his famous contact transformation, which was an important initial geometrical discovery—it was a first step toward his later development of the theory of Lie groups. The Franco-Prussian War erupted in the same year, and Lie was arrested as a spy while hiking through the countryside. He was soon freed and manged to escape France before the blockade of Paris. In 1871 he returned to Oslo, where he taught at Nissen's Private Latin School. He obtained his doctorate in 1872.

At this time Lie developed the integration theory of partial differential equations, which is still taught as a classical method in mathematics texts. His initial work on differential geometry later led to his important work on transformation groups and differential equations. The transformation group, later known as the Lie group, brought algebraic tools to bear on geometric and analytic problems, and in particular resulted in his powerful approach to partial differential equations. Although these ideas were not initially accepted—largely due to the cumbersome style of presenting analytic ideas that was fashionable at the time—their significance to modern mathematics cannot be overestimated.

He completed his work on Lie groups in the 1870s, but their publication took several decades of effort.

In 1872 a chair in mathematics was created for Lie at Christiania University. Besides the above-mentioned research on contact transformations, he was busy editing the collected works of NIELS HENRIK ABEL. Lie married Anna Birch in 1874, and together they raised two sons and one daughter.

In Oslo Lie was isolated from other mathematicians; he had no pupils, and only two mathematicians—Klein and Emile Picard—paid attention to his work. Friedrich Engel assisted Lie in the publication of a lengthy text on transformation groups, which appeared in three parts between 1888 and 1893. His parallel work on contact transformation and partial differential equations with Felix Hausdorff was not completed. In 1886 Lie came to Leipzig, succeeding Klein, and his collaborative situation improved.

Lie's health had been excellent, and he was described as an openhearted man of huge stature. However, in 1889 he was struck with mental illness. When he resumed work in 1890 his character had changed greatly—now he was paranoid and belligerent. Eventually he returned to Christiania University with the lure of a special chair in 1898. He died a year later on February 18, 1899, in Oslo from anemia.

Lie's work revolutionized the study of geometry and differential equations, since group theoretic and algebraic techniques could now solve problems. The study of Lie groups eventually became a discipline of its own. The appreciation for Lie's work grew gradually. Initially Engel and Issai Schur further developed his ideas, and later Picard, Killing, ÉLIE CARTAN, and HERMANN WEYL continued Lie's theoretical work in the 20th century. In the early 20th century Lie algebras were discovered, and Lie's original work has been generalized in many ways. One reason for the enduring popularity of his thought is the application of Lie groups to quantum physics.

Further Reading

Ackerman, M., and R. Hermann. *Sophus Lie's 1880 Transformation Group Paper*. Brookline, Mass.: Math Sci Press, 1975.

Fritzsche, B. "Sophus Lie: A Sketch of His Life and Work," *Journal of Lie Theory* 9, no. 1 (1999): 1–38.

Hermann, R. *Lie Groups: History, Frontiers and Applications*. Brookline, Mass.: Math Sci Press, 1979.

Yaglom, I. *Felix Klein and Sophus Lie: Evolution of the Idea of Symmetry in the Nineteenth Century*. Boston: Birkhäuser, 1988.

⊠   **Liouville, Joseph**
(1809–1882)
French
Analysis, Mechanics, Geometry, Number Theory

Joseph Liouville played an important role in the advancement and promotion of 19th-century mathematics, accomplished through his own publications as well as his editing of the influential *Journal de Liouville* (Liouville's Journal). He principally researched analysis, geometry, and number theory, publishing a series of numerous short notes and papers. Through the academic positions that he held, Liouville was able to mold the mathematical interests of the next generation.

Joseph Liouville was born on March 24, 1809, in St.-Omer, France. He was the second son of Claude-Joseph Liouville, an army captain, and Thérèse Balland, both of whom came from the province of Lorraine. He initially studied in the towns of Commercy and Toul before attending the École Polytechnique in 1825. He transferred to the École des Ponts et Chaussées in 1827, where he began original research in mathematics. During the next few years, Liouville presented several memoirs to the Academy of Sciences, treating heat, electricity, and mathematical analysis. These were favorably received, and enabled Liouville to obtain a teaching position at the École Polytechnique in 1831, following his graduation the previous year. Also in 1831 he married his cousin Marie-Louise Balland. They would have three daughters and one son.

Liouville remained in the teaching profession for 50 years, and he was able to teach pure and applied mathematics at the leading institutions of Paris. In 1838 he occupied a chair of analysis and mechanics at the École Polytechnique, and in 1851 gained the chair of mathematics at the Collège de France, remaining there until 1879. Meanwhile, he taught classes at a more elementary level, and dabbled in politics—he was elected to the Constituent Assembly in 1848, but left his political career after an 1849 defeat. Liouville earned his doctorate on the applications of Fourier series to mathematical physics in 1836, which allowed him to teach at the university level. In 1857 he simultaneously taught mechanics at the Paris Faculty of Sciences.

While he was teaching, Liouville also participated in several societies, such as the Academy of Sciences and the Bureau des Longitudes, and most importantly launched the *Journal of Pure and Applied Mathematics* (later known as *Liouville's Journal*) in 1836. This forum, created after the demise of two influential journals, was crucial for the dissemination of mid-19th-century mathematics. As the journal's editor, Liouville was able to affect the development of mathematics at that time; he remained the chief editor until 1874.

His initial research interests focused on mathematical analysis. Most important, Liouville dealt with such topics as the classification of algebraic functions (he defined the Liouvillian number, an example of a transcendental number),

the theory of elliptic functions (building on the work of NIELS HENRIK ABEL and CARL JACOBI), and differential equations. Between 1832 and 1837 he formulated a notion of fractional derivative; he also extended the knowledge of oscillations, and contributed the theories of electricity and heat. Liouville's work was quite interdisciplinary, and he took an interest in the applications of mathematical methods to problems in celestial mechanics.

Liouville also contributed to algebra, furnishing a new proof of the fundamental theorem of algebra as well as proving one of Cauchy's theorems. More important, he publicized the works of EVARISTE GALOIS, exposing them to a wider audience of mathematicians, and thus ushered in new techniques that would become classical in modern algebra and group theory. Liouville wrote numerous papers on geometry, studying the calculus of variations, geodesic lines of ellipsoids, and properties of polygons. He introduced the new notion of total curvature, and studied the deformations of a surface.

In addition to these studies, Liouville later became interested in number theory. From 1858 to 1865 he published several theorems that all belong to analytic number theory—some of the first publications in this new field of inquiry. In his later years Liouville's research focused on more particular problems outside the mainstream, and was of less interest to other mathematicians.

Liouville lived a quiet, studious life. He died on September 8, 1882, in Paris. He was able to affect the development of mathematics through his distinguished academic career. His promotion of the work of Galois, and more generally his encouragement of younger mathematicians through his journal, changed the landscape of mathematics. His own research contributions were significant in their scope and maturity, excepting his later work in number theory toward the end of his life.

Further Reading

Chrystal, G. "Joseph Liouville," *Proceedings of the Royal Society of Edinburgh* 14 (1888): 83–91.

Lützen, J. *Joseph Liouville, 1809–1882, Master of Pure and Applied Mathematics*. New York: Springer-Verlag, 1990.

Stander, D. "Makers of Modern Mathematics: Joseph Liouville," *Bulletin of the Institute of Mathematics and Its Applications* 24, nos. 3–4 (1988): 59–60.

⊠ Lipschitz, Rudolf (Rudolf Otto Sigismund Lipschitz)
(1832–1903)
German
Analysis, Geometry

Rudolf Lipschitz was an important analyst and geometer in the latter half of the 19th century who advanced the knowledge of Riemannian manifolds, differential forms, and continuous functions, thereby contributing to the foundations of much of 20th-century mathematics. His research interests were quite broad, but his labors in geometry (building on BERNHARD RIEMANN's work) are most noteworthy.

Rudolf Lipschitz was born on May 14, 1832, in Königsberg, Germany. His father was a landholder, and Lipschitz received a good education. He began his study of mathematics at the University of Königsberg at age 15, but later went to Berlin where he became GUSTAV PETER LEJEUNE DIRICHLET's pupil. He suffered a delay in his studies due to illness, but was able to complete his doctorate at the University of Berlin in 1853.

After several years teaching at local Gymnasiums, Lipschitz obtained a position at the University of Berlin in 1857, and in the same year he married Ida Pascha. He first became a professor at the University of Breslau in 1862, and then at the University of Bonn in 1864. Lipschitz was a member of several academies, and was distinguished by the variety and depth of his research.

Lipschitz investigated number theory, Bessel functions, Fourier series, differential equations, and mechanics. Most important was his work on high dimensional differential forms and their relationships to the calculus of variations and geometry. In this area, Lipschitz developed the early ideas of Riemann and was able to develop a new area of mathematics that has proved to have enduring interest and relevance in the 20th century.

Lipschitz also wrote a book, *Foundation of Analysis*, which gathered together various topics of mathematical research in one work and was the first of its kind written in German. He formulated a continuity condition for functions called the Lipschitz condition that has proved to be important in function theory and approximation theory, and relates to questions of existence and uniqueness of solutions of differential equations.

Lipschitz's work on differential forms was done in collaboration with the mathematician Elwin Christoffel. Lipschitz obtained many significant results concerning the curvature of Riemannian manifolds and submanifolds. His investigations were later continued by Gregorio Ricci-Curbastro, and implemented by Albert Einstein in his theory of general relativity.

Lipschitz died on October 7, 1903, in Bonn. His principal contribution lies in the foundation of the theory of differential forms; this branch of mathematics is both elegant and useful for understanding high-dimensional geometries. His work on manifolds was indicative of the direction that geometrical inquiry would soon take.

Further Reading

Scharlau, W. "The Mathematical Correspondence of Rudolf Lipschitz," *Historia Mathematica* 13, no. 2 (1986): 165–167.

⊠ **Lobachevsky, Nikolai (Nikolai Ivanovich Lobachevsky)**
(1792–1856)
Russian
Geometry

A major paradigm shift in geometrical intuition took place in the 19th century, when CARL FRIEDRICH GAUSS, JÁNOS BOLYAI, and Lobachevsky each independently developed alternative geometries to flat space. Lobachevsky was the first to publish this discovery. His generalizations of the intuitive notion of space have since proved extremely relevant within mathematics (paving the way for the abstract definition and study of geometry) and physics, through the modeling of gravity's effect on the shape of the universe.

Nikolai Lobachevsky was born on December 2, 1792, in Gorki, Russia. His father, Ivan

Nikolai Lobachevsky invented an alternative, consistent geometry known as hyperbolic geometry. *(Library of Congress, courtesy of AIP Emilio Segrè Visual Archives)*

Maksimovich, was a clerk, and his mother was named Praskovia Aleksandrovna Lobachevskaya. In 1800 Lobachevsky's mother moved, together with Lobachevsky and his two brothers, to Kazan. There the three boys were enrolled in the Gymnasium on scholarships. In 1807 Lobachevsky entered Kazan University, where he studied mathematics and physics, obtaining his master's degree in 1812.

In 1814 Lobachevsky lectured on mathematics and mechanics as an adjunct, and became a professor the same year; he was promoted in 1822, and served a variety of positions at Kazan University, including dean of the department of physics and mathematics, librarian of the university, rector, and assistant trustee for the Kazan district. His first major work, written in 1823, was called *Geometriya* (Geometry), and its basic geometrical studies led Lobachevsky to his later researches into non-Euclidean geometry. He reported his early discoveries in 1826, and published these ideas in 1829–30.

Lobachevsky initially attempted to prove the fifth postulate of EUCLID OF ALEXANDRIA, as many before him (including CLAUDIUS PTOLEMY, Thabit ibn Qurra, ABU ALI AL-HAYTHAM, ADRIEN-MARIE LEGENDRE, and JOHN WALLIS) had tried and failed to accomplish. He soon turned to the construction of a more general geometry that did not require the fifth postulate, which states that given a line and a distinct point, there exists a unique line through the point that is parallel to the given line. The resulting geometry, which he named "imaginary geometry," allowed for the construction of multiple distinct parallel lines through the given point. From here he was able to deduce several interesting properties: most important, the geometry was consistent (there was no contradiction in its rules, however counterintuitive its characteristics). Curiously, the sum of angles in a triangle is less than 180 degrees; Lobachevsky later attempted to deduce the geometry of the universe by measuring the angles of a vast cosmic triangle spanned by distant stars. He concluded that, within the margins of measurement error, the angles summed to 180 degrees, and hence the universe is Euclidean.

Lobachevsky produced several more papers on this subject, including the above stellar computation; he gave both an axiomatic and a constructive definition of his "pangeometry," which later came to be known as hyperbolic geometry. His ideas were not initially accepted abroad, although he was promoted at Kazan and made into a nobleman in 1837. He married a wealthy aristocrat, the Lady Varvara Aleksivna Moisieva, in 1832, and they had seven children.

Besides his important geometrical work, Lobachevsky contributed to algebra, infinite series, and the theory of integration. However, this work was flavored by his geometrical ideas and was related to his "imaginary geometry." Gauss appreciated Lobachevsky's efforts, which were similar to his own work on non-Euclidean geometry, and assisted his election to the Göttingen Academy of Science after 1842.

Lobachevsky, despite his advantageous marriage, experienced financial difficulties in his later years, due to the cost of his large family and the maintenance of his estate. His eyes deteriorated with age until he became totally blind. He died on February 24, 1856, in Kazan.

Recognition of Lobachevsky's pioneering work came slowly. Many mathematicians, such as Arthur Cayley, failed to comprehend its significance, and denigrated it. In the 1860s the works of Bolyai and Lobachevsky gained increasing renown among the French, and Eugenio Beltrami later gave a construction of Lobachevskian geometry on a closed circle of the plane. After 1870 KARL WEIERSTRASS and FELIX KLEIN became interested in Lobachevsky's work, and Klein eventually formulated the various geometries—elliptic, flat, and hyperbolic—in terms of invariants of group transformations. Lobachevskian geometry was later shown to be

a special case of Cayley geometries. JULES-HENRI POINCARÉ, together with Klein, further built on the ideas of BERNHARD RIEMANN and Lobachevsky. In the 20th century non-Euclidean geometry was shown to be relevant to the general theory of relativity. It is intriguing that the space of the universe was later demonstrated to have variable curvature, with the warp and woof of its fabric defined by gravitational forces. This reality is modeled by Lobachevsky's geometry.

Further Reading

Bonola, R. *Non-Euclidean Geometry: A Critical and Historical Study of Its Developments.* New York: Dover Publications, 1955.

Halsted, G. "Biography. Lobachevsky," *The American Mathematical Monthly* 2 (1895): 137.

Householder, A. "Dandelin, Lobachevskii, or Gräffe?" *The American Mathematical Monthly* 66 (1959): 464–466.

Kagan, V. N. *Lobachevsky and His Contribution to Science.* Moscow: Foreign Languages Publishing House, 1957.

Vucinich, A. "Nicolai Ivanovich Lobachevskii: The Man behind the First Non-Euclidean Geometry," *Isis* 53 (1962): 465–481.

⊠ **Lovelace, Augusta Ada Byron
(Ada Lovelace)**
(1815–1852)
British
Logic, Algebra

Computers, and the theory accompanying them, have been one of the most significant intellectual developments of the latter half of the 20th century. However, the history of the computer goes back several centuries to the first calculators, developed by BLAISE PASCAL and others; later, in the early 19th century, the first primitive computer was developed by CHARLES BABBAGE, and the first work on computer science was written by Ada Lovelace.

Ada Lovelace was born on December 10, 1815, in Piccadilly, England, with the name Augusta Ada Byron. Her mother was Anne Isabelle Milbanke, and her father was George Gordon, Lord Byron, the famous poet. Lovelace's parents were separated shortly after her birth, and her manipulative mother kept the identity of Lovelace's father a secret. Byron died in Greece when Lovelace was eight years old. Lady Byron was determined that her daughter would not become a poet like her father, and so trained her in mathematics, a subject to which she had predilection herself.

Thus Lovelace's early education, overseen by her mother, had an intense focus on mathematics. In fact, it seems that Lady Byron was overbearing and tyrannical in her efforts; however, Lovelace's native mathematical talent did eventually flower in the latter portion of her life. Lovelace herself preferred geography to arithmetic, and only became interested in science and mathematics after meeting Babbage in 1833, when she learned about his difference engine.

In 1835 Lovelace married William King, who was made the earl of Lovelace in 1838; thus, Ada Lovelace gained the name by which she is commonly referred. The next few years were spent in childbearing (she had two boys and a girl), and Lovelace began an earnest study of mathematics only in 1841. Her advanced studies were guided by AUGUSTUS DE MORGAN.

In 1842 she published a translation of Luigi Menabrea's description of Babbage's analytical engine, and she added much of her own material to the original text. Lovelace's notes entered deeply into the abstract algebraic questions raised by the engine, which essentially attempted to map algebraic operations into the mechanical actions of moving machine parts. She also described how the engine could be manipulated, in essence presenting the first computer program ever written. It is interesting that Lovelace was very optimistic about the capabilities of the engine, believing that every algebraic operation could be mechanized and computed. Modern computer science theory has further explored what types of mathematical operations can be performed by a computer program (or at least by a Turing machine); much present effort is focused on the design of quantum computers with the capability of performing different operations (or performing the classical ones faster). Lovelace, together with Babbage, was the progenitor of this intellectual journey.

Although she published under a pseudonym, Lovelace enjoyed some recognition among her friends. However, her troubled personal life interfered with further contributions. Lovelace became involved in several marital scandals, developed addictions to gambling, alcohol, and opium, and suffered health problems. She was afflicted with cancer, and its effects interfered with her ability to concentrate. After several years of struggle, she died on November 27, 1852, in London.

Lovelace might well have contributed more to the foundations of computer science and abstract algebra if she had lived longer. Nevertheless, her one published work presented the first explicit computer program (in a primitive form), and she gave the mathematical justification for the analytical engine. Therefore, she is remembered for pioneering this branch of abstract algebra, which eventually would become the separate field of computer science in the 20th century.

Further Reading

Angluin, D. "Lady Lovelace and the Analytical Engine," *Association for Women in Mathematics Newsletter* 6 (1976): 6–8.

Babbage, C. *Passages from the Life of a Philosopher.* London: Dawsons, 1968.

Baum, J. *The Calculating Passion of Ada Byron.* Hamden, Conn.: Archon Books, 1986.

Elwin, M. *Lord Byron's Family: Annabelle, Ada, and Augusta, 1816–1824.* London: J. Murray, 1975.

Moore, D. *Ada, Countess of Lovelace: Byron's Legitimate Daughter.* London: John Murray General Publishing Division, 1977.

Morrison, P., and E. Morrison. *Charles Babbage and His Calculating Engines.* New York: Dover Publications, 1961.

Stein, D. *Ada: A Life and a Legacy.* Cambridge, Mass.: MIT Press, 1985.

Toole, B. *Ada, the Enchantress of Numbers: Prophet of the Computer Age, a Pathway to the 21st Century.* Mill Valley, Calif.: Strawberry Press, 1998.

M

Maclaurin, Colin
(1698–1746)
British
Calculus, Geometry

England suffered a drought of mathematicians in the latter portion of the 18th century, and Maclaurin represents the last great mathematician of the Newtonian era. He contributed to the defense of SIR ISAAC NEWTON's calculus and made some impressive discoveries of his own, including the series expansion of a function.

Colin Maclaurin was born in February 1698, in Kilmodan, Scotland. He was the youngest of three sons, and his father, John Maclaurin, was the local minister. Soon after Maclaurin was born, his father died, and his mother died when he was nine. After the death of his parents, Maclaurin was raised by his uncle. In 1709 Maclaurin entered the University of Glasgow, where he became interested in mathematics. He defended his thesis in 1715 *On the Power of Gravity*, obtaining his master's degree. In 1717 he was appointed as professor of mathematics at Marischal College, although he was still quite young.

He visited London in 1719 and made the acquaintance of Newton, whose work made a profound impression on him. By 1720 Maclaurin published his *Geometrica organica* (Organic geometry), which contained many proofs of

Newton's unproved results, as well as many of Maclaurin's own discoveries. His approach, like Newton's, was highly geometrical.

In 1722 Maclaurin left Scotland to serve as tutor to the son of Lord Polwarth. They traveled in France, where Maclaurin continued his research, winning a prize from the French Academy of Sciences in 1724. In this year, his pupil died unexpectedly, and Maclaurin was obliged to return to Scotland, where he obtained the chair of mathematics at the University of Edinburgh through the intervention of Newton. There, Maclaurin lectured on EUCLID OF ALEXANDRIA, spherical trigonometry, conic sections, fortification, astronomy, and perspective. He was also one of the foremost expositors of Newton's calculus. In 1733 he married Anne Stewart, with whom he raised seven children.

In 1742 Maclaurin published his *Treatise on Fluxions*, which was a defense of Newton's methods and a response to the criticism of George Berkeley. Many scientists and mathematicians were skeptical of infinitesimals, and Maclaurin undertook to provide the theory of fluxions with a rigorous logical foundation. It is noteworthy that Maclaurin rejected the advantageous notation of GOTTFRIED WILHELM VON LEIBNIZ in favor of Newton's clumsier nomenclature, due to his loyalty and partisanship. As a result, the Newtonian style came to dominate thought in

England, and consequently impaired the computational and analytical abilities of subsequent mathematicians. In this sense, Maclaurin was to some extent responsible for retarding mathematical progress in England.

The treatise contained the solutions of a number of problems in geometry, statics, and infinite series. It contained Maclaurin's test for convergence and, more important, the series expansion of a differentiable function around the origin. Although the Taylor series is more general, Maclaurin's series was the first step in developing an analytical tool of great utility.

Maclaurin also investigated bodies of attraction, and he competed for a French prize with his "On the Tides" in 1740, sharing the award with LEONHARD EULER and DANIEL BERNOULLI. He is also remarkable for being the first mathematician to correctly distinguish between the maxima and minima of a function. He was a skilled experimentalist and inventor, and he performed astronomical observations and actuarial computations. In 1745 a Highland army marched on Edinburgh, and Maclaurin vigorously organized the defense of the city. As a result of his exertions, his health began to fail. He died on January 14, 1746, in Edinburgh.

Maclaurin was described as a benevolent and pious man, and in his controversies he was polite to his adversaries. His defense of Newtonian methods and notation partially led to the English neglect of calculus, which deprived England of good analysts for the next century. Nevertheless, he positively contributed to the rigorous development of Newtonian calculus, and he was easily one of the most talented British mathematicians of his own day.

Further Reading

Giorello, G. "The 'Fine Structure' of Mathematical Revolutions: Metaphysics, Legitimacy, and Rigour, The Case of the Calculus from Newton to Berkeley and Maclaurin," in *Revolutions in Mathematics*. New York: Oxford University Press, 1995.

Schlapp, R. "Colin Maclaurin: A Biographical Note," *Edinburgh Mathematical Notes* 37 (1949): 1–6.

Turnbull, H. "Colin Maclaurin," *The American Mathematical Monthly* 54 (1947).

⊠ Madhava of Sangamagramma
(ca. 1350–ca. 1425)
Indian
Trigonometry, Analysis

The great European mathematicians had many predecessors within the Arabian, Indian, and Chinese cultures, but the latter groups are not typically acknowledged as the original discoverers because their knowledge was not disseminated as broadly. Madhava of Sangamagramma is an example of this, as he began the exploration of infinitesimal calculus and so-called Taylor expansions two centuries before COLIN MACLAURIN began his investigations. In this sense, Madhava must be recognized as the first analyst, even though his ideas did not blossom as fully in India.

None of the original works of Madhava remain, and his life and mathematical contributions must be reconstructed from the accounts of later Indian mathematicians. He was born around 1350 in Sangamagramma, in the state of Kerala, India. In about 1400 Madhava discovered the series expansion for various trigonometric functions, such as the sine and cosine. These formulas are similar to the Taylor series that were later discovered in Europe, and can be used to develop computable approximations to sines and cosines of angles.

Madhava came from a tradition of mathematics that emphasized finite procedures; the very idea of an infinite sum of terms is a novel innovation that completely departs from preceding concepts of mathematics. Madhava applied these series to trigonometry, developing highly accurate tables for trigonometric values. In developing the infinite series for the arcsine function, Madhava was able to produce an excellent approximation for pi, producing its value to 11 decimal places. He also analyzed the remainder terms when the exact infinite series is truncated to a finite sum. Scholars believe that Madhava used the method of continued fractions to derive these remainder terms.

Again, little is known of Madhava's life, but it is thought that he died around 1425 in India. It is amazing that Madhava developed such techniques far before the Europeans did, given that they had the benefit of an intellectual progression. In Europe the progress toward calculus can be traced through several characters who each participated in this mathematical process. In India the scholastic community was sparser, and there was less of a concerted effort to produce mathematics useful to science. Many historians believe that Madhava's discovery of infinite series expansions is akin to a term-by-term integration technique of calculus—a few hundred years before the official discovery of calculus!

Further Reading

Joseph, G. *The Crest of the Peacock: Non-European Roots of Mathematics*. London: Penguin Books, 1990.

⊠ **Markov, Andrei**
(1856–1922)
Russian
Probability

The theory of probability, which had its foundation in the 17th-century studies of BLAISE PASCAL and PIERRE DE FERMAT, became one of the most important and influential mathematical subjects in the 20th century. The work of Andrei Markov contributed some fundamental concepts to the discipline of probability, and so-called Markov chains have been one of the most widely used probabilistic concepts in science and statistics.

Andrei Markov was born on June 14, 1856, in Ryazan, Russia. He graduated from Saint Petersburg University in 1878, and became a professor of mathematics there in 1886. His early research efforts focused on number theory and analysis, dealing with such topics as continued fractions and convergence of infinite series.

After 1900 Markov turned increasingly to probability theory, wherein he would achieve his greatest work. Following in the footsteps of his teacher PAFNUTY LVOVICH CHEBYSHEV, Markov applied his knowledge of continued fractions to probability. He began the study of relationships between dependent random variables, which would become quite important to later work on stochastic processes. For example, Markov was able to prove the central limit theorem, the most important result of mathematical statistics, under more general assumptions on the dependence structure of the random variables being summed.

These results are of fundamental importance to the study of time series, or chronologically ordered data, where future values depend, in a stochastic manner, upon present and past data. In particular, Markov invented and studied Markov chains, which are essentially sequences of random variables where the probabilistic structure of a future value only depends on its immediate predecessor. This simple structure has since proved to be applicable to a variety of scientific problems, while at the same time being mathematically tractable. The invention of Markov chains constitutes a first step in the study of stochastic processes, and so Markov is arguably the founder of this important branch of probability. Later in the early 20th century, NORBERT WIENER and Andrei Kolmogorov would generalize Markov's early work on stochastic processes.

Markov died on July 20, 1922, in St. Petersburg, Russia. He represents an important link in the sequence of great Russian probabilists, including Chebyshev and Kolmogorov. Markov's work is heavily cited in the theory of probability, and is now classical in its importance and influence.

Further Reading

Sheynin, O. "A. A. Markov's Work on Probability," *Archive for History of Exact Sciences* 39 (1988): 337–377.

⊠ **Menelaus of Alexandria**
(ca. 70–ca. 130)
Greek
Geometry

Menelaus of Alexandria, one of the later great Greek mathematicians, is the founder of spherical trigonometry (the study of triangles defined on spheres). Both Earth and the heavens are spherical, so this subject is relevant to navigation, geography, and the study of the calendar. By defining spherical triangles properly, Menelaus greatly advanced this subject, thereby also advancing astronomy.

Only scraps of information are available on the life of Menelaus, and only one of his works has survived. Scholars believe that he was born in approximately the year 70 in Alexandria, Egypt, and later spent much of his adult life in Rome. Based on historical records, he made astronomical observation in Rome on January 14, 98. Plutarch records a conversation between Menelaus and another man long after the year 75 in Rome, concerning the reflection of light. These facts constitute the only evidence of his activity in Rome.

Menelaus wrote several books, including *Sphaerica (The Book of Spherical Propositions), On the Knowledge of the Weights and Distribution of Different Bodies,* and *The Book on the Triangle.* Only the first of these has survived. He was the first to write down the definition of a spherical triangle as the figure enclosed by the intersection of three great circles on a sphere (a great circle on a sphere is a circle of maximal diameter).

Menelaus proceeded in analogy with EUCLID OF ALEXANDRIA's treatment of plane geometry, and established many basic results. His success was due to his superior definition of a triangle, as previous works utilized lesser circles. In fact, it is now known that great circles are geodesics, the equivalent of straight lines on a plane (they give the shortest path between two points). Hence, triangles should have sides determined by geodesics, and this is exactly how Menelaus proceeded.

In paralleling Euclid's *Elements,* Menelaus proved many propositions. It is interesting that he rejected the *reductio ad absurdum* argument, which involves an infinite chain of arguments leading to an absurdity. Menelaus instead used other techniques that he believed to be more rigorous, and his treatment of the spherical trigonometry is somewhat more complete than that of Euclid for the plane trigonometry.

The second part of *Sphaerica* gives the applications of spherical trigonometry to astronomy, and the third part presents Menelaus's theorem, which was a generalization to spherical trigonometry of a plane geometry result concerning the intersection of a line with the sides of a triangle.

Menelaus's *Sphaerica* comes to the modern reader through several Arab translators and commentators and, unfortunately, their accounts of the book differ somewhat. Menelaus's other works, listed above, were referenced by Arabs such as Thabit ibn Qurra. Only fragments of the original remain. The Arab commentators also mentioned Menelaus's work on mechanics—apparently he studied the balances devised by ARCHIMEDES OF SYRACUSE.

Scholars believe that Menelaus died around 130. It seems that he was somewhat well known as a mathematician in his own time, and the later Arab mathematicians certainly referenced him heavily. Menelaus's most important contribution lies in his solid definition of spherical triangles, which allowed the field of astronomy to progress further.

Further Reading

Heath, T. A *History of Greek Mathematics*. Oxford: Clarendon Press, 1921.

Neugebauer, O. A *History of Ancient Mathematical Astronomy*. New York: Springer-Verlag, 1975.

⊠ Minkowski, Hermann
(1864–1909)
Lithuanian
Geometry, Analysis

Albert Einstein's special theory of relativity posited space and time as a unified structure with its own geometry. The work of Hermann Minkowski, building on the general geometrical theories formulated by BERNHARD RIEMANN, formed the mathematical basis for this model of the universe.

Hermann Minkowski was born on June 22, 1864, in Alexotas, part of the Russian Empire. Now the town is known as Kaunas, and is part of Lithuania. Minkowski pursued mathematical studies at the universities of Berlin and Königsberg, receiving his doctorate from the latter institution in 1885. Following graduation, Minkowski taught at several schools, including Bonn, Zurich, and Königsberg.

Minkowski accepted a chair at the University of Göttingen in 1902, where he stayed for the remainder of his career. There he learned mathematical physics from DAVID HILBERT, and filled in the rest of his scientific education. His main contribution to mathematics arrived through his realization that Einstein's work in physics could be mathematically formulated as a non-Euclidean (that is, nonflat) space that could be completely described through Riemann's metric description of manifolds. Minkowski viewed time and space as a joint continuum that could not be thought of as being formally independent; the dependence of time and space was developed through Einstein's study of special relativity, and Minkowski supplied

Hermann Minkowski developed the geometrical foundations of the special theory of relativity. *(H.S. Lorentz, A. Einstein, H. Minkowski, Das Relatitätsprinzip, 1915, courtesy of AIP Emilio Segrè Visual Archives)*

the appropriate geometrical construction that illustrated this dependence. Minkowski's four-dimensional manifold was summarized by a four-dimensional space-time metric, later known as the Lorentz metric. This space-time continuum is sometimes referred to as Minkowski space, in recognition of his contributions to this field, which are summarized in his 1907 *Space and Time*.

In addition, Minkowski developed a four-dimensional treatment of electrodynamics, exposited in his 1909 *Zwei Abhandlungen über die Grundgleichungen der Elektrodynamik* (Two papers on the principal equations of electrodynamics). He is less well known for his work in pure mathematics, to which he devoted most of his attention. Minkowski investigated quadratic forms and continued fractions, and he discovered an important inequality in analysis. He made original discoveries on the geometry of numbers, which led to the study of packing problems—the question of how many objects of a given shape can be packed into a given space. Packing problems have become a significant area of research in the 20th century, due to their intuitive appeal and easily realizable applications.

Minkowski died on January 12, 1909, in Göttingen of a ruptured appendix. His primary achievement lay in his foundation of the mathematical study of packing problems, though he is more famous for his geometric contributions to the theory of special relativity. These early studies of special relativity led to the promulgation of mathematical methods in the general theory of relativity, developed by Albert Einstein.

Further Reading

Hancock, H. *Development of the Minkowski Geometry of Numbers*. New York: Dover Publications, 1964.

Pyenson, L. "Hermann Minkowski and Einstein's Special Theory of Relativity," *Archive for History of Exact Sciences* 17, no. 1 (1977): 71–95.

⊠ **Möbius, August (August Ferdinand Möbius)**
(1790–1868)
German
Topology, Geometry, Number Theory

August Möbius was an excellent mathematician who pioneered many ideas in topology, the study of continuous maps acting on high-dimensional surfaces. This field of mathematics was studied piecemeal in the early 19th century, and indeed would only receive systematic investigation by JULES-HENRI POINCARÉ, LUITZEN EGBERTUS JAN BROUWER, and others in the early 20th century. Möbius's research presented the first investigations of orientation, one-sided surfaces, and homogeneous coordinates.

August Möbius was born on November 17, 1790, in Schulpforta, Germany. His father, Johann Heinrich Möbius, was a dance instructor who died when Möbius was only three years old. He was raised by his mother, a descendant of Martin Luther, and was educated by her until he was 13. Möbius pursued further study at the local college, and he matriculated at the University of Leipzig in 1809.

At Leipzig Möbius followed his family's preference for him to study law, but after his first year abandoned this program to pursue mathematics, physics, and astronomy instead. There Karl Mollweide, an astronomer with mathematical inclinations, influenced Möbius. In 1813 he traveled to the University of Göttingen for graduate studies, and was taught by CARL FRIEDRICH GAUSS himself. As a result of having this great mentor, Möbius had a solid background in mathematics and astronomy. In 1815 Möbius completed his doctoral thesis, which concerned the occultation of the fixed stars, and next commenced his postdoctoral research. Although his work at this time was in the field of astronomy, it was highly mathematical in flavor.

Avoiding the possibility of being drafted into the Prussian army, Möbius completed his second thesis on trigonometric equations, and he was soon appointed as professor of astronomy at Leipzig in 1816. Möbius's career advancement came slowly, essentially due to his poor lecturing abilities, even though his mathematical work was of high quality and originality.

Möbius worked quietly and steadily on a variety of mathematical projects, producing finished works of great quality and completeness. Besides his papers on celestial mechanics and astronomical principles, Möbius wrote about projective geometry, number theory, topology, and polyhedra. His classic work on analytical geometry of 1827 introduced homogeneous coordinates (a way of describing projective surfaces) and the Möbius net (a certain configuration in projective space). This research was foundational to more modern studies in projective geometry. The Möbius function and Möbius inversion formula are both significant in the study of prime numbers and factorization in number theory. But in the budding field of topology Möbius demonstrated his creative genius, with innovative investigations of one-sided surfaces and the topic of orientation (the determination of clockwise versus counterclockwise directions upon a surface). In particular, he rediscovered the so-called Möbius strip in 1858 (it had previously been explored by Johann Listing). This object is essentially a twisted strip of paper that has only one side.

In 1844 Möbius became a full professor at Leipzig. In the meantime he took on astronomical duties, overseeing the local observatory's reconstruction from 1818 to 1821. He married in 1820, and had one daughter and two sons. Also in 1844 he interacted briefly with HERMANN GUNTER GRASSMANN, whose work on topology and algebraic geometry was quite similar to that of Möbius. Möbius died on September 26, 1868, in Leipzig, Germany.

Möbius is perhaps most well known for the Möbius strip and the Möbius inversion formula, although his most important work was probably in projective geometry. His work was distinguished in its originality and cohesion, as well as the depth of penetration into the material.

Further Reading
Fauvel, J., R. Flood, and R. Wilson. *Möbius and His Band*. Oxford: Oxford University Press, 1993.

Moivre, Abraham de
(1667–1754)
French
Probability, Analysis, Statistics, Geometry

Abraham de Moivre was an influential French mathematician who took some of the important initial steps in probability and statistics. He was a contemporary of SIR ISAAC NEWTON, and participated in the calculus priority debate. In addition, he advanced analytic geometry and made some elegant discoveries in complex analysis.

Abraham de Moivre was born on May 26, 1667, in Vitry, France, into a Protestant family, and later in life was persecuted for his religious beliefs. His early education was at a Protestant academy at Sedan. In 1682 he studied logic at the school of Saumur, and two years later came to Paris to study mathematics at the Collège de Harcourt.

In 1685 the Edict of Nantes (a 1598 decree that granted French Protestants the liberty to worship God as they pleased) was revoked, which signified a resumption of hostilities toward the Huguenots. De Moivre fled to England, where he unsuccessfully attempted to secure a position as a mathematics professor. Instead he became a private tutor—a profession he pursued until the end of his life. Meanwhile, de Moivre continued his own private researches in the area of analytic geometry, but made a more significant mark in the field of probability. He studied basic games of chance, and from his work formulated the first, most basic version of the central limit theorem, easily the most important result of probability and statistics. The theorem states that sample proportions (the proportion of times a certain event is observed to occur within a determined number of repeated trials of measurements) are close to the underlying probabilities that they estimate, assuming that the amount of information is sufficiently large. For example, the proportion of heads observed in a sequence of coin tosses should approximate the true probability of one-half. Moreover, the error in estimating a probability with a proportion can be quantified, having an approximately bell-shaped distribution.

De Moivre's work in probability was summarized in his 1718 book *The Doctrine of Chance*.

This work was well received by the scientific community, and greatly advanced the knowledge of probability and statistics. Generalizations of his first central limit theorem would later become a keystone in the theory of statistical estimation—the central limit theorem would be used to compute probabilities of statistics such as the sample mean. De Moivre first introduced the concept of statistical independence, which has been a crucial concept for statistical inference up to the present day. He explored his new concepts through several examples from dice games, but he also investigated mortality statistics and founded actuarial science as a statistical subject.

His later *Miscellanea Analytica* (Analytical Miscellany) of 1730 contained the famous Stirling formula, which gives an asymptotic expression for $n!$ 5 n $(n2\,1)$ $(n2\,2)$ . . . 1 for large integers n. This formula has been wrongly attributed to James Stirling, who generalized de Moivre's original result. De Moivre used this formula to derive the approximation of the bell-shaped distribution from the binomial distribution.

De Moivre is also famous for his work in complex analysis—he gives an expression for the higher powers of certain trigonometric functions. In fact, an arbitrary complex number could be expressed with trigonometric functions; thus, he was able to connect trigonometry to analysis.

Despite his poverty and French origins, de Moivre was elected to the Royal Society in 1697, and in 1710 he was asked to adjudicate over a heated dispute between Newton and GOTTFRIED WILHELM VON LEIBNIZ. Both men claimed to have been the original inventors of calculus, but due to the lateness in their publishing and the distance of their native countries (Newton was British and Leibniz was German), there was some confusion about which one had priority. De Moivre was already a friend of Newton, and he was selected in order to prejudice the verdict toward the English favorably; as expected, de Moivre ruled in favor of Newton.

De Moivre died in financial dearth on November 27, 1754, in London. Some said that he predicted the date of his own death, having observed that his slumber was steadily lengthening by 15 minutes each night. He is an important character in the history of mathematics, most especially for his pioneering work in probability, statistics, and actuarial science. In these areas he showed the most originality, but he was an excellent all-around analyst, and his complex variables formula is of classical importance to the subject.

Further Reading

Stigler, S. *The History of Statistics: The Measurement of Uncertainty before 1900*. Cambridge, Mass.: Belknap Press of Harvard University Press, 1986.

Walker, H. "Abraham De Moivre," *Scripta Mathematica* 2 (1934): 316–333.

Monge, Gaspard
(1746–1818)
French
Geometry

Gaspard Monge was an important mathematician of the late 18th century who also played a significant political role during the French Revolution. He is considered to be the father of differential geometry and was renowned for his creative intellect. Monge diverged from the standard modes of mathematical thought and was equally adept at theoretical and applied problems.

Gaspard Monge was born on May 9, 1746, in Beaune, France, to Jacques Monge, a merchant from southeastern France, and Jeanne Rousseaux, a native of the province of Burgundy. Raised in the same region, Monge attended the Oratorian College, a school intended for young noblemen; here Monge received education in the humanities, history, natural sciences, and mathematics. He first showed his brilliance at this school, and in 1762 he continued his studies at the Collège de la Trinité. A year later he was placed in charge of a physics course, although he was only 17 at the time. By 1764 he was finished with his education, and he returned to Beaune to draw up a plan for the city.

His plan was recognized for its genius, and he was appointed as a draftsman at the École Royale du Génie at Mézières in 1765. This post brought him into contact with Charles Bossut, the professor of mathematics. Meanwhile, Monge was developing his own ideas about geometry in private. The next year, he solved a problem involving the construction of a fortification, and he utilized his geometrical ideas in the solution. After this event, the faculty of the École Royale du Génie recognized Monge's abilities as a mathematician. In 1771 Monge read an important paper before the French Academy of Sciences. The work generalized certain results of CHRISTIAAN HUYGENS on space curves, and it was favorably accepted by the academy.

In 1769 Monge replaced Bossut, who had moved away to Paris, and also received a position as an instructor in experimental physics. He sought out the great Parisian mathematicians in an effort to advance his career, and through Marie-Jean Condorcet's assistance, he was able to present to the Academy his research on the calculus of variations, partial differential equations, infinitesimal geometry, and combinatorics. During the next few years he continued to contribute in the area of partial differential equations, which he approached from a geometrical perspective. At this time his academic interests expanded to include problems in physics and chemistry.

In 1777 he married Catherine Huart, owner of a forge, and researched metallurgy at the forge. Later he organized a chemistry laboratory at the École Royale du Génie. In 1780 he held an adjunct position at the Academy of Sciences, and eventually resigned his job at Mézières in 1784 when he became the examiner of naval cadets.

During the next five years, he researched topics in chemistry, the generation of curved surfaces, finite difference equations, partial differential equations, and refraction, as well as a variety of other scientific topics.

The French Revolution struck Paris in 1789, and Monge became deeply involved. He was highly sympathetic to the republican cause, although he became a staunch supporter of Bonaparte in the later years of his life. Monge was involved in various societies that supported the Revolution, and when a republic was formed in 1792, Monge was appointed as minister of the navy. His tenure was unsuccessful, largely due to the fickle nature of the new republic, and he resigned in 1793. He briefly returned to the Academy of Sciences (until it was abolished), and played a prominent role in the founding of the École Polytechnique. During this time, Monge wrote papers on military topics, such as ballistics and explosives, and gave courses in these subjects. He trained future teachers, and his lectures on geometry were later published in his text *Application de l'analyse à la géométrie* (Application of analysis to geometry).

From 1796 to 1797 Monge was in Italy, overseeing the plundering of Italian art by the French. While there he became acquainted with Napoleon Bonaparte, who exerted a tremendous influence on Monge through his superlative charisma. After some time spent in Paris and Rome, Monge accompanied Bonaparte on the ill-fated Egyptian expedition. After the French fleet was wiped out, Monge was appointed president of the *Institut d'Egypte* in Cairo in 1798. The mathematical division of the institute had 12 members, which included Monge and JEAN-BAPTISTE-JOSEPH FOURIER.

In 1799 Monge returned to Paris with Bonaparte, who soon held absolute power. Monge became director of the École Polytechnique, and after the consulate was established, was appointed a senator. Monge abandoned his republican views when Bonaparte showered him with honors—Monge was made into the Count of Péluse in 1808. During this first decade of the 19th century, Monge's research activity in mathematics tapered off as he focused more on pedagogical concerns. Later, in 1809, his health declined. After the failure of Bonaparte's Russian expedition, Monge's health collapsed, and he ultimately fled before the emperor's abdication in 1814. Upon Bonaparte's escape from Elba in 1815, Monge rallied to his support, but after Waterloo he fled the country. Monge returned to France in 1816, but his life was difficult, as his political enemies harassed him. He died in Paris on July 28, 1818.

Monge is considered one of the principal founders of differential geometry, through his pioneering work *Application de l'analyse à la géométrie*. Here he introduces the concept of a line of curvature on a surface in a three-dimensional space. Besides this important theoretical work, he developed what came to be known as descriptive geometry, which was essentially a way of giving a graphical description of a solid object. Modern mechanical drawing utilizes Monge's method of orthographic projection. His fresh, nonstandard approach to geometry greatly stimulated the subject, and his impact on mathematics has endured far longer than his political and pedagogical efforts.

Further Reading

Bikerman, J. "Capillarity before Laplace: Clairaut, Segner, Monge, Young," *Archive for History of Exact Sciences* 18, no. 2 (1977/78): 103–122.

Coolidge, J. *A History of Geometrical Methods*. New York: Dover Publications, 1963.

N

Napier, John
(1550–1617)
British
Analysis

In a time of great mathematical ignorance, John Napier made an outstanding contribution through his discovery of the logarithm. Not only did this discovery provide an algorithm that simplified arithmetical computation, but it also presented a transcendental function that has fascinated mathematicians for centuries. Napier was regarded as one of the most impressive intellects of his time, and his creative genius ranks him among the best mathematicians of all time.

John Napier was born in 1550, in Merchiston Castle of Edinburgh, Scotland. His father was Archibald Napier, a Scottish aristocrat (he was knighted in 1565), and his mother was Janet Bothwell, the sister of the bishop of Orkney. John Napier received his early education at home, and began studying at St. Andrew's University in 1563. Soon afterward his mother died. It was at St. Andrew's that Napier became passionately intrigued by theology, which would remain an enduring interest throughout his life. Indeed, it is ironic that Napier regarded his principal contributions as theological, since the world remembers him for his mathematical work.

Napier probably journeyed to Europe to continue his education, acquiring knowledge of classical literature and mathematics; no records exist, but it is likely that he studied at the University of Paris. Napier returned to Scotland by 1571 to attend his father's remarriage. He also was married in 1573, and took up residence with his wife in his family's Gartness estate in 1574. Here Napier occupied himself with running his estates, proving to be a talented inventor and innovator in agricultural methods. A fervent Protestant, he was also active in the religious controversies of the time. In 1593 he published a work that he considered to be his best: *The Plaine Discovery of the Whole Revelation of St. John.* This work, written to combat the spread of Roman Catholicism, gained Napier a reputation on the Continent.

Napier did much of his work on logarithms while at Gartness. His purpose was to simplify multiplications by transforming them into additions. The result was Napier's logarithm. Today, this logarithmic function has the property that products are transformed into sums, and it is easily one of the most important and useful mathematical tools. Napier's logarithm was slightly different from the modern definition, since his was motivated by analogy with dynamics rather than by pure algebra. Napier's first public discourse on logarithms appeared in *Mirifici logarithmorum*

John Napier, inventor of logarithms *(Courtesy of the Library of Congress)*

known as "Napier's bones." These bones were actually ivory rods with numbers inscribed, and products could be read off by arranging the rods in certain patterns. His great intellect and creativity gave Napier the reputation among locals of being a warlock, especially since he used to walk about in his nightgown. The rumors gave rise to the belief that Napier was in league with the devil.

Napier died on April 4, 1617, in Edinburgh, Scotland. His invention of the logarithm was a great aid to later calculators and mathematicians, who were able to carry out multiplications with increased speed and accuracy. The logarithm later became an important building stone in the foundation of modern analysis, and has continued to be widely used by mathematicians.

Further Reading

Leybourn, W. *The Art of Numbring by Speaking Rods, Vulgarly Termed Nepeirs Bones [sic].* 1667 Ann Arbor, Mich.: University Microfilms, 1968.

Smith, R. *Teacher's Guide to Napier's Bones.* Burlington, N.C.: Carolina Biological Supply Company, 1995.

canonis descriptio (Description of the marvelous canon of logarithms) in 1614. One difficulty with his definition was that the logarithm of one was not zero, which was desirable so that the logarithm could be interpreted as the inverse of exponentiation.

Henry Briggs, who read Napier's Latin discourse, communicated with him about making logarithms to have base 10; this would put a convenient interpretation on logarithms, since our numerical system involved 10 digits. If $\log x = y$, then y is equal to the number of powers of 10 needed to obtain x. The revised logarithm also gave the log of one the value zero. Napier and Briggs worked in tandem on new logarithmic tables through 1616, but the collaboration was interrupted by Napier's death in 1617.

Besides his work on the logarithm, Napier was also the inventor of a calculational aid

⊠ Navier, Claude-Louis-Marie-Henri
(1785–1836)
French
Mechanics, Differential Equations

Claude Navier is most famous today for the Navier-Stokes equations, which describe the dynamics of an incompressible fluid. He is responsible for introducing analytical techniques into civil engineering, and the cross-fertilization between mathematics and engineering that Navier initiated benefited both disciplines.

Claude Navier was born on February 10, 1785, in Dijon, France. He was raised amidst the furor of the French Revolution. His father was a lawyer and a member of the National Assembly. Navier's father died when he was only eight years old, and his mother retired to the countryside, leaving Navier in Paris in the care of his great-uncle Emiland Gauthey. Gauthey was the most renowned civil engineer of that time, and he may have exerted some influence on the young Navier.

Navier entered the École Polytechnique in 1802, barely making the entrance requirements due to his scholastic mediocrity. However, he made tremendous progress in his first year, rising to the top 10 of his class. One of Navier's teachers was JEAN-BAPTISTE-JOSEPH FOURIER, who had a significant impact on Navier's mathematical development. The two men remained lifelong friends. In 1804 Navier matriculated at the École des Ponts et Chaussées; he graduated two years later. When Emiland Gauthey died soon afterward, the Corps des Ponts et Chaussées asked Navier to edit his great-uncle's collected works. In doing so, Navier gained an appreciation for civil engineering as an application of mechanics, and he inserted many elements of mathematical analysis into Gauthey's writings.

During the next decade Navier became recognized as a leading scholar on engineering science, and he took a position at the École des Ponts et Chaussées in 1819. Navier placed a strong emphasis on the mathematical and analytical foundation of engineering, and this was evident in his teaching style. He was named professor there in 1830, and replaced AUGUSTIN-LOUIS CAUCHY at the École Polytechnique in 1831.

Navier had special expertise in building bridges. Traditionally, bridges were built on empirical principles, but Navier developed a mathematical theory for suspension bridges. He attempted to test his ideas by building a suspension bridge over the Seine, but the municipal council countered his efforts and eventually dismantled his partially completed bridge.

During his lifetime, Navier was recognized as a leading civil engineer, but he is famous today for his pioneering mathematical work on fluid mechanics. Navier worked on applied mathematical problems, such as elasticity, the motion of fluids, and applications of Fourier series to engineering questions. In 1821 he gave the Navier-Stokes differential equations for the motion of incompressible fluids. Today his derivation is known to be incorrect, as he neglected to consider the effect of shear forces; nevertheless, his equations were, providentially, correct.

Navier was not especially active in politics, though he favored a socialist position, aligning himself with social philosophers such as Auguste Comte. Navier believed in the power of science and technology to solve societal problems. As Franz Kafka later pointed out, the mechanization of society addresses materialistic concerns while leaving humankind spiritually alienated; from today's perspective, Navier's positivist philosophy seems naive. Navier did oppose the propagation of violence through the military complex, and in particular withstood the warmongering of Napoleon.

Navier received many honors in his life, including being elected to the Academy of Sciences in 1824. From 1830 onward, Navier worked as a government consultant on how science and technology could be used to improve the country. He died on August 21, 1836, in Paris, France. His most important contribution lies in the Navier-Stokes equations for fluid flow, which were heavily studied in physics and engineering, and applied in many technical arenas. Fluid mechanics is certainly one of the most difficult branches of applied mathematics, and is still not completely understood. Navier must also be remembered for his introduction of mathematics and physics to civil engineering, which resulted in a more modern, effective science.

Further Reading

Anderson, J. *A History of Aerodynamics and Its Impact on Flying Machines*. Cambridge, U.K.: Cambridge University Press, 1997.

Picon, A. "Navier and the Introduction of Suspension Bridges in France," *Construction History* 4 (1988): 21–34.

Newton, Sir Isaac
(1643–1727)
British
*Calculus, Geometry, Mechanics,
Differential Equations*

Sir Isaac Newton may well have been the greatest scientist of Western civilization. He made outstanding contributions to optics, mechanics, gravitation, and astronomy, using his newly discovered "method of fluxions"—a geometric form of differential calculus—to support his original conclusions. Newton not only unified many branches of physics through the umbrella of his differential calculus, which provided a quantitative tool of great power to explain physical phenomena, but he also made amazing discoveries that revolutionized the way scientists understood the natural world. His intellect was highly creative, and his genius was able to see to the heart of a scientific problem to provide a novel and viable explanation.

Sir Isaac Newton, cofounder of calculus and one of the greatest scientists ever, studied optics, gravity, mechanics, and astronomy. *(Courtesy of the Library of Congress)*

Isaac Newton was born on January 4, 1643, in Woolsthorpe, England. His father, also named Isaac Newton, came from a long line of wealthy farmers. He died a few months before the birth of his son. Young Isaac's mother, Hannah Ayscough, soon remarried, and this resulted in an unhappy childhood for the young boy—he was essentially treated as an orphan. Newton was sent to live with his maternal grandparents, and apparently he disliked his grandfather. He was also embittered toward his mother, and later threatened to burn her together with her new husband. Newton was of a volatile temper, prone to fits of capricious rage.

When Newton's stepfather died in 1653, he lived with his mother, half-brother, and two half-sisters for a time. At this time he began attending the Free Grammar School in Grantham, but the initial reports indicated that Newton was a poor, inattentive student. His mother inflicted a hiatus on Newton's education, bringing him home to manage her estate. This was another failure, as Newton had no interest in business affairs, and he resumed his education in 1660. Having shown a bit more promise in his latter years at Grantham, Newton was allowed to pursue further university education. Due to his mother's interference, he was older and less prepared than most students at Trinity College of Cambridge in 1661.

Despite his mother's extensive property and wealth, Newton became a sizar at Cambridge—a servant of the other students. He pursued a degree in law and became familiar with the classical philosophy of Aristotle and Plato, as well as the more modern ideas of RENÉ DESCARTES. Newton's personal scientific journal, *Certain Philosophical Questions*, reveals the early formulation of his most profound ideas. Newton's passion for scientific truth (in those days, scientific inquiry was dogmatically restricted to the development of Aristotle's ideas) played a role in his remarkable profundity as a thinker.

Newton's interest in mathematics developed later; the story is recounted that in 1663 he purchased an astrology text that was incomprehensible to him. This experience prompted Newton to pursue geometry, commencing with EUCLID OF ALEXANDRIA's *Elements*. Next he devoured the geometrical works of Descartes and FRANÇOIS VIÈTE, as well as JOHN WALLIS's *Algebra*. In 1663 ISAAC BARROW took up a professorship at Cambridge, and there exerted some influence over the young Newton. However, Newton's genius did not emerge at this time. This flowering of his intellect occurred after his 1665 graduation, when he returned home for the summer to escape a plague that shut Cambridge down. During the next two years at Lincolnshire, Newton achieved tremendous scientific breakthroughs in mathematics, physics, optics, and astronomy.

Newton's development of differential calculus took place at this time, well before GOTTFRIED WILHELM VON LEIBNIZ made similar, independent discoveries. Newton called his calculus the "method of fluxions," and it was very geometric (whereas Leibnizian calculus is more algebraic); central to Newton's technique was the realization of differentiation and integration as inverse processes. His method was able to solve many classical problems in a more elegant, unified fashion, while also being capable of solving wholly new problems unapproachable by older methodologies. The result of his labors, *De Methodis Serierum et Fluxionum* (On the methods of series and fluxions), was not published until 1736, many years after his death.

Cambridge was reopened in 1667 after cessation of the plague, and Newton obtained a minor fellowship, shortly afterward obtaining his master's degree and the Lucasian chair in 1669, which had been freshly vacated by Barrow. Barrow perused much of Newton's work, and helped to disseminate the novel ideas. He also assisted Newton in obtaining his new position. In 1670 Newton turned to optics, advancing a particle theory of light as well as the notion that white light was actually composed of a spectrum of different colors. Both of these ideas went counter to existing beliefs on the nature of light, but they were still well received. Newton was elected to the Royal Society in 1672 after donating a reflecting telescope of his own invention. Some controversy erupted over his ideas, and Newton did not handle the criticism well. Throughout his life, he experienced a tension between his desire to publish and gain recognition for his genius, and his loathing of the bickering and politics of the academic arena.

In 1678 Newton suffered a nervous breakdown, probably the result of overwork combined with the stress of his scholastic debates. The following year his mother died, and Newton removed himself even further from society. His work in gravity and celestial mechanics has gained him the most renown, and his early ideas on these topics date back to 1666. Based on his own law of centrifugal force and Kepler's third law of planetary motion, Newton was able to deduce his inverse square law for the force of gravity between two objects. This work was published in the *Philosophiae naturalis principia mathematica* (Mathematical principles of natural philosophy) in 1687, commonly known as the *Principia*. This work is thought by many to be the greatest scientific treatise of all time: It presents an analysis of centripetal forces, with applications to projectiles and pendulums. Newton demonstrated the inverse square law for gravitational force and formulated the general (and universal) principle of gravity as a fundamental artifact of our universe. Centuries later, Einstein would describe the force of gravity as the fabric of space itself. Of course, the *Principia* was an enormous success, and Newton became the most famous scientist of his age.

In the latter portion of his life, Newton fell away from scientific research and became involved in government. When James I attempted to appoint underqualified Catholics to university professorships, Newton (who was a fervent Protestant) withstood him publicly. After the king's deposition in 1689, Newton was elected to Parliament and recognized as an academic hero. He suffered a second emotional breakdown in 1693, perhaps brought on by laboratory chemicals, and officially retired from research. He became warden of the mint in 1696 and master of the mint in 1699, and in this capacity he worked diligently to prevent counterfeiting of the new coinage.

Scientists and mathematicians throughout Europe recognized Newton as one of the greatest intellects, although the controversy with Leibniz that erupted over the issue of priority in the invention of calculus detracted from his intellectual reign. Much of his energy was devoted to this protracted debate, carried on by the disciples of both men, and certainly Newton's ferocious temperament was conspicuous in his treatment of his competitor. (The details of this argument are given in the biography of Leibniz.) Newton held the presidency of the Royal Society from 1703 until his death, and he also holds the distinction of being the first Englishman to be knighted (in 1705 by Queen Anne) for scientific achievements. He died on March 21, 1727, in London, England.

It is hard to overestimate the importance of Newton's work, so great has its impact on science and mathematics been. It must be understood that his invention of calculus was born out of a long progression of intellectual endeavor by such figures as ARCHIMEDES OF SYRACUSE, BLAISE PASCAL, and Wallis, among others. However, Newton's voice rang like a clarion call through a babble of disorganized and incoherent voices; his calculus not only provided a general system that revealed prior methodologies to be variations on a theme, but also was a practical and powerful tool capable of tackling thorny scientific questions. His calculus placed the sciences further under the shadow of mathematics and quantitative reasoning, and thus increased the precision and rigor of physics and astronomy. For

his mathematics alone, Newton would have been considered one of the greatest minds of human history.

Further Reading

Bechler, Z. *Newton's Physics and the Conceptual Structure of the Scientific Revolution*. Boston: Kluwer Academic Publishers, 1991.

Brewster, D. *Memoirs of the Life, Writings, and Discoveries of Sir Isaac Newton*. New York: Johnson Reprint Corp., 1965.

Chandrasekhar, S. *Newton's "Principia" for the Common Reader*. New York: Oxford University Press, 1995.

Christianson, G. *In the Presence of the Creator: Isaac Newton and His Times*. New York: Free Press, 1984.

Cohen, I. *Introduction to Newton's "Principia."* Cambridge, U.K.: Cambridge University Press, 1978.

Gjertsen, D. *The Newton Handbook*. New York: Routledge & Kegan Paul, 1986.

Hall, A. *Isaac Newton, Adventurer in Thought*. Oxford: Blackwell, 1992.

Meli, D. *Equivalence and Priority: Newton versus Leibniz; Including Leibniz's Unpublished Manuscripts on the "Principia."* Oxford: Clarendon Press, 1993.

Turnbull, H. *The Mathematical Discoveries of Newton*. London: Blackie and Son Ltd., 1945.

Westfall, R. *Never at Rest: A Biography of Isaac Newton*. New York: Cambridge University Press, 1980.

———. *The Life of Isaac Newton*. New York: Cambridge University Press, 1993.

⊠ **Noether, Emmy (Amalie Emmy Noether)**
(1882–1935)
German
Algebra

Emmy Noether was an exceptional mathematician who was able to overcome gender and ethnic obstacles to make outstanding contributions to abstract algebra. She is best known for her early work on ring theory. Her results on ideals in rings were instrumental to the later development of modern algebra.

Emmy Noether was born on March 23, 1882, in Erlangen, a town in the German province of Bavaria, to Max Noether, a notable mathematician at the University of Erlangen, and Ida Kaufmann. Both of her parents were of Jewish descent, which would later be a source of persecution for Noether. Emmy Noether was the eldest of four children—her younger siblings were all boys.

Noether studied at the Höhere Töchter Schule in Erlangen from 1889 until 1897, where she studied languages and arithmetic. She originally intended to become a language teacher, and became certified in 1900 to teach English and French in Bavarian schools. However, Noether instead pursued the difficult path of mathematics, and began attending lectures at the University of Erlangen in 1900. Women were allowed to study only unofficially, and Noether had to obtain permission to attend classes. She also studied at Göttingen under DAVID HILBERT and FELIX KLEIN.

In 1904 Noether was allowed to matriculate at Erlangen, and she obtained her doctorate in 1907 under the direction of Paul Gordan. Her thesis constructed several algebraic invariants, which was a constructive approach to Hilbert's basis theorem of 1888. Unable to progress further in an academic career due to her gender, Noether spent the next few years assisting her father in his research. She also turned toward Hilbert's more abstract approach to algebra, and made many contributions of her own. Gradually she gained recognition from the mathematical community through her publications, and in 1915 Hilbert and Klein invited her to Göttingen as a lecturer. It is a testimony to her talent that Hilbert and Klein fought long and hard with the university administration to grant Noether a position, which was finally obtained in 1919.

Noether's first work in Göttingen was a theorem of theoretical physics—sometimes referred to as Noether's theorem—which relates particle symmetries to conservation principles. Albert Einstein later praised this contribution to general relativity for its penetration and value. After 1919 Noether shifted from invariant theory to ideals, which are certain special subsets of rings, a generalization of Euclidean space viewed from an algebraic perspective. One of her most important papers, published in 1921, gave a fundamental decomposition for these ideals. Her work on ring theory was of great significance to later developments in modern algebra; in 1927 Noether investigated noncommutative rings (rings in which the commutative law does not hold). These algebraic spaces have become very important for theoretical physics, where the interactions between particles follow noncommutative laws.

For her outstanding work, Noether received much recognition; in 1932 she shared the Alfred Ackermann-Teubner Memorial Prize for the Advancement of Mathematical Knowledge with Emil Artin. However, her Jewish ethnicity made her a target of Nazi prejudice in 1933, and she was forced to flee to the United States, where she lectured at the Institute for Advanced Study at Princeton.

Noether died on April 14, 1935, in Bryn Mawr, Pennsylvania. Her colleagues recognized her as an exceptional mathematician who did much to advance the knowledge of algebra. Her fundamental results in the theory of rings and invariants left an enduring legacy in abstract algebra, and her success in the presence of discrimination and persecution testifies to her spirited determination and firm character.

Further Reading
Byers, N. "The Life and Times of Emmy Noether; Contributions of E. Noether to Particle Physics," in *History of Original Ideas and Basic Discoveries in Particle Physics*. New York: Plenum, 1996.

————. "E. Noether's Discovery of the Deep Connection between Symmetries and Conservation Laws," *Israel Mathematical Conference Proceedings* 12 (1999).

Dick, A. *Emmy Noether, 1882–1935.* Boston: Birkhäuser, 1981.

Kimberling, C. "Emmy Noether and Her Influence," in *Emmy Noether: A Tribute to Her Life and Work.* New York: Marcel Dekker, 1981.

Srinivasan, B., and J. Sally. *Emmy Noether in Bryn Mawr.* New York: Springer-Verlag, 1983.

O

**Oresme, Nicole (Nicole d'Oresme,
Nicholas Oresme)**
(1323–1382)
French
Geometry

Nicole Oresme was an excellent all-around scholar who proposed several ideas, in a primitive form, centuries before the persons to whom they are usually credited. In particular, he was a predecessor to RENÉ DESCARTES in his graphical depiction of functional relationships.

Oresme was born in 1323 in Allemagne, France. There is no information about his early life, but it is known that he was of Norman ancestry. He attended the University of Paris in the 1340s, studying the arts under the philosopher Jean Buridan. This teacher encouraged Oresme's interests in natural philosophy and pushed him to question the ideas of Aristotle.

Oresme later earned a degree in theology at the College of Navarre in 1348, and he became a master in theology in 1355. This led to his appointment as grand master of the College of Navarre in 1356. During this time he befriended the future king Charles V. This friendship was born of similar intellectual interests, and continued through both of their lives.

Oresme took on increasingly prestigious religious positions, culminating in his appointment as royal chaplain to the king in 1364. From 1370 onward he resided in Paris and busied himself advising the king and translating several of Aristotle's works into French. Oresme challenged some of Aristotle's revered notions, redefining time and space in terms closer to what is accepted today.

Oresme contributed to mathematics through the invention of a type of coordinate geometry that traced the relationship between a table of paired values (such as for a function's independent and dependent variables) and a two-dimensional plot. This concept anticipates Descartes's more sophisticated analytic geometry by three centuries; it is likely that Descartes was familiar with Oresme's widely read *Tractatus de configurationibus qualitatum et motuum* (Treatise on the configurations of qualities and motions).

Oresme was also the first mathematician to use the fractional exponent (though in a different notation), and made primitive investigations into infinite series. He posited the question whether the ratio of periods of two heavenly bodies could be an irrational number; this fairly deep question of irrational periodicities has been explored in the nonlinear dynamical studies of the 20th century. Besides these mathematical discoveries, Oresme also did some initial thinking (although he did not completely formulate a theory) on scientific problems, proposing the law of freefall, the rotation of the Earth, and the structural theory of chemical compounds. After being appointed a bishop in 1377, Oresme died on July 11, 1382, in Lisieux, France.

Oresme was an excellent scholar of the 14th century who made several innovative scientific and philosophic advances. In mathematics, he invented coordinate geometry, which was a step toward the full theory of analytic geometry popularized in the 17th century. His widely read works probably influenced later mathematicians.

Further Reading

Clagett, M. *Nicole Oresme and the Medieval Geometry of Quantities and Motions*. Madison: University of Wisconsin Press, 1968.

Coopland, G. *Nicole Oresme and the Astrologers: A Study of His "Livre de Divinacions."* Liverpool: The University Press, 1952.

Grant, E. "Nicole Oresme and the Commensurability or Incommensurability of Celestial Motions," *Archive for History of Exact Sciences* 1 (1961).

———. "Nicole Oresme and His De Proportionibus Proportionum," *Isis* 51 (1960): 293–314.

P

Pappus of Alexandria
(ca. 290–ca. 350)
Greek
Geometry

Pappus of Alexandria is the last of the great Greek mathematicians. He is principally known for considering certain geometrical questions that blossomed into the field of projective geometry. Virtually nothing is known of his personal life.

Pappus of Alexandria was born in approximately 290 in Alexandria, Egypt. The ancient sources describing the dates of his activity are in conflict, but the consensus of scholars indicates that he was active from 284 to 305, during the reign of the emperor Diocletian. However, this may also be too early, as it is now known that Pappus's *Almagest* was written after 320. His death is conjectured to have occurred around 350 in Alexandria.

Apparently Pappus lived in Alexandria all of his life. He had a family, for he dedicates one of his books to his son Hermodorus. Pappus also discusses his philosopher friend Heirius, and it seems that Pappus headed a school in Alexandria.

Pappus's major work on geometry is called the *Mathematical Collection* and is thought to have been written around 340. A handbook of geometry designed to revive interest in the classical works, this volume is divided into several books. Book I, on arithmetic, is lost, and Book II treats APOLLONIUS OF PERGA's notation for expressing large numbers. Book II discusses the harmonic, geometric, and arithmetic means and their accompanying constructions, as well as some geometric paradoxes. In Book IV Pappus treats some special curves, such as the spiral and quadratrix. He divides geometric problems into plane, solid, and linear problems. Book V describes the construction of honeycombs by bees and the optimality of the circle for enclosing maximal area with a minimal perimeter. He reviews the 13 semiregular solids of ARCHIMEDES OF SYRACUSE and proves results relating surface area and volume for several types of solids. Book VI considers astronomy, reviewing the works of EUCLID OF ALEXANDRIA, ERATOSTHENES OF CYRENE, and Apollonius.

Book VII contains the "Treasury of Analysis," in which Pappus sets out the method of analysis and synthesis encountered in the classic works of Euclid and others. He describes analysis as a breakdown of a problem into simpler, related problems; these are then synthesized into the final solution. This method of thought was distinctively Greek, and was later mastered by the European mathematicians who studied the classics. Pappus also lays out the so-called Pappus problem, which has greatly influenced the evolution of geometry—RENÉ DESCARTES and SIR ISAAC NEWTON later discussed this topic of geometry. Book VIII treats mechanics, which Pappus defines as the study of motion and force. The work as a whole demonstrates Pappus's mastery of many mathematical sciences, and his exposition is fairly good.

Besides the *Mathematical Collection*, Pappus wrote several commentaries of variable quality, including those on CLAUDIUS PTOLEMY's *Almagest* and Euclid's *Elements*. Pappus also wrote a work on geography, and he may well have written about music and hydrostatics, but the primary sources have not survived.

Pappus was influential on later European mathematicians, since he gave an insightful overview of all the older Greek mathematical works. After reading Pappus, a mathematician could track down the original sources of such great mathematicians as Euclid and Archimedes; in this sense Pappus was quite influential. His own mathematical discoveries seem limited, though the Pappus problem can be viewed as the foundation of projective geometry.

Further Reading

Bulmer-Thomas, I. *Selections Illustrating the History of Greek Mathematics*. Cambridge, Mass.: Harvard University Press, 1980.

Heath, T. A *History of Greek Mathematics*. Oxford: Clarendon Press, 1921.

Neugebauer, O. A *History of Ancient Mathematical Astronomy*. New York: Springer-Verlag, 1975.

Tahir, H. "Pappus and Mathematical Induction," *The Australian Mathematical Society Gazette* 22, no. 4 (1995): 166–167.

⊠   Pascal, Blaise
(1623–1662)
French
Geometry, Probability, Mechanics, Calculus

Blaise Pascal, a geometer who formulated early notions of calculus, is also viewed as a founder of the theory of probability. *(Courtesy of the Library of Congress)*

Blaise Pascal is famous for his brilliant foundational work in probability, geometry, and hydrostatics, as well as for his insightful thoughts on philosophy and religion. Pascal's work in the mathematics of gambling, along with that of PIERRE DE FERMAT, laid the basis for modern theory of probability and statistics and sparked a movement in western Europe toward a "stochasticized" society. His labors in the arena of hydrostatics were groundbreaking, providing much of the theory behind modern hydraulics technology, while his efforts in Christian apologetics are notable for their clarity of thought and insight into human nature.

Pascal was born on June 19, 1623, in Clermont (now Clermont-Ferrand) in the Auvergne region of France. Blaise was the third child of Étienne Pascal, a mathematician, who educated his only son himself. Antoinette Begon, his mother, died when Pascal was only three years old. Interestingly, the young Pascal was not permitted to study mathematics until age 12, when he began reading EUCLID OF ALEXANDRIA's *Elements*. However, even before this time, the precocious child was investigating geometry on his own.

Blaise would accompany his father to meetings held in Paris by Marin Mersenne, a priest who greatly promoted the spread and communication of mathematics. In this context Pascal further developed his mathematical abilities, being influenced by the thought of GIRARD DESARGUES. Pascal soon became Desargues's main disciple in the study of geometry, and in June 1639 he discovered the "mystic hexagram." He had found that the opposite sides of a hexagon inscribed in a conic section form three points that are collinear.

In December 1639 the Pascal family moved to Rouen, where Étienne had an appointment as tax collector. In 1640 Blaise published his first work, *Essay on Conic Sections,* an outline of a treatise on conics. Soon afterward, in 1642, he began an attempt to mechanize addition and subtraction, in order to assist his father with his accounting calculations. By 1645 Pascal had completed the construction of the first digital calculator (although Wilhelm Schickard had designed an earlier prototype in 1623, it was not manufactured). The device, although unsuccessful financially due to the expense of construction, was quite similar to a mechanical calculator of the 1940s. After several experiments in atmospheric pressure, Pascal concluded that as altitude increases the pressure of air decreases, and that a vacuum exists above the atmosphere. Although true, these findings, published in 1647 as *New Experiments Concerning Vacuums,* were controversial in the scientific community, and there was some debate over who had priority in the discoveries, as several

scientists were researching hydrostatics. Hydrostatics is the study of fluids at rest and the pressures they exert, and Pascal's 1654 *Treatise on the Equilibrium of Liquids* gave a rigorous account of the topic. This treatise clearly demonstrated the effects of the weight of the air, as well as several laws of hydrostatics, including Pascal's law of pressure. This principle, which states that fluid in a closed vessel transmits pressure undiminished (or, in other words, the fluid is incompressible), is the basis of the hydraulic press—essentially a type of lever. His treatment gave a synthesis of prior knowledge and new work, and lucidly presented the concept of pressure.

The young Pascal had been interested in religion since 1646, and when his father died in 1651, he became deeply contemplative about spiritual matters. His ideas would later be published in his philosophical work *Pensées de Monsieur Pascal sur la religion et sur quelques autres sujets* (Monsieur Pascal's thoughts on religion and some other subjects) of 1670. His work on projective geometry, the mathematical study of perspective, led to *The Generation of Conic Sections* (1654). *Conic section* is the name for a curve obtained by slicing a cone by a plane at certain angles. This great work dealt with the projective generation of conics and their properties, the definition of the mystic hexagram, and the projective theory of centers and diameters. In addition, his *Treatise on the Arithmetical Triangle* appeared in the same year, dealing with the so-called Pascal's triangle, a triangle of numbers, in which each entry is obtained by summing the two entries above it. Although he did not invent the arithmetical triangle, his work was quite influential on the development of the general binomial theorem.

In 1654 Pascal was working on some gambling problems with Fermat. The two main questions they investigated were, the problem of the dice, calculating the probability of obtaining a pair of sixes in a given number of throws; and the problem of the stakes, concerned with how to divide the pot fairly to the players if a game of chance is interrupted. In formulating these types of problems, Pascal became a founding father of the Western theory of probability. In the succeeding centuries, Western culture would become increasingly quantitative, embracing a stochastic (i.e., relating to probability and chance) approach to phenomena; it became apparent, after these humble origins, that reliable information could be obtained from uncertain events, as long as a large number of repeated trials could be performed and measured. Pascal worked on a calculus of probabilities, using inductive reasoning to find solutions. His work in games seems to have affected Pascal's view of Christian apologetics (rhetorical or rational defenses of a belief), since *Pensées* includes the famous "Pascal's wager":

> If God does not exist, one will lose nothing by believing in him, while if he does exist, one will lose everything by not believing.

Indeed, Pascal's approach to probability foreshadows the modern theory of decision, in which choice is intimately connected with the probability of uncertain events; one can see Pascal's apologetic method as a classic problem in decision theory.

Pascal had long suffered from ill health (indigestion and constant headaches), being sickly from his youth, and he had not long to live. In 1654 he was drawn more deeply into religious concerns; on the night of November 23, designated as his "night of fire," he experienced a second conversion to Christianity; from this time, he would turn away from science and mathematics toward religion and epistemology (the study of knowledge and belief structures). In 1656 and 1657 he composed his *Lettres provinciales* (Provincial letters), a Jansenist polemic against the Jesuits. They were published anonymously, and it is said that their rigor of thought and clarity of presentation dealt a wound to

Jesuitism from which it has never recovered. His defense of Christianity to unbelievers, formulated in the *Pensées*, was written at this time.

Encouraged even by his Jansenist friends, Pascal did some final work in mathematics. In 1657 he prepared the *Elements of Geometry*, which unfortunately was not completed. His last work in 1658 and 1659 was on the cycloid, a curve traced out by the path of a marked point on the circumference of a rolling circle. In his investigations of this curve, he developed the "theory of indivisibles," which was a forerunner of the integral calculus soon formulated by SIR ISAAC NEWTON and GOTTFRIED WILHELM VON LEIBNIZ. Pascal considered such problems as calculating areas under curves, centers of gravity for surfaces, and volumes beneath surfaces of revolution (the surface obtained by rotating a curve about a fixed axis). Interestingly, it seems that this work developed over the course of several public mathematical contests, in which Pascal posed calculus problems to the community.

In 1659 Pascal fell gravely ill and sought solitude, devoting himself to charitable works. His last project was the development of a public transportation project in Paris that involved horse-drawn carriages. He died at age 39 in great pain, on August 19, 1662, in Paris. For his contributions to mathematics, as well as physics and religion, Pascal ranks as one of the greatest intellects of the West. It seems that his soul was torn between pride over his intellectual abilities and accomplishments and self-denial of an austere Augustinian brand, but perhaps it was this very tension that produced such brilliant work. Though some mathematicians may exceed Pascal in terms of originality, profundity, or volume, Pascal's systemization of much of science and mathematics must draw attention and admiration.

Further Reading

Adamson, D. *Blaise Pascal: Mathematician, Physicist, and Thinker about God.* New York: St. Martin's, 1995.

Coleman, F. *Neither Angel nor Beast: The Life and Work of Blaise Pascal*. New York: Routledge and Kegan Paul, 1986.

Edwards, A. *Pascal's Arithmetical Triangle*. New York: Oxford University Press, 1987.

Hooper, A. *Makers of Mathematics*. New York: Random House, 1958.

Krailsheimer, A. *Pascal*. New York: Oxford University Press, 1980.

Mesnard, J. *Pascal*. Paris: Hatier, 1951.

Mortimer, E. *Blaise Pascal: The Life and Work of a Realist*. New York: Harper, 1959.

⊠   **Peano, Giuseppe**
(1858–1932)
Italian
Logic, Differential Equations

Giuseppe Peano was one of the most talented mathematicians of the late 19th century; he was conspicuous for his attention to rigor and detail. His work on mathematical logic and set theory has earned him fame, but he also contributed to pedagogical projects that proved to be unimportant. Peano's creative genius gave birth to the famous Peano curve, and he also constructed the Peano axioms.

Giuseppe Peano was born on August 27, 1858, in Cuneo, Italy. His parents were farmers, and Peano traveled by foot each day to the school in Cuneo. Peano's uncle was a priest who recognized the boy's natural talents and took him to Turin in 1870 to prepare him for university studies. Peano started at the University of Turin in 1876, and there studied mathematics. Peano received his doctorate in 1880.

Peano had a remarkable skill for detecting the logical flaws in arguments. Upon graduation he was appointed assistant to Angelo Genocchi, and Peano soon detected an error in the textbook for one of the courses. Peano largely taught Genocchi's classes, since the older professor was ill, and in 1884 published a text of the course

notes. Peano had also published several research papers after 1880, and became qualified to teach at the university level in 1884.

In 1886 Peano researched questions of existence and uniqueness in the theory of differential equations, and next developed a method for solving such equations using successive approximations. He was also teaching at the Military Academy at this time, and was later appointed to Genocchi's chair at Turin upon his death in 1889. Peano meanwhile published *Geometrical Calculus* in 1888, which began with a chapter on mathematical logic, and developed HERMANN GÜNTER GRASSMANN's concept of a vector space. Peano used a modern notation for this work, which built upon the ideas of CHARLES PEIRCE and GEORGE BOOLE. In 1889 he published his famous Peano axioms, which defined the natural numbers in terms of sets, and he defined in a rigorous fashion such ideas as proof by induction. This was a significant contribution to the foundations of mathematics, and it would be exploited and developed by many of Peano's successors.

Peano is also famous for his "space-filling curves." He defined a continuous mapping of the unit interval onto the unit square, in essence constructing a one-dimensional curve that filled up a two-dimensional space. This mapping does not have a continuous inverse, since that would be tantamount to establishing that the line and the plane have equal dimension. Nevertheless, many mathematicians were disturbed by the pathological result, which followed in the same spirit of the work of GEORG CANTOR.

Once appointed to his new post at the University of Turin, Peano founded the journal *Rivista de matematica* in 1891. As editor of the journal, Peano was able to ensure that high standards of rigor were maintained. In 1892 he embarked on a new project—the *Formulario matematico* (Mathematical formulary), which was to be a collection of definitions, theorems, and methods of all mathematical subjects, that could be used as a basic text for every mathematics course. This monumental effort was not completed until 1908. It turned out to have little popularity, since this meticulous approach to mathematics did not facilitate learning. Peano was considered a good teacher prior to his implementation of the *Formulario;* afterward, students and fellow faculty members complained of the boring exactness of his method.

One of the high points of Peano's career was the International Congress of Philosophy held in Paris during 1900. Peano's logical training enabled him to shine among his less rigorous philosopher colleagues, as he was able to win all the philosophical arguments in which he became embroiled. His presence there made a great impression on the young BERTRAND RUSSELL, who was excited by the power of Peano's notation and methodology. Peano also attended a similar congress of mathematicians, at which DAVID HILBERT stated his famous 23 problems for the 20th century. Peano was intrigued by Hilbert's problem on the axioms of arithmetic.

Peano's last years were spent on a new project—the construction of a new language based on French, Latin, English, and German. The resultant *"Latino sine flexione"*—later called Interlingua—has seen little use, and is irrelevant to the development of mathematics. Peano died on April 20, 1932, in Turin, Italy. He was a brilliant mathematician of great precision, setting standards of rigor that were uncommon at the time; his meticulousness seems more appropriate for the present age of mathematics. Although his work on the *Formulario* and *Latino sine flexione* can be seen as distractions, his contributions to mathematics are highly significant nonetheless. Peano must be regarded as one of the early founders of mathematical logic—his work on the Peano axioms was well known to his descendants. The Peano curve is also an important contribution to topology and the study of fractal geometry.

Further Reading

Gillies, D. *Frege, Dedekind, and Peano on the Foundations of Arithmetic.* Assen, the Netherlands: Van Gorcum, 1982.

Kennedy, H. *Peano: Life and Works of Giuseppe Peano.* Dordrecht, the Netherlands: D. Reidel Publishing Company, 1980.

———. "Peano's Concept of Number," *Historia Mathematica* 1 (1974): 387–408.

⊠ **Pearson, Egon Sharpe**
(1895–1980)
British
Statistics

Egon Pearson is ranked among the greatest mathematicians of modern times due to his work, together with Jerzy Neyman, on hypothesis testing. Their work formulated the classical statistical decision theory familiar to most scientists.

Egon Sharpe Pearson was born on August 11, 1895, in Hampstead, England. His father was the famous statistician Karl Pearson, who first invented the correlation statistic to quantify linear relationship between two statistical variables. His mother was Maria Sharpe. Pearson was the middle child of the three children. His childhood was somewhat sheltered, and he grew to admire and revere the outstanding work of his father.

Pearson attended the Dragon School in Oxford from 1907 to 1909, and later studied at Winchester College, from which he graduated in 1914. At this time World War I erupted, but Pearson did not serve in the military due to his poor health—he had a heart murmur. Instead, he pursued university studies at Trinity College, although during his first year he was incapacitated by influenza. Determined to contribute to the war effort, Pearson left Trinity to work for the Admiralty; he resumed his undergraduate studies after conclusion of hostilities, and earned his diploma through a special test for veterans in 1920.

In the next phase of his life, Pearson took up graduate-level research at Cambridge, originally studying solar physics. In his astronomical studies he encountered a substantial amount of statistical theory, and in 1921 he joined his father's Department of Applied Statistics at University College of London as a lecturer. However, Pearson's father ensured that his son did little real lecturing; instead, his time was spent attending talks and conducting research. He began to produce a significant quantity of statistical research papers, and in 1924 also became an assistant editor of *Biometrika*, his father's statistical journal.

Meanwhile, Pearson became emotionally involved in one of the most heated statistical controversies of the time. SIR RONALD AYLMER FISHER, who was also at the same department, promoted the small-sample approach to statistical problems. He emphasized the computation of exact distributions, and more generally attempted to ground statistical practice in rigorous mathematics. Karl Pearson's approach emphasized large-sample statistics and asymptotic theory instead; these differing viewpoints, coupled with Fisher's pugnacious personality, led to a savage public debate. Egon Pearson was caught between paternal fidelity and the realization that Fisher, antagonistic as he was, seemed to be correct. After Karl Pearson's death years later, Fisher continued his statistical agenda in print, an ongoing source of irritation for Egon Pearson.

In 1925 Pearson met with Neyman, another young statistician, and initiated a fruitful collaboration with him. This work continued on into 1927, resulting in excellent research into the theory of hypothesis testing (that is, how to test scientific hypotheses with quantitative data in such a way as to minimize mistakes). Their research in this area has now become a classical segment of basic statistical theory, although much of the current work is focused on the Bayesian approach to inference and the resolution of hypotheses. Pearson and Neyman continued to collaborate, mostly by voluminous correspondence, over the next decade. Also at this time, Pearson began working closely with WILLIAM GOSSET.

Pearson began lecturing in 1926. His father retired in 1933 from his position as the Galton Chair of Statistics, and University College decided to split the department into two sections: Fisher became head of the Department of Eugenics, and Pearson was head of the Department of Applied Statistics. In 1934 Pearson married (he had two daughters), and after his father's death in 1936 he took over managing and editing *Biometrika*. In this year Neyman also visited Pearson's department, sparking further joint work. He was recognized for his exceptional labors through the 1935 Weldon Prize.

Another great achievement of Pearson's was the editing of his father's substantial *Tables for Statisticians and Biometricians*, published in two volumes in 1954 and 1972 with Hartley. These tables were easy to use, and became models for statistical figures. In the advent of World War II, Pearson shifted the thrust of his research to topics applicable to the war, such as the statistical analysis of the fragmentation of shells. Pearson was later recognized with a government award for his service.

He was a quiet, introverted man who had led a somewhat sheltered life. Pearson's difficult relations with Fisher were ameliorated in 1939, after Fisher moved away from London. Pearson was struck by personal tragedy in 1949, when his wife, Eileen, died of pneumonia. He continued his prodigious contributions to the theory of statistics, and retired from University College in 1961. In 1966 he was belatedly elected to the Royal Society, and he died on June 12, 1980, in Midhurst, England.

One of the greatest mathematicians, Pearson was an extremely renowned and noteworthy statistician who introduced many mathematical ideas into the practice of science and statistics. Most remarkable is his joint work with Neyman on hypothesis testing.

Further Reading

David, H. "Egon S. Pearson, 1895–1980," *The American Statistician* 35, no. 2 (1981): 94–95.

Johnson, N., and S. Kotz. "Egon Sharpe Pearson," in *Leading Personalities in Statistical Sciences*. New York: John Wiley, 1997.

Moore, P. "A Tribute to Egon Sharpe Pearson," *Journal of the Royal Statistical Society. Series A* 138, no. 2 (1975): 129–130.

Pearson, E. *The Selected Papers of E. S. Pearson.* Berkeley: University of California Press, 1966.

Reid, C. *Neyman—from Life.* New York: Springer-Verlag, 1982.

⊠ Peirce, Charles
(1839–1914)
American
Logic, Topology

There were few American mathematicians of note before the 20th century, when Americans came to dominate the mathematical scene. One exception is Charles Peirce, a notable mathematician who was active in the latter half of the 19th century.

Charles Peirce was born on September 10, 1839, in Cambridge, Massachusetts. His father was the mathematician Benjamin Peirce, whose work he later extended, and his mother was Sarah Mills. Charles Peirce was educated at Harvard University, and after graduation in 1859 became active on the Coast and Geodetic Survey.

After one year with the survey, Peirce entered the Lawrence Scientific School of Harvard University, where he studied chemistry. He continued his work for the survey as a computing aide to his father, who was also involved. Charles Peirce contributed to the determination of the Earth's ellipticity, and used the swinging of a pendulum to measure the force of gravity. Despite his brilliant work for the survey, Peirce was in constant conflict with the administrators, who viewed his careful and meticulous preparation of reports as procrastination. He eventually resigned in 1891, and thereafter had no steady employment or income.

Peirce is primarily known as a logician, though he was also interested in topological and geometrical problems. In connection with his work on geodesy, he became interested in conformal mappings, and he invented a quincuncial projection that involved elliptic functions. Later Peirce tackled the famous four color problem, which asks whether a political map can be colored with only four colors, such that no two neighboring states have the same color. Peirce was intrigued by a wide selection of topological problems, such as those found in the theory of knots. He extended his father's work on associative algebras, and made original contributions to mathematical logic and set theory.

Peirce did not attain an academic career—there were no chairs in logic at that time in the United States—although he briefly taught courses in logic at Johns Hopkins University from 1879 to 1884. He supported himself through odd jobs and the generosity of his friends. Peirce was an early member of the American Mathematical Society, where he retained his membership despite being unable to pay his dues. He was admired for his brilliance, although he often shrugged off mathematical details as unimportant.

Peirce identified logic with semiotics, the theory of signs (symbols that signify something). These ideas were summarized in his unfinished work *A System of Logic, Considered as Semiotic*. Peirce contributed to deductive logic, but his primary interest lay in induction, or in his own words, abduction—the formation of a hypothesis in order to explain some strange observation. Due to this unique emphasis in the theory of logic, it is easy to see how Peirce was interested in science, broadly speaking, since scientific investigations gave an application of the concept of abduction. He was also well known as a philosopher, contributing to the philosophy of pragmatism, which he identified with abduction.

Peirce was married twice: to Harriet Melusina Fay in 1862, who abandoned him in 1876, and to Juliette Pourtalai in 1883. He had no children, and spent the final years of his life on a farm in Pennsylvania. In his last years, he fell seriously ill, and was also afflicted by poverty. Peirce died on April 19, 1914, in Milford, Pennsylvania. He was a famous logician, highly regarded by American mathematicians. Although he has not left an outstanding intellectual legacy, Peirce was one of the first notable American mathematicians; he flourished at a time when American mathematics was in its infancy.

Further Reading

Brent, J. *Charles Sanders Peirce: A Life*. Bloomington: Indiana University Press, 1998.

Debrock, G., and M. Hulswit. *Living Doubt: Essays concerning the Epistemology of Charles Sanders Peirce*. Dordrecht, the Netherlands: Kluwer Academic Publishers, 1994.

Deledalle, G. *Charles S. Peirce, 1839–1914: An Intellectual Biography*. Amsterdam, the Netherlands: J. Benjamins Publishing Company, 1990.

Eisele, C., and R. Martin. *Studies in the Scientific and Mathematical Philosophy of Charles S. Peirce*. New York: Mouton, 1979.

Kevelson, R. *Charles S. Peirce's Method of Methods*. Amsterdam, the Netherlands: J. Benjamins Publishing Company, 1987.

Roberts, D. *The Existential Graphs of Charles S. Peirce*. The Hague, the Netherlands: Mouton, 1973.

⊠   Poincaré, Jules-Henri
(1854–1912)
French
Topology, Geometry, Complex Analysis, Differential Equations

Henri Poincaré has been described as the last of the great mathematicians adept in several branches of mathematics and science; however, a similar claim could be made about DAVID HILBERT. Poincaré was a genius of the first rank, whose innovative contributions shaped (and in some cases, essentially founded) several areas of mathematics, including algebraic geometry, algebraic topology, the theory of automorphic functions in complex analysis, and nonlinear dynamics. His work continues to exert a profound influence on modern studies in topology and geometry.

Jules-Henri Poincaré was born on April 29, 1854, in Nancy, France, to Léon Poincaré, a professor of medicine at the University of Nancy, and Eugénie Launois. Henri Poincaré

Jules Henri Poincaré used algebraic methods to solve geometrical problems and formulated the yet unproved Poincaré conjecture. *(Courtesy of the Library of Congress)*

was physically weak, suffering from nearsightedness and a lack of coordination; he was ill for a time from diphtheria. However, his intellectual gifts more than compensated for these deficiencies. His mother taught him to write at a young age, and Poincaré later became a powerful author.

When Poincaré was still young, he started at the local school in Nancy in 1862 (this school was later renamed Lycée Henri Poincaré in his honor). During the next 11 years, Poincaré proved to be the top student, excelling in all subjects, especially mathematics—he often won first prize in competitions. He entered the École Polytechnique in 1873, and graduated two years later. Poincaré was far beyond his fellow students in most of the intellectual subjects; he also had a strong interest in music, especially the piano. He read widely in science, and thus obtained a thorough knowledge of electricity, optics, and thermodynamics.

Next Poincaré pursued further studies at the École des Mines, and briefly worked as a mining engineer while working on his doctorate at the University of Paris. His mentor was CHARLES HERMITE, and Poincaré completed a thesis on differential equations in 1879. From here, Poincaré went through several appointments: a teacher of analysis at the University of Caen, a chair at the Faculty of Science in Paris in 1881, and the chair of mathematical physics and probability at the Sorbonne in 1886. His lectures were disorganized, but addressed new material each year; Poincaré seasoned his mathematical topics with applications from optics, astronomy, electricity, and other cognate sciences.

Besides his scientific work, which includes contributions to celestial mechanics, fluid mechanics, and the philosophy of science—he was also credited as a coinventor of the special theory of relativity along with Albert Einstein—Poincaré delved deeply into several of the major branches of pure mathematics. His thesis work led to the definition of an automorphic

function, which is now a classical component of the theory of complex analysis (automorphisms also play a substantial role in abstract algebra). These are complex functions whose values are invariant under certain groups of transformations of the domain space. Poincaré corresponded heavily with FELIX KLEIN regarding these new and intriguing functions, which had connections to non-Euclidean geometry.

Poincaré's *Analysis Situs* (Site analysis) of 1895 was a systematic treatment of topology (the study of continuous mappings operating on high-dimensional surfaces), a fledgling subject in the late 19th century. In this and in other papers over the next decade, Poincaré developed the subject of algebraic topology. Essentially, this subject uses algebraic tools—such as groups and rings—to describe and classify topological objects. For example, Poincaré's homotopy group consisted of equivalence classes of twisted circles embedded on a manifold (a high-dimensional space); this afforded a method of classifying manifolds. The famous Poincaré conjecture, still unproved a century later, states that any three-dimensional manifold with homotopy group equal to that of a sphere must be topologically equivalent (that is, it can be continuously deformed without tearing) into a three-dimensional sphere. Poincaré conjectured this after proving it in the intuitive two-dimensional setting, and conjectured it for dimension three. It is intriguing that the conjecture has been verified for higher dimensions, but a proof for dimension three has eluded a century of effort. Poincaré's work dominated the scene of algebraic topology for the next four decades: his methods, his questions, and his results were all enormously influential.

Poincaré initiated the study of functions of several complex variables through his 1883 work involving the Dirichlet principle. This difficult subject is still being studied today. He labored in the field of algebraic geometry, the study of manifolds given as the solution of algebraic equations in several variables. In 1910 and 1911 he developed powerful methods that allowed him to prove previously conjectured results concerning algebraic curves embedded in algebraic surfaces. Poincaré studied number theory in 1901, examining Diophantine equations. He later stated that an axiomatic approach to the foundations of arithmetic would be unable to furnish a rigorous proof of the consistency of number theory; his opinion was vindicated decades later through the work of KURT GÖDEL.

Poincaré also studied optics, electricity, telegraphy, capillarity, elasticity, thermodynamics, potential theory, quantum theory, and the theory of relativity and cosmology. In an 1889 competition in Sweden, he developed new ideas in nonlinear dynamics concerning the three-body problem of celestial mechanics. Although he won the prize, a perceived error in his manuscript led to an extensive correspondence with the mathematician Magnus Mittag-Leffler. Some date the birth of chaos theory to this communication. Besides his other work on fluid mechanics, Poincaré also wrote scientific articles aimed at a popular audience, and went a long way toward making mathematics and science of interest to the common people of France.

Poincaré also contributed to the philosophy of science, and he was a guiding influence in mathematical logic, where he stressed the importance of intuition over axiomatization. The thought process of Poincaré was the subject of a psychological study by Toulouse, who described him as a true genius reliant on an amazing mathematical intuition. Poincaré would leave problems for a time, letting his mind ruminate subconsciously over the issues; then, he would return to a project in force, making sudden leaps of the intellect. In this way he was able to achieve a remarkable diversity and profundity of mathematical material. Thus, logic alone was unfruitful, according to Poincaré, and was only useful as a tool for the correction of intuition. This mentality is quite similar to the philosophy of LUITZEN EGBERTUS JAN BROUWER.

Poincaré was highly honored during his lifetime, receiving many awards—he was elected to the Academy of Sciences in 1887 and became the president in 1906. Due to the breadth of his research, Poincaré was the only member of the academy elected to all five sections—geometry, physics, geography, navigation, and mechanics. He died somewhat prematurely on July 17, 1912, in Paris, France. Although his contributions to mathematics were phenomenal, he did not have his own school since he did not mentor students. Nevertheless, Poincaré's ideas and methods have proven to be enduringly influential to modern mathematics—especially in algebraic topology, complex analysis, and differential geometry.

Further Reading

Barrow-Green, J. *Poincaré and the Three Body Problem*. Providence, R.I.: American Mathematical Society, 1997.

Browder, F. *The Mathematical Heritage of Henri Poincaré*. Providence, R.I.: American Mathematical Society, 1983.

Miller, A. *Imagery in Scientific Thought: Creating 20th-Century Physics*. Cambridge, Mass.: MIT Press, 1986.

———. *Insights of Genius: Imagery and Creativity in Science and Art*. New York: Copernicus, 1996.

⊠ Poisson, Siméon-Denis
(1781–1840)
French
Probability, Differential Equations

Siméon-Denis Poisson was one of the great French mathematicians active during the early part of the 19th century. He was recognized as one of the most brilliant young Frenchmen of his time, and his work in several branches of mathematics has had an enduring influence; his name is attached to numerous mathematical objects.

Siméon-Denis Poisson advanced the fields of mechanics, algebra, and probability, and formulated the law of large numbers and the Poisson distribution. *(Courtesy of the Library of Congress)*

Poisson was born on June 21, 1781, in Pithiviers, France. His father was a former soldier, who was embittered toward the nobility for discrimination he had suffered while in the army. At the time of Poisson's birth, he worked as a government official. Poisson had many brothers and sisters, some of whom died young; Poisson himself suffered from poor health throughout his life, and was somewhat clumsy. Poisson's father oversaw his early education, teaching him to read and write.

When the French Revolution struck in 1789, Poisson's father's antiaristocratic outlook led to his appointment as president of the district of Pithiviers. He originally intended Poisson to be a surgeon, but the boy's physical awkwardness made this idea impracticable. When Poisson enrolled in the École Central in 1796, his exceptional aptitude for mathematics became apparent to his teachers. Shortly

thereafter he earned first place in the entrance exams for the École Polytechnique. Poisson started there in 1798, and was finished by 1800. Although his background was not as thorough as that of other young men, Poisson made exceptional progress in his studies. He wrote his first paper on finite differences at age 18, which attracted the attention of ADRIEN-MARIE LEGENDRE; PIERRE-SIMON LAPLACE and JOSEPH-LOUIS LAGRANGE, who were among his teachers, were also duly impressed with his talent. In his final year, Poisson substituted a paper of the theory of equations for his final examination and was appointed to a position at the École Polytechnique. Attaining a post in Paris at such a young age was unheard of.

Poisson gained a professorship there in 1802, and he spent all his energies on mathematical research. Most of his work pertained to the theory of partial differential equations and the mathematical aspects of various scientific problems, such as the motion of the pendulum. He was averse to physical experiment and graphical drawings due to his lack of manual dexterity. Poisson's success led to new appointments: He was made astronomer at the Bureau des Longitudes in 1808 and chair of mechanics at the Faculté des Sciences in 1809.

In 1808 Poisson published *Sur les inégalités des moyens mouvement des planets* (On the inequalities of planetary movements), which used series expansions to solve problems in celestial mechanics raised by Laplace and Lagrange. The next year he followed with two important papers that utilized Lagrange's method of variation. Poisson also published *Treatise on Mechanics* in 1811, a lucid presentation of his course notes.

Poisson also won the grand prize, set by the Paris Institute in 1811, on the topic of how electrical fields are distributed over surfaces. Poisson won the prize, and earned a place in the institute as a result. He became increasingly busy over the next years, but never slowed the pace of his investigations. Poisson would work on only one mathematical problem at a time; he would write new ideas in his wallet and put them away for later development when he could devote his full attention. In 1815 he became an examiner for the École Militaire. He married Nancy de Bardi in 1817.

Poisson's work focused on solving thorny mathematical problems in developed fields, and thus he did not create any new branch of research. However, his theorems and constructions propelled mathematics forward and assisted the general progress of knowledge. Some of Poisson's important areas of work were electricity, magnetism, elasticity, and heat. Again, his work was highly theoretical even though it concerned scientific topics. Poisson's work on the velocity of sound was motivated by Laplace's research, and GEORGE GREEN later drew inspiration from Poisson's results on attractive forces. In 1837 Poisson produced an important book on probability—*Recherches sur la probabilité des jugements en matière criminelle et en matière civile* (Research in the probability of criminal and civil verdicts), in which he introduced the Poisson distribution—a tool that has been heavily used in probability and statistics. This distribution models the likelihood of seeing repeated rare events in a small window of time. He introduced the terminology for the law of large numbers, which is concerned with arithmetic means of independent random quantities.

Poisson died on April 25, 1840, in Sceaux, France. He was mainly influential in advancing developed areas of mathematics. His name is attached to a wide variety of mathematical objects, indicating the scope of his research: the Poisson integral, the Poisson differential equation of potential theory, the Poisson bracket (and algebraic object), and the Poisson distribution. His work was well known by his own teachers and also by foreign mathematicians, but many of his countrymen failed to recognize Poisson's merit until after his death.

Further Reading

Geller, B., and Y. Bruk. "A Portrait of Poisson," *Quantum* (1991): 21–25.

⊠ **Pólya, George**
(1887–1985)
Hungarian
Probability

George Pólya is one of the best-known figures of the 20th century to mathematicians, due to his pedagogical work on problem solving. His remarkably diverse mathematical work, which achieved notable results in probability and combinatorics, among other fields, merits him a place among the top researchers of his time.

George Pólya was born on December 13, 1887, in Budapest, Hungary, to Jakab Pólya and Anna Deutsch. Pólya's parents were Hungarian Jews who had changed their last name to Pólya from Pollák for political reasons—Pólya sounded more Magyar than Pollák. Pólya's father had originally been a lawyer, but he was more interested in academics, and obtained a post at the University of Budapest while George Pólya was still young. Pólya had an older brother, Jenö, two older sisters, Ilona, and Flóra, and a younger brother, Láslò.

Although Pólya's parents were Jewish, the whole family converted to Roman Catholicism before Pólya was born. His father died when Pólya was 10 years old, and the whole family labored to assist with Pólya's education. Pólya performed well in elementary school, but he was indifferent to mathematics; he later claimed that his mathematics teachers were terrible. He enrolled in the University of Budapest in 1905, supported by his older brother, Jenö, who was now a surgeon. Pólya's mother encouraged him to study law, but he found the subject boring and he turned to languages, literature, and philosophy instead. His philosophy teachers informed Pólya that he lacked an adequate background in mathematics and physics, so he studied these subjects next. He later attended the University of Vienna from 1910 to 1911, and upon his return to Budapest was granted a doctor's degree for solving a problem in probability. He spent the years 1912 and 1913 at the University of Göttingen, pursuing further studies under such mathematicians as FELIX KLEIN, DAVID HILBERT, and HERMANN WEYL.

Pólya's experience in Germany greatly advanced his development as a mathematician, but he was forced to leave Göttingen after being involved in lawlessness. On a train he became involved in an altercation with a young man, and Pólya boxed his ears to further provoke him. The young man was a student at Göttingen, and his father was a political official with the power to bar Pólya from the campus. Later, Pólya amended his feisty temperament, becoming a pacifist and draft dodger by the start of World War I.

Pólya did some more traveling, visiting the mathematicians Émile Picard and Jacques Hadamard in Paris. He later received an appointment at the University of Zürich in 1914, where he collaborated with Adolf Hurwitz, whose work he found quite influential. Pólya also had Weyl and ERNST ZERMELO as colleagues, and his research was quite fruitful at this time. When World War I erupted, Pólya avoided military service in his native Hungary through a previous soccer injury; later, he was drafted anyway but refused to serve, becoming a Swiss citizen instead. He married Stella Vera Weber, the daughter of a physics professor, in 1918.

Pólya had met the mathematician Gábor Szego in 1913 in Budapest, and soon after the war contacted him with the idea of writing a book on mathematical problem solving. Although there are many such books now, their 1925 *Aufgaben und Lehrsätze aus der Analysis* (Problems and theorems of analysis) was the first text of its kind. The authors classified problems in analysis in a novel manner: They grouped the material according to the method of solution rather than the natural and historical development. This book was a great success, and helped Pólya to achieve some fame.

In 1920 Pólya was promoted to professor, and in 1924 obtained a fellowship to work with GODFREY HAROLD HARDY at Cambridge; they (along with Littlewood) started work on the book *Inequalities*, later published in 1934. Pólya published more than 30 papers between 1926 and 1928 on a wide range of mathematical topics, and he was promoted to full professor in 1928 as a result. Pólya's research touched on probability, geometry, complex analysis, physics, and combinatorics. He also worked on number theory, astronomy, and many applied problems, such as the mathematics of voting. Some of his research accomplishments include the study of the random walk, Fourier analysis applied to probability, the central limit theorem, and geometric tilings. The random walk is a model of motion, where an object on a line moves either forward or backward with equal chances. This can be generalized to higher-dimensional spaces, giving the random walks on the plane and in space. Pólya showed that a random walker returns to his initial location only if the dimension of the random walk is at least three—one can get lost in space but not on a line or in a plane.

Pólya's work on geometric configurations in the plane was related to the various tilings of the plane—a partition of the plane into figures (such as triangles or hexagons) that were invariant under certain rotations and shifts. M. C. Escher later used Pólya's ideas to create his beautiful artwork. Pólya greatly added to the knowledge of this discipline, called crystallography, which has many applications in chemistry and art. In combinatorics, Pólya's greatest result was his enumeration theorem, which provided a method for counting objects that share certain properties; this later led to the new field of enumerative graph theory. In complex analysis, Pólya contributed to potential theory and conformal mappings and explored the singularities of power series.

Pólya visited Princeton in 1933 on another fellowship, and while in the United States he also visited Stanford. By 1940 the political climate in Europe led Pólya to emigrate, and he worked first at Brown University before settling at Stanford. Around this time Pólya was getting his new book, *How to Solve It,* published, and it became an instant success among mathematicians. Pólya stressed the idea of learning heuristic—the collection of methods and techniques that are used to solve classes of problems. This was a landmark in the theory of mathematics education, and over the years Pólya followed it with similar books. One of his main theses was that mathematics involves thinking; it is a deeply intellectual subject, not a mechanical collection of methods and techniques. The mechanistic approach prevalent in U.S. secondary schools today differs greatly from Pólya's philosophy, and the consequences of this departure are only beginning to be experienced.

Pólya received many awards and honors throughout his life, including election to the National Academy of Sciences and membership in various mathematical societies. He retired from Stanford in 1953, but he continued to research mathematics, being especially interested in mathematics education. The last course he taught was a combinatorics lecture at Stanford in 1978, when he was more than 90 years old. He died on September 7, 1985, in Palo Alto, California.

Pólya was one of the most talented mathematicians of the 20th century, as his diverse and profound research achievements can attest. His work on mathematical learning and teaching was profound, and he is perhaps the father of the modern studies in this area. His problem-solving books are still classics, and his influence endures to the present day.

Further Reading

Albers, D., and G. Alexanderson. *Mathematical People: Profiles and Interviews.* Chicago: Contemporary Books, 1985.

Alexanderson, G. *The Random Walks of George Pólya.* Washington, D.C.: Mathematical Association of America, 2000.

———, and L. Lange. "Obituary: George Pólya," *The Bulletin of the London Mathematical Society* 19, no. 6 (1987): 559–608.

⊠ Poncelet, Jean-Victor
(1788–1867)
French
Geometry

Jean-Victor Poncelet was one of the founders of modern projective geometry, a subject that intrigued many mathematicians in the 19th century. This subject, originally of interest to Renaissance painters attempting to generate an aesthetically pleasing perspective, was picked up by modern mathematicians for its relevance to geometry.

Jean-Victor Poncelet was born on July 1, 1788, in Metz, France. As a young man, he studied under GASPARD MONGE at the École Polytechnique, where he learned analytic geometry and a wide range of mathematics. He was trained as an engineer, and took part in the disastrous 1812 march to Russia. After the destruction of the French army by the Russian winter, Poncelet was left for dead at the town of Krasnoy, and was subsequently imprisoned by the Russians. He spent the next two years studying projective geometry while in prison; Poncelet returned to France in 1814.

This period of study resulted in his *Treatise on the Projective Properties of Figures* (1822). In this paper Poncelet developed fundamental ideas, such as polar lines of conics, the principle of duality, the cross-ratio, involution, and circular points at infinity. For example, the point at infinity for an unbounded plane enables one to represent the plane as a sphere (minus its north pole); it can also be represented as a closed circle—a model that has proved useful in hyperbolic geometry. These original ideas became very influential in the evolution of projective geometry, and his work has also influenced the development of algebraic geometry more generally. He also wrote a treatise on analytic geometry (*Applications of Analysis and Geometry*), but this was not published until 1862.

Poncelet served as a military engineer in Metz from 1815 to 1825, and from 1825 to 1835 was professor of mechanics there. He applied his knowledge of mechanics to improve the efficiency of waterwheels and turbines. Poncelet proposed the first inward-flow turbine in 1826, and it was finally built in 1838. From 1838 to 1848 he was professor at the Faculty of Sciences, and from 1848 to 1850 was commander of the École Polytechnique, where he held the rank of general. He died on December 22, 1867, in Paris.

Poncelet's innovative contributions to projective geometry establish him as one of the founders of the modern theory of the subject. His work certainly stimulated later mathematicians, such as JAKOB STEINER.

Further Reading
Bos, H., et al. "Poncelet's Closure Theorem," *Expositiones Mathematicae. International Journal for Pure and Applied Mathematics* 5, no. 4 (1987): 289–364.

⊠   Ptolemy, Claudius
(ca. 85–ca. 165)
Greek
Trigonometry

The name of Ptolemy is associated with the geocentric theory of the cosmos. But to some scholars, he is also perceived as an unethical scientist; he was accused by several mathematicians of falsifying his data in order to fit the theory

Claudius Ptolemy developed an Earth-centered theory of the universe that was supported mathematically. *(Courtesy of the Library of Congress)*

that he proposed. Ptolemy developed a very complete system of mathematics, including original contributions to trigonometry that were used in his cosmic system.

Ptolemy's life is mostly constructed from secondary sources, so modern knowledge of him is scanty and unreliable. Ptolemy was born approximately in the year 85, in Alexandria, Egypt. He may have been of Greek descent, but his first name was Roman, and he may have been a Roman citizen as well.

Ptolemy made celestial observations between the years 127 and 141 in Alexandria. Apparently he obtained some of his data from Theon of Smyrna, who was likely his mentor as well. Ptolemy's early works were dedicated to Syrus, an individual of whom nothing else is known—he may have been another of Ptolemy's teachers. Even though Theon did not understand astronomy very well, Ptolemy had access to the outstanding library of Alexandria, from which he may well have gained his extensive knowledge.

Ptolemy's most important work was the *Almagest,* a 13-book work that advanced his geocentric conception of the universe. In the *Almagest* he presents a mathematical theory of the motion of Sun, Moon, and Earth that was unsurpassed until Copernicus's 1543 heliocentric theory. Thus this work, although incorrect, long remained the definitive masterpiece in astronomy, much as EUCLID OF ALEXANDRIA's *Elements* dominated geometry. This success was partly due to Ptolemy's masterful development of an extensive mathematical theory for his system.

In particular, Ptolemy developed trigonometric functions similar to the familiar sine and cosine, and proved various trigonometric identities to assist with computations. He also derived an accurate approximation to pi—namely 3 + 17/120—and the square root of three. Using these tools, Ptolemy went on to describe the motions of the celestial bodies and the lengths of seasons. In some of his observations Tycho Brahe and SIR ISAAC NEWTON later discovered gross inaccuracies; the latter accused Ptolemy of falsification of his data. However, scholars have since found it more likely that Ptolemy was innocent of deliberate fraud, but merely made errors in judgment due to the lack of statistical methodology.

The motion of the Sun was circular, with the Earth off-center; for the motion of the moons Ptolemy followed HIPPARCHUS OF RHODES. From here he describes eclipses and the motions of the five known planets. This latter model was a sophisticated mathematical masterpiece to which there was no equal predecessor.

Besides the *Almagest,* Ptolemy wrote the *Handy Tables*—a compilation of expanded trigonometric tables—and a popular scientific account of his geocentric theory. He wrote about astrology—the application of the celestial theory to people's personal lives—and methods for constructing a sundial. Ptolemy also gives an early account of the method of stereographic projection, a commonly used projection of the sphere onto the plane used to make maps of the Earth. His efforts in geography were feeble, due to the dearth of reliable cartographic data during his times. In Ptolemy's studies of optics, he advanced the concept that theory should be established by empirical evidence and experiment—a radical departure from the Greek epistemology of natural philosophy of the previous centuries.

Ptolemy died sometime around 165 in Alexandria. Although his theory of the motion of the heavens was distinctly incorrect, his mathematical system was exceptional in its detail and sophistication. His work on trigonometry represented an early effort in this subject, and his tables are the first of their kind in the ancient world.

Further Reading

Dreyer, J. *A History of Astronomy from Thales to Kepler.* New York: Dover Publications, 1953.

Gingerich, O. *The Eye of Heaven: Ptolemy, Copernicus, Kepler.* New York: American Institute of Physics, 1993.

Grasshoff, G. *The History of Ptolemy's Star Catalogue.* New York: Springer-Verlag, 1990.

Heath, T. *A History of Greek Mathematics.* Oxford: Clarendon Press, 1921.

———. *A Manual of Greek Mathematics.* Oxford: Clarendon Press, 1931.

Newton, R. *The Crime of Claudius Ptolemy.* Baltimore: Johns Hopkins University Press, 1977.

Petersen, O. *A Survey of the Almagest.* Odense, Denmark: Odense Universitetsforlag, 1974.

Smith, A. "Ptolemy's Theory of Visual Perception," *Transactions of the American Philosophical Society* 86, pt. 2 (1996).

Toomer, G. *Ptolemy's Almagest.* London: Duckworth, 1984.

⊠ **Pythagoras of Samos**
(ca. 569 B.C.E.–ca. 475 B.C.E.)
Greek
Number Theory, Geometry

Pythagoras of Samos was one of the earliest Greek mathematicians, and is certainly one of the most famous of all time due to the well-known Pythagorean theorem. However, very little is known of his life, and what details exist are reconstructed from several secondary sources; he left no writings of his own behind him.

Pythagoras of Samos was born around 569 B.C.E. on the island of Samos, Greece. His father, Mnesarchus, was a Phoenician merchant who earned citizenship at Samos by delivering a shipment of grain during a time of famine. His mother was Pythais, a native of Samos.

Pythagoras was a philosopher who believed numbers had personalities. His cult formulated and proved the Pythagorean theorem. *(Courtesy of the National Library of Medicine)*

Pythagoras received the best education, being trained in poetry and music, and later in philosophy. He had two brothers, and the family traveled extensively during Pythagoras's youth, visiting Italy and Tyre.

Pythagoras was later taught by THALES OF MILETUS and his pupil Anaximander; from Thales he gained an appreciation for geometry, and he traveled to Egypt in 535 B.C.E. to further his studies. Before he left, the tyrant Polycrates took over Samos, and Pythagoras's friendship with him facilitated his introduction into Egyptian society, since Polycrates had an alliance with Egypt. Pythagoras visited with the priests there, but was admitted only to the temple of Diospolis, where he was inducted into the religious mysteries. It seems that many of Pythagoras's later beliefs, as well as the rites of the cult he would later found, were drawn from his time among the Egyptian clerics—for instance, his vegetarianism and stress on ethical purity can be traced to his time in Egypt. In terms of mathematics, it is not likely that he learned much more there than Thales would have taught him.

In 525 B.C.E., the Babylonian emperor Cambyses invaded Egypt and sacked Heliopolis and Memphis; Pythagoras was taken as a prisoner of war to Babylon. There he communed further with the magi and Chaldeans, learning further religious mysteries. More important, he studied all the Babylonian mathematical sciences, becoming an expert in arithmetic and the mathematical theory of music (Pythagoras was skilled at the lute). Somehow he obtained his freedom and returned to Samos in 520 B.C.E.

In his hometown, Pythagoras founded a school called the semicircle, which taught ethics, philosophy, and mathematics. Pythagoras himself dwelled in a cave outside the city, where he researched the uses of mathematics.

In 518 B.C.E. Pythagoras left Samos for Italy, arriving at the town of Croton. His ostensible reason for departure was the rudeness with which his novel teaching methods were treated; however, it is more likely that he left in a desire to avoid public duty, being under continual pressure to execute diplomatic missions. In Croton, a town in southeastern Italy, Pythagoras founded the cult that later came to be known as the Pythagoreans. The inner circle, known as the *mathematikoi*, held to principles of communal property, vegetarianism, secrecy, and a strict ethical code. They also investigated various aspects of mathematics in a novel manner: Rather than merely formulating practical rules, they explored mathematical objects—such as triangles, circles, and numbers—as concrete, real things. They abstracted the known mathematical relationships into pure formulas and theorems, and then claimed that these things were as real as the material world. But their beliefs also took on a religious aspect, since they held that reality was, at its foundation, constructed out of numbers.

The outer circle of the cult was known as the *akousmatics*. They were allowed to own property and eat meat. This group produced a great quantity of mathematical knowledge, the most famous of which is the Pythagorean theorem: The square on the hypotenuse of a right triangle is equal to the sum of the squares on the legs. For the Greeks, this would have been conceived in terms of actual geometric squares rather than the second power of an abstract number. It is unclear whether the proof of this result (it was known to the Egyptians and to the Babylonians centuries earlier) was due to Pythagoras or his followers. Other discoveries of the cult include the irrational numbers, the fact that the sum of the angles of a triangle are 180 degrees, and the five regular solids.

Pythagoras's belief in the primacy of number stemmed from his observations of mathematical structure in music and astronomy. It is interesting that today the modern culture is exceedingly quantitative, even perceiving mathematical relationships in human relationships (economics) and the human brain (cognitive science). So in some sense, the cult of Pythagoras endures to the present era. However, Pythagoras's views were a bit different—he held that each number had its own personality, complete with gender and character traits.

Besides his mathematical research, Pythagoras was a famous philosopher who emphasized the importance of the ethical life. He taught a cosmology with the Earth at the center of the universe, and believed the soul to be a form of number that moved through various reincarnation toward complete purity.

Despite Pythagoras's aversion to politics, the cult was involved in Croton's attack and defeat of the neighboring city Sybaris in 510 B.C.E. In 508 B.C.E., an obnoxious nobleman by the name of Cylon, incensed at his exclusion from the *mathematikoi*, attacked the Pythagoreans. As a result, Pythagoras fled the city, and some accounts say that he died in exile in Metapontium. Other sources say that he survived the persecution to return to Croton, and that he died much later, around 475 B.C.E.

The cult itself flourished around 500 B.C.E., spreading to other cities. It later became politically oriented, and split into various factions; in 460 B.C.E. the members were again violently persecuted. Nevertheless, Pythagoras's ideas permeated much of the Greek mathematical community, and affected later thinkers such as EUCLID OF ALEXANDRIA. Pythagoras is most remarkable for his mathematical abstraction; he was certainly one of the first thinkers in the world to conceive of mathematics in this abstract form.

Further Reading

Brumbaugh, R. *The Philosophers of Greece*. New York: Crowell, 1964.

Heath, T. *A History of Greek Mathematics*. Oxford: Clarendon Press, 1921.

Laertius, D. *Lives, Teachings, and Sayings of Famous Philosophers*. Cambridge, Mass.: Harvard University Press, 1959.

O'Meara, D. *Pythagoras Revived: Mathematics and Philosophy in Late Antiquity*. New York: Oxford University Press, 1989.

Russell, B. *History of Western Philosophy and Its Connection with Political and Social Circumstances from the Ancient Times to the Present Day*. London: Allen and Unwin, 1961.

Vogel, C. de. *Pythagoras and Early Pythagoreanism*. Assen, the Netherlands: Van Gorcum, 1966.

van der Waerden, B. *Science Awakening*. Leyden, the Netherlands: Noordhof International, 1975.

R

Ramanujan, Srinivasa Aiyangar
(1887–1920)
Indian
Number Theory

The Indian mathematician Ramanujan led a short life full of mathematics. From a highly disadvantageous background, he was able to make substantial contributions to number theory. His feverish preoccupation with mathematics, bordering on obsession, is remarkable for its intensity and devotion. He is remembered as one of India's greatest mathematical geniuses.

Srinivasa Aiyangar Ramanujan was born in Erode, Madras Province, India, on December 22, 1887. Although descended from the Brahman caste, his family was quite poor, as his father was a bookkeeper for a local cloth merchant. He excelled in his early education, and in 1900 he began his own investigations of mathematics. In 1903 he borrowed G.S. Carr's *Synopsis of Pure Mathematics*, which contained thousands of theorems. Ramanujan quickly devoured this book, and mathematics became his sole interest.

It is said of Ramanujan that he was quiet and meditative, with a fondness for numerical calculations and an unusual memory. In 1904 he won a fellowship at Government College, but failed to graduate due to his neglect of English. For a time he was without a definite occupation; he spent his time jotting down results and computations in a little notebook. In 1909, at age 22, he married, at the arrangement of his mother, a 9-year old girl. Shortly thereafter he secured a job as a clerk, and in 1912 worked at the Madras Port Trust. At this time, his first publication appeared, titled *Some Properties of Bernoulli Numbers* (1911), a communication on series, infinite products, and a geometric approximate construction of pi. In the Madras area, he was increasingly recognized for his brilliant work.

Ramanujan's famous correspondence with the British mathematician GODFREY HAROLD HARDY, a specialist in analytic number theory, initiated the next phase of his life. In a letter to Hardy, he outlined some of his principal results, and Hardy responded with enthusiasm. Through this credential, Ramanujan was able to obtain a two-year fellowship at the University of Madras. In 1914 Ramanujan came to Trinity College in England at Hardy's invitation, and in the next five years would produce 21 research papers on a variety of topics: approximations to pi, highly composite (that is, not prime) numbers, and the average number of prime divisors. Most important in terms of intellectual legacy, Ramanujan studied partition of numbers into summands. He proved many properties of this partition function using elliptic function theory, and stimulated later work in this area. In addition, he labored in many other areas, such as combinatorics and function theory.

The remarkable thing about Ramanujan's achievement is his lack of formal training. At the time of Hardy's correspondence, there were large gaps in Ramanujan's knowledge of mathematics, and his concept of proof was nebulous. His arguments were built from intuition and induction, and lacked the characteristic rigor of European thought. Though his mastery of continued fractions and elliptic integrals was extensive, Ramanujan's ignorance of other aspects of mathematics was startling; some of his theorems about prime numbers were completely wrong. Nevertheless, his contributions to elliptic functions, continued fractions, and infinite series were profound.

He had struggled with ill health for many years, and in 1917 he fell ill again, perhaps with tuberculosis. In 1918 he was elected as a fellow to the Royal Society of London, the first Indian to receive that honor, and the accolades seemed to improve his health. The following year he returned to India with the prospect of a professorship at the University of Madras. Unfortunately, his health worsened and he refused medical aid. Ramanujan continued his mathematical research until his last days, and he died on April 26, 1920, in Chetput, India.

Mathematicians recognized Ramanujan as one of the greatest geniuses of all time. Given the lack of appropriate resources, the depth of his mathematical talent was truly exceptional. His most famous work addressed the topic of the partition of numbers, but his results on hypergeometric series have also fueled further research.

Further Reading

Hardy, G. *Ramanujan: Twelve Lectures on Subjects Suggested by His Life and Work*. New York: Chelsea Publishing Company, 1959.

Kanigel, R. *The Man Who Knew Infinity: A Life of the Genius Ramanujan*. New York: Scribner's, 1991.

Ranganathan, S. *Ramanujan: The Man and the Mathematician*. London: Asia Publishing House, 1967.

Regiomontanus, Johann Müller
(1436–1476)
German
Trigonometry

The 15th century was a slow time for mathematics in Europe, during which the knowledge of trigonometry gradually broadened. Some of this development was motivated by navigation and astronomy, two sciences that heavily utilized trigonometry. A century before GEORG RHETICUS's trigonometric tables were introduced, Johann Regiomontanus introduced trigonometric methods that could be used to form accurate astronomical predictions.

Johann Müller Regiomontanus was born on June 6, 1436, in Königsberg, Germany. His last name is the Latin translation of his hometown, Königsberg, which means "king's mountain." Regiomontanus studied under Georg Peurbach, a professor of astronomy, at the University of Vienna. It is unknown when he finished his studies, but in 1461 he was appointed to Peurbach's position after the death of Peurbach. In 1468 Regiomontanus became the royal astronomer to King Mathias Corvinus of Hungary.

Regiomontanus was an excellent scholar who translated and published many documents. He advanced the knowledge of trigonometry in Europe by giving a systematic method for solving triangles by determining all the sides and angles given some of them. This theory was developed in his *De triangulis omnimodis* (On triangles of all kinds) of 1464. He applied these mathematics to assist with the prediction of astronomical orbits, such as Halley's comet. With financial support from Corvinus, Regiomontanus built an observatory in Nuremberg in 1471 with a workshop to produce instruments. The following year he made highly accurate observations of a certain comet, which 210 years later was verified to be the same as Halley's comet.

Regiomontanus was also interested in the Moon, observing several eclipses. He invented the idea of using lunar distances as a navigational aid, although the full details of the method were not worked out until later, when the position of the Moon could be measured with sufficient accuracy. He also worked on calendar reform, and in 1475 was summoned to Rome by the pope to give advice on this subject and to accept an appointment as bishop of Regensburg. However, Regiomontanus died on July 9, 1476, in Rome before he could take office; some accounts say he was poisoned by political enemies, while others claim that he died from the plague.

Regiomontanus died before his time, but was still a significant figure in the history of mathematics. His work on trigonometry was certainly an advance, especially in light of the dark intellectual times.

Further Reading

Kren, C. "Planetary Latitudes, the Theorica, and Regiomontanus," *Isis* 68 (1977): 194–205.

Zinner, E. *Regiomontanus: His Life and Work.* Amsterdam: North-Holland, 1990.

⊠ Rheticus, Georg (Georg Joachim von Lauchen Rheticus)
(1514–1574)
German
Trigonometry

Georg Rheticus is known primarily for his trigonometric tables, being one of the first Europeans to produce such an item. He was an intense, busy man who advanced the cause of mathematics in Europe at a time when there was little intellectual activity.

Rheticus was born on February 16, 1514, in Feldkirch, Austria. His father was named Georg Iserin and his mother was Thomasina de Porris. Rheticus's father was the town doctor, as well as a government official. When Rheticus was only 14 years old, his father was tried and executed for the crime of sorcery in 1528. As a consequence of the sentence, Rheticus was not allowed to use his father's name; instead, he took his mother's maiden name, (which means "of the leeks") and translated it from Italian into German, resulting in "von Lauchen." He later added the name "Rheticus," which referred to the Roman province of Rhaetia in which he had been born.

Rheticus's father was succeeded by Achilles Masser as the town doctor, and this man supported Rheticus's further studies. Rheticus went on to study at Zurich from 1528 to 1531 after finishing his classical Latin education at Feldkirch. He entered the University of Wittenberg in 1533 and graduated with a master's degree in 1536. At this point, Rheticus obtained an appointment to lecture at the University of Wittenberg with the assistance of Philipp Melanchthon, a friend of Martin Luther who reorganized Germany's educational system. Rheticus first taught mathematics and astronomy at Wittenberg. In 1538 he traveled for a year, visiting various other scholars, and in 1539 journeyed to Frauenberg, where he was to spend the next two years studying with Copernicus. This was a valuable friendship for Rheticus, who eagerly devoured the astronomical and mathematical knowledge of the venerable Copernicus. In 1539 Rheticus also visited Danzig and procured funding for the publication of Copernicus's book *Narratio Prima* (The first account of the book on the revolution). This was essentially a work written by Rheticus, containing a mathematical presentation of Copernicus's research.

Rheticus also obtained permission in 1541 to publish another of Copernicus's works (*De Revolutionibis*) through an interesting gift to the duke of Prussia—a map of Prussia and a device that could determine the time of day (a prototype of the clock). The duke also requested that Rheticus return to his chair at Wittenberg, and Rheticus was there elected dean of the faculty of the arts. In the same year Rheticus published the trigonometric tables of *De Revolutionibis*, supplemented with his own calculations. This was the first such table of its kind in Europe, and the utility of this knowledge has helped to secure Rheticus's position in history.

Melanchthon again assisted Rheticus to attain a position at the University of Leipzig in 1542 as a professor of higher mathematics. After three years, Rheticus began another period of travel, visiting GIROLAMO CARDANO in Italy as well as Feldkirch. His physical health deteriorated in 1547 at Lindau, and he also suffered from mental problems. Once he recovered, he went on to Zurich to study medicine. When he finally returned to Leipzig in 1548, he was appointed a member of the theological faculty.

Rheticus was very productive during these years, not merely in the area of mathematics, but more widely; for instance, he produced a calendar for 1550 and 1551. He was soon involved in a scandal at Leipzig: he was accused of having a homosexual affair with one of his students, and Rheticus chose to flee rather than defend himself. As a result, his friends (such as Melanchthon) abandoned him, and he was sentenced to 101 years of exile. Meanwhile, Rheticus arrived at Prague, where he continued his medical studies. He used his knowledge of medicine mainly to treat patients rather than conduct original research.

Rheticus was offered a post as mathematics professor at the University of Vienna, but he instead moved to Krakow in 1554 where he set up a practice as a doctor. He remained in Krakow for the next 20 years. While there, he continued his mathematical research, using his trigonometric tables to conduct further studies on astronomy and alchemy. He obtained funding for his projects from Emperor Maximilian II, and employed six research assistants. Rheticus's most important work on trigonometry, the *Opus Palatinum de triangulis* (The Palatine work on triangles), describes the use of the six main trigonometric functions: sine, cosine, tangent, cotangent, secant, and cosecant. Further trigonometric tables for these functions were published in 1596, years after his death.

Rheticus died on December 4, 1574, in Kassa, Hungary. Besides the mathematical work on trigonometric tables, he also completed a book on mapmaking as well as devising various navigational instruments, such as sea compasses. Rheticus was an intellectual of broad interests who traveled widely to further his diverse scholarly inclinations; his investigations were characterized by an uncommon vitality and energy. From the perspective of mathematics, he is an important figure for his formation of trigonometric tables, which were extremely useful for the pursuit of astronomy and the other sciences.

Further Reading

Archibald, R. "The Canon Doctrinae Triangulorum (1551) of Rheticus (1514–1576)," *Mathematical Tables and Other Aids to Computation* 7 (1953): 131.

———. "Rheticus, with Special Reference to His Opus Palatinum," *Mathematical Tables and Other Aids to Computation* 3 (1949): 552–561.

Riemann, Bernhard (Georg Friedrich Bernhard Rieman)
(1826–1866)
German
Complex Analysis, Differential Equations, Geometry, Number Theory

Few mathematicians can compare to Bernhard Riemann in terms of creativity and depth of insight. Not only did Riemann found the new discipline of Riemannian geometry that would become so important to the theory of general relativity a century later, but he significantly

Bernhard Riemann, a founder of differential geometry, also contributed to complex analysis, topology, and the theory of integration. *(Courtesy of the Library of Congress)*

advanced several other fields of mathematics, including complex analysis, the theory of elliptic functions, differential equations, the theory of integration, and topology. He is perhaps most famous for discovering the Riemann zeta function, which is important to analytic number theory. Like those of many a genius, Riemann's ideas were so advanced that few were able to accept them immediately; after his early death, the impact of his research began to be appreciated.

Georg Friedrich Bernhard Riemann, commonly known as Bernhard Riemann, was born on September 17, 1826, in Breselenz, Germany. His mother was Charlotte Ebell, and his father was Friedrich Bernhard Riemann. Riemann maintained a close relationship with his father, a Lutheran minister, throughout his life. Riemann was the second of six children. His father educated him personally until he was 10 years old,

and in 1842 the boy joined the Johanneum Gymnasium in Lüneburg. Riemann was a good pupil, but did not yet show extraordinary talent in mathematics. Although his main studies were classics and theology, he became interested in mathematics after quickly devouring a number theory book by ADRIEN-MARIE LEGENDRE.

In 1846 Riemann enrolled at the University of Göttingen, where he pursued further study in mathematics. Although CARL FRIEDRICH GAUSS was teaching there at the time, he did not recognize Riemann's talent, as did some of his other teachers. The next year Riemann transferred to the University of Berlin, where he was able to study under CARL JACOBI and GUSTAV PETER LEJEUNE DIRICHLET; the latter was especially influential on Riemann, who adopted Dirichlet's intuitive, noncomputational approach to mathematical ideas. Much of Riemann's work lacked the precise rigor common at that time—he focused his energies on developing the correct concepts and frameworks to understand mathematics. During this time, Riemann formulated the basic principles of his theory of complex variables.

Riemann returned to Göttingen in 1849 for doctoral work, and he submitted his thesis, conducted under Gauss's supervision, in 1851. This work introduces the geometrical objects that came to be known as Riemann surfaces. Riemann was influenced by ideas from theoretical physics and topology, and he brought these techniques to bear in his analysis of these surfaces, building upon AUGUSTIN-LOUIS CAUCHY's more basic theory of complex variables. Some of his results were proved using a variational technique known as Dirichlet's principle (Riemann attributed the method to Dirichlet, although it had been developed by Gauss and others previously). This thesis was striking for its originality—even the sovereign Gauss was impressed.

For his postdoctoral work, Riemann began investigating the representation of functions in terms of a basis of trigonometric functions

(Fourier analysis); in the course of his research, he developed a rigorous theory of integration, constructing what later came to be known as the Riemann integral of a function. He was working at Göttingen, and Gauss required him to give a lecture on geometry for completion of his fellowship; Riemann's lecture on geometry later became very famous, as he laid down the basic principles and key ideas behind the theory of differential geometry. This 1854 lecture developed general concepts of space, dimension, straight lines, metrics, angles, and tangent places for curved surfaces. The result of this remarkably original exposition was the establishment of differential geometry as a major field of mathematical inquiry (there were earlier works on differential geometry, but Riemann planted the major ideas that would continue to guide the subject throughout the next century), which later turned out to have a remarkable application to the general theory of relativity—Albert Einstein, in the early 20th century, described the force of gravity as essentially a curvature of space, and Riemann's geometrical theory was the perfect mathematical basis for this important new branch of physics.

This lecture probed the fundamental concept of space to a remarkable depth, and few scientists and mathematicians were able to appreciate the extraordinary genius of Riemann's penetrating thought; perhaps Gauss alone was able to truly grasp the significance of the new paradigm. Riemann next turned to the theory of partial differential equations, on which topic he gave a sparsely attended course. He obtained a professorship at Göttingen in 1857, the same year he published *The Theory of Abelian Functions*. This work further investigates the topological properties of Riemann surfaces, as well as so-called inversion problems. Although other mathematicians—including KARL WEIERSTRASS—were working in this area, Riemann's work was so far-reaching that he became a leading thinker in this branch of mathematics.

Riemann again used the Dirichlet principle for his results, and Weierstrass declared it to be invalid for Riemann's applications. The search for an alternative proof during the next several decades led to several other fruitful algebraic developments; DAVID HILBERT eventually gave the correct formulation and proof of Riemann's results around the turn of the century. As a result of Weierstrass's correct critique, many mathematicians abandoned the theories developed by Riemann, who maintained that they were true.

In 1858 Riemann was visited by ENRICO BETTI, who imported Riemann's topological ideas into his own work. The next year Dirichlet died, and Riemann replaced him as the chair of mathematics at Göttingen; Riemann was also elected to the Berlin Academy of Sciences through the strong recommendations of ERNST EDUARD KUMMER and Weierstrass. Riemann's next area of inquiry was number theory: he explored the zeta function, already defined by LEONHARD EULER, by first extending it to the complex plane. This zeta function gives the sum of various infinite series and was already known to be related to the set of prime numbers. Riemann's work greatly extended the knowledge of this function, as well as its applications; the famous Riemann hypothesis, which remains unsolved today, states that all the nontrivial roots of the zeta function lie on the line in the complex plane defined by the complex numbers whose real part is equal to one-half. This bizarre conjecture has been extensively verified numerically, but a complete proof has escaped the concerted efforts of hundreds of mathematicians. The zeta function has various applications to analytic number theory, such as estimating the number of primes less than a given integer.

Riemann suffered from poor health throughout his life. His weak constitution would later impede his research and take his life prematurely. Riemann married Elise Koch in 1862, but soon afterward he contracted a cold and then developed tuberculosis. He spent much of his time over the next few years abroad in Italy, in the hope that the milder climate would soothe his illness. Riemann returned to Göttingen in 1865, and his health declined rapidly thereafter; he traveled to Italy in 1866 again for reasons of health, but did not recover. He died on July 20, 1866, in Selasca, Italy.

Riemann was easily one of the most influential and creative mathematicians of the 19th century, and indeed of all history. He significantly affected geometry and complex analysis above all, essentially providing the framework through which these subjects are studied today. And the deep questions and issues that he addressed in the field of geometry are extremely relevant to modern conceptions of the physical universe. His work in number theory has spurred an unparalleled research effort—investigation of Riemann's zeta function must be one of the busiest arenas of mathematical activity. Gauss would concur that Riemann was certainly one of the greatest mathematicians this world has seen.

Further Reading

Klein, F. *Development of Mathematics in the 19th Century*. Brookline, Mass.: Math Sci Press, 1979.

Monastyrsky, M. *Rieman, Topology and Physics*. Boston: Birkhäuser, 1987.

Weil, A. "Riemann, Betti and the Birth of Topology," *Archive for History of Exact Sciences* 20, no. 2 (1979): 91–96.

⊠   Riesz, Frigyes
(1880–1956)
Hungarian
Analysis

Frigyes Riesz was one of the principal founders of functional analysis in the early 20th century, as he essentially invented operator theory and introduced many important concepts. His work had important applications to physics—to quantum mechanics in particular—and many of the ramifications of his theories were worked out over the ensuing decades.

Frigyes Riesz was born on January 22, 1880, in Györ, Hungary. At the time of his birth, Györ was part of the Austro-Hungarian Empire. Riesz's father was Ignácz Riesz, a doctor; he had a younger brother, Marcel, who also became a famous mathematician. After his preliminary education, Riesz traveled to Budapest to study, and later journeyed to the Universities of Göttingen and Zurich for further knowledge. He returned to Hungary to obtain his doctorate from the University of Budapest in 1902; his thesis topic was geometry.

After completing his doctorate, Riesz taught at local schools before obtaining a university position. In 1911 he finally earned a chair at the University of Kolozsvár in Hungary. His main work was in functional analysis, and he built upon the work of RENÉ-MAURICE FRÉCHET, building on his idea of distance in a function space. Between 1907 and 1909 Riesz developed some representation theorems that expressed functionals in terms of integrals of other functions. Later he introduced the notion of weak convergence for a sequence of functions; this presented a convenient topology for the function spaces commonly used in physics and engineering. Riesz also developed Lebesgue integration theory, which facilitated the construction of orthonormal bases in Hilbert spaces.

In 1910 Riesz's work marked the birth of operator theory; operators are the analogs of matrices in infinite-dimensional function spaces. The study and use of operators has continued into the present time, and they are certainly one of the most effective mathematical tools of statistics and engineering. In 1918 Riesz developed rigorous foundations for Banach spaces, which were axiomatically defined by STEFAN BANACH two years later.

In 1920 the territory of Hungary was severely reduced as part of the aftermath of World War I; as a result, Kolozsvár became located in Romania. The university that had been in

Kolozsvár was relocated to Szeged, and Riesz moved with it. In 1922 Riesz founded the János Bolyai Mathematical Institute and soon became editor of the *Acta Scientiarum Mathematicarum*, which became a renowned mathematical journal. Riesz later became the chair of mathematics at the University of Budapest in 1945.

Riesz's research was important to the field of functional analysis, but he also did work in ergodic theory (he proved the mean ergodic theorem in 1938) and topology, the study of continuously deformed surfaces. One of his most important results, the Riesz-Fischer theorem of 1907, is of great importance in Fourier analysis, which is used in engineering and physics. Besides being an excellent researcher, Riesz was appreciated as a clear expositor of mathematics; his style was lucid, with frequent reference to relevant applications. He received many honors and prizes throughout his life, including election to the Hungarian Academy of Sciences.

Riesz died on February 28, 1956, in Budapest. He principally contributed to functional analysis, where his ideas were foundational; the techniques and concepts that he developed continue to have an impact and influence on mathematics, physics, engineering, and statistics.

Further Reading

Bernkopf, M. "The Development of Functional Spaces," *Archive for History of Exact Sciences* 3 (1966–67): 1–96.

Rogosinski, W. "Frederic Riesz," *Journal of the London Mathematical Society* 31, no. 4 (1956): 508–512.

Russell, Bertrand (Bertrand Arthur William Russell)
(1872–1970)
British
Logic

Bertrand Russell was one of the more colorful mathematical personalities of the 20th century, and he is ranked among the most important logicians of the modern era. He believed in the potential for all of mathematics to be reduced to logic, and exerted much effort to validate this paradigm. Russell was also an active philosopher and social revolutionary, applying his logical ideas to science, ethics, and religion.

Bertrand Russell was born on May 18, 1872, in Ravenscroft, Wales. He was the grandson of Lord John Russell. His mother and father died in 1874 and 1876, respectively, so his grandparents raised him. This grandfather had twice served as prime minister under Queen Victoria, but he died in 1878 and Russell's grandmother continued the boy's education. He received private education at first, and later was instructed at Trinity College, Cambridge, where he attained first marks in mathematics.

Russell became an academic, eventually being elected to the Royal Society in 1908. He spent his early years pursuing his program of logicism, which believed that all of mathematics could be reduced to logical statements. In this sense, Russell was a follower of FRIEDRICH LUDWIG GOTTLOB FREGE, who held a similar philosophy. Russell's 1910 work on the *Principia Mathematica* (The principles of mathematics), written together with Alfred Whitehead, established that mathematical proofs could be reduced to logical proofs. The first volumes of this work dealt with set theory, arithmetic, and measure theory; a fourth volume, on geometry, was not completed. Part of this approach, inspired by the ideas of Frege, was to express numbers and other mathematical objects as sets of classes that share a common property. This ambitious project lost steam in later years, probably due to philosophical trends leading away from logicism.

Prior to the *Principia*, Russell acquired fame through construction of the so-called

Russell paradox. He formed the set (set A) of all sets having the property that they are not members of themselves. Then one asks the question: Is A (viewed as an element) a member of the set A? This cannot be resolved as either true or false, since either answer leads to a contradiction. This demonstrated the fundamental problem with taking collections of sets and assuming that such a collection is itself a set; more generally, it pointed out the difficulties with self-reference in mathematics and philosophy. This concept of self-reference would later be utilized by KURT GÖDEL to produce his incompleteness theorems.

Russell's solution to the paradox was to develop his theory of types, mainly fleshed out in his 1908 *Mathematical Logic as Based on the Theory of Types*. Therein Russell described a hierarchy of classes, for which the idea of set is specially defined at each level. Other resolutions of the paradox have resulted from weakening the power of the basic axiom of comprehension formulated by GEORG CANTOR, which states that one can always gather objects sharing a common property into a set. The immediate consequence of the paradox was to cast doubt on the logic program espoused by DAVID HILBERT, which sought to rigorously establish the foundations of mathematical logic and set theory. It seemed that even the intuitive concept of a set was cast in shadow.

Besides these important contributions to logic, Russell was also famous for his "analytic philosophy," which attempted to cast philosophical questions in the rigorous framework of mathematical logic. Of course, this computational approach to philosophy has a long history, going back to RENÉ DESCARTES and other mathematicians.

Russell's personal and public life both interfered with his career advancement. He was convicted of antiwar activity in 1916, and this resulted in his dismissal from Trinity College.

Two years later he was again convicted and sentenced to a short prison term. During his incarceration, he wrote his famous *Introduction to Mathematical Philosophy* (1919). He stumbled through four marriages that were rife with extramarital affairs, and was even fired from a teaching position at City College of New York in 1940 after a judge ruled that he was morally unfit. He ran (but failed to be elected) for Parliament three times; Russell became Earl Russell in 1931 after the death of his brother. He opened an experimental school with his second wife in the late 1920s. His antiwar sentiments gained better reception in the 1950s and 1960s, when he was recognized as a leader in the anti–nuclear proliferation movement. The Russell-Einstein manifesto of 1955 called for the abandonment of nuclear weapons. In 1957 Russell organized the Pugwash Conference, a convention of scientists against nuclear weapons, and he became president of the Campaign for Nuclear Disarmament in 1958. In his 80s Russell was arrested again in 1961 for nuclear protests.

After a full life of mathematics, philosophy, and public protest, Russell died on February 2, 1970, in Penrhyndeudraeth, Wales. Russell was recognized for his extensive contributions to literature and science, winning the Nobel Prize for literature in 1950. He is best known for his paradox and its subsequent resolution through the theory of types, but also through his later investigations of logicism and the issue of incompleteness studied by Gödel. Russell's thought has been enormously influential on logic, mathematics, and philosophy, as well as ethics, religion, and social responsibility.

Further Reading

Ayer, A. *Bertrand Russell*. Chicago: University of Chicago Press, 1988.

Clark, R. *The Life of Bertrand Russell*. New York: Knopf, 1976.

————. *Bertrand Russell and His World*. New York: Thames and Hudson, 1981.

Hardy, G. *Bertrand Russell and Trinity*. Cambridge: University Press, 1942.

Klemke, E. *Essays on Bertrand Russell*. Urbana: University of Illinois Press, 1970.

Kuntz, P. *Bertrand Russell*. Boston: Twayne Publishers, 1986.

Monk, R. *Bertrand Russell: The Spirit of Solitude*. New York: Free Press, 1996.

Watling, J. *Bertrand Russell*. Edinburgh: Oliver and Boyd, 1970.

Seki Takakazu Kowa
(1642–1708)
Japanese
Algebra, Calculus

Seki Takakazu was a singular figure in the history of mathematics: At a time when mathematical activity in Japan was quite limited, Seki made amazing discoveries, rivaling those of Western mathematicians such as GOTTFRIED WILHELM VON LEIBNIZ. His achievements are remarkable in light of the fact that Seki could not benefit from a mathematical culture and colleagues with whom to exchange ideas.

Seki was born in March 1642 in Fujioka, Japan. His family was of the samurai caste, but a family of the nobility, known as Seki Gorozayemon, adopted Seki. Afterward, he was identified by this adopted surname. Seki was a child prodigy in mathematics. A household servant introduced him to the subject when he was nine years old, and Seki taught himself from that time. As he became an adult, Seki built up a library of Chinese and Japanese mathematical books, and was gradually recognized as an expert—he became known as the "Arithmetical Sage." He attracted a body of pupils and sparked an upsurge in mathematical activity in Japan.

Seki served as an examiner of accounts for the lord of Koshu, and when his master was promoted Seki became a shogunate samurai in 1704. He was later advanced to master of ceremonies in the shogun's household.

Seki's mathematical work, building upon former Chinese mathematicians, represented a considerable advance in knowledge. He published *Hatsubi Sampo* in 1674, a work that treated and solved algebraic equations. In his exposition, Seki shows himself to be a careful and thorough teacher, accounting for his popularity with pupils. In 1683 Seki studied matrix determinants, which were not examined in the West until a decade later, when Leibniz used them to solve certain problems. The so-called Bernoulli numbers, named for JAKOB BERNOULLI, were investigated antecedently by Seki. He utilized the concept of negative numbers in solving equations, but had no knowledge of complex numbers. Seki also researched magic squares, following the work of YANG HUI, and used the Newton-Raphson method for solving algebraic equations, discovered independently of SIR ISAAC NEWTON. His work on Diophantine equations was also considerable.

Little else is known of Seki, except that he died on October 24, 1708, in Tokyo, Japan. It is difficult to determine the extent to which his school was familiar with calculus, but it seems that

Seki made some progress in this area. This is amazing, since Japan did not have the historical tradition that Europeans could claim—namely, the geometrical works of the earlier Greek and Arab civilizations. Seki should be viewed in the lineage of Chinese mathematicians, even though he was Japanese, since he thoroughly studied the prior mathematics of the mainland.

Further Reading

Mikami, Y. *The Development of Mathematics in China and Japan.* New York: Chelsea Publishing Company, 1974.

Smith, D., and Y. Mikami. *A History of Japanese Mathematics.* Chicago: Open Court Publishing Company, 1914.

Yosida, K. "A Brief Biography of Takakazu Seki (1642?–1708)," *The Mathematical Intelligencer 3* (1981): 121–122.

⊠   **Steiner, Jakob**
(1796–1863)
Swiss
Geometry

Jakob Steiner made several important contributions to projective geometry, the study of spaces made up of lines rather than points. This subject was historically of interest to artists, who in the medieval age required knowledge of projection in order to correctly render perspective; in the 19th century the subject was pursued largely for its own beauty.

Jakob Steiner was born on March 18, 1796, in Utzenstorf, Switzerland. His farmer parents discouraged him from pursuing education, and Steiner did not learn to read and write until age 14. When he was 18, he went to school for the first time, and attended the Universities of Heidelberg and Berlin. In light of this late start, his considerable achievement in abstract mathematics is all the more remarkable. His parents did not endorse his pursuit of mathematics, and

Steiner was forced to support himself through tutoring.

By 1824 Steiner had already studied a series of geometric transformations that he formulated into the theory of inversive geometry, a type of non-Euclidean geometry. Steiner published many of his writings in *Crelle's Journal,* the first periodical entirely devoted to mathematics. His work focused on projective geometry, and he discovered the Steiner surface—a surface that receives considerable attention from geometers—as well as the Steiner theorem, which describes the projective properties of conic sections. The Poncelet-Steiner theorem is another famous result, which states that only a circle and a straight edge are necessary to complete the various Euclidean constructions. His colleagues' recognition of his substantial efforts in projective geometry resulted in an appointment to a chair at the University of Berlin in 1834.

Steiner was awarded an honorary doctorate for his geometric discoveries from the University of Königsberg in 1832, and two years later he took up a chair of mathematics at the University of Berlin, where he remained until his death. His various contributions were published after his death, in 1881 in the *Collected Works.*

In terms of his mathematical philosophy, Steiner avoided computation and algebra, believing that true insight came through geometrical understanding rather than mindless calculations. He suffered from rheumatism in his later years, resulting in a characteristic pained facial expression. Steiner died on April 1, 1863, in Bern, Switzerland.

Steiner's work on projective geometry helped to establish that discipline as a major branch of mathematical inquiry. He was influenced by JEAN-VICTOR PONCELET, whose work he further developed. The Steiner surface continues to be an object of study today, and Steiner's results are now of classical importance in current studies.

⊠   Stevin, Simon
(1548–1620)
Belgian
Trigonometry, Mechanics, Algebra

The late 16th and early 17th centuries were an exciting time for Europe, as science and mathematics began to flourish during this period. Simon Stevin was a Belgian engineer who made innovative contributions to a variety of different fields of knowledge, including mathematics. It is interesting that many of the notations and concepts he introduced have become indispensable to the modern presentation of mathematics.

Simon Stevin was born in 1548 in Bruges, Belgium. Little is known of his early years. He did not have a formal university education; he pursued higher learning only later in his life. Stevin first worked as a bookkeeper in Antwerp, and later as a tax clerk in Bruges. Later he moved to Leiden, and began to study at the University of Leiden in 1583. At some point after graduation, Stevin became a quartermaster in the Dutch army.

Stevin's diverse scientific accomplishments are described in his 11 books. He essentially founded the science of hydrostatics, discovering that the pressure exerted by water upon a surface principally depends on the height of the water and the surface area. He defended the heliocentric conception of the universe propounded by Copernicus, and discovered (prior to GALILEO GALILEI) that objects of diverse weight fell at the same rate, thus arriving at the uniform acceleration due to gravity. He made numerous contributions to navigation, geography, mechanics, and the science of fortification.

Stevin was also an accomplished engineer, having constructed numerous windmills, locks, and ports. He was an advisor on the project of building military fortifications, and mastered the art of opening sluices in order to flood the lowlands before the advance of an invading army. He also invented a 26-passenger carriage equipped with sails for use along the seashore.

In terms of mathematical achievements, Stevin promulgated the use of the decimal system into European mathematics (it had been previously discovered and used by Arabic mathematicians) through his exposition of decimal fractions in his 1585 book *The Tenth*, and in his work on algebra he introduced the modern symbols for plus, minus, and multiplication. His notion of real number, which includes the irrational numbers in addition to the rationals, became widely accepted and facilitated the progress of European mathematics beyond the knowledge of the Greeks. In particular, Stevin accepted and used negative numbers, already advocated by LEONARDO FIBONACCI and JOHN NAPIER, and other contemporary mathematicians took up his ideas. He formulated mathematical theorems that influenced the development of statics and the study of physical forces. His 1586 *Statics and Hydrostatics* presented the theorem relating forces via a triangle, equivalent to the parallelogram diagram of forces.

Stevin died in 1620 in The Hague, the Netherlands. He is remembered for his contributions to algebra, trigonometry, and hydrostatics. His confidence in the decimal system as possessing fundamental importance for continued developments in mathematics proved to be well founded, as history has subsequently established.

Further Reading
Struik, D. *The Land of Stevin and Huygens*. Dordrecht, the Netherlands: D. Reidel Publishing Company, 1981.

⊠   Stokes, George Gabriel
(1819–1903)
Irish
Mechanics

George Stokes made important contributions to the mathematical theory of hydrodynamics, coderiving the famous Navier-Stokes equations. His work extends to optics, gravity, and the study

George Stokes contributed to the mathematical theory of hydrodynamics and derived the Stokes theorem of vector calculus. *(Courtesy of AIP Emilio Segrè Visual Archives, E. Scott Bar Collection)*

of the Sun; his mathematical work in the area of vector calculus is familiar to modern undergraduates.

George Gabriel Stokes was born on August 13, 1819, in Skreen, Ireland. His father was Gabriel Stokes, a Protestant minister, and his mother was a minister's daughter. Due to his parents' backgrounds, Stokes and his brothers received a very religious upbringing; he was the youngest of six children, and his three older brothers all became clergy. His childhood was happy, full of physical and mental activity. Stokes learned Latin from his father at an early age, and in 1832 pursued further studies in Dublin. During the next three years at Dublin, Stokes lived with his uncle and developed his natural mathematical talents. His father died during this period, which greatly affected Stokes.

In 1835 Stokes entered Bristol College in England, and he won several mathematical prizes with his native intelligence. His teachers encouraged Stokes to pursue a fellowship at Trinity College, but Stokes instead matriculated at Pembroke College, Cambridge, in 1837. Upon entering, he had little formal knowledge of differential calculus, although under the tutelage of William Hopkins he quickly filled the gaps in his education; Hopkins stressed the importance of astronomy and optics. In 1841 Stokes graduated first place in his class, and the college awarded him a fellowship. At this point, Stokes decided to work as a private tutor and conduct his own private mathematical research.

Stokes first began research into hydrodynamics, familiarizing himself with the work of GEORGE GREEN. In 1842 he published a work on the motion of incompressible fluids, which he later discovered was quite similar to the results of Jean Duhamel; however, Stokes's formulation was sufficiently original to merit public dissemination. His 1845 work on hydrodynamics rediscovered CLAUDE-LOUIS NAVIER's equations, but Stokes's derivation was more rigorous. Part of the reason for this duplication of research was the lack of communication between British and continental mathematicians. At this time Stokes also contributed to the theory of light and the theory of gravity.

Stokes became recognized as a leading mathematician in Britain: He was appointed Lucasian professor of mathematics at Cambridge in 1849 and elected to the Royal Society in 1851. To supplement his income, he also accepted a professorship of physics at the Government School of Mines in London. Stokes next published an important work treating the motion of a pendulum in a viscous fluid, and made significant contributions to the theory of the diffraction of light; Stokes's mathematical methods in this area became classical. In 1852 he explained and named the phenomenon of fluorescence, basing this on his elastic theory of the ether.

In 1857 Stokes moved into administrative and empirical work, leaving his more theoretical studies behind. This was partly due to his 1857 marriage to Mary Susanna Robinson, who provided him with a distraction from his intense speculations. Stokes performed an important function in the Royal Society, operating as secretary from 1854 to 1885, and presiding as president afterward until 1890. Stokes received the Copley Medal from the Royal Society in 1893 and served as master of Pembroke College from 1902 to 1903. All of this administrative work seriously distracted him from his original research, but at that time it was not atypical for great scientists to obtain financial support through a variety of positions, since there was no public funding for research.

Stokes died on February 1, 1903, in Cambridge, England. He was a profound influence on the subsequent generation of Cambridge scientists, such as James Maxwell, and formed an important link with the previous French mathematicians working on scientific problems, such as AUGUSTIN-LOUIS CAUCHY, SIMÉON-DENIS POISSON, Navier, JOSEPH-LOUIS LAGRANGE, PIERRE-SIMON LAPLACE, and JEAN-BAPTISTE-JOSEPH FOURIER. His mathematical work, which mainly focused on applied physics problems, later became a standard element of the modern calculus curriculum.

Further Reading

Kinsella, A. "Sir George Gabriel Stokes: The Malahide Connection," *Irish Mathematical Society Bulletin* 35 (1995): 59–62.

Larmor, J. *Memoir and Scientific Correspondence of the Late Sir George Gabriel Stokes.* Cambridge, U.K.: Cambridge University Press, 1907.

Tait, P. "Scientific Worthies V—George Gabriel Stokes," *Nature* 12 (July 15, 1875): 201–202.

Wilson, D. *Kelvin and Stokes: A Comparative Study in Victorian Physics.* Bristol: A. Hilger, 1987.

Wood, A. "George Gabriel Stokes 1819–1903, an Irish Mathematical Physicist," *Irish Mathematical Society Bulletin* 35 (1995): 49–58.

T

Tartaglia, Niccolò (Niccolò Fontana Tartaglia)
(1499–1557)
Italian
Algebra

Niccolò Tartaglia is one of the notable Italian mathematicians of the early 16th century, and he figures as a prominent character in one of the most pugnacious mathematical feuds of history. He independently discovered a method for solving a general cubic equation, and for this achievement he is principally known.

Tartaglia was born in 1499 in Brescia, Italy (then the Republic of Venice). His last name means "stammerer," which he received as a nickname due to his slow and difficult speech. Tartaglia's father was a mail rider. Little is known of his early childhood. In 1512 French marauders captured his hometown, and Tartaglia suffered severe sword wounds to his face; he survived the ordeal only through his mother's tender care, and he forever afterward wore a beard to disguise the scars.

Tartaglia taught himself mathematics, having no money for formal education, and supported himself as a private mathematics teacher in Venice and Verona. He increased his meager reputation by participating in several public mathematics debates, in which he was quite successful.

SCIPIONE DEL FERRO's student Antonio Fior acquired his master's secret of solving the cubic equation, and with this armory challenged Tartaglia to a contest in 1535. Confident in his superior mathematical ability, Tartaglia accepted, but was soon bewildered by Fior's cubic equations. Fior made little progress on Tartaglia's problems due to his ignorance of negative numbers, but in a flash of inspiration Tartaglia discovered the secret to solving the cubic on the last evening of the competition. After obtaining the key formula, he was easily able to solve all of Fior's problems, demonstrating that he was clearly superior.

Tartaglia's contemporary GIROLAMO CARDANO, already interested in the cubic equation himself, attempted to learn the method from Tartaglia, communicating with him in 1539. However, Tartaglia jealously guarded his knowledge, and divulged his secrets only after repeated coercion from Cardano; he made Cardano swear an oath not to reveal the secret formula. The relationship between the two men later deteriorated, as Tartaglia became embittered over revealing his hidden knowledge. This hatred came to a head in 1545, when Cardano published the secret formula after learning that del Ferro was the previous discoverer.

In the ensuing feud, which was carried out in print and involved personal insults and childish bickering, Cardano's assistant LUDOVICO FERRARI

Niccolò Tartaglia solved the cubic equation. *(Courtesy of the Library of Congress)*

challenged Tartaglia to a debate. Tartaglia wished to spar with Cardano, but he accepted Ferrari's challenge in order to secure a lectureship at Brescia. On August 10, 1548, the debate took place, and Tartaglia was defeated, despite his extensive debate experience. As a result, he lost his lectureship at Brescia and returned home to Venice in shame.

Besides his work on the cubic, Tartaglia is also known for his early work on ballistics and artillery fire, presenting the first known firing tables. He provided the first Italian translation of EUCLID OF ALEXANDRIA's *Elements* in 1543, and published Latin editions of ARCHIMEDES OF SYRACUSE's works.

Tartaglia died on December 13, 1557, in Venice. Although he did not attain glory or preeminence in his lifetime, he is remembered today for his codiscovery of the formula for the roots of the cubic equation (with rational coefficients), now known as the Cardan-Tartaglia formula.

Further Reading

Drake, S., and I. Drabkin. *Mechanics in 16th-Century Italy: Selections from Tartaglia, Benedetti, Guido Ubaldo, and Galileo.* Madison: University of Wisconsin Press, 1969.

⊠ **Thales of Miletus**
(ca. 625 B.C.E.–547 B.C.E.)
Greek
Arithmetic

Thales is credited with founding the study of mathematics in Greece, though much of his history is questionable due to the lack of reliable records. At a time when many in Greece were more concerned with mere survival, Thales devoted his energies to contemplating science and, in particular, mathematics. Perhaps he should be remembered best as introducing a logical structure to mathematical investigations, and he is responsible for the concept of proof. To the Greeks of the classical era, Thales was an exalted figure, ranking among the Seven Sages.

It is thought that Thales was born around 625 B.C.E., in the city of Miletus. Even though this town was located in what is today Turkey, at the time it was inhabited by Grecian peoples, and it was a thriving economic center. His parents were Examyes and Cleobuline, who were probably members of a distinguished Milesian family. It is recorded that he died in his 78th year.

Little is known of his youth and early years. Apparently Thales was fairly successful as a merchant, as he had the leisure to pursue natural philosophy and early science. The tale is told that he made his fortune by buying up all the surrounding olive presses; in any event, he spent some time in Egypt while trading. There was no formal mathematics in Egypt, but the Egyptians did possess certain rules of thumb about "earth measurements," which consisted of practical geometrical knowledge useful for demarking the frequently flooded Nile River area. What Thales brought from Egypt he called *geometry*, which is Greek for "earth measurement." In the process, he transformed a loose bunch of facts and statements into a cohesive discipline. He introduced abstraction into the study of geometry, so that one could make general statements, and he utilized deductive reasoning, what is known now as a mathematical proof, as a means to true knowledge. It is hard to appreciate the conceptual leap involved in this change of thinking. The Egyptians had long known that the numbers 3, 4, 5 form the sides of a right triangle, but they were not concerned with *why* it was true. The Greek mentality was different; their intellectual curiosity propelled their mathematical culture far beyond that of their predecessors, and Thales was the father of this movement.

Several other tales are told of Thales. Certainly he was interested in astronomy, and he is credited with introducing that science to Greece from Babylonia, where he may well have traveled. Reputedly he foretold an eclipse of the Sun using a Babylonian calendar of lunar months and computed the height of the Egyptian pyramids via the length of their shadows. Apparently he also wore a politician's hat, persuading the surrounding states to form a confederacy. The Greeks also claim him as the author of a work on navigation, *The Nautical Star Guide*, and he would calculate the distance from shore to a ship out at sea via the angle-side-angle theorem on the congruency of triangles. Later Greeks, such as Eudemus, credit Thales with various theorems, such as the statement that the circle is bisected by its diameter.

Thales is also known as the founder of natural philosophy, which seeks to explain the phenomena of the world without reference to mysterious mystical forces and spirits. He postulated that the world floated on water, the primordial element, which gave an explanation for earthquakes that did not depend upon Poseidon, the Earth-shaker. This approach represented a paradigm shift in thinking about reality, and would serve as a foundation for centuries of Greek philosophy and science. Indeed, Thales is said to be the first philosopher holding a belief in an innate structure to the world.

As for mathematics, it owes its current form and method to Thales. Many cultures, such as Egypt, India, and the Mayans, had pursued what might be called "mathematics," but their investigations were limited to practical rules, and there was no method for establishing the validity of those rules. Deductive reasoning—starting from acceptable axioms and proceeding to conclusions through carefully constructed logical steps—made mathematics into a credible science, and this vital contribution is due to Thales.

Further Reading

Anglin, W., and J. Lambek. *The Heritage of Thales.* New York: Springer, 1995.

Brumbaugh, R. *The Philosophers of Greece.* New York: Crowell, 1964.

Guthrie, W. *The Greek Philosophers: From Thales to Aristotle.* New York: Harper and Row, 1960.

Heath, T. *A History of Greek Mathematics.* Oxford: Clarendon Press, 1921.

Hooper, A. *Makers of Mathematics.* New York: Random House, 1958.

Laertius, D. *Lives, Teachings, and Sayings of Famous Philosophers.* Cambridge, Mass.: Harvard University Press, 1959.

Russell, B. *History of Western Philosophy and Its Connection with Political and Social Circumstances from the Ancient Times to the Present Day.* London: Allen and Unwin, 1961.

Tsu Ch'ung-Chih (Zhu Chongzhi)
(ca. 429–ca. 500)
Chinese
Geometry

Also known as Zhu Chongzhi, Tsu Ch'ung-Chih was an early Chinese mathematician whose main contribution was to improve the approximation of pi. Little is known of his life, and his works have not survived to the present age.

Tsu Ch'ung-Chih was employed in the service of the emperor Hsiao-wu, who reigned from 454 to 464, and it has been deduced that he was born around 429. Tsu Ch'ung-Chih first served as an officer in the province of Kiangsu, and later as a military officer in the capital city of Nanking. Apparently, he completed several works on mathematics and astronomy during this employment. When the emperor died in 464, he left the government in order to focus entirely on science.

Several standard Chinese mathematical works were probably familiar to Tsu Ch'ung-Chih. He was particularly interested in finding a better approximation of pi, since his predecessors had given the values 3, 92/29, and 142/35 in their attempts. The better value of 22/7 was also known since the fourth century. Tsu Ch'ung-Chih attempted to produce a better calculation, and it is recorded by Chinese historians that he constructed a circle of vast diameter and arrived at upper and lower bounds of 3.1415927 and 3.1415926, respectively. It seems that he was the first (in the East) to formulate upper and lower bounds this way; it is curious that, believing pi must be a ratio, he concluded that the exact value should be 355/133, but that 22/7 could be used as a convenient approximation.

Unfortunately, nothing is known of Tsu Ch'ung-Chih's methods, but the seventh-century Chinese historian Wei Cheng guessed that he developed and solved a system of linear equations to arrive at the ratio 355/133. Another historian supposed that Tsu Ch'ung-Chih's method lay in computing the area of a many-sided polygon that was inscribed in the circle. Whatever the case, it seems that Tsu Ch'ung-Chih's works were lost due to their advanced nature—they were inaccessible to contemporary mathematicians, and hence were not preserved.

Tsu Ch'ung-Chih also produced works on astronomy and calendar reform. Although his new calendar year was more precise, it was not implemented due to the opposition of Tsu Ch'ung-Chih's political enemies. He is believed to have died around 500. Tsu Ch'ung-Chih is principally known for his improvement of the value of pi, and is one of the early great Chinese mathematicians.

Further Reading

Chen, C. "A Comparative Study of Early Chinese and Greek Work on the Concept of Limit," in *Science and Technology in Chinese Civilization*. Singapore: World Scientific, 1987.

Dennis, D., V. Kreinovich, and S. Rump. "Intervals and the Origins of Calculus," *Reliable Computing* 4, no. 2 (1998): 191–197.

Martzloff, J. *A History of Chinese Mathematics*. Berlin/Heidelberg: Springer-Verlag, 1997.

V

Venn, John
(1834–1923)
British
Probability, Logic

John Venn contributed to both probability and logic through his research, and was one of the first mathematicians to introduce the symbolism of logic into the study of probability. He is most well known for the Venn diagrams that are useful in the study of logic.

John Venn was born on August 4, 1834, in Hull, England. His family belonged to the evangelical wing of the Church of England, and Venn became a minister briefly. He attended the two London schools of Highgate and Islington, and studied at Cambridge from 1853 to 1857. He was elected a fellow of his college, and he retained this fellowship all his life.

Venn took holy orders in 1859 and worked for a short time as a minister before returning to Cambridge as a lecturer on moral philosophy. He resigned his clerical orders in 1883, due to his increasing disagreement with Anglican dogma, although Venn remained a devout church member. In the same year he was also elected to the Royal Society.

Venn wrote several texts on probability and logic, and these were quite popular in the late 19th and early 20th centuries. Venn's *Logic of Chance* offered criticism of AUGUSTUS DE MORGAN and GEORGE BOOLE—he was especially critical of Boole's algebraic approach to logic. Venn also constructed the empirical definition of probability, which states that the chance of an event occurring is defined to be the long-term limit of the ratio of times it historically occurred. This definition has many advantages over the more classical approach, as it allows for events that are not equally likely. However, one drawback is that the notion of such a limit is not well defined. This led to later work on laws of large numbers and the modern (or axiomatic) formulation of probability theory.

Venn's works on logic also contain geometric diagrams to represent logical situations—he was not the first to use such diagrams, as GOTTFRIED WILHELM VON LEIBNIZ had previously used them systematically, and LEONHARD EULER developed the notion further. Venn's diagrams were therefore based on an existing historical tradition of such geometric aids; nevertheless, Venn systematically developed these geometrical representations. These drawings have been used extensively in elementary mathematics to give young students training in logic.

Venn died on April 4, 1923, in Cambridge. Besides his efforts on improving the foundations of logic, his work on diagrammatic representations of logical events and their applications to probability is most noteworthy. His approach has become fairly standard in elementary studies in probability.

Further Reading

Salmon, W. "John Venn's Logic of Chance," in *Proceedings of the 1978 Pisa Conference on the History and Philosophy of Science*. Dordrecht, the Netherlands: D. Reidel Publishing Company, 1981.

⊠ Viète, François
(1540–1603)
French
Algebra, Geometry

François Viète, along with PIERRE DE FERMAT, RENÉ DESCARTES, and BLAISE PASCAL, was one of the principal founders of European mathematics. He is known as the "father of algebra" due to his introduction of so many important concepts and notations that are still in use. However, his mathematical work was not limited to algebra—he also contributed to geometry, trigonometry, and analysis.

Viète was born in 1540 in Fontenay-le-Comte, a town in the province of Poitou, France. His father, Étienne Viète, was a lawyer in Fontenay-le-Comte, and his mother was Marguerite Dupont. Viète followed his father's profession, graduating with a law degree from the University of Poitiers in 1560. He pursued a legal career for four years before abandoning it to pursue science and mathematics. Viète became a tutor to a nobleman's daughter in the town of La Rochelle.

In the ensuing years, the French Wars of Religion continued to rage between Roman Catholics and Protestants. Viète was a Huguenot, and so naturally sided with the Protestants. Later in his life he became a victim of religious persecution. Before 1570, when he left La Rochelle for Paris, Viète worked on various topics of mathe-matics and science, and he published his first mathematical work, the *Canon Mathematicus seu ad triangular* (Mathematical laws applied to triangles), in 1571. This book was designed to provide introductory mathematical material pertinent to astronomy; it included various trigonometric tables, as well as techniques for studying flat and spherical triangles. Herein Viète first gives a notation for decimal fractions that is a precursor of modern notations. Notation, especially at this immature stage in the history of mathematics, was tremendously important for the advancement of knowledge, since it gave a convenient and appropriate language to express subtle ideas. Arguably, good notation is still vitally important for modern abstract mathematics. A salient example of this point is the Arabic numeral system, which is essentially a notation that has greatly facilitated calculation and number theory; another example is the notations of algebraic equations (with exponents for powers of unknown quantities and letters to designate variables or constants) largely introduced by Viète himself.

In 1572 King Charles IX authorized the massacre of the Huguenots, but Viète escaped and was appointed as a counselor to the government of Brittany in 1573. In the ensuing years of political unrest, Viète worked for Henry III and, after his assassination, for Henry IV. Viète was first appointed as a royal counselor to Henry III in 1580 but, after the rise of Roman Catholic power in Paris, was banished in 1584 for his Protestant faith. Viète spent the next five years at Beauvoir-sur-Mer, devoting himself to mathematical pursuits.

He focused his initial labors on astronomy, and Viète desired to publish a major book, the *Ad harmonicon coeleste* (The celestial harmony), on astronomy. This was never completed, but four manuscript versions have survived the ravages of time. These manuscripts show that Viète was mainly concerned with geometry and the planetary theories of Copernicus and CLAUDIUS PTOLEMY.

In 1588 the Catholics forced Henry III to flee Paris, and he sent for Viète to accompany him in exile. Viète was made a member of the king's parliament in his government at Tours. A Catholic friar murdered Henry III in 1589, and Viète entered the service of the heir, Henry IV. Henry IV, formerly a Protestant, relied heavily on the abilities of Viète, who eventually decoded the secret transmissions of the king of Spain, who was plotting an invasion of France. It is interesting that the Spanish king Philip II, confident in his cipher, thought the French cognizance of his military plans was accomplished through black magic. In this case, it was mathematics rather than sorcery.

These events took place in 1590, and Viète meanwhile gave lectures at Tours. His lectures concerned various supposed advances in mathematics—for example, there was a proof that the circle could be squared—and Viète demonstrated that these arguments were faulty. Perhaps it shows a weakness of character in Viète that he converted to Roman Catholicism in 1593, following the lead of his liege, who probably converted for political reasons. As a result, Viète returned to Paris.

Shortly thereafter, Viète entered a competition with the Dutch mathematician Adriaan von Roomen, who posed a problem involving a degree 45 equation. Viète solved this problem and posed a geometrical question of his own. As a result of this interchange, a friendship arose between Roomen and Viète. Viète continued in the king's service until his dismissal in 1602. He died on December 13, 1603, in Paris, France.

Viète is considered to be the preeminent founder of algebra. Of course, there are numerous Arabic mathematicians (not to mention Greeks) who made pivotal contributions by shaping conceptions of what constitutes arithmetic (for instance, the introduction of zero and negative numbers). However, Viète certainly produced the first complete algebraic system with a consistent notation. In *Introduction to the Analytic Art*, published in Tours in 1591, Viète used familiar alphabetic symbols to designate variables and constants, using vowels for unknowns and consonants for knowns. Descartes later introduced the convention that letters from the end of the alphabet (such as x, y, and z) should designate unknowns, whereas letters from the beginning of the alphabet (such as a, b, and c) should denote known quantities. Nevertheless, Viète made a convincing case for his notational system; previous literature on algebraic equations relied on inconvenient expressions, and often equations were described with sentences rather than abstract symbols. The use of symbols facilitated computation.

Viète made little use of Arabic mathematics, preferring the style of the Italian algebraists like GIROLAMO CARDANO. He should have investigated the Arabic writings more carefully, as many of the ideas Viète introduced were already known to the Arabs. However, Viète made a superior algebraic framework generally available to European mathematicians. He further developed the theory of algebraic equations, although he still attached a geometrical interpretation to quantities, much as the Greeks did. This in essence limited the types of equations that he could examine (for example, homogeneous equations). The next level of algebraic abstraction was ushered in by the next generation, including Descartes and Fermat. Nevertheless, Viète's notation for algebraic equations was adopted with minor adjustment by these successors. One may measure his influence by noting that the term *coefficient* for the known constant multiplying an unknown variable is due to Viète.

Besides the strictly algebraic work, Viète also researched analysis, geometry, and trigonometry. He produced early numerical methods for solving algebraic equations, gave a new decimal approximation for pi (as well as an infinite product characterization of it), and presented geometrical methods for doubling the cube and trisecting an angle.

Viète's mathematical work is clearly part of an intellectual movement from Arabia to Italy to France, and his ideas were dependent on various contemporaries as well as predecessors such as Cardano and LEONARDO FIBONACCI. But his algebraic system represents the next stage in mathematical thinking about algebra, as it provided a foundation for future exploration and generalization. Even though he regarded himself as an amateur (and indeed he lacked formal training in mathematics), Viète was able to make intellectual contributions that would effect a paradigm shift in mathematical circles.

Further Reading

Crossley, J. *The Emergence of Number*. Victoria, Australia: Upside Down A Book Company, 1980.

⊠ Volterra, Vito
(1860–1940)
Italian
Analysis

Vito Volterra helped to extend the ideas of differential and integral calculus from sets to spaces of functions. His work on biology also brought mathematical concepts, such as partial differential equations, to bear on predator-prey relationships. He is most famous for his work on integral equations, producing the "integral equations of Volterra type," which were widely applied to mechanical problems.

Vito Volterra was born on May 3, 1860, in Ancona (a town in the Papal States of Italy) to a poor family. His father died when Volterra was only two years old, and his early education is unknown. He became interested in mathematics after reading ADRIEN-MARIE LEGENDRE's *Geometry* at age 11, and two years later he began studying the three-body problem, an outstanding question in the theory of dynamical systems.

Volterra attended lectures in Florence, and later matriculated at Pisa in 1878; there he studied under the direction of Betti, and obtained his doctorate in 1882 with a thesis treating hydrodynamics. Betti died the next year, and Volterra succeeded him as professor of mathematics at the University of Pisa. He went on to serve at both Turin and Rome.

Volterra was the first mathematician to conceive of what later came to be known as the "functional," a function of real-valued functions. An example of a functional (this terminology was later introduced by Jacques Hadamard) is the operation of integration, which produces a real value for every input function. Volterra was able to extend the integral methods of SIR WILLIAM ROWAN HAMILTON and CARL JACOBI for differential equations to other problems of mechanics, and he developed a wholly new functional calculus to perform the necessary computations. Hadamard, RENÉ-MAURICE FRÉCHET, and other thinkers later developed this original idea.

From 1892 to 1894 Volterra moved on to partial differential equations, investigating the equation of the cylindrical wave. His most famous results were in the area of integral equations, which relate the integrals of various unknown functions. After 1896 Volterra published several papers in this area; he studied what came to be known as "integral equations of the Volterra type." He was able to apply his functional analysis to these integral equations with considerable success.

Despite his age, Volterra joined the Italian air force during World War I, assisting with the development of blimps into weapons of war. Afterward he returned to the University of Rome. He promoted scientific collaboration and later turned to the predator-prey equations of biology, studying the logistic curve. In 1922 fascism spread through Italy, and Volterra fought vehemently against this tide of oppression as a member of the Italian parliament. In 1830 the Fascists gained control, and Volterra was forced to flee Italy. He spent the rest of his life abroad in France and Spain. However, he returned to Italy before his death on October 11, 1940, in Rome.

Volterra was important as a founder of functional analysis, which has been one of the most applied branches of mathematics in the 20th century. Integral equations have been successfully employed to solve many scientific problems, and Volterra's work greatly advanced the knowledge of these equations.

Further Reading

Allen, E. "The Scientific Work of Vito Volterra," *The American Mathematical Monthly* 48 (1941): 516–519.

Fichera, G. "Vito Volterra and the Birth of Functional Analysis," in *Development of Mathematics 1900–1950*. Basel, Switzerland: Birkhäuser, 1994.

W

Wallis, John
(1616–1703)
British
Calculus, Geometry, Algebra

John Wallis was the greatest English mathematician of his time; in fact, he is the first significant British mathematician of the 17th century. He not only stimulated the study of mathematics, making it an attractive subject for others to pursue, but directly influenced SIR ISAAC NEWTON through his early discoveries in the area of differential calculus.

John Wallis was born on November 23, 1616, in Ashford, England. His father, also called John Wallis, was a widely respected minister in Ashford. Wallis's mother, Joanna Chapman, was the second wife of Wallis's father, and Wallis was the third of her five children. Wallis's father died when Wallis was six years old.

Wallis's early education was at Ashford, but when the plague struck his mother sent him to James Movat's grammar school in 1625. He first displayed his potential as a scholar there, training both his memory and his understanding. Throughout life, Wallis was able to achieve great feats of mental calculation, even taking the square roots of irrational numbers in his mind. Next Wallis attended Martin Holbeach's school in Felsted from 1631 to 1632, where he mastered

Greek, Latin, and Hebrew. Although he learned logic there, he received no training in mathematics until his brother taught him the rules of arithmetic during Christmas vacation. The subject appealed to him as a diversion, but he did not pursue mathematics formally.

Wallis next came to Emanual College, Cambridge, in 1632, where he studied ethics, metaphysics, geography, astronomy, and medicine. He later defended his teacher Glisson's new theory of the circulation of the blood in public debate. Wallis completed his bachelor's degree in 1637 and his master's degree in 1640. He was then ordained, and served as a chaplain at various posts over the next few years.

Wallis's career took a turn when he successfully deciphered an encoded Royalist message in only two hours. This made him popular with the Parliamentarians, and Wallis continued to provide them with cryptographical service throughout the Civil War. As a reward for his work, Wallis was awarded care of the church of St. Gabriel of Fenchurch Street in London in 1643. His mother died that year, leaving Wallis a considerable inheritance.

Wallis briefly held a fellowship at Cambridge in 1644, but he was forced to forsake this when he married Susanna Glyde in 1645. In London he began to meet regularly with a group of scientists interested in discussing medicine, geometry,

John Wallis obtained early results in calculus.
(Courtesy of the Library of Congress)

astronomy, and mechanics; this group later evolved into the Royal Society. Through the meetings he encountered William Oughtred's *Clavis Mathematica* (The key to mathematics) in 1647, which he devoured in a few weeks. This work stimulated Wallis's love for mathematics, and encouraged him to begin his own investigations.

Wallis first wrote the *Treatise on Angular Sections,* and discovered methods for solving equations of degree four. In 1649 Oliver Cromwell appointed him to the Savilian chair of geometry at Oxford; his opponents contended that he secured this position through politics, though it seems that the appointment was justified, based on the exceptional service that Wallis provided. Wallis held the post for more than 50 years, until his death; he was also made keeper of the university archives in 1657. In 1648 Wallis publicly disagreed with the motion to execute Charles I. As a result, Charles II rewarded Wallis when the

monarchy was restored: His appointment as the Savilian chair was continued, and he was also made royal chaplain.

Wallis's primary mathematical contribution lies in his work on the foundations of calculus. He first studied the work of Johannes Kepler and RENÉ DESCARTES, and then extended their early results. His *Arithmetica Infinitorum* (The arithmetic of infinitesimals) of 1657 establishes an infinite product expansion for half of pi, which Wallis discovered in the course of computing a certain integral. Wallis discovered how to integrate functions of the form $1 - x^2$ that were raised to an integer power, and extended his rules to fractional powers via interpolation, relying on Kepler's notions of continuity. His work in this area would later influence Newton, who carried the basics of calculus to a much greater extent.

Wallis's *Tract on Conic Sections* of 1655 presented parabolas and circles as sets of points satisfying abstract algebraic equations. This approach, familiar to the modern reader, differs from the classical definition, which describes these curves as the intersection of tilted planes with a cone (they are conic sections). Thus Wallis's style was reminiscent of Descartes's analytic geometry. Wallis's 1685 *Treatise of Algebra* shows his acceptance of negative and complex roots. Herein Wallis solves many algebraic equations, and provides a wealth of historical material. He restored some of the ancient Greek texts, including works by ARISTARCHUS OF SAMOS and ARCHIMEDES OF SYRACUSE.

Besides Wallis's mathematical work, he wrote on a variety of other topics, including etymology, logic, and grammar. He became involved in a feisty dispute with the philosopher Thomas Hobbes, who in 1655 claimed to have squared the circle, which was tantamount to discovering a rational number whose square was pi. Wallis refuted this false claim publicly, and a rather nasty dispute followed that ended only with Hobbes's death.

Wallis slept badly, perhaps because his active mind could not easily find rest. He died on October 28, 1703, in Oxford, England. He is principally remembered for his work on the foundations of calculus, which influenced later mathematicians such as Newton; however, his mathematical labors extended to geometry and algebra as well. It is also notable that Wallis was the first great English mathematician; he had no predecessors or teachers, but in his wake mathematics became a more popular subject.

Further Reading

Scott, J. "The Reverend John Wallis, F.R.S.," *Notes and Records of the Royal Society of London* 15 (1960–61): 57–68.

Scriba, C. "The Autobiograhy of John Wallis, F.R.S.," *Notes and Records of the Royal Society of London* 25 (1970): 17–46.

———. "A Tentative Index of the Correspondence of John Wallis, F.R.S.," *Notes and Records of the Royal Society of London* 22 (1967): 58–93.

———. "Wallis and Harriot," *Centaurus* 10 (1965): 248–257.

⊠ **Weierstrass, Karl (Karl Theodor Wilhelm Weierstrass)**
(1815–1897)
German
Analysis, Complex Analysis

Karl Weierstrass has been described as the father of modern analysis. Indeed, his exacting standards of rigor have become embedded in the modern discipline of analysis, and many of the methods and topics are due to him. Weierstrass also made fundamental contributions to complex analysis and the theory of elliptic functions.

Karl Theodor Wilhelm Weierstrass was born on October 31, 1815, in Ostenfelde, Germany. His father, Wilhelm Weierstrass, was a highly

Karl Weierstrass, father of modern real analysis, made the subject rigorous and introduced new topics, such as functions that are continuous but nondifferentiable. *(Courtesy of AIP Emilio Segrè Visual Archives)*

educated civil servant. Weierstrass's mother was named Theodora Vonderforst, and Weierstrass was her eldest child of four. When Weierstrass was eight years old, his father became a tax inspector, which involved constant relocation. In 1827 Weierstrass's mother died.

The family settled down in 1829 when Weierstrass's father secured a more permanent position in Paderborn, and Weierstrass attended the local high school. There he excelled at mathematics above all subjects, and developed an unusual facility and love for the discipline. He was already reading *Crelle's Journal* in 1834 when he entered a finance program at the University of Bonn. The career of finance was not Weierstrass's choice, but rather his father's; in rebellion and vexation of spirit, Weierstrass wasted his college years in excessive drinking and fencing. Although he was truant from most of his classes, Weierstrass continued his private study of mathematics, and decided that he would devote his life to this one branch of knowledge. As a result of his squandered time, he was unable to pass his examinations (he never even took the tests), and he instead enrolled at the academy in Münster in 1839 in order to become a secondary school teacher. His father was deeply disappointed with his son's change of direction, but it was a fortunate decision for the history of mathematics.

In 1840 Weierstrass passed his exams with excellent results, having proved a certain derivation of NIELS HENDRIK ABEL's from a differential equation; his examiner thought the proof worthy of publication. Weierstrass went on to teach at the high school in Münster, and he wrote three papers between 1841 and 1842 on complex variables. In these papers Weierstrass reformulated the concept of an analytic function in terms of convergent power series, as opposed to the typical approach through differentiation. Meanwhile, Weierstrass taught a variety of subjects, such as history, geography, and even gymnastics, and was utterly bored. The workload was quite heavy, because he conducted research into theoretical mathematics in every spare moment. This busyness may have caused his subsequent health problems, which started in 1850: he suffered from attacks of dizziness, followed by nausea.

Weierstrass worked in Brauensberg from 1848, but after the 1854 publication of his *Toward the Theory of Abelian Functions*, which was widely acclaimed by mathematicians, he received several offers from prominent universities. This paper sketched the representation of abelian functions as convergent power series, and the University of Königsberg conferred an honorary doctorate on him in 1854. ERNST EDUARD KUMMER attempted to procure a post for Weierstrass at the University of Breslau, but this attempt failed. Weierstrass remained as senior lecturer at Brauensberg until 1856, when he accepted his dream job at the University of Berlin. In the meantime he published a follow-up to his 1854 paper, which gave the full details of his method of inversion of hyperelliptic integrals.

Weierstrass's tenure at Berlin, together with Kummer and LEOPOLD KRONECKER, made that school the mathematical mecca of Germany at that time. Weierstrass's well-attended lectures of the next few years give insight into the diversity and profundity of his mathematical research: In 1856 he discussed the theory of elliptic functions applied to geometry and mechanics, in 1859 he tackled the foundations of analysis, and in 1860 he lectured on integral calculus. His investigations produced a continuous function that was nowhere differentiable; the existence of such a bizarre function shattered most analysts' overreliance on intuition, since until that time mathematicians could only conceive of nondifferentiability occurring at isolated points. Weierstrass's 1863 course founded the theory of real numbers—an area that other mathematicians such as RICHARD DEDEKIND and GEORG CANTOR would also work on. He proved that the complex numbers are the only commutative algebraic extension of the real numbers—a result that CARL FRIEDRICH GAUSS previously stated but never proved.

Weierstrass's health problems continued, and he experienced a total collapse in 1861; he took the next year off to recover, but he was never the same. From that time, he had an assistant to write his lectures, and chronic chest pains replaced his dizziness.

Weierstrass organized his various lectures into four main courses: analytic functions, elliptic functions, abelian functions, and the calculus of variations. The courses were fresh and stimulating, since much of the material was his own innovative research. It is a testimony to the legacy of his style that modern courses in analysis follow Weierstrass's progression of topics, including the power series concept of a function, continuity and differentiability, and analytic continuation.

Weierstrass collaborated with Kummer and Kronecker profitably for many years, but later he and Kronecker parted ways over the radical ideas of Cantor; Weierstrass was supportive of Cantor's innovative ideas in set theory, but Kronecker could not accept the pathological constructions. Weierstrass had many excellent students, some of whom became famous mathematicians themselves, such as Cantor, SOPHUS LIE, and FELIX KLEIN. He privately instructed SOFIA KOVALEVSKAYA, who was not allowed to formally enroll due to her gender. Weierstrass had great intellectual rapport with this woman, whom he assisted in finding a suitable position.

Weierstrass was very concerned with mathematical rigor. His high standards became impressed on the succeeding generation, and sparked intensive research into the foundations of mathematics, such as the construction of the real number system. Weierstrass's studies of convergence led him to distinguish different types, thus sparking research into various topologies for function spaces. He studied the concept of uniform convergence, which preserves continuity, and devised various tests for the convergence of infinite series and products. His approach to publishing was careful and methodical, so that his publications were few but extremely deep and exact.

Weierstrass continued to teach until 1890. His last years were devoted to publishing the collected works of JAKOB STEINER and CARL JACOBI. He died of pneumonia on February 19, 1897, in Berlin, Germany. His contributions to mathematics, in particular to real and complex analysis, were extensive and far-reaching, earning him the epithet of "father of modern analysis." His influence was also extended through the large number of talented students whom he mentored and who further developed his ideas in various new directions. From his humble beginnings as a high school teacher, Weierstrass accomplished great things for the field of mathematics.

Further Reading
Manning, K. "The Emergence of the Weierstrassian Approach to Complex Analysis," *Archive for History of Exact Sciences* 14, no. 4 (1975): 297–383.

⊠ Weyl, Hermann
(1885–1955)
German
Geometry, Number Theory

Hermann Weyl, one of the great mathematicians of the early 20th century, successfully developed the ideas of others into rigorous theories. His papers were remarkable for their originality and depth of insight, and his work is quite influential on present research.

Hermann Weyl was born on November 9, 1885, in Elmshorn, Germany. As a boy he attended the Gymnasium at Altona, and entered the University of Göttingen at age 18. He remained there for several years, studying mathematics. After obtaining his degree, he became a professor at the University of Zurich in 1913.

Weyl had studied under DAVID HILBERT at Göttingen and was surely one of his most talented pupils. Weyl's first major work, in 1910, was on the spectral theory of differential equations, which was an area that Hilbert was also investigating. In 1911 Weyl began studying the spectral theory of certain operators in so-called Hilbert spaces. His methods provided some geometric insight into these abstract spaces, and became important techniques in functional analysis.

In 1916 Weyl published a famous paper on analytic number theory, treating the distribution of certain special sequences of numbers. With characteristic ingenuity, Weyl gave a novel solution to the unsolved questions by making connections with integration theory. His techniques have remained relevant to the additive theory of numbers.

After this work in number theory, Weyl turned back to geometry (he had previously, in 1913, given a rigorous foundation for the intuitive definition of a Riemannian manifold). In 1915 he attacked a problem concerned with certain deformations of convex surfaces, and outlined a method of proof that would eventually prove fruitful. Weyl was interrupted by World War I, but was freed from military duty in 1916. In Zurich he worked with Albert Einstein, and consequently became interested in the general theory of relativity. Weyl set out to provide a mathematical foundation for the physical ideas, discovering the concept of a linear connection—ÉLIE CARTAN further developed this important idea.

In the 1920s Weyl became interested in Lie groups, and his papers on this subject are probably his most important and influential. Part of the genius of his approach was the use of topological methods on algebraic objects such as Lie groups. SOPHUS LIE had introduced Lie groups as an interesting new field of mathematics, but Weyl greatly advanced this branch through his new methodology.

As a mathematician, Weyl believed in the importance of abstract theories, and he believed that they were capable of solving classical problems when combined with careful, penetrating thought. He differed with the formalist Hilbert on the philosophy of mathematical foundations, and instead accepted LUITZEN EGBERTUS JAN BROUWER's intuitionism. However, in many other aspects he displayed Hilbert's influence. In 1930 he succeeded Hilbert at Göttingen, but decided to leave Nazi Germany in 1933, arriving at Princeton's Institute for Advanced Study. He remained in the United States until he retired in 1951. He divided the last years of his life between Princeton and Zurich. He died on December 8, 1955.

Hermann Weyl made several significant contributions to number theory, geometry, and differential equations. When he solved a difficult problem, he often devised some wholly new technique for the proof; these new methods often became standard tools, or sometimes led to new areas of research. His work on the theory of Lie groups provided a foundation for later advances.

Further Reading

van Dalen, D. "Hermann Weyl's Intuitionistic Mathematics," *Bulletin of Symbolic Logic* 1, no. 2 (1995): 145–169.

Newman, M. "Hermann Weyl," *Journal of the London Mathematical Society* 33 (1958): 500–511.

Wheeler, J. "Hermann Weyl and the Unity of Knowledge," *American Scientist* 74, no. 4 (1986): 366–375.

⊠ **Wiener, Norbert**
(1894–1964)
American
Probability, Statistics

Norbert Wiener was one of the great American mathematicians of the 20th century. His ideas were profound and rich, if poorly expressed, and revolutionized the theory of communications as well as harmonic analysis. Wiener is also famous for founding the discipline of cybernetics, or the application of statistical ideas to communication.

Norbert Wiener was born on November 26, 1894, in Columbia, Missouri. His father, Leo Wiener, was a Russian Jew who had immigrated to the United States, and was a professor of modern languages at the University of Missouri at the time of his son's birth. Wiener's mother was a German Jew originally named Bertha Kahn. He had one younger sister. Due to his father's extensive intellectual interests (he published several books and was widely read in the sciences), Wiener received an excellent home education that placed him far beyond boys his own age. In fact, Wiener started high school at the age of nine and graduated in 1906.

Norbert Wiener researched statistics and harmonic analysis and solved the signal extraction problem in the theory of stationary time series. *(Massachusetts Institute of Technology Museum and Historical Collections, courtesy of AIP Emilio Segrè Visual Archives)*

It seems that Wiener's father was largely responsible for the development of his child's genius. As a boy, Wiener was quite clumsy and suffered from poor eyesight; when the doctor recommended that Wiener cease reading for six months, his father continued his mathematical education. As a result, Wiener developed great capacities for memorization and mental calculation at a young age. Wiener's family had moved to Boston—Leo Wiener taught at Harvard—and the boy attended Tufts College. He graduated in 1909 with a degree in mathematics, and commenced graduate school at Harvard at only 14 years of age.

Originally Wiener studied zoology, but later changed to philosophy, earning his doctorate from Harvard at age 18. Wiener then journeyed to England to continue his philosophical studies with BERTRAND RUSSELL, who told him that he needed to learn more mathematics. So Wiener studied under GODFREY HAROLD HARDY, and spent most of 1914 at the University of Göttingen studying differential equations under DAVID HILBERT. He

returned to the United States before the outbreak of World War I, and worked a number of odd jobs: He taught philosophy at Harvard, worked for General Electric, and was also a staff writer for the *Encyclopedia Americana*. At the end of the war he obtained a position at the Massachusetts Institute of Technology (MIT).

It was at MIT that Wiener first began studying Brownian motion, an important concept in probability (it is a continuous time stochastic process used to model a variety of phenomena, from the motion of small particles to the evolution of the stock market) and other topics of probability. He also investigated harmonic analysis and its application to the statistical theory of time series. Much of the work that Wiener found resulted from conversations with his engineering colleagues, who were eager to obtain mathematical assistance with their own engineering problems.

Wiener frequently traveled to France, Germany, and England in order to collaborate with European mathematicians—he worked with RENÉ-MAURICE FRÉCHET and PAUL LÉVY. He married Margaret Engemann in 1926. He spent 1931–32 in England working with Hardy, where he also met KURT GÖDEL.

Wiener's genius certainly fulfilled many of the common stereotypes of mathematicians. His papers were often difficult to read, with brilliant discoveries given inadequate proof; sometimes, he would launch into great detail over trivial matters. Despite his poor writing skills, Wiener's contributions were outstanding. His 1921 work on Brownian motion set this important idea of particle physics on a solid theoretical foundation; his further research into the space of continuous one-dimensional curves led to the intuitively appealing so-called Wiener measure, which facilitated the calculation of probabilities of the Brownian motion paths. In 1923 he investigated the partial differential equation known as Dirichlet's problem, and this led to great advances in potential theory. From 1930 he labored in harmonic analysis, winning the Bôcher prize from the American Mathematical Society in 1933. Wiener delved into the various applications of the Fourier transform—one large application was the so-called spectral analysis of time series. With the tools that Wiener developed, it was possible to filter, forecast, and smooth data streams. His 1948 *Cybernetics: Or, Control and Communication in the Animal and the Machine* applied ideas from mechanical systems to biology, such as feedback, stability, and filtering. Apparently this work was a chaotic mess of poorly written text and brilliant flashes of insight.

Wiener died on March 18, 1964, in Stockholm, Sweden. This child prodigy was a notoriously poor lecturer, sloppy writer, and outstanding thinker. His most important work was in probability theory and harmonic analysis, and his influence is still felt today in such subjects as partial differential equations, stochastic processes, and the statistical analysis of time series.

Further Reading

Heims, S. *John Von Neumann and Norbert Wiener: From Mathematics to the Technologies of Life and Death*. Cambridge, Mass.: MIT Press, 1980.

Jerison, D., and D. Stroock. "Norbert Wiener," *Notices of the American Mathematical Society* 42 (1995): 430–438.

Mandrekar, V. "Mathematical Work of Norbert Wiener," *Notices of the American Mathematical Society* 42 (1995): 664–669.

Wiener, N. *Ex-Prodigy: My Childhood and Youth*. New York: Simon and Schuster, 1953.

———. *I Am a Mathematician*. Garden City, N.Y.: Doubleday, 1956.

Y

Yang Hui
(ca. 1238–ca. 1298)
Chinese
Arithmetic

Yang Hui was a Chinese official who developed a decimal system of numbers. The 10-digit number system had already arrived in China through India, but the use of decimals to represent fractions was previously unknown.

Little is known of Yang Hui's life, but his birth is dated around 1238 in China (the location is unknown). A minor government official, Yang found time to write two books in 1261 and 1275 that advanced the decimal representation of fractions, represented in the modern formulation. Apparently he relied on the 11th-century work of Jia Xian, who devised a method of calculating the roots of polynomials. Jia used the so-called Pascal's triangle to extend the computation of square and cube roots to higher-degree polynomials. Yang was familiar with Jia's work, and discusses his methods in his own books.

Yang's 1275 book, *Alpha and Omega of Variations on Multiplication and Division,* provides an interesting document on mathematics education. Herein Yang emphasizes the importance of true understanding over rote memorization, which would characterize modern approaches to mathematics education in China and the East. Yang died sometime around 1298 in China.

Yang Hui did not contribute extensively to mathematics, but he is notable for his introduction of decimals into Chinese mathematics, centuries before such an advance was made in Europe.

Further Reading
Lam, L. *A Critical Study of the "Yang Hui Suan fa": A Thirteenth-Century Chinese Mathematical Treatise.* Singapore: Singapore University Press, 1977.

Needham, J. *Science and Civilisation in China.* Cambridge, U.K.: Cambridge University Press, 1959.

Yativrsabha
(ca. 500–570)
Indian
Number Theory

Mathematics in the sixth century in India was developed under the Jain culture; Yativrsabha, who was a Jain intellectual, developed current mathematics and also tied his work to the older traditions.

Little is known of Yativrsabha's life, but he lived in the sixth century, which is known because he refers to the termination of the Gupta dynasty, which occurred in 551. He studied under

Arya Manksu and Nagahastin, and he compiled several works that expounded Jain traditions. He is also dated by the fact that Jinabhadra Ksamasramana references Yativrsabha's work in 609; also, Yativrsabha refers to a work by Sarvanandin in 458.

Yativrsabha's main work, the *Tiloyapannatti*, contains a description of the universe and certain mathematical formulas that are typical of this era in India; his mathematics is representative of the progress in Jain mathematical thought that had developed from the older canonical works. The book describes various units for measuring distance and time, notable for their massive scale. In fact, Yativrsabha's system gives a first concept for measuring infinite distances. In the Jaina cosmology, the universe was infinite in space and time; Yativrsabha's work provided a method for measuring these increasingly larger quantities.

Yativrsabha's mathematics are surely a product of his own Jain culture, and this comfort with infinity facilitated the development of transfinite mathematics. Centuries before GEORGE CANTOR, Yativrsabha first dabbled with the concept that there were varying degrees of infinity, and this hierarchy could be measured and studied. However, he exerted little lasting influence in this direction since the study of infinity would not be resumed until the 17th and 18th centuries in Europe.

Further Reading

Jain, L. "Aryabhata I and Yativrsabha—a Study in Kalpa and Meru," *Indian Journal of History of Science* 12, no. 2 (1977): 137–146.

⊠ **Yule, George Udny**
(1871–1951)
British
Statistics

George Yule was an important statistician of the early 20th century who stimulated a generation of students and contributed to a wide range of topics. His work on correlation, regression, and time series is most noteworthy.

George Udny Yule was born on February 18, 1871, in Morham, Scotland. His father, who shared the same name, was a colonial administrator in India; he was later knighted for his services. Yule received a good education, and he attended Winchester College until 1887. Next he went on to study engineering at University College, London, graduating in 1890. Yule spent the next two years working in an engineering lab, but this vocation failed to stimulate him, and he soon turned to experimental physics. In 1892 Yule resided in Bonn, studying physics under the guidance of Heinrich Hertz, and published four papers on electricity.

Despite having a good start in physics, Yule was dissatisfied, and in 1893 he returned to University College as a demonstrator—a position that Karl Pearson had procured for him. With Pearson, Yule worked on the notion of correlation coefficient and related this important statistic to linear regression. His 1895 work *On the Correlation of Total Pauperism with Proportion of Outrelief* addressed these topics, and its excellence heralded Yule's election to the Royal Statistical Society that same year. Yule's subsequent works were very influential in the social sciences, where in the following decades his methods came to predominate. He was advanced to assistant professor at University College in 1896, but three years later left for a better-paid position at the City and Guilds London Institute.

Yule continued to produce a large volume of papers, and his annual Newmarch lectures at University College became incorporated into his widely read *Introduction to the Theory of Statistics* (1911). The text was a great success, and in 1911 Yule was awarded the Royal Statistical Society's highest award, the Guy Medal in Gold. Yule was intimately connected to the Royal Statistical Society, since he served as secretary from 1907 to 1919 and president from 1924 to 1926. In 1912 he accepted a post at Cambridge and dwelled at St. John's College for most of his remaining life. Besides these activities, Yule served as a statistician in the army during World War I.

During the 1920s Yule was especially productive: He introduced the correlogram and measures of serial correlation to the statistical study of time series. In addition, he promulgated autoregressive time series models that are still widely used today. He retired from Cambridge in 1930, but he continued to make new editions for his enduringly popular *Introduction to the Theory of Statistics*. An aficionado of fast cars, Yule was determined to obtain a pilot's license for his retirement. Unfortunately, he suffered a heart ailment in 1931 that incapacitated him. He died on June 26, 1951, in Cambridge, England.

Yule was a kind man who was very accessible to students. Besides his contributions to the concept of correlation and regression, Yule was important for the impetus that he gave to mathematical statistics through his textbook and his interactions with his colleagues.

Further Reading

Johnson, N., and S. Kotz. "George Udny Yule," in *Leading Personalities in Statistical Sciences*. New York: John Wiley, 1997.

Kendall, M. "George Udny Yule, 1871–1951," *Journal of the Royal Statistical Society* 115 (1952): 156–161.

Stigler, S. *The History of Statistics: The Measurement of Uncertainty before 1900*. Cambridge, Mass.: Belknap Press of Harvard University Press, 1986.

Yates, F. "George Udny Yule," *Obituary Notices of Fellows of the Royal Society of London* 8 (1952): 309–323.

Z

Zeno of Elea
(ca. 490 B.C.E.–ca. 425 B.C.E.)
Greek
Logic

The classical Greek mathematicians shied away from the study of infinity, both the infinitely large and the infinitely small (the infinitesimal). Infinitesimals are the cornerstone of calculus, and many Greeks, such as ARCHIMEDES OF SYRACUSE, made the first faltering steps toward a full discovery of calculus. However, the majority rejected the notion of infinitely divisible quantities, such as a continuum, and this reaction was largely due to the paradoxes of Zeno.

Zeno of Elea was born in approximately 490 B.C.E. in Elea, Italy. He was of Greek descent despite his birth in Italy, and he is classed with the Greek philosophers. There exists very little reliable information on his life, but it is said that his father was Telautagoras. Zeno eventually studied at the school of philosophy at Elea, where he met his master Parmenides. The Eleatic school, founded by Parmenides, taught monism—the concept that all is one. This philosophy influenced Zeno to formulate various paradoxes that challenged the concepts of infinite divisibility.

Plato claims that Zeno and Parmenides traveled to Athens in 450 B.C.E., where they met the young Socrates and discussed philosophy with him. Before traveling to Athens, Zeno had already acquired some fame through the publication of his book (which has not survived) containing 40 paradoxes. These paradoxes form a deeply stimulating dissection of the concept of the continuum, thereby disturbing comfortable notions of such common things as motion, time, and space. One of Zeno's assumptions is that of divisibility: If a magnitude can be divided in two, then it can be divided forever. The work of RICHARD DEDEKIND would later establish this continuum property for the real numbers. Zeno also assumed that any object of zero magnitude (he did not express it this way, since the Greeks did not have zero) does not exist.

In the paradox labeled "The Dichotomy," Zeno states that in order to traverse a distance, it is first necessary to traverse half that distance; but to get halfway, it is first required to go a quarter of the way. Continuing this reasoning indefinitely, Zeno concludes that to begin is impossible, and that therefore motion is impossible. This paradox is typically resolved by summing the geometric series of reciprocal power of two. In "The Arrow," Zeno states that motion is impossible, because (assuming that the current "now" instance of time is indivisible) if an arrow moves some distance in an indivisible instant of time, then it moved half that distance in half the time, thereby resulting in a division of the instant. This can be resolved by allowing time to be a continuum—infinitely divisible.

Zeno's most famous paradox is that of Achilles: It states that a race between the Greek hero Achilles and a tortoise is run, and the slow tortoise is given a head start. After some time has elapsed, Achilles catches up half the intervening distance. But the tortoise has meanwhile moved on; Achilles then runs half the remaining intervening distance, but again the tortoise has advanced farther. Carrying this argument on infinitely far, Zeno concludes that Achilles can never catch up! This, too, can be resolved by setting up an appropriate geometric series. However, the resolutions of these paradoxes rely on certain notions of infinity and properties of the continuum. The mathematical structure behind these concepts was not developed until many centuries later. SIR ISAAC NEWTON, GOTTFRIED WILHELM VON LEIBNIZ, and BLAISE PASCAL laid the modern foundations of calculus, along with a host of others discussed in this book. More advanced work on the continuum, as well as the basic properties of the real numbers, was conducted in the late 19th century by GEORG CANTOR, FRIEDRICH LUDWIG GOTTLOB FREGE, and BERTRAND RUSSELL, among others. Thus, Zeno's influence was far-reaching, in that he asked some very deep questions about time, space, and motion.

Zeno died sometime around 425 B.C.E., and a questionable source relates that he was executed after a failed attempt to remove a tyrant of Elea. Although he was a philosopher, Zeno's ideas sparked a mathematical revolution millennia later, since his paradoxes pointed to the need to provide a rigorous foundation to intuitive concepts of space and time. His paradoxes concerning motion demonstrated the difficulties of considering velocity as distance divided by time, since this ratio appears to become zero divided by zero when the elapsed time of travel

is reduced to zero; only with the discovery of limits and infinitesimals in the discipline of differential calculus was this conundrum resolved. Besides providing a plethora of mental obstacles for later intellectuals, Zeno also served to inhibit the growth of Greek mathematics to encompass the infinite; thus, he was a retarding influence classically, but millennia later became an impetus for mathematical development.

Further Reading

Barnes, J. *The Presocratic Philosophers*. London: Routledge and Kegan Paul, 1982.

Grunbaum, A. *Modern Science and Zeno's Paradoxes*. London: Allen and Unwin, 1968.

Guthrie, W. *A History of Greek Philosophy*. Cambridge, U.K.: Cambridge University Press, 1981.

Heath, T. *A History of Greek Mathematics*. Oxford: Clarendon Press, 1921.

Kirk, G., J. Raven, and M. Schofield. *The Presocratic Philosophers: A Critical History with a Selection of Texts*. Cambridge: Cambridge University Press, 1983.

Laertius, D. *Lives, Teachings, and Sayings of Famous Philosophers*. Cambridge, Mass.: Harvard University Press, 1959.

Russell, B. *The Principles of Mathematics*. London: G. Allen and Unwin, 1964.

Salmon, W. *Zeno's Paradoxes*. Indianapolis: Bobbs-Merrill, 1970.

Sorabji, R. *Time, Creation and the Continuum*. Ithaca, N.Y.: Cornell University Press, 1983.

⊠ Zermelo, Ernst (Ernst Friedrich Ferdinand Zermelo)
(1871–1953)
German
Logic

The revolution in mathematical logic and set theory that took place in the early 20th century had many important participants, including Ernst Zermelo. His axiomatic construction of set theory has been of great importance for the development of mathematics, since all of modern mathematics is now built upon set theoretic foundations.

Ernst Zermelo was born on July 27, 1871, the son of Ferdinand Rudolf Theodor Zermelo, a college professor, and Maria Augusta Elisabeth Zieger. The young Zermelo received his secondary education in Berlin, and he pursued the study of mathematics, philosophy, and physics at schools in Berlin, Halle, and Freiburg. His teachers included Georg Frobenius, Max Planck, and Herman Schwartz. In 1894 he obtained his doctorate at the University of Berlin with a thesis studying the calculus of variations. Even though Zermelo would obtain fame through his researches into set theory, he maintained his interest and knowledge of the calculus of variations throughout his life.

After working for several years on hydrodynamics, Zermelo obtained a position at the University of Göttingen in 1899, and he became titular professor there a year after his 1904 proof of the well-ordering theorem. This result, which earned Zermelo instant recognition among contemporary mathematicians, stated that any set could be well ordered (that is, one can construct an ordering relation that allows one to compare any two elements of the set, and determine which comes first). This surprising theorem says that any set looks like the set of real numbers (where the ordering is the "less than" symbol $<$).

Zermelo was interested in physics, and had a knack for finding applications of mathematics to practical problems. For example, he analyzed the strength of chess competitors and studied the fracture of a sugar cube. In 1900 he began lecturing on GEORG CANTOR's set theory, which he had carefully digested; a few years later he produced his well-ordering theorem,

and in 1908 produced a second proof. In the same year Zermelo set up an axiom system for Cantor's set theory that is commonly used today. The axioms carefully avoid Russell's paradox, but employ the controversial axiom of choice, which states that any disjoint union of nonempty sets has a subset containing exactly one element from each of the original sets. The provability of the famous continuum hypothesis is contingent on this axiom of choice. Some mathematicians dispense with it, while most view it as intuitive.

In 1910 Zermelo accepted a professorship at Zürich, but he retired six years later due to poor health. From 1916 to 1926 he lived in the Black Forest of Germany, regaining his health. He next came to the University of Freiburg im Breisgau. (He broke off connection with the school in 1935 in protest against the Nazi regime. After World War II he was reinstated.) Meanwhile, the logicians Adolf Fraenkel and Thoralf Skolem had made certain criticisms of Zermelo's system, pointing out the weakness of the seventh axiom of infinity. In 1929 Zermelo responded to this critique with an axiomatization of the property of definiteness, which is used to define sets through the common properties of their elements.

Zermelo made a few additional contributions to set theory, attempting to abolish proof theory in 1935, but he had already accomplished his most important work. He died at the University of Freiburg im Breisgau on May 21, 1953. Although Zermelo's proof of the well-ordering theorem was important, he is remembered principally for his axiomatic formulation of set theory, which is still widely influential today. Besides providing a rigorous set theoretic foundation for most (or all) of modern mathematics, his work initiated pure research in mathematical set theory. Today, many mathematicians are investigating the consequences of various systems of axioms, testing them for their strengths and weaknesses in terms of consistency and completeness.

Further Reading

van Heijenoort, J. *From Frege to Gödel: A Source Book of Mathematical Logic*. Cambridge, Mass.: Harvard University Press, 1967.

Moore, G. "Ernst Zermelo, A. E. Harward, and the Axiomatization of Set Theory," *Historia Mathematica* 3, no. 2 (1976): 206–209.

Peckhaus, V. "Ernst Zermelo in Göttingen," *History and Philosophy of Logic* 11, no. 1 (1990): 19–58.

ENTRIES BY FIELD

ALGEBRA
Abel, Niels Henrik
Aryabhata I
Brahmagupta
Cardano, Girolamo
Ch'in Chiu-Shao
Chu Shih-Chieh
Ferrari, Ludovico
Ferro, Scipione del
Galois, Evariste
Hermite, Charles
Jordan, Camille
al-Karaji, Abu
al-Khwarizmi, Abu
Klein, Felix
Kummer, Ernst
Li Chih
Liouville, Joseph
Noether, Emmy
Seki Takakazu Kowa
Tartaglia, Niccolò
Viète, François

ANALYSIS
Agnesi, Maria Gaetana
Babbage, Charles
Baire, René-Louis
Banach, Stefan
Bessel, Friedrich Wilhelm
Birkhoff, George David
Bolzano, Bernhard

Borel, Émile
Dedekind, Richard
Eudoxus of Cnidus
Fatou, Pierre-Joseph-Louis
Fourier, Jean-Baptiste-Joseph
Fréchet, René-Maurice
Fredholm, Ivar
Fubini, Guido
Jacobi, Carl
Lebesgue, Henri-Léon
Liouville, Joseph
Lipschitz, Rudolf
Napier, John
Riesz, Frigyes
Volterra, Vito
Weierstrass, Karl

ARITHMETIC
Adelard of Bath
Bacon, Roger
Fibonacci, Leonardo
Thales of Miletus
Yang Hui

CALCULUS
Barrow, Isaac
Carnot, Lazare
Green, George
Gregory, James
Leibniz, Gottfried
      Wilhelm von

Maclaurin, Colin
Newton, Sir Isaac
Wallis, John

COMPLEX ANALYSIS
Cauchy, Augustin-Louis
Hamilton, Sir William Rowan
Riemann, Bernhard

DIFFERENTIAL EQUATIONS
Bernoulli, Jakob
Bernoulli, Johann
Kovalevsky, Sonya

GEOMETRY
Apollonius of Perga
Archimedes of Syracuse
Bolyai, János
Cartan, Élie
Cavalieri, Bonaventura
Democritus of Abdera
Desargues, Girard
Descartes, René
Eratosthenes of Cyrene
Euclid of Alexandria
Grassmann, Hermann Günter
al-Haytham, Abu Ali
Hippocrates of Chios
Ibrahim, ibn Sinan
Leonardo da Vinci
Lie, Sophus

Lobachevsky, Nikolai
Menelaus of Alexandria
Minkowski, Hermann
Monge, Gaspard
Oresme, Nicole
Pappus of Alexandria
Pascal, Blaise
Poncelet, Jean-Victor
Steiner, Jakob
Tsu Ch'ung Chi
Weyl, Hermann

LOGIC
Boole, George
Brouwer, Luitzen
    Egbertus Jan
Cantor, Georg
De Morgan, Augustus
Frege, Friedrich Ludwig
    Gottlob
Gödel, Kurt Friedrich
Hilbert, David
Lovelace, Augusta Ada Byron
Peano, Giuseppe
Peirce, Charles
Russell, Bertrand
Zeno of Elea
Zermelo, Ernst

MECHANICS
Alembert, Jean d'
Bernoulli, Daniel

Galilei, Galileo
Gibbs, Josiah Willard
Heaviside, Oliver
Huygens, Christiaan
Lagrange, Joseph-Louis
Navier, Claude-Louis-Marie-
    Henri
Stokes, George Gabriel

NUMBER THEORY
Diophantus of Alexandria
Dirichlet, Gustav Peter
    Lejeune
Euler, Leonhard
Fermat, Pierre de
Germain, Sophie
Goldbach, Christian
Hardy, Godfrey
    Harold
Kronecker, Leopold
Legendre, Adrien-Marie
Pythagoras of Samos
Ramanujan, Srinivasa
    Aiyangar
Yativrsabha

PROBABILITY
Bayes, Thomas
Chebyshev, Pafnuty
    Lvovich
Laplace, Pierre-Simon
Lévy, Paul-Pierre

Markov, Andrei
Moivre, Abraham de
Poisson, Siméon-Denis
Pólya, George
Venn, John
Wiener, Norbert

STATISTICS
Fisher, Sir Ronald
    Aylmer
Gauss, Carl Friedrich
Gosset, William
Pearson, Egon Sharpe
Yule, George Udny

TOPOLOGY
Betti, Enrico
Hopf, Heinz
Möbius, August
Poincaré, Jules-Henri

TRIGONOMETRY
Aristarchus of Samos
Bhaskara II
Hipparchus of Rhodes
Madhava of
    Sangamagramma
Ptolemy, Claudius
Regiomontanus, Johann
    Müller
Rheticus, Georg
Stevin, Simon

Entries by Country of Birth

ARABIA
al-Haytham, Abu Ali
Ibrahim, ibn Sinan
al-Karaji, Abu
al-Khwarizmi, Abu

AUSTRIA
Gödel, Kurt Friedrich

BELGIUM
Stevin, Simon

CHINA
Ch'in Chiu-Shao
Chu Shih-Chieh
Li Chih
Tsu Ch'ung Chi
Yang Hui

CZECHOSLOVAKIA
Bolzano, Bernhard

FRANCE
Alembert, Jean d'
Baire, René-Louis
Borel, Émile
Carnot, Lazare
Cartan, Élie
Cauchy, Augustin-Louis
Desargues, Girard
Descartes, René

Fatou, Pierre-Joseph-Louis
Fermat, Pierre de
Fourier, Jean-Baptiste-Joseph
Fréchet, René-Maurice
Galois, Evariste
Germain, Sophie
Hermite, Charles
Jordan, Camille
Laplace, Pierre-Simon
Lebesgue, Henri-Léon
Legendre, Adrien-Marie
Lévy, Paul-Pierre
Liouville, Joseph
Moivre, Abraham de
Monge, Gaspard
Navier, Claude-Louis-Marie-Henri
Oresme, Nicole
Pascal, Blaise
Poincaré, Jules-Henri
Poisson, Siméon-Denis
Poncelet, Jean-Victor
Viète, François

GERMANY
Bessel, Friedrich Wilhelm
Cantor, Georg
Dedekind, Richard
Dirichlet, Gustav Peter Lejeune

Frege, Friedrich Ludwig Gottlob
Gauss, Carl Friedrich
Goldbach, Christian
Grassmann, Hermann Günter
Hilbert, David
Hopf, Heinz
Jacobi, Carl
Klein, Felix
Kronecker, Leopold
Kummer, Ernst
Leibniz, Gottfried Wilhelm von
Lipschitz, Rudolf
Möbius, August
Noether, Emmy
Regiomontanus, Johann Müller
Rheticus, Georg
Riemann, Bernhard
Weierstrass, Karl
Weyl, Hermann
Zermelo, Ernst

GREAT BRITAIN
Adelard of Bath
Babbage, Charles
Bacon, Roger
Barrow, Isaac
Bayes, Thomas
Boole, George

262

Fisher, Sir Ronald
    Aylmer
Gosset, William
Green, George
Gregory, James
Hardy, Godfrey Harold
Heaviside, Oliver
Lovelace, Augusta
    Ada Byron
Maclaurin, Colin
Napier, John
Newton, Sir Isaac
Pearson, Egon Sharpe
Russell, Bertrand
Venn, John
Wallis, John
Yule, George Udny

GREECE
Apollonius of Perga
Archimedes of Syracuse
Aristarchus of Samos
Democritus of Abdera
Diophantus of
    Alexandria
Eratosthenes of Cyrene
Euclid of Alexandria
Eudoxus of Cnidus
Hipparchus of Rhodes
Hippocrates of Chios
Menelaus of Alexandria
Pappus of Alexandria
Ptolemy, Claudius
Pythagoras of Samos
Thales of Miletus
Zeno of Elea

HOLLAND/NETHERLANDS
Bernoulli, Daniel
Brouwer, Luitzen Egbertus Jan
Huygens, Christiaan

HUNGARY
Bolyai, János
Pólya, George
Riesz, Frigyes

INDIA
Aryabhata I
Bhaskara II
Brahmagupta
De Morgan, Augustus
Madhava of
    Sangamagramma
Ramanujan, Srinivasa
    Aiyangar
Yativrsabha

IRELAND
Hamilton, Sir William Rowan
Stokes, George Gabriel

ITALY
Agnesi, Maria Gaetana
Betti, Enrico
Cardano, Girolamo
Cavalieri, Bonaventura
Ferrari, Ludovico
Ferro, Scipione del
Fibonacci, Leonardo
Fubini, Guido
Galilei, Galileo
Lagrange, Joseph-Louis

Leonardo da Vinci
Peano, Giuseppe
Tartaglia, Niccolò
Volterra, Vito

JAPAN
Seki Takakazu Kowa

NORWAY
Abel, Niels Henrik
Lie, Sophus

POLAND
Banach, Stefan

RUSSIA AND THE SOVIET UNION
Chebyshev, Pafnuty Lvov
Kovalevskaya, Sonya
Lobachevsky, Nikolai
Markov, Andrei
Minkowski, Hermann

SWITZERLAND
Bernoulli, Jakob
Bernoulli, Johann
Euler, Leonhard
Steiner, Jakob

SWEDEN
Fredholm, Ivar

UNITED STATES
Birkhoff, George David
Gibbs, Josiah Willard
Peirce, Charles
Wiener, Norbert

Entries by Country of Major Scientific Activity

ARABIA
al-Haytham, Abu Ali
Ibrahim ibn Sinan
al-Karaji, Abu
al-Khwarizmi, Abu

BELGIUM
Stevin, Simon

CHINA
Ch'in Chiu-Shao
Chu Shih-Chieh
Li Chih
Tsu Ch'ung Chi
Yang Hui

CZECHOSLOVAKIA
Bolzano, Bernhard

EGYPT
Apollonius of Perga
Diophantus of Alexandria
Eratosthenes of Cyrene
Euclid of Alexandria
Pappus of Alexandria
Ptolemy, Claudius

FRANCE
Alembert, Jean d'

Baire, René-Louis
Borel, Émile
Carnot, Lazare
Cartan, Élie
Cauchy, Augustin-Louis
Desargues, Girard
Fatou, Pierre-Joseph-Louis
Fermat, Pierre de
Fourier, Jean-Baptiste-Joseph
Fréchet, René-Maurice
Galois, Evariste
Germain, Sophie
Hermite, Charles
Jordan, Camille
Lagrange, Joseph-Louis
Laplace, Pierre-Simon
Lebesgue, Henri-Léon
Legendre, Adrien-Marie
Lévy, Paul-Pierre
Liouville, Joseph
Monge, Gaspard
Navier, Claude-Louis-Marie-
    Henri
Oresme, Nicole
Pascal, Blaise
Poincaré, Jules-Henri
Poisson, Siméon-Denis
Poncelet, Jean-Victor
Viète, François

GERMANY
Bernoulli, Johann
Bessel, Friedrich
    Wilhelm
Cantor, Georg
Dedekind, Richard
Dirichlet, Gustav Peter
    Lejeune
Frege, Friedrich Ludwig
    Gottlob
Gauss, Carl Friedrich
Grassmann, Hermann
    Günter
Hilbert, David
Jacobi, Carl
Klein, Felix
Kronecker, Leopold
Kummer, Ernst
Leibniz, Gottfried
    Wilhelm von
Lie, Sophus
Lipschitz, Rudolf
Minkowski, Hermann
Möbius, August
Noether, Emmy
Regiomontanus, Johann
    Müller
Rheticus, Georg
Riemann, Bernhard

Weierstrass, Karl
Weyl, Hermann
Zermelo, Ernst

GREAT BRITAIN
Adelard of Bath
Babbage, Charles
Bacon, Roger
Barrow, Isaac
Bayes, Thomas
De Morgan, Augustus
Fisher, Sir Ronald
    Aylmer
Green, George
Gregory, James
Hardy, Godfrey Harold
Heaviside, Oliver
Lovelace, Augusta
    Ada Byron
Maclaurin, Colin
Moivre, Abraham de
Napier, John
Newton, Sir Isaac
Pearson, Egon Sharpe
Ramanujan, Srinivasa
    Aiyangar
Russell, Bertrand
Stokes, George Gabriel
Venn, John
Wallis, John
Yule, George Udny

GREECE
Aristarchus of Samos
Democritus of Abdera
Eudoxus of Cnidus
Hipparchus of Rhodes
Hippocrates of Chios

Thales of Miletus
Zeno of Elea

HOLLAND/NETHERLANDS
Brouwer, Luitzen
    Egbertus Jan
Descartes, René
Huygens, Christiaan

HUNGARY
Bolyai, János
Riesz, Frigyes

INDIA
Aryabhata I
Bhaskara II
Brahmagupta
Madhava of Sangamagramma
Yativrsabha

IRELAND
Boole, George
Gosset, William
Hamilton, Sir William
    Rowan

ITALY
Agnesi, Maria Gaetana
Archimedes of Syracuse
Betti, Enrico
Cardano, Girolamo
Cavalieri, Bonaventura
Ferrari, Ludovico
Ferro, Scipione del
Fibonacci, Leonardo
Fubini, Guido
Galilei, Galileo
Leonardo da Vinci

Menelaus of Alexandria
Peano, Giuseppe
Pythagoras of Samos
Tartaglia, Niccolò
Volterra, Vito

JAPAN
Seki Takakazu Kowa

NORWAY
Abel, Niels Henrik

RUSSIA AND THE SOVIET UNION
Banach, Stefan
Bernoulli, Daniel
Chebyshev, Pafnuty
    Lvovich
Euler, Leonhard
Goldbach, Christian
Lobachevsky, Nikolai
Markov, Andrei

SWITZERLAND
Bernoulli, Jakob
Hopf, Heinz
Pólya, George
Steiner, Jakob

SWEDEN
Fredholm, Ivar
Kovalevskaya, Sonya

UNITED STATES
Birkhoff, George David
Gibbs, Josiah Willard
Gödel, Kurt Friedrich
Peirce, Charles
Wiener, Norbert

ENTRIES BY YEAR OF BIRTH

1641–1660
Bernoulli, Jakob
Leibniz, Gottfried
    Wilhelm von
Newton, Sir Isaac
Seki Takakazu
    Kowa

1661–1680
Bernoulli, Johann
Moivre, Abraham de

1681–1700
Goldbach, Christian
Maclaurin, Colin
Newton, Sir Isaac

1701–1720
Agnesi, Maria
    Gaetana
Alembert, Jean d'
Bayes, Thomas
Bernoulli, Daniel
Euler, Leonhard

1721–1740
Lagrange, Joseph-Louis

1741–1760
Carnot, Lazare
Laplace, Pierre-Simon
Legendre, Adrien-Marie
Monge, Gaspard

1761–1780
Fourier, Jean-Baptiste-Joseph
Gauss, Carl Friedrich
Germain, Sophie

1781–1800
Babbage, Charles
Bessel, Friedrich Wilhelm
Bolzano, Bernhard
Cauchy, Augustin-Louis

Green, George
Lobachevsky, Nikolai
Möbius, August
Navier, Claude-Louis-Marie-
    Henri
Poisson, Siméon-Denis
Poncelet, Jean-Victor
Steiner, Jakob

1801–1810
Abel, Niels Henrik
Bolyai, János
De Morgan,
    Augustus
Dirichlet, Gustav Peter
    Lejeune
Grassmann, Hermann
    Günter
Hamilton, Sir William
    Rowan
Jacobi, Carl
Kummer, Ernst
Liouville, Joseph

1811–1820
Boole, George
Galois, Evariste
Lovelace, Augusta
    Ada Byron
Stokes, George Gabriel
Weierstrass, Karl

1821–1830
Betti, Enrico
Chebyshev, Pafnuty
    Lvovich
Hermite, Charles
Kronecker, Leopold
Riemann, Bernhard

1831–1840
Dedekind, Richard
Gibbs, Josiah
    Willard

Jordan, Camille
Lipschitz, Rudolf
Peirce, Charles
Venn, John

1841–1850
Cantor, Georg
Frege, Friedrich Ludwig
    Gottlob
Heaviside, Oliver
Klein, Felix
Kovalevskaya, Sonya
Lie, Sophus

1851–1860
Markov, Andrei
Peano, Giuseppe
Poincaré, Jules-Henri
Volterra, Vito

1861–1870
Cartan, Élie
Fredholm, Ivar
Hilbert, David
Minkowski, Hermann

1871–1880
Baire, René-Louis
Borel, Émile
Fatou, Pierre-Joseph-
    Louis
Fréchet, René-Maurice
Fubini, Guido
Gosset, William
Hardy, Godfrey
    Harold
Lebesgue, Henri-Léon
Riesz, Frigyes
Russell, Bertrand
Yule, George Udny
Zermelo, Ernst

1881–1890
Birkhoff, George David

Brouwer, Luitzen
    Egbertus Jan
Fisher, Sir Ronald
    Aylmer
Lévy, Paul-Pierre
Noether, Emmy

Pólya, George
Ramanujan, Srinivasa Aiyangar
Weyl, Hermann

1891–1900
Banach, Stefan

Hopf, Heinz
Pearson, Egon Sharpe
Wiener, Norbert

1901–1910
Gödel, Kurt Friedrich

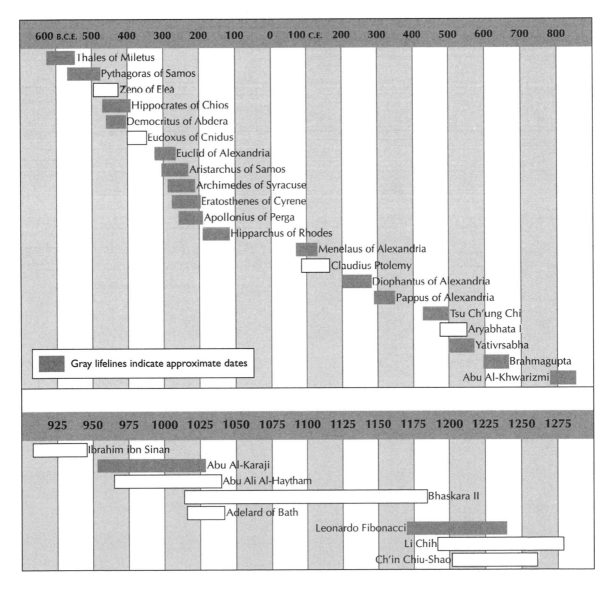

600 B.C.E.	500	400	300	200	100	0	100 C.E.	200	300	400	500	600	700	800

Thales of Miletus

Pythagoras of Samos

Zeno of Elea

Hippocrates of Chios

Democritus of Abdera

Eudoxus of Cnidus

Euclid of Alexandria

Aristarchus of Samos

Archimedes of Syracuse

Eratosthenes of Cyrene

Apollonius of Perga

Hipparchus of Rhodes

Menelaus of Alexandria

Claudius Ptolemy

Diophantus of Alexandria

Pappus of Alexandria

Tsu Ch'ung Chi

Aryabhata I

Yativrsabha

Brahmagupta

Abu Al-Khwarizmi

Gray lifelines indicate approximate dates

925	950	975	1000	1025	1050	1075	1100	1125	1150	1175	1200	1225	1250	1275

Ibrahim ibn Sinan

Abu Al-Karaji

Abu Ali Al-Haytham

Bhaskara II

Adelard of Bath

Leonardo Fibonacci

Li Chih

Ch'in Chiu-Shao

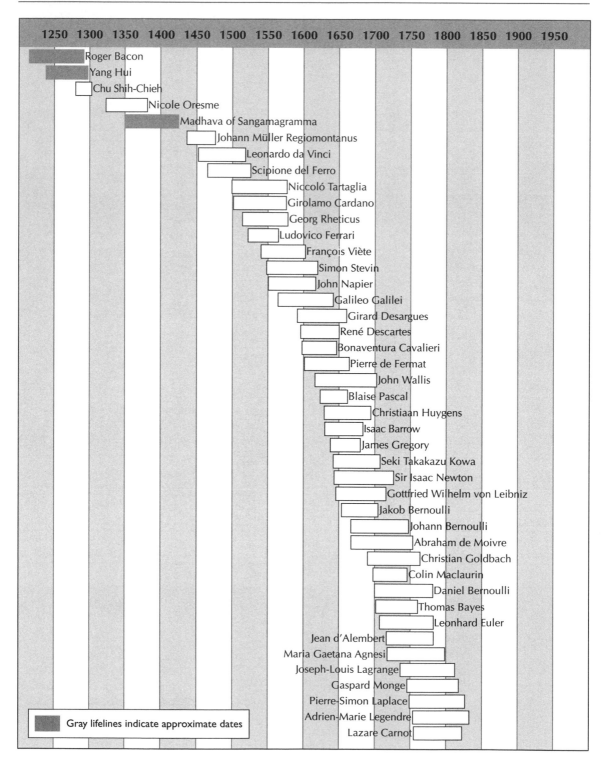

	1250	1300	1350	1400	1450	1500	1550	1600	1650	1700	1750	1800	1850	1900	1950

Roger Bacon
Yang Hui
Chu Shih-Chieh
Nicole Oresme
Madhava of Sangamagramma
Johann Müller Regiomontanus
Leonardo da Vinci
Scipione del Ferro
Niccoló Tartaglia
Girolamo Cardano
Georg Rheticus
Ludovico Ferrari
François Viète
Simon Stevin
John Napier
Galileo Galilei
Girard Desargues
René Descartes
Bonaventura Cavalieri
Pierre de Fermat
John Wallis
Blaise Pascal
Christiaan Huygens
Isaac Barrow
James Gregory
Seki Takakazu Kowa
Sir Isaac Newton
Gottfried Wilhelm von Leibniz
Jakob Bernoulli
Johann Bernoulli
Abraham de Moivre
Christian Goldbach
Colin Maclaurin
Daniel Bernoulli
Thomas Bayes
Leonhard Euler
Jean d'Alembert
Maria Gaetana Agnesi
Joseph-Louis Lagrange
Gaspard Monge
Pierre-Simon Laplace
Adrien-Marie Legendre
Lazare Carnot

Gray lifelines indicate approximate dates

	1250	1300	1350	1400	1450	1500	1550	1600	1650	1700	1750	1800	1850	1900	1950

Jean-Baptiste-Joseph Fourier

Sophie Germain

Carl Friedrich Gauss

Bernhard Bolzano

Siméon-Denis Poisson

Friedrich Wilhelm Bessel

Claude-Louis-Marie-Henri Navier

Jean-Victor Poncelet

Augustin-Louis Cauchy

August Möbius

Charles Babbage

Nikolai Lobachevsky

George Green

Jakob Steiner

Niels Henrik Abel

János Bolyai

Carl Jacobi

Gustav Peter Lejeune Dirichlet

Sir William Rowan Hamilton

Augustus De Morgan

Hermann Günter Grassmann

Joseph Liouville

Ernst Kummer

Evariste Galois

George Boole

Augusta Ada Byron Lovelace

Karl Weierstrass

George Gabriel Stokes

Pafnuty Lvovich Chebyshev

Charles Hermite

Enrico Betti

Leopold Kronecker

Bernhard Riemann

Richard Dedekind

Rudolf Lipschitz

John Venn

Camille Jordan

Josiah Willard Gibbs

Charles Peirce

Sophus Lie

Georg Cantor

Friedrich Ludwig Gottlob Frege

Felix Klein

	1250	1300	1350	1400	1450	1500	1550	1600	1650	1700	1750	1800	1850	1900	1950

Oliver Heaviside

Sonya Kovalevskaya

Jules-Henri Poincaré

Andrei Markov

Giuseppe Peano

Vito Volterra

David Hilbert

Hermann Minkowski

Ivar Fredholm

Élie Cartan

Émile Borel

George Udny Yule

Ernst Zermelo

Bertrand Russell

René-Louis Baire

Henri-Léon Lebesgue

William Gosset

Godfrey Harold Hardy

Pierre-Joseph-Louis Fatou

René-Maurice Fréchet

Guido Fubini

Frigyes Riesz

Luitzen Egbertus Jan Brouwer

Emmy Noether

George Birkhoff

Hermann Weyl

Paul-Pierre Lévy

George Pólya

Srinivasa Aiyangar Ramanujan

Sir Ronald Aylmer Fisher

Stefan Banach

Heinz Hopf

Norbert Wiener

Egon Sharpe Pearson

Kurt Friedrich Gödel

Aaboe, A. *Episodes from the Early History of Mathematics.* Washington, D.C.: Mathematical Association of America, 1964.

Ackerman, M., and R. Hermann. *Sophus Lie's 1880 Transformation Group Paper.* Brookline, Mass.: Math Sci Press, 1975.

Adamson, D. *Blaise Pascal: Mathematician, Physicist, and Thinker about God.* New York: St. Martin's, 1995.

Albers, D., and G. Alexanderson. *Mathematical People: Profiles and Interviews.* Chicago: Contemporary Books, 1985.

Alexander, D. *A History of Complex Dynamics: From Schröder to Fatou and Julia.* Braunschweig/ Wiesbaden: Friedrich Vieweg and Sohn, 1994.

Alexanderson, G. *The Random Walks of George Pólya.* Washington, D.C.: Mathematical Association of America, 2000.

Alexanderson, G., and L. Lange. "Obituary: George Pólya," *Bulletin of the London Mathematical Society* 19, no. 6 (1987): 559–608.

Allen, E. "The Scientific Work of Vito Volterra," *The American Mathematical Monthly* 48 (1941): 516–519.

Amir-Moéz, A., and J. Hamilton. "Hippocrates," *Journal of Recreational Mathematics* 7, no. 2 (1974): 105–107.

Anderson, J. *A History of Aerodynamics and Its Impact on Flying Machines.* Cambridge, U.K.: Cambridge University Press, 1997.

Anderson, K. "Cavalieri's Method of Indivisibles," *Archive for the History of Exact Sciences* 31, no. 4 (1985): 291–367.

Angelelli, I. *Studies on Gottlob Frege and Traditional Philosophy.* Dordrecht, the Netherlands: Kluwer Academic Publishers Group, 1967.

Anglin, W., and J. Lambek. *The Heritage of Thales.* New York: Springer, 1995.

Angluin, D. "Lady Lovelace and the Analytical Engine," *Association for Women in Mathematics Newsletter* 6 (1976): 6–8.

Arago, F. "Joseph Fourier," in *Biographies of Distinguished Scientific Men.* Boston: Ticknor and Fields, 1859.

Archibald, R. "The Canon Doctrinae Triangulorum (1551) of Rheticus (1514–1576)," *Mathematical Tables and Other Aids to Computation* 7 (1953): 131.

———. "The First Translation of Euclid's Elements into English and Its Source," *The American Mathematical Monthly* 57 (1950): 443–452.

———. "Rheticus, with Special Reference to His Opus Palatinum," *Mathematical Tables and Other Aids to Computation* 3 (1949): 552–561.

Ariotti, P. "Bonaventura Cavalieri, Marin Mersenne, and the Reflecting Telescope," *Isis* 66 (1975): 303–321.

Arunachalam, P. "W. R. Hamilton and His Quaternions," *Mathematical Education* 6, no. 4 (1990): 261–266.

Asimov, I. *Asimov's Biographical Encyclopedia of Science and Technology.* Garden City, N.Y.: Doubleday, 1982.

Ayer, A. *Bertrand Russell.* Chicago: University of Chicago Press, 1988.

Ayoub, R. "Euler and the Zeta Function," *The American Mathematical Monthly* 81 (1974): 1067–1086.

Babbage, C. *Passages from the Life of a Philosopher.* London: Dawsons, 1968.

Babbage, H. *Babbage's Calculating Engines.* Los Angeles: Tomash, 1982.

Baltus, C. "Continued Fractions and the Pell Equations: The Work of Euler and Lagrange," *Communications in the Analytic Theory of Continued Fractions* 3 (1994): 4–31.

Barnard, G. "Thomas Bayes—a Biographical Note," *Biometrika* 45 (1958): 293–315.

Barnes, J. *The Presocratic Philosophers.* London: Routledge and Kegan Paul, 1982.

Barrow-Green, J. *Poincaré and the Three Body Problem.* Providence, R.I.: American Mathematical Society, 1997.

Barry, P. *George Boole: A Miscellany.* Cork, Ireland: Cork University Press, 1969.

Barth, M. "Huygens at Work: Annotations in His Rediscovered Personal Copy of Hooke's 'Micrographia,'" *Annals of Science* 52, no. 6 (1995): 601–613.

Baum, J. *The Calculating Passion of Ada Bryon.* Hamden, Conn.: Archon Books, 1986.

Bechler, Z. *Newton's Physics and the Conceptual Structure of the Scientific Revolution.* Boston: Kluwer Academic Publishers, 1991.

Behnke, H., and F. Hirzebruch. "In Memoriam Heinz Hopf," *Mathematische Annalen* 196 (1972): 1–7.

Belhoste, B. *Augustin-Louis Cauchy. A Biography.* New York: Springer-Verlag, 1991.

Bell, A. *Christian Huygnes* [sic] *and the Development of Science in the Seventeenth Century.* London: E. Arnold, 1950.

Bell, E. *Men of Mathematics.* New York: Simon and Schuster, 1965.

Berg, J. *Bolzano's Logic.* Stockholm: Almqvist and Wiksell, 1962.

Berggren, J., and R. Thomas. *Euclid's "Phaenomena": A Translation and Study of a Hellenistic Treatise in Spherical Astronomy.* New York: Garland Publishing, 1996.

Bernays, P. "David Hilbert," *Encyclopedia of Philosophy III.* New York: Macmillan, 1967.

Bernkopf, M. "The Development of Functional Spaces," *Archive for History of Exact Sciences* 3 (1966–67): 1–96.

Bikerman, J. "Capillarity before Laplace: Clairaut, Segner, Monge, Young," *Archive for History of Exact Sciences* 18, no. 2 (1977/78): 103–122.

Bonola, R. *Non-Euclidean Geometry; a Critical and Historical Study of Its Developments.* New York: Dover Publications, 1955.

Bos, H., et al. "Poncelet's Closure Theorem," *Expositiones Mathematicae. International Journal for Pure and Applied Mathematics* 5, no. 4 (1987): 289–364.

Bose, A. "Fourier, His Life and Work," *Bulletin of the Calcutta Mathematical Society* 7 (1915–6): 33–48.

———. "Fourier Series and Its Influence on Some of the Developments of Mathematical Analysis," *Bulletin of the Calcutta Mathematical Society* 9 (1917–18): 71–84.

Boswell, T. "The Brothers James and John Bernoulli on the Parallelism between Logic and Algebra," *History and Philosophy of Logic* 11, no. 2 (1990): 173–184.

Box, J. R. A. *Fisher: The Life of a Scientist.* New York: John Wiley, 1978.

Boyer, C. "Carnot and the Concept of Deviation," *The American Mathematical Monthly* 61 (1954): 459–463.

Brent, J. *Charles Sanders Peirce: A Life.* Bloomington: Indiana University Press, 1998.

Brewster, D. *Memoirs of the Life, Writings, and Discoveries of Sir Isaac Newton.* New York: Johnson Reprint Corp., 1965.

Bridges, J. *The Life and Work of Roger Bacon: An Introduction to the Opus Majus*. Merrick, N.Y.: Richwood Publishing Company, 1976.

Broad, C., and C. Lewy. *Leibniz: An Introduction*. London: Cambridge University Press, 1975.

Browder, F. *The Mathematical Heritage of Henri Poincaré*. Providence, R.I.: American Mathematical Society, 1983.

Brumbaugh, R. *The Philosophers of Greece*. New York: Crowell, 1964.

Bucciarelli, L. *Sophie Germain: An Essay in the History of the Theory of Elasticity*. Boston, Mass.: Kluwer, 1980.

Bühler, W. *Gauss: A Biographical Study*. New York: Springer-Verlag, 1981.

Bulmer-Thomas, I. *Selections Illustrating the History of Greek Mathematics*. Cambridge, Mass.: Harvard University Press, 1980.

Bumstead, H. "Josiah Willard Gibbs," *American Journal of Science* 4, no. 16 (September 1903).

Burkill, J. "Henri Lebesgue," *Journal of the London Mathematical Society* 19 (1944): 56–64.

———. "Obituary: Henri Lebesgue, 1875–1941," *Obituary Notices of Fellows of the Royal Society of London* 4 (1944): 483–490.

Burnett, C. *Adelard of Bath: An English Scientist and Arabist of the Early Twelfth Century*. London: Warburg Institute, University of London, 1987.

Busard, H. *The Latin Translation of the Arabic Version of Euclid's "Elements" Commonly Ascribed to Gerard of Cremona*. Leiden, the Netherlands: Brill, 1984.

Butler, L. "George David Birkhoff," *American National Biography 2*. New York: Oxford University Press, 1999.

Butzer, P. "Dirichlet and His Role in the Founding of Mathematical Physics," *Archives Internationales d'Histoire des Sciences* 37, no. 118 (1987): 49–82.

Butzer, P., and F. Jongmans. "P. L. Chebyshev (1821–1894): A Guide to His Life and Work," *Journal of Approximation Theory* 96, no. 1 (1999): 111–138.

———. "P. L. Chebyshev (1821–1894) and His Contacts with Western European Scientists," *Historia Mathematica* 16 (1989): 46–68.

Buxton, H. *Memoir of the Life and Labors of the Late Charles Babbage Esq., F.R.S.* Los Angeles: Tomash, 1988.

Byers, N. "Emmy Noether's Discovery of the Deep Connection between Symmetries and Conservation Laws," *Israel Mathematical Conference Proceedings* 12 (1999).

———. "The Life and Times of Emmy Noether; Contributions of E. Noether to Particle Physics," in *History of Original Ideas and Basic Discoveries in Particle Physics*. New York: Plenum Press, 1996.

Calinger, R. *Classics of Mathematics*. Upper Saddle River, N.J.: Prentice Hall, 1995.

———. "The Mathematics Seminar at the University of Berlin: Origins, Founding, and the Kummer-Weierstrass Years," in *Vita Mathematica*. Washington, D.C.: Mathematical Association of America, 1996.

Campanella, T. *A Defense of Galileo, the Mathematician from Florence*. Notre Dame, Ind.: University of Notre Dame Press, 1994.

Cannell, D. *George Green: Mathematician and Physicist 1793–1841: The Background to His Life and Work*. London: Athlone Press, 1993.

Cannell, D., and N. Lord. "George Green, Mathematician and Physicist 1793–1841," *Mathematical Gazette* 66 (1993): 26–51.

Cannon, J., and S. Dostrovsky. *The Evolution of Dynamics: Vibration Theory from 1687 to 1742*. New York: Springer-Verlag, 1981.

Cartan, H. "Heinz Hopf (1894–1971)," *International Mathematical Union* (1972): 1–7.

Chan, L. "Godfrey Harold Hardy (1877–1947)— the Man and the Mathematician," *Menemui Matematik. Discovering Mathematics* 1, no. 3 (1979): 1–13.

Chandrasekhar, S. Newton's "Principia" for the Common Reader. New York: Oxford University Press, 1995.

Chatterjee, B. "Al-Biruni and Brahmagupta," Indian Journal of History of Science 10, no. 2 (1975): 161–165.

Chen, C. "A Comparative Study of Early Chinese and Greek Work on the Concept of Limit," in Science and Technology in Chinese Civilization. Singapore: World Scientific, 1987.

Chern, S., and C. Chevalley. "Elie Cartan," American Mathematical Society Bulletin 58 (1952).

Chong, P. "The Life and Work of Leonardo of Pisa," Menemui Matematik. Discovering Mathematics 4, no. 2 (1982): 60–66.

Christianson, G. In the Presence of the Creator: Isaac Newton and His Times. New York: Free Press, 1984.

Chrystal, G. "Joseph Liouville," Proceedings of the Royal Society of Edinburgh 14 (1888): 83–91.

Clagett, M. Nicole Oresme and the Medieval Geometry of Quantities and Motions. Madison: University of Wisconsin Press, 1968.

Clark, K. Leonardo da Vinci. London: Viking, 1975.

Clark, R. Bertrand Russell and His World. New York: Thames and Hudson, 1981.

———. The Life of Bertrand Russell. New York: Knopf, 1976.

Clarke, D. Descartes' Philosophy of Science. University Park: Pennsylvania State University Press, 1982.

Clerke, A. A Popular History of Astronomy during the Nineteenth Century. London: A. and C. Black, 1902.

Cohen, I. Introduction to Newton's "Principia." Cambridge, U.K.: Cambridge University Press, 1978.

Cole, T. "Democritus and the Sources of Greek Anthropology," Amer. Philos. Ass. Monograph (1967).

Coleman, F. Neither Angel nor Beast: The Life and Work of Blaise Pascal. New York: Routledge and Kegan Paul, 1986.

Collingwood, E. "Émile Borel," Journal of the London Mathematical Society 34 (1959): 488–512.

Cooke, R. The Mathematics of Sonya Kovalevskaya. New York: Springer-Verlag, 1984.

Coolidge, J. A History of Geometrical Methods. New York: Dover Publications, 1963.

Coopland, G. Nicole Oresme and the Astrologers: A Study of His "Livre de Divinacions." Liverpool: The University Press, 1952.

Coxeter, H. "Gauss as a Geometer," Historia Mathematica 4, no. 4 (1977): 379–396.

Crosland, M. The Society of Arcueil: A View of French Science at the Time of Napoleon I. Cambridge, Mass.: Harvard University Press, 1967.

Crossley, J. The Emergence of Number. Victoria, Australia: Upside Down A Book Company, 1980.

Crowther, J. Famous American Men of Science. Freeport, N.Y.: Books for Libraries Press, 1969.

Dale, A. "Thomas Bayes: A Memorial," The Mathematical Intelligencer 11, no. 3 (1989): 18–19.

van Dalen, D. "Hermann Weyl's Intuitionistic Mathematics," Bull. Symbolic Logic 1, no. 2 (1995): 145–169.

———. Mystic, Geometer, and Intuitionist: The Life of L. E. J. Brouwer. Oxford: Clarendon Press, 1999.

Dalmedico, A. "Sophie Germain," Scientific American 265 (1991): 117–122.

Datta, B. "Brahmagupta," Bulletin of the Calcutta Mathematical Society 22 (1930): 39–51.

———. "The Two Bhaskaras," Indian Historical Quarterly 6 (1930): 727–736.

Dauben, J. Georg Cantor: His Mathematics and Philosophy of the Infinite. Cambridge, Mass.: Harvard University Press, 1979.

David, H. "Egon S. Pearson, 1895–1980," The American Statistician 35, no. 2 (1981): 94–95.

Dawson, J. "Kurt Gödel in Sharper Focus," *The Mathematical Intelligencer* 6, no. 4 (1984): 9–17.

Deakin, M. "Euler's Invention of Integral Transforms," *Archive for History of Exact Sciences* 33, no. 4 (1985): 307–319.

Debrock, G., and M. Hulswit. *Living Doubt: Essays Concerning the Epistemology of Charles Sanders Peirce*. Dordrecht, the Netherlands: Kluwer Academic Publishers, 1994.

Dehn, M., and E. Hellinger. "Certain Mathematical Achievements of James Gregory," *The American Mathematical Monthly* 50 (1943): 149–163.

Deledalle, G. *Charles S. Peirce, 1839–1914: An Intellectual Biography*. Amsterdam: J. Benjamins Publishing Company, 1990.

Dennis, D., V. Kreinovich, and S. Rump. "Intervals and the Origins of Calculus," *Reliab. Comput.* 4, no. 2 (1998): 191–197.

Dick, A. *Emmy Noether, 1882–1935*. Boston: Birkhäuser, 1981.

Dicks, D. *The Geographical Fragments of Hipparchus*. London: Athlone Press, 1960.

Dijksterhuis, E. *Archimedes*. Copenhagen: E. Munksgaard, 1956.

———. "Christiaan Huygens," *Centaurus* 2 (1953): 265–282.

Doob, J. "Obituary: Paul Lévy," *Journal of Applied Probability* 9 (1972): 870–872.

Drake, S. *Galileo at Work: His Scientific Biography*. Chicago: University of Chicago Press, 1978.

———. *Galileo Studies: Personality, Tradition, and Revolution*. Ann Arbor: University of Michigan Press, 1970.

———. *Galileo*. New York: Hill and Wang, 1980.

———. *Galileo: Pioneer Scientist*. Toronto: University of Toronto Press, 1990.

Drake, S., and I. Drabkin. *Mechanics in 16th-Century Italy: Selections from Tartaglia, Benedetti, Guido Ubaldo, and Galileo*. Madison: University of Wisconsin Press, 1969.

Dreyer, J. *A History of Astronomy from Thales to Kepler*. New York: Dover Publications, 1953.

Dubbey, J. "Cauchy's Contribution to the Establishment of the Calculus," *Annals of Science* 22 (1966): 61–67.

———. *The Mathematical Work of Charles Babbage*. Cambridge, U.K.: Cambridge University Press, 1978.

Dummett, M. *Frege: Philosophy of Language*. Cambridge, Mass.: Harvard University Press, 1981.

———. *Frege: Philosophy of Mathematics*. London: Ducksworth, 1991.

———. *The Interpretation of Frege's Philosophy*. Cambridge, Mass.: Harvard University Press, 1981.

Dunham, W. *Euler: The Master of Us All*. Washington, D.C.: The Mathematical Association of America, 1999.

Dunnington, G. *Carl Friedrich Gauss, Titan of Science*. New York: Hafner, 1955.

Dupre, H. *Lazare Carnot, Republican Patriot*. Philadelphia: Porcupine Press, 1975.

Easton, S. *Roger Bacon and His Search for a Universal Science: A Reconsideration of the Life and Work of Roger Bacon in the Light of His Own Stated Purposes*. Westport, Conn.: Greenwood Press, 1970.

Edge, D. "The Omission of George Green from 'British Mathematics (1800–1830),'" *Bulletin of the Institute of Mathematics and Its Applications* 16, no. 2–3 (1980): 37.

Edwards, A. *Pascal's Arithmetical Triangle*. New York: Oxford University Press, 1987.

Edwards, H. "An Appreciation of Kronecker," *The Mathematical Intelligencer* 9 (1987): 28–35.

———. "Dedekind's Invention of Ideals," *Bulletin of the London Mathematical Society* 15, no. 1 (1983): 8–17.

———. "Euler and Quadratic Reciprocity," *Mathematics Magazine* 56, no. 5 (1983): 285–291.

———. *Fermat's Last Theorem: A Genetic Introduction to Algebraic Number Theory*. New York: Springer-Verlag, 1977.

————. "Kronecker's Place in History," in *History and Philosophy of Modern Mathematics*. Minneapolis: University of Minnesota Press, 1988.

————. "Mathematical Ideas, Ideals, and Ideology," *The Mathematical Intelligencer* 14 (1992): 6–18.

————. "On the Kronecker Nachlass," *Historia Mathematica* 5, no. 4 (1978): 419–426.

Eisele, C., and R. Martin. *Studies in the Scientific and Mathematical Philosophy of Charles S. Peirce*. New York: Mouton, 1979.

Elwin, M. *Lord Byron's Family: Annabelle, Ada, and Augusta, 1816–1824*. London: J. Murray, 1975.

Etherington, I. "Obituary: George David Birkhoff," *Edinburgh Mathematical Notes* 36 (1947): 22–23.

Ewing, J. "Leonhard Euler," *The Mathematical Intelligencer* 5, no. 3 (1983): 5–6.

Fantoli, A. *Galileo: For Copernicanism and for the Church*. Vatican City: Vatican Observatory Publications, 1994.

Fauvel, J., R. Flood, and R. Wilson. *Möbius and His Band*. Oxford: Oxford University Press, 1993.

Fearnley-Sander, D. "Hermann Grassmann and the Creation of Linear Algebra," *The American Mathematical Monthly* 86, no. 10 (1979): 809–817.

————. "Hermann Grassmann and the Prehistory of Universal Algebra," *The American Mathematical Monthly* 89, no. 3 (1982): 161–166.

Feingold, M. *Before Newton: The Life and Times of Isaac Barrow*. New York: Cambridge University Press, 1990.

————. "Newton, Leibniz, and Barrow Too: An Attempt at a Reinterpretation," *Isis* 84, no. 2 (1993): 310–338.

Ferreirós, J. "On the Relations between Georg Cantor and Richard Dedekind," *Historia Mathematica* 20 (1993): 343–363.

Feys, R. "Boole as a Logician," *Proceedings of the Royal Irish Academy. Section A. Mathematical and Physical Sciences* 57 (1955): 97–106.

Fichera, G. "Vito Volterra and the Birth of Functional Analysis," in *Development of Mathematics 1900–1950*. Basel: Birkhäuser, 1994.

Field, J. *The Invention of Infinity: Mathematics and Art in the Renaissance*. New York: Oxford University Press, 1997.

————. "Linear Perspective and the Projective Geometry of Girard Desargues," *Istituto e Museo di Storia della Scienza Firenze. Nuncius. Annali di Storia della Scienza* 2, no. 2 (1987): 3–40.

Field, J., and J. Gray. *The Geometrical Work of Girard Desargues*. New York: Springer-Verlag, 1987.

Fierz, M. *Girolamo Cardano, 1501–1576: Physician, Natural Philosopher, Mathematician, Astrologer, and Interpreter of Dreams*. Boston: Birkhäuser, 1983.

Finkel, B. "Biography: Leonard Euler," *The American Mathematical Monthly* 4 (1897): 297–302.

Fischer, H. "Dirichlet's Contribution to Mathematical Probability Theory," *Historia Mathematica* 21 (1994): 39–63.

Fisher, G. "Cauchy's Variables and Orders of the Infinitely Small," *British Journal for the Philosophy of Science* 30, no. 3 (1979): 261–265.

Fletcher, C. "G. H. Hardy-Applied Mathematician," *Bulletin of the Institute of Mathematics and Its Applications* 16, nos. 2–3 (1980): 61–67.

Forbes, E. "The Astronomical Work of Carl Friedrich Gauss (1777–1855)," *Historia Mathematica* 5, no. 2 (1978): 167–181.

————. "Gauss and the Discovery of Ceres," *Journal for the History of Astronomy* 2, no. 3 (1971): 195–199.

Fowler, D. *The Mathematics of Plato's Academy: A New Reconstruction*. Oxford: Clarendon Press, 1999.

Franchella, M. "L. E. J. Brouwer: Toward Intuitionistic Logic," *Historia Mathematica* 22, no. 3 (1995): 304–322.

Fraser, C. "Isoperimetric Problems in the Variational Calculus of Euler and Lagrange," *Historia Mathematica* 19, no. 1 (1992): 4–23.

Fraser, P. *Ptolemaic Alexandria*. Oxford: Clarendon Press, 1972.

Frei G., and U. Stammbach. "Heinz Hopf," in *History of Topology*. Amsterdam: Elsevier Science B.V., 1999.

Fricke, W. "Friedrich Wilhelm Bessel (1784–1846)," *Astrophysics and Space Science* 110, no. 1 (1985): 11–19.

Fritzsche, B. "Sophus Lie: A Sketch of His Life and Work," *J. Lie Theory* 9, no. 1 (1999): 1–38.

Garding, L. *Mathematics and Mathematicians: Mathematics in Sweden before 1950*. Providence, R.I.: American Mathematical Society, 1998.

Gaukroger, S. *Descartes: Philosophy, Mathematics, and Physics*. Sussex: Harvester Press, 1980.

Geller, B., and Y. Bruk. "A Portrait of Poisson," *Quantum* (1991): 21–25.

George, R. "Bolzano's Concept of Consequence," *Journal of Philosophy* 83, no. 10 (1986): 558–564.

———. "Bolzano's Consequence, Relevance, and Enthymemes," *Journal of Philosophical Logic* 12, no. 3 (1983): 299–318.

Geymonat, L. *Galileo Galilei*. Turin: Piccola Biblioteca Einaudi, 1969.

Gies, J., and F. Gies. *Leonard of Pisa and the New Mathematics of the Middle Ages*. New York: Crowell, 1969.

Gillies, D. *Frege, Dedekind, and Peano on the Foundations of Arithmetic*. Assen, the Netherlands: Van Gorcum, 1982.

———. "Was Bayes a Bayesian?" *Historia Mathematica* 14, no. 4 (1987): 325–346.

Gillispie, C. *Dictionary of Scientific Biography*. New York: Scribner, 1970.

———. *Pierre-Simon Laplace, 1749–1827: A Life in Exact Science*. Princeton, N.J.: Princeton University Press, 1997.

Gingerich, O. *The Eye of Heaven: Ptolemy, Copernicus, Kepler*. New York: American Institute of Physics, 1993.

Giorello, G. "The 'Fine Structure' of Mathematical Revolutions: Metaphysics, Legitimacy, and Rigour, The Case of the Calculus from Newton to Berkeley and Maclaurin," in *Revolutions in Mathematics*. New York: Oxford University Press, 1995.

Gjertsen, D. *The Newton Handbook*. New York: Routledge and Kegan Paul, 1986.

Goldstein, B. "Eratosthenes on the 'Measurement' of the Earth," *Historia Mathematica* 11, no. 4 (1984): 411–416.

Gorini, Catherine A. *The Facts On File Geometry Handbook*. New York: Facts On File, 2003.

Gower, B. "Planets and Probability: Daniel Bernoulli on the Inclinations of the Planetary Orbits," *Studies in History and Philosophy of Science* 18, no. 4 (1987): 441–454.

Gower, J. "Ronald Aylmer Fisher 1890–1962," *Mathematical Spectrum* 23 (1990–91): 76–86.

Grabiner, J. *The Origins of Cauchy's Rigorous Calculus*. Cambridge, Mass.: MIT Press, 1981.

———. "Who Gave You the Epsilon? Cauchy and the Origins of Rigorous Calculus," *The American Mathematical Monthly* 90, no. 3 (1983): 185–194.

Grant, E. "Nicole Oresme and His *De Proportionibus Proportionum*," *Isis* 51 (1960): 293–314.

———. "Nicole Oresme and the Commensurability or Incommensurability of Celestial Motions," *Archive for History of Exact Sciences* 1 (1961).

Grasshoff, G. *The History of Ptolemy's Star Catalogue*. New York: Springer-Verlag, 1990.

Grattan-Guinness, I. "Bolzano, Cauchy and the 'New Analysis' of the Early Nineteenth Century," *Archive for History of Exact Sciences* 6 (1970): 372–400.

————. *The Development of the Foundations of Mathematical Analysis from Euler to Riemann.* Cambridge, Mass.: MIT Press, 1970.

————. *Joseph Fourier, 1768–1830: A Survey of His Life and Work.* Cambridge, Mass.: MIT Press, 1972.

————. "Towards a Biography of Georg Cantor," *Annals of Science* 27 (1971): 345–391.

Graves, R. *Life of Sir William Rowan Hamilton.* New York: Arno Press, 1975.

Grimsley, R. *Jean d'Alembert, 1717–83.* Oxford: Clarendon Press, 1963.

Grinstein, L., and P. Campbell. *Women of Mathematics.* New York: Greenwood Press, 1987.

Grunbaum, A. *Modern Science and Zeno's Paradoxes.* London: Allen and Unwin, 1968.

Gupta, R. C. "Aryabhata, Ancient India's Great Astronomer and Mathematician," *Mathematical Education* 10, no. 4 (1976): B69–B73.

————. "A Preliminary Bibliography on Aryabhata I," *Mathematical Education* 10, no. 2 (1976): B21–B26.

Guthrie, W. *The Greek Philosophers: From Thales to Aristotle.* New York: Harper and Row, 1960.

————. *A History of Greek Philosophy.* Cambridge, U.K.: Cambridge University Press, 1981.

Hacking, I. "Jacques Bernoulli's 'Art of Conjecturing,'" *British Journal for the Philosophy of Science* 22 (1971): 209–229.

Hahm, D. "Chrysippus' Solution to the Democritean Dilemma of the Cone," *Isis* 63, no. 217 (1972): 205–220.

Haldane, E. *Descartes: His Life and Times.* London: J. Murray, 1905.

Hall, A. *Isaac Newton, Adventurer in Thought.* Oxford: Blackwell, 1992.

Hall, T. *Carl Friedrich Gauss: A Biography.* Cambridge, Mass.: MIT Press, 1970.

Halsted, G. "Biography: De Morgan," *The American Mathematical Monthly* 4 (1897): 1–5.

————. "Biography. Lobachevsky," *The American Mathematical Monthly* 2 (1895): 137.

————. "Biography. Professor Felix Klein," *The American Mathematical Monthly* 1 (1894): 416–420.

Hamel, J. *Friedrich Wilhelm Bessel.* Leipzig: BSB B.G. Teubner, 1984.

Hancock, H. *Development of the Minkowski Geometry of Numbers.* New York: Dover Publications, 1964.

Hankins, L. *Sir William Rowan Hamilton.* Baltimore: Johns Hopkins University Press, 1980.

Hankins, T. *Jean d'Alembert: Science and the Enlightenment.* Oxford: Clarendon Press, 1970.

Hardy, G. *Bertrand Russell and Trinity.* Cambridge, U.K.: University Press, 1942.

————. *Ramanujan: Twelve Lectures on Subjects Suggested by His Life and Work.* New York: Chelsea Publishing Company, 1959.

Hawkins, T. "Jacobi and the Birth of Lie's Theory of Groups," *Archive for History of Exact Sciences* 42, no. 3 (1991): 187–278.

Heath, A. "Hermann Grassmann, The Neglect of His Work," *Monist* 27 (1917): 1–56.

Heath, T. *Aristarchus of Samos, the Ancient Copernicus.* Oxford: Clarendon Press, 1966.

————. *Diophantus of Alexandria: A Study in the History of Greek Algebra.* New York: Dover Publications, 1964.

————. *A History of Greek Mathematics.* Oxford: Clarendon Press, 1921.

————. *A Manual of Greek Mathematics.* Oxford: Clarendon Press, 1931.

————. *The Thirteen Books of Euclid's Elements.* New York: Dover Publications, 1956.

————. *Treatise on Conic Section.* New York: Barnes and Noble, 1961.

van Heijenoort, J. *From Frege to Gödel: A Source Book of Mathematical Logic.* Cambridge, Mass.: Harvard University Press, 1967.

Heims, S. *John Von Neumann and Norbert Wiener: From Mathematics to the Technologies of Life and Death.* Cambridge, Mass.: MIT Press, 1980.

Hellman, C. "Legendre and the French Reform of Weights and Measures," *Osiris* 1 (1936): 314–340.

Herivel, J. "The Influence of Fourier on British Mathematics," *Centaurus* 17, no. 1 (1972): 40–57.

———. *Joseph Fourier: The Man and the Physicist.* Oxford: Clarendon Press, 1975.

Hermann, R. *Lie Groups: History, Frontiers and Applications.* Brookline, Mass.: Math Sci Press, 1979.

Hill, L. "Fraenkel's Biography of Georg Cantor," *Scripta Mathematica* 2 (1933): 41–47.

Hoare, G., and N. Lord. "Stefan Banach (1892–1945): A Commemoration of His Life and Work," *The Mathematical Gazette* 79 (1995): 456–470.

Hofstadter, D. *Gödel, Escher, Bach: An Eternal Golden Braid.* New York: Basic Books, 1999.

Hogendijk, J. "Al-Khwarizmi's Table of the 'Sine of the Hours' and the Underlying Sine Table," *Historia Scientiarum* 42 (1991): 1–12.

———. "Arabic Traces of Lost Works of Apollonius," *Archive for History of Exact Sciences* 35, no. 3 (1986): 187–253.

———. *Ibn al-Haytham's "Completion of the Conics."* New York: Springer-Verlag, 1985.

Hollingdale, S. "Archimedes of Syracuse: A Tribute on the 22nd Century of His Death," *Bulletin of the Institute of Mathematics and Its Applications* 25, no. 9 (1989): 217–225.

———. "Isaac Barrow (1630–1677)," *Bulletin of the Institute of Mathematics and Its Applications* 13, nos. 11–12 (1977): 258–262.

Hooper, A. *Makers of Mathematics.* New York: Random House, 1958.

Hostler, J. *Leibniz's Moral Philosophy.* London: Duckworth, 1975.

Householder, A. "Dandelin, Lobachevskii, or Gräffe?" *The American Mathematical Monthly* 66 (1959): 464–466.

Hughes, B. "Hippocrates and Archytas Double the Cube: A Heuristic Interpretation," *The College Mathematics Journal* 20, no. 1 (1989): 42–48.

Huxley, G. "Eudoxian Topics," *Greek, Roman and Byzantine Studies* 4 (1963): 83–96.

Hyman, A. *Charles Babbage: Pioneer of the Computer.* Princeton, N.J.: Princeton University Press, 1982.

Ifrah, G. *A Universal History of Numbers: From Prehistory to the Invention of the Computer.* New York: John Wiley, 2000.

Indorato, L., and P. Nastasi. "The 1740 Resolution of the Fermat-Descartes Controversy," *Historia Mathematica* 16, no. 2 (1989): 137–148.

Ishiguro, H. *Leibniz's Philosophy of Logic and Language.* New York: Cambridge University Press, 1990.

Jain, L. "Aryabhata I and Yativrsabha—A Study in Kalpa and Meru," *Indian Journal of History of Science* 12, no. 2 (1977): 137–146.

Jerison, D., and D. Stroock. "Norbert Wiener," *Notices of the American Mathematical Society* 42 (1995): 430–438.

Johnson, D. "The Correspondence of Camille Jordan," *Historia Mathematica* 4 (1977): 210.

Johnson, N., and S. Kotz. *Leading Personalities in Statistical Sciences.* New York: John Wiley, 1997.

Joseph, G. *The Crest of the Peacock: Non-European Roots of Mathematics.* London: Penguin Books, 1990.

Kagan, V. N. *Lobachevsky and His Contribution to Science.* Moscow: Foreign Languages Publishing House, 1957.

Kanigel, R. *The Man Who Knew Infinity: A Life of the Genius Ramanujan.* New York: Scribner's, 1991.

Kauza, R. *Through a Reporter's Eyes: The Life of Stefan Banach.* Boston: Birkhäuser, 1996.

Kemp, M. *Leonardo da Vinci: The Marvelous Works of Nature and Man.* London: J. M. Dent, 1981.

Kendall, D. "Obituary: Maurice Fréchet, 1878–1973," *Journal of the Royal Statistical Society. Series A. Statistics in Society* 140, no. 4 (1977): 566.

———. "Obituary: Paul Lévy," *Journal of the Royal Statistical Society. Series A. Statistics in Society* 137 (1974): 259–260.

Kendall, M. "George Udny Yule 1871–1951," *Journal of the Royal Statistical Society* 115 (1952): 156–161.

Kennedy, A., and W. Ukashah. "Al-Khwarizmi's Planetary Latitude Tables," *Centaurus* 14 (1969): 86–96.

Kennedy, D. *Little Sparrow: A Portrait of Sophia Kovalevsky*. Athens: Ohio University Press, 1983.

Kennedy, E. "Al-Khwarizmi on the Jewish Calendar," *Scripta Mathematica* 27 (1964): 55–59.

Kennedy, H. "Peano's Concept of Number," *Historia Mathematica* 1 (1974): 387–408.

———. *Peano, Life and Works of Giuseppe Peano*. Dordrecht, the Netherlands: D. Reidel Publishing Company, 1980.

Kenney, E. "Cardano: 'Arithmetic Subtlety' and Impossible Solutions," *Philosophia Mathematica II* (1989): 195–216.

Kenny, A. *Frege*. London: Penguin Books, 1995.

Kevelson, R. *Charles S. Peirce's Method of Methods*. Amsterdam: J. Benjamins Publishing Company, 1987.

Kimberling, C. *Emmy Noether: A Tribute to Her Life and Work*. New York: Marcel Dekker, 1981.

Kinsella, A. "Sir George Gabriel Stokes: The Malahide Connection," *Irish Mathematical Society Bulletin* 35 (1995): 59–62.

Kirk, G., J. Raven, and M. Schofield. *The Presocratic Philosophers: A Critical History with a Selection of Texts*. Cambridge, U.K.: Cambridge University Press, 1983.

Klein, F. *Development of Mathematics in the 19th Century*. Brookline, Mass.: Math Sci Press, 1979.

Klein, J. *Greek Mathematical Thought and the Origin of Algebra*. Cambridge, Mass.: MIT Press, 1968.

Klemke, E. *Essays on Bertrand Russell*. Urbana: University of Illinois Press, 1970.

Kneale, W. "Boole and the Revival of Logic," *Mind* 57 (1948): 149–175.

Knorr, W. "What Euclid Meant: On the Use of Evidence in Studying Ancient Mathematics," in *Science and Philosophy in Classical Greece*. New York: Garland, 1991.

Koblitz, A. *A Convergence of Lives. Sofia Kovalevskaia: Scientist, Writer, Revolutionary*. Boston: Birkhäuser, 1983.

Koch, H. "Gustav Peter Lejeune Dirichlet," in *Mathematics in Berlin*. Boston: Birkhäuser Verlag, 1998.

Koetsier, T. "Joseph Louis Lagrange (1736–1813): His Life, His Work and His Personality," *Nieuw Archief voor Wiskunde* 4, no. 3 (1986): 191–205.

Krailsheimer, A. *Pascal*. New York: Oxford University Press, 1980.

Kuntz, P. *Bertrand Russell*. Boston: Twayne Publishers, 1986.

Laertius, D. *Lives, Teachings, and Sayings of Famous Philosophers*. Cambridge, Mass.: Harvard University Press, 1959.

Laird, W. "Archimedes among the Humanists," *Isis* 82, no. 314 (1991): 629–638.

Lam, L. *A Critical Study of the "Yang Hui Suan fa": A Thirteenth-Century Chinese Mathematical Treatise*. Singapore: Singapore University Press, 1977.

Langermann, Y. *Ibn al-Haytham's "On the Configuration of the World."* New York: Garland, 1990.

Larmor, J. *Memoir and Scientific Correspondence of the Late Sir George Gabriel Stokes*. Cambridge, U.K.: Cambridge University Press, 1907.

Lawrynowicz, K. *Friedrich Wilhelm Bessel, 1784–1846*. Basel: Birkhäuser Verlag, 1995.

Lewis, D. "David Hilbert and the Theory of Algebraic Invariants," *Irish Mathematical Society Bulletin* 33 (1994): 42–54.

Leybourn, W. *The Art of Numbring by Speaking Rods, Vulgarly Termed Nepeirs Bones* [sic]. Ann Arbor, Michigan: University Microfilms, 1968.

Lindberg, D. *Roger Bacon's Philosophy of Nature: A Critical Edition*. Oxford: Clarendon Press, 1983.

———. "Science as Handmaiden: Roger Bacon and the Patristic Tradition," *Isis* 78, no. 294 (1987): 518–536.

Lützen, J. *Joseph Liouville, 1809–1882, Master of Pure and Applied Mathematics*. New York: Springer-Verlag, 1990.

MacDuffee, C. "Algebra's Debt to Hamilton." *Scripta Mathematica* 10 (1944): 25–35.

MacHale, D. *George Boole: His Life and Work*. Dublin: Boole Press, 1985.

Malet, A. "Barrow, Wallis, and the Remaking of Seventeenth Century Indivisibles," *Centaurus* 39, no. 1 (1997): 67–92.

Mancosu, P. *From Brouwer to Hilbert: The Debate on the Foundations of Mathematics in the 1920s*. New York: Oxford University Press, 1998.

Mandrekar, V. "Mathematical Work of Norbert Wiener," *Notices of the American Mathematical Society* 42 (1995): 664–669.

Manning, K. "The Emergence of the Weierstrassian Approach to Complex Analysis," *Archive for History of Exact Sciences* 14, no. 4 (1975): 297–383.

Maor, Eli. *The Facts On File Calculus Handbook*. New York: Facts On File, 2003.

Martzloff, J. *A History of Chinese Mathematics*. Berlin Heidelberg: Springer-Verlag, 1997.

May, K. "Biographical Sketch of Henri Lebesgue," in *Measure and the Integral by Henri Lebesgue*. San Francisco: Holden-Day, 1966.

McLanathan, R. *Images of the Universe; Leonardo da Vinci: The Artist as Scientist*. Garden City, N.Y.: Doubleday, 1966.

Meli, D. *Equivalence and Priority: Newton versus Leibniz; Including Leibniz's Unpublished Manuscripts on the "Principia."* Oxford: Clarendon Press, 1993.

Merz, J. *Leibniz*. Edinburgh: Blackwood, 1884.

Mesnard, J. *Pascal*. Paris: Hatier, 1951.

Mikami, Y. *The Development of Mathematics in China and Japan*. New York: Chelsea Publishing Company, 1974.

Miller, A. *Imagery in Scientific Thought: Creating 20th Century Physics*. Cambridge, Mass.: MIT Press, 1986.

———. *Insights of Genius: Imagery and Creativity in Science and Art*. New York: Copernicus, 1996.

Milne, E. "Obituary: Godfrey Harold Hardy," *Royal Astronomical Society. Monthly Notices* 108 (1948): 44–46.

Monastyrsky, M. *Rieman, Topology and Physics*. Boston: Birkhäuser, 1987.

Monk, R. *Bertrand Russell: The Spirit of Solitude*. New York: Free Press, 1996.

Moody, D., and M. Clagett. *The Medieval Science of Weights*. Madison: University of Wisconsin Press, 1960.

Moore, D. *Ada, Countess of Lovelace: Byron's Legitimate Daughter*. London: J. Murray, 1977.

Moore, G. "Ernst Zermelo, A. E. Harward, and the Axiomatization of Set Theory," *Historia Mathematica* 3, no. 2 (1976): 206–209.

Moore, P. "A Tribute to Egon Sharpe Pearson," *Journal of the Royal Statistical Society. Series A. Statistics in Society* 138, no. 2 (1975): 129–130.

Morrison, P., and E. Morrison. *Charles Babbage and His Calculating Engines*. New York: Dover Publications, 1961.

Morse, M. "George David Birkhoff and His Mathematical Work," *American Mathematical Society. Bulletin. New Series* 52 (1946): 357–391.

Mortimer, E. *Blaise Pascal: The Life and Work of a Realist*. New York: Harper, 1959.

Nahin, P. *Oliver Heaviside, Sage in Solitude: The Life, Work, and Times of an Electrical Genius* of the Victorian Age. New York: IEEE Press, 1988.

Needham, J. Science and Civilisation in China. Cambridge, U.K.: Cambridge University Press, 1959.

Nemeth, L. "The Two Bolyais," The New Hungarian Quarterly 1 (1960).

Neugebauer, O. "Archimedes and Aristarchus," Isis 34 (1942): 4–6.

———. The Exact Sciences in Antiquity. Providence, R.I.: Brown University Press, 1957.

———. A History of Ancient Mathematical Astronomy. New York: Springer-Verlag, 1975.

Newman, M. "Godfrey Harold Hardy, 1877–1947," The Mathematical Gazette 32 (1948): 50–51.

———. "Hermann Weyl," Journal of the London Mathematical Society 33 (1958): 500–511.

Newton, R. The Crime of Claudius Ptolemy. Baltimore: Johns Hopkins University Press, 1977.

Ng, L. "Evariste Galois," Mathematical Medley 22, no. 1 (1995): 32–33.

O'Meara, D. Pythagoras Revived: Mathematics and Philosophy in Late Antiquity. New York: Oxford University Press, 1989.

Ore, O. Cardano, the Gambling Scholar. Princeton, N.J.: Princeton University Press, 1953.

———. Niels Henrik Abel, Mathematician Extraordinary. Minneapolis: University of Minnesota Press, 1974.

Osborne, C. "Archimedes on the Dimension of the Cosmos," Isis 74, no. 272 (1983): 234–242.

Papini, P. "Guido Fubini 1879–1943," European Mathematical Society Newsletter 9 (1993): 10.

Pappas, J. Voltaire and d'Alembert. Bloomington: Indiana University Press, 1962.

Parshall, K. "The Art of Algebra from al-Khwarizmi to Viète: A Study in the Natural Selection of Ideas," History of Sciences 26, nos. 72, 2 (1988): 129–164.

Patwardhan, K., S. Naimpally, and S. Singh. Lilavati of Bhaskaracarya. Delhi: Motilal Banarsidass Publications, 2001.

Pearl, L. Descartes. Boston: Twayne Publishers, 1977.

Pearson, E. The Selected Papers of E. S. Pearson. Berkeley: University of California Press, 1966.

Peckhaus, V. "Ernst Zermelo in Göttingen," History and Philosophy of Logic 11, no. 1 (1990): 19–58.

Petersen, O. A Survey of the Almagest. Odense, Denmark: Odense Universitetsforlag, 1974.

Picon, A. "Navier and the Introduction of Suspension Bridges in France," Construction History 4 (1988): 21–34.

Pieper, H. "Carl Gustav Jacob Jacobi," in Mathematics in Berlin. Berlin: Birkhäuser Verlag, 1998.

Pintz, J. "On Legendre's Prime Number Formula," The American Mathematical Monthly 87, no. 9 (1980): 733–735.

Plackett, R. "The Influence of Laplace and Gauss in Britain," Bulletin de l'Institut International de Statistique 53, no. 1 (1989): 163–176.

Pyenson, L. "Hermann Minkowski and Einstein's Special Theory of Relativity," Archive for History of Exact Sciences 17, no. 1 (1977): 71–95.

Ranganathan, S. Ramanujan: The Man and the Mathematician. London: Asia Publishing House, 1967.

Rashed, R. The Development of Arabic Mathematics: Between Arithmetic and Algebra. Boston: Kluwer Academic, 1994.

Rawlins, D. "Eratosthenes' Geodest Unraveled: Was There a High-Accuracy Hellenistic Astronomy," Isis 73 (1982): 259–265.

Redondi, P. Galileo Heretic. Princeton, N.J.: Princeton University Press, 1987.

Reid, C. Hilbert-Courant. New York: Springer-Verlag, 1986.

———. Neyman—from Life. New York: Springer-Verlag, 1982.

Rescher, N. *Leibniz: An Introduction to His Philosophy.* Oxford: Blackwell, 1979.

Ribenboim, P. "Kummer's Ideas on Fermat's Last Theorem," *L'Enseignement Mathématique. Revue Internationale. Deuxième Série* 2, no. 29 (1–2) (1983): 165–177.

Rice, A. "Augustus De Morgan: Historian of Science," *History of Science* 34 (1996): 201–240.

———. "Augustus De Morgan (1806–1871)," *The Mathematical Intelligencer* 18, no. 3 (1996): 40–43.

Richards, J. "Augustus De Morgan, the History of Mathematics, and the Foundations of Algebra," *Isis* 78, no. 291 (1987): 7–30.

Ritagelli, L. *Evariste Galois (1811–1832).* Boston: Springer-Verlag, 1996.

Roberts, D. *The Existential Graphs of Charles S. Peirce.* The Hague, the Netherlands: Mouton, 1973.

Rogosinski, W. "Frederic Riesz," *Journal of the London Mathematical Society* 31, no. 4 (1956): 508–512.

Ronan, C. *Galileo.* New York: Putnam, 1974.

van Rootselaar, B. "Bolzano's Theory of Real Numbers," *Archive for History of Exact Sciences* 2 (1964/1965): 168–180.

Rose, P. *The Italian Renaissance of Mathematics: Studies on Humanists and Mathematicians from Petrarch to Galileo.* Geneva: Droz, 1975.

Rosen, M. I. "Niels Henrik Abel and the Equation of the Fifth Degree," *The American Mathematical Monthly* 102 (1995): 495–505.

Ross, G. *Leibniz.* New York: Oxford University Press, 1984.

Rowe, D. "David Hilbert on Poincaré, Klein, and the World of Mathematics," *The Mathematical Intelligencer* 8, no. 1 (1986): 75–77.

———. "The Early Geometrical Works of Sophus Lie and Felix Klein," in *The History of Modern Mathematics.* Boston: Academic Press, 1989.

———. "Gauss, Dirichlet and the Law of Biquadratic Reciprocity," *The Mathematical Intelligencer* 10 (1988): 13–26.

———. "Klein, Hilbert, and the Göttingen Mathematical Tradition," *Osiris* 2, no. 5 (1989): 186–213.

———. "The Philosophical Views of Klein and Hilbert: The Intersection of History and Mathematics," *Science Networks. Historical Studies* 15 (1994): 187–202.

Rukeyser, M. *Willard Gibbs.* Garden City, N.Y.: Doubleday, Doran and Company, 1942.

Russell, B. *History of Western Philosophy and Its Connection with Political and Social Circumstances from the Ancient Times to the Present Day.* London: Allen and Unwin, 1961.

———. *The Principles of Mathematics.* London: G. Allen and Unwin, 1964.

Rutherford, D. *Leibniz and the Rational Order of Nature.* New York: Cambridge University Press, 1995.

Sabra, A. *The Optics of ibn al-Haytham.* London: Warburg Institute, University of London, 1989.

Salmon, W. "John Venn's Logic of Chance," in *Proceedings of the 1978 Pisa Conference on the History and Philosophy of Science.* Dordrecht, the Netherlands: D. Reidel Publishing Company, 1981.

———. *Zeno's Paradoxes.* Indianapolis: Bobbs-Merrill, 1970.

Sarton, G. *A History of Science.* Cambridge, Mass.: Harvard University Press, 1959.

———. "Lagrange's Personality (1736–1813)," *Proc. Amer. Philos. Soc.* 88 (1944): 457–496.

Savage, L. *The Foundations of Statistics.* New York: Dover Publications, 1972.

Scharlau, W. "The Mathematical Correspondence of Rudolf Lipschitz," *Historia Mathematica* 13, no. 2 (1986): 165–167.

Schlapp, R. "Colin Maclaurin: A Biographical Note," *Edinburgh Mathematical Notes* 37 (1949): 1–6.

Scott, J. "The Reverend John Wallis, F.R.S.," *Notes and Records of the Royal Society of London* 15 (1960–61): 57–68.

———. *The Scientific Work of René Descartes.* New York: Garland, 1987.

Scriba, C. "The Autobiography of John Wallis, F.R.S.," *Notes and Records of the Royal Society of London* 25 (1970): 17–46.

———. "A Tentative Index of the Correspondence of John Wallis, F.R.S.," *Notes and Records of the Royal Society of London* 22 (1967): 58–93.

———. "Wallis and Harriot," *Centaurus* 10 (1965): 248–257.

Seeger, R. J. *Willard Gibbs, American Mathematical Physicist par Excellence.* Oxford: Pergamon Press, 1974.

Sesiano, J. *Books IV to VII of Diophantus' "Arithmetica" in the Arabic Translation Attributed to Qusta ibn Luqa.* New York: Springer-Verlag, 1982.

Shea, W. *Galileo's Intellectual Revolution: Middle Period, 1610–1632.* New York: Science History Publications, 1977.

———. *The Magic of Numbers and Motion: The Scientific Career of René Descartes.* Canton, Mass.: Science History Publications, 1991.

Shen, K. "Historical Development of the Chinese Remainder Theorem," *Archive for History of Exact Sciences* 38, no. 4 (1988): 285–305.

Sheynin, O. "A. A. Markov's Work on Probability," *Archive for History of Exact Sciences* 39 (1988): 337–377.

———. "C. F. Gauss and the Theory of Errors," *Archive for History of Exact Sciences* 20, no. 1 (1979): 21–72.

Singh, S. *Fermat's Last Theorem: The Story of a Riddle That Confounded the World's Greatest Minds for 358 Years.* London: Fourth Estate, 1998.

Smith, A. "Ptolemy's Theory of Visual Perception," *Transactions of the American Philosophical Society* 86, pt. 2 (1996).

Smith, D., and Y. Mikami. *A History of Japanese Mathematics.* Chicago: Open Court Publishing Company, 1914.

Smith, G. "Thomas Bayes and Fluxions," *Historia Mathematica* 7, no. 4 (1980): 379–388.

Smith, P. "Josiah Willard Gibbs," *American Mathematical Society. Bulletin. New Series* 10 (1903).

Smith, R. *Teacher's Guide to Napier's Bones.* Burlington, N.C.: Carolina Biological Supply Company, 1995.

Snow, C. "Foreword," in *A Mathematician's Apology* by G. H. Hardy. Cambridge, U.K.: Cambridge University Press, 1967.

Sorabji, R. *Time, Creation and the Continuum.* Ithaca, N.Y.: Cornell University Press, 1983.

Sorell, T. *Descartes.* New York: Oxford University Press, 1987.

Sprott, D. "Gauss's Contributions to Statistics," *Historia Mathematica* 5, no. 2 (1978): 183–203.

Srinivasan, B., and J. Sally. *Emmy Noether in Bryn Mawr.* New York: Springer-Verlag, 1983.

Stander, D. "Makers of Modern Mathematics: Charles Hermite," *Bulletin of the Institute of Mathematics and Its Applications* 24, nos. 7–8 (1988): 120–121.

———. "Makers of Modern Mathematics: Joseph Liouville," *Bulletin of the Institute of Mathematics and Its Applications* 24, nos. 3–4 (1988): 59–60.

———. "Makers of Modern Mathematics: Niels Henrik Abel," *Bulletin of the Institute of Mathematics and Its Applications* 23, nos. 6–7 (1987): 107–109.

———. "Makers of Modern Mathematics: Pafnuty Liwowich Chebyshev," *Bulletin of the Institute of Mathematics and Its Applications* 26, nos. 1–2 (1990): 18–19.

Stein, D. *Ada: A Life and a Legacy.* Cambridge, Mass.: MIT Press, 1985.

Stein, H. "Eudoxos and Dedekind: On the Ancient Greek Theory of Ratios and Its

Relation to Modern Mathematics," *Synthese* 84, no. 2 (1990): 163–211.

Stigler, S. "Gauss and the Invention of Least Squares," *The Annals of Statistics* 9, no. 3 (1981): 465–474.

———. *The History of Statistics: The Measurement of Uncertainty before 1900.* Cambridge, Mass.: Belknap Press of Harvard University Press, 1986.

———. "Laplace's Early Work: Chronology and Citations," *Isis* 69, no. 247 (1978): 234–254.

———. "Studies in the History of Probability and Statistics XXXII: Laplace, Fisher, and the Discovery of the Concept of Sufficiency," *Biometrika* 60 (1973): 439–445.

———. "Thomas Bayes's Bayesian Inference," *Journal of the Royal Statistical Society. Series A. Statistics in Society* 145, no. 2 (1982): 250–258.

van Stigt, W. "L. E. J. Brouwer: Intuitionism and Topology," *Proceedings, Bicentennial Congress Wiskundig Genootschap* (1979): 359–374.

———. "L. E. J. Brouwer 'Life, Art and Mysticism,'" *Notre Dame Journal of Formal Logic* 37, no. 3 (1996): 389–429.

Struik, D. *The Land of Stevin and Huygens.* Dordrecht, the Netherlands: D. Reidel Publishing Company, 1981.

Swift, J. "Diophantus of Alexandria," *The American Mathematical Monthly* 63 (1956): 163–170.

Synge, J. "The Life and Early Work of Sir William Rowan Hamilton," *Scripta Mathematica* 10 (1944): 13–24.

Tahir, H. "Pappus and Mathematical Induction," *Australian Mathematical Society. Gazette* 22, no. 4 (1995): 166–167.

Tait, P. "Scientific Worthies V—George Gabriel Stokes," *Nature* 12 (July 15, 1875), 201–202.

Taylor, A. "A Study of Maurice Fréchet I," *Archive for History of Exact Sciences* 27 (1982): 233–295.

———. "A Study of Maurice Fréchet II," *Archive for History of Exact Sciences* 34 (1985): 279–380.

———. "A Study of Maurice Fréchet III," *Archive for History of Exact Sciences* 37 (1987): 25–76.

Taylor, G. "George Boole, 1815–1864," *Proceedings of the Royal Irish Academy. Section A. Mathematical and Physical Sciences* 57 (1955): 66–73.

Todd, Deborah. *The Facts On File Algebra Handbook.* New York: Facts On File, 2003.

Toole, B. *Ada, the Enchantress of Numbers: Prophet of the Computer Age, a Pathway to the 21st Century.* Mill Valley, Calif.: Strawberry Press, 1998.

Toomer, G. *Ptolemy's Almagest.* London: Duckworth, 1984.

Truesdell, C. "Correction and Additions for Maria Gaetana Agnesi," *Archive for History of Exact Sciences* 43 (1991): 385–386.

Turnbull, H. "Colin Maclaurin," *The American Mathematical Monthly* 54 (1947).

———. *The Mathematical Discoveries of Newton.* London: Blackie and Son, 1945.

Ulam, S. *Adventures of a Mathematician.* Berkeley: University of California Press, 1991.

Vogel, C. de *Pythagoras and Early Pythagoreanism.* Assen, the Netherlands: Van Gorcum, 1966.

Vucinich, A. "Nicolai Ivanovich Lobachevskii: The Man behind the First Non-Euclidean Geometry," *Isis* 53 (1962): 465–481.

van der Waerden, B. "The 'Day of Brahman' in the Work of Aryabhata," *Archive for History of Exact Sciences* 38, no. 1 (1988): 13–22.

———. *Science Awakening.* Leyden, the Netherlands: Noordhof International, 1975.

Walker, H. "Abraham De Moivre," *Scripta Mathematica* 2 (1934): 316–333.

Wang, H. "Kurt Gödel's Intellectual Development," *The Mathematical Intelligencer* 1, no. 3 (1978): 182–185.

———. *Reflections on Kurt Gödel.* Cambridge, Mass.: MIT Press, 1987.

————. "Some Facts about Kurt Gödel," *Journal of Symbolic Logic* 46, no. 3 (1981): 653–659.

Watling, J. *Bertrand Russell*. Edinburgh: Oliver and Boyd, 1970.

Weil, A. "Euler," *The American Mathematical Monthly* 91, no. 9 (1984): 537–542.

————. "Riemann, Betti and the Birth of Topology," *Archive for History of Exact Sciences* 20, no. 2 (1979): 91–96.

Weiner, J. *Frege*. New York: Oxford University Press, 1999.

Westfall, R. *The Life of Isaac Newton*. New York: Cambridge University Press, 1993.

————. *Never at Rest: A Biography of Isaac Newton*. New York: Cambridge University Press, 1980.

Weyl, H. "David Hilbert and His Mathematical Work," *American Mathematical Society. Bulletin. New Series* 50 (1944): 612–654.

Wheeler, J. "Hermann Weyl and the Unity of Knowledge," *Amer. Sci.* 74, no. 4 (1986): 366–375.

Wheeler, L. *Josiah Willard Gibbs: The History of a Great Mind*. New Haven, Conn.: Yale University Press, 1962.

Wiener, N. *Ex-Prodigy: My Childhood and Youth*. New York: Simon and Schuster, 1953.

————. *I Am a Mathematician*. Garden City, N.Y.: Doubleday, 1956.

Wilkes, M. "Babbage as a Computer Pioneer," *Historia Mathematica* 4, no. 4 (1977): 415–440.

Williams, H. *The Great Astronomers*. New York: Simon and Schuster, 1930.

Wilson, C. "D'Alembert versus Euler on the Precession of the Equinoxes and the Mechanics of Rigid Bodies," *Archive for History of Exact Sciences* 37, no. 3 (1987): 233–273.

Wilson, D. *Kelvin and Stokes: A Comparative Study in Victorian Physics*. Bristol, U.K.: A. Hilger, 1987.

Wood, A. "George Gabriel Stokes, 1819–1903, an Irish Mathematical Physicist," *Irish Mathematical Society Bulletin* 35 (1995): 49–58.

Wright, C. *Frege's Conception of Numbers as Objects*. Aberdeen, U.K.: Aberdeen University Press, 1983.

Yaglom, I. *Felix Klein and Sophus Lie: Evolution of the Idea of Symmetry in the Nineteenth Century*. Boston: Birkhäuser, 1988.

Yates, F. "George Udny Yule," *Obituary Notices of Fellows of the Royal Society of London* 8 (1952): 309–323.

Yavetz, I. *From Obscurity to Enigma: The Work of Oliver Heaviside, 1872–1889*. Boston: Birkhäuser Verlag, 1995.

Yoder, J. *Unrolling Time: Christiaan Huygens and the Mathematization of Nature*. New York: Cambridge University Press, 1988.

Yosida, K. "A Brief Biography of Takakazu Seki (1642?–1708)," *The Mathematical Intelligencer* 3 (1981): 121–122.

Yuan, W. *Goldbach Conjecture*. Singapore: World Scientific, 1984.

Zubov, V. *Leonardo da Vinci*. Cambridge, Mass: Harvard University Press, 1968.

INTERNET RESOURCES

Eisenhower National Clearinghouse for Mathematics and Science Education. Available online. URL: http://www.enc.org. Downloaded on June 2, 2003. As its name implies, this site is a clearinghouse for a comprehensive set of links to interesting sites in math and science.

Electronic Bookshelf. Available online. URL: http://hilbert.dartmouth.edu/~matc/eBookshelf/art/index.html. Updated on May 21, 2002. This site is maintained by Dartmouth College. It is both visually beautiful and informative, and it has links to many creative presentations on computer science, the history of mathematics, and mathematics. It also treats a number of other topics from a mathematical perspective.

Eric Weisstein's World of Mathematics. Available online. URL: http://mathworld.wolfram.com. Updated on April 10, 2002. This site has brief overviews of many topics in mathematics. The level of presentation varies substantially from topic to topic.

Faber, Vance, et al. This Is MEGA Mathematics! Available online. URL: http://www.c3. lanl.gov/mega-math. Downloaded June 2, 2003. Maintained by the Los Alamos National Laboratories, one of the premier scientific establishments in the world, this site has a number of unusual offerings.

Fife, Earl, and Larry Husch. Math Archives. "History of Mathematics." Available online. URL:http://archives.math.utk.edu/topics/ history.htm. Updated January 2002. Information on mathematics, mathematicians, and mathematical organizations.

Gangolli, Ramesh. *Asian Contributions to Mathematics*. Available online. URL: http://www.pps.k12.or.us/depts-c/mc-me/be-as-ma.pdf. Downloaded on June 2, 2003. As its name implies, this well-written online book focuses on the history of mathematics in Asia and its effect on the world history of mathematics. It also includes information on the work of Asian Americans, a welcome contribution to the field.

INDEX

Note: Page numbers in **boldface** indicate main topics. Page numbers in *italic* refer to illustrations.

C